Race, Resistance and the Ainu of Japan

Dispossessed and marginalised during the colonisation of their homeland, the Ainu have been categorised as an inferior and subordinate 'race' by the immigrant Japanese majority. Challenging the perceived ethnic homogeneity of Japanese society, the Ainu are reasserting both their culture and their claims to be the 'indigenous' people of Japan.

Race, Resistance and the Ainu of Japan traces the history of the Ainu and explores the ways in which competing versions of Ainu identity have been constructed and articulated since the Ainu people were dispossessed during the colonisation of their homeland. This study places the development of Ainu–Japanese relations within the broader currents of race and racism, revealing the social and cultural diversity of Japan while exposing the myths of Japanese homogeneity.

Richard Siddle is a Research Fellow, School of East Asian Studies, University of Sheffield.

Sheffield Centre for Japanese Studies/Routledge Series

Series editor: Glenn D. Hook, Professor of Japanese Studies, University of Sheffield

This series, publishing by Routledge in association with the Centre for Japanese Studies at the University of Sheffield, will make available both original research on a wide range of subjects dealing with Japan and will provide introductory overviews of key topics in Japanese studies.

The Internationalization of Japan
Edited by Glenn D. Hook and Michael Weiner

Race and Migration in Imperial Japan
Michael Weiner

Greater China and Japan
Prospects for an economic partnership in East Asia
Robert Taylor

The Steel Industry in Japan
A comparison with Britain
Harukiyo Hasegawa

Race, Resistance and the Ainu of Japan

Richard Siddle

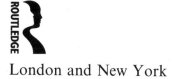

ROUTLEDGE
London and New York

First published 1996
by Routledge
11 New Fetter Lane, London EC4P 4EE

Routledge is an International Thomson Publishing company

Simultaneously published in the USA and Canada
by Routledge
29 West 35th Street, New York, NY 10001

Typeset in Times by LaserScript, Mitcham, Surrey
Printed and bound in Great Britain by
TJ Press (Padstow) Ltd, Padstow, Cornwall

British Library Cataloguing in Publication Data
A catalogue record for this book is available from the British Library

Library of Congress Cataloging in Publication Data
Siddle, Richard, 1959–
Race, resistance, and the Ainu of Japan / Richard Siddle.
p. cm. – (Sheffield Centre for Japanese Studies/Routledge series)
Includes bibliographical references.
1. Ainu–History. 2. Ainu – Ethnic identity. 3. Japan – Ethnic relations. I. Title. II. Series.
DS832.S59 1996
952′.004946–dc20 95-48243
CIP

ISBN 0–415–13228–2

For Yoshiko, Mariya and Hugo

Contents

Acknowledgements

This book is the outcome of years of endeavour, during which I have incurred many debts. At the School of East Asian Studies at Sheffield University, where this project was conceived and gestated as a Ph.D. dissertation, Mike Weiner was instrumental in providing intellectual focus and inspiration. His incisive and often withering criticisms have shaped this study in many ways. The advice and electronic expertise of my colleague Trevor Astley have also been much appreciated. In Japan, John Maher of International Christian University has been a constant mentor and friend. The Japan Foundation Endowment Committee twice provided generous financial support, as well as additional funds for a final research trip in the summer of 1995. I am further grateful to the editors of *Asian Cultural Studies* for permission to use material previously published in Issue 21 of their journal. At Routledge, thanks are due both to the editor for patience and encouragement, and to the anonymous reviewer who provided suggestions for revision.

Most of the research for this book was undertaken at the Hokkaidō University of Education in Iwamizawa, thanks to a Japanese Ministry of Education Scholarship which enabled me to spend eighteen months there under the patient guidance of Professor Tabata Hiroshi. I owe much of my understanding of Hokkaidō and Ainu history to his impressive, but always quietly and modestly expressed, knowledge of these subjects. A number of scholars at the University and other institutions also gave generously of their time and academic expertise, in particular Aiuchi Toshikazu, Kimi Nobuhiko, Ogawa Masahito, Okuda Osami, Satō Tomomi, Satō Yū and Takegahara Yukio. I am deeply indebted to Amano Tetsuya of Hokkaidō University, without whose friendship and initial interest in this project I may never have been able to continue. It is also my pleasure to recall the many happy hours spent in the company of Ishihara Makoto and Ishihara Itsuko, the owners of the incomparable Sapporo-dō Shoten bookshop. In Tokyo, Uemura Hideaki and other staff of the *Shimin Gaikō Sentā* provided invaluable advice and assistance. Needless to say, any errors or misinterpretations are mine alone.

During my involvement with the Ainu people I spent considerable time in the office of the Utari Kyōkai, at various functions, and with delegations in Geneva; I am grateful to Nomura Giichi, Sasamura Jirō, Satō Yukio and all the office staff, and I sincerely hope I did not overly try their patience. Many other Ainu in various organisations and communities contributed, with varying degrees of willingness, to this study. Although they may disagree with my findings, I am grateful to them all.

While professional and personal indebtedness are often difficult to separate, this project was only completed thanks to the support of friends and relatives. My parents provided me with a quiet place to work during a crucial few months, while my father-in-law, Gotō Sadakichi, encouraged me throughout. Friends in Tokyo and elsewhere gave generously of their hospitality and support in times of crisis, particularly during the early days. Without them, my career would have been over almost before it began. My children, who grew somewhat faster than this book, had to put up with their father's frequent absence and almost permanent preoccupation. Finally, my greatest debt is to my wife, Yoshiko, without whom, quite simply, it could never have happened.

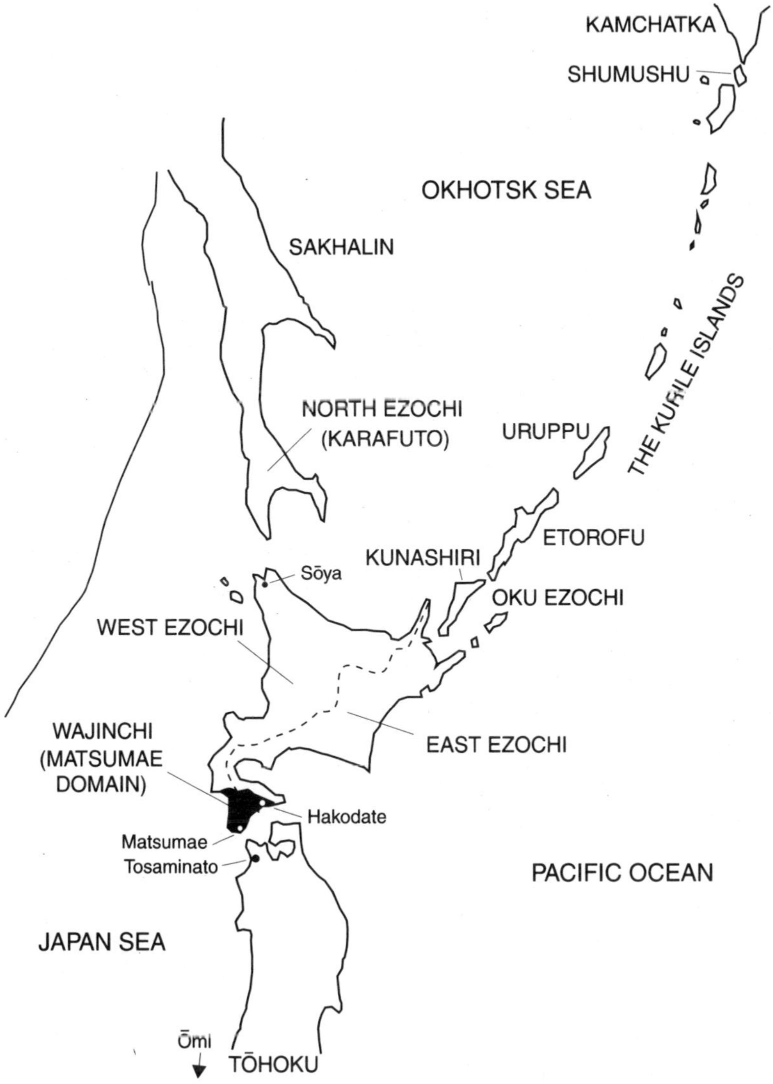

The northern regions before 1868

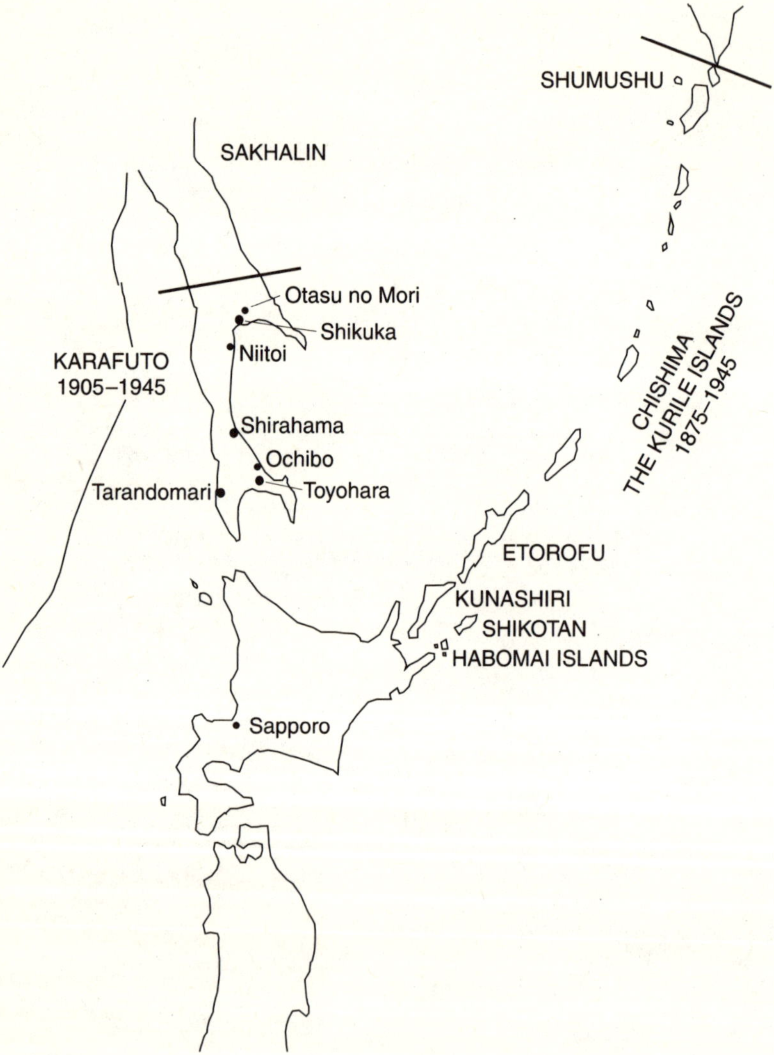

Hokkaidō and surrounding areas, 1869–1945

Modern Hokkaidō

Introduction

On 10 December 1992 an elderly man stepped up to the podium of the General Assembly of the United Nations in New York. It was, he later recalled, the proudest moment of his life. It is not often that private citizens are given leave to address the General Assembly, and although an accomplished public speaker, the man could not hide his nervousness and emotion. The occasion was the inauguration of the United Nations International Year of the World's Indigenous People, and the speaker was Nomura Giichi, a representative of the Ainu nation. In his speech, Nomura drew the attention of other delegates to the marginalisation and prejudice that the Ainu, the indigenous people of Japan, have suffered as a consequence of the Japanese colonisation of Hokkaidō. Reiterating Ainu support for the efforts of indigenous peoples worldwide to obtain the right to self-determination under international law, Nomura then called upon the government of Japan to enter into a 'new partnership' with the Ainu for the 'development and realization of a society in which all peoples can live together in dignity'. His short speech ended with words of thanks in the Ainu language.[1]

In Japan, Nomura's appeal fell largely on deaf ears. Voices that celebrate ethnic diversity and opposition are all but overwhelmed by the master narrative of seamless national homogeneity that dominates Japan's discursive space. Nomura's portrayal of an oppressed and ethnically distinct 'indigenous people' in northern Japan runs contrary to the common-sense understanding of most Japanese. Both official and popular versions of the history of Hokkaidō and its adjoining territories emphasise peaceful 'development' (*kaitaku*) in virgin lands made possible by the heroic sacrifices of Japanese pioneers, and the government of Japan has yet to officially recognise the Ainu as an indigenous people. This is partly because the idea of 'indigenous peoples' itself, however self-evident it may appear, is a relatively recent construct of the global postwar movement for decolonisation. But, more importantly, the denial of Ainu existence is a manifestation of a deeper discursive trend in Japanese society. Prime Minister Nakasone Yasuhiro's public comments in 1986 that Japan has no 'racial minorities', for instance, was only one in a long sequence of official statements invoking Japanese homogeneity.[2] In Hokkaidō itself, once the ancestral homeland of the Ainu, visitors today encounter them primarily within the context of a handful of tourist villages that convey the pitiful impression of 'relic[s] of a not quite dead culture'.[3] It comes as no real surprise that Western students of Japan have tended to accept dominant Japanese views of a 'vanishing people' well on the way to 'cultural extinction'.[4]

This study investigates these conflicting narratives of identity, history and contemporary reality. While broadly tracing the outlines of Ainu history and the colonisation of Hokkaidō, the main focus is on the making and remaking of Ainu identity by both the dominant Japanese and the Ainu themselves. It explores the ways in which competing versions of Ainu identity have been articulated and rearticulated during different historical periods, and how these identities – 'racial' and 'ethnic' – have served to shape relations between Ainu and Japanese. (Both 'race' and 'ethnicity' are regarded here not as primordial entities but as socially constructed categories, and are enclosed in quotation marks – along with other contested terms like 'native' – to indicate their problematic status.) By focusing on the dynamics between racialisation and ethnic mobilisation within the context of colonial relations of domination, this study considers Ainu 'ethnicity' as a creative response to marginalisation and racism. To borrow from Attwood's study of the Australian Aborigines, to understand the position of the Ainu nation in modern Japan means concentrating 'not on their "being" but their "becoming"' – the ways that the Ainu have been made, and have made themselves.[5] Entering the modern period as 'barbarians', the Ainu have transformed themselves into an 'indigenous people'.

When considered at all, the Ainu have usually been regarded as passive and marginal participants in Japanese history and society. While there is no doubt that the Ainu are a small and marginalised minority group, it would be a mistake to underestimate their significance for the study of modern Japan. Japan's transition to modernity was characterised, among other things, by the forging of a strong sense of 'nation' and the creation of a colonial empire. As these pages will show, a consideration of Ainu history can shed light on both these processes. From another perspective, the present Ainu struggle for ethnic identity and expression highlights the social and cultural diversity of Japan while simultaneously exposing the hollowness of myths of Japanese homogeneity.

Ainu history invites the scholar to discard notions of Japanese uniqueness and seek parallels with Western imperialism and the experiences of other indigenous peoples. How does the Ainu story differ from that of, say, the Australian Aborigines or the Lakota Sioux? While such comparisons are not explicitly drawn, a basic premise of this study, explored in Chapter 1, is that the development of relations between Japanese and Ainu over the last one hundred and fifty years does not reflect uniquely Japanese cultural mores and political institutions. Instead, the colonisation of Hokkaidō and subsequent dispossession of its 'native' inhabitants can be located within the broader historical contexts of nation- and empire-building that created 'indigenous' peoples from the Arctic to the South Pacific during the nineteenth and early twentieth centuries. The motives, means and ideologies that drove Japanese colonial expansion and informed the treatment of subordinated populations had precedents or parallels in other empires. Racism, in particular, usually associated only with Western imperialism, was a defining feature of the Japanese Empire as notions of Japanese 'racial' superiority served to explain and justify Japan's colonial mission in Hokkaidō and other territories.

While the prevalence of 'racial' discourse in nineteenth and early twentieth century Japan is generally acknowledged, there have been few systematic attempts to assess the significance of 'race' in structuring relations between social collectivities defined in those terms. The first main theme of this study, taken up in Chapters 2 to 4, explores the centrality of 'race' in the Ainu, and by extension the Japanese, experience of modernity. Japan was an ardent student of Western scientific knowledge at the height of its infatuation with the Darwinian paradigm of evolution. The discourse of 'race' and Social Darwinian notions of social evolution soon became a prominent feature of the Japanese intellectual landscape. The divisions between populations of human beings, although socially constructed and transmitted, came to be perceived as 'natural' and inevitable. The 'scientific principle' of the 'survival of the fittest' ruled the day. As the sense of 'nation' took root among Japanese in the late Meiji period it became increasingly identified with the 'Yamato race'. In a racialised world both collective Self and Other, Japanese and non-Japanese, were perceived as hierarchically ordered 'racial' communities. As a result, the dispossession and marginalisation of the Ainu during the colonisation of Hokkaidō were paralleled by their categorisation as a subordinate and inferior 'racial' population – a 'dying race' – by all sectors of the Japanese immigrant community. Such perceptions directly influenced policies that furthered Ainu subordination. Moreover, in the context of debates over Japan's identity and place in a world dominated by Europe and the USA, the Ainu provided an initial 'native' Other as a foil not only for Japan's own emerging national (and 'racial') identity, but against which Japan's modernity and progress towards civilisation could be measured.

On the other hand, the Ainu have not merely been the passive victims of this historical process. Although organised military resistance had ceased in the eighteenth century, Ainu leaders and communities continued to react in different ways to their changing circumstances. Many sought accommodation, while others clung stubbornly to their old ways. Yet others sought to mobilise politically. Ainu responses to subordination, and particularly the struggle to challenge dominant images of their inferiority and remake themselves as an ethnic community, form the second main theme of this study. Early resistance, described in Chapter 5, was expressed through involvement in self-help organisations, culminating in the establishment of the Ainu Kyōkai (Ainu Association) in 1930. These early pioneers aimed to influence the ideological and institutional structures through which they were controlled by placing emphasis on enlightenment, education and assimilation. The final chapters examine how, after a lull in the early postwar period, Ainu political activity resurfaced from the late 1960s in the form of ethnic identification and the creation of an 'Ainu nation'. Ainu leaders are presently confronting the Japanese state by means of a political struggle waged around a separate Ainu identity as 'indigenous people', a struggle that aims to increase Ainu access to power and resources as a minority group within Japanese society. Among other things, this entails contesting the official narratives of Japanese history and homogeneity. While originating in the mood of social activism that swept Japan in the late 1960s and early 1970s, the Ainu struggle has transcended the narrowly Japanese context to reflect the concerns and strategies of the worldwide movement of indigenous peoples for decolonisation.

This study is based on a wide range of sources. While rejecting deterministic structural analyses, the discussion recognises that racisms and other ideological forms are articulated by groups located within specific historical and material circumstances that shape, and are further shaped by, discursive activity itself. I have therefore relied on the excellent Japanese scholarship that exists on Hokkaidō and Ainu history when sketching out the economic and political terrain. Analysis of the construction of the Ainu as a racialised Other draws on contemporary sources from the eighteenth to the early twentieth centuries; official documents, travellers accounts, semi-official and popular journals, newspapers, popular literature, academic writings, and transcripts of Diet debates. Conscious of the need to be wary of assigning too much influence to ideological forms, a partial attempt has also been made to incorporate the attitudes held by the 'average person' through recourse to personal and oral histories. The second major theme of this study, Ainu response and ethnic mobilisation, relies in similar fashion on both official and popular contemporary sources, as well as the writings of Ainu leaders and activists themselves.

Finally, a note on terminology and conventions. Most scholars concerned with the relations between immigrants and indigenous people in Hokkaidō use the terms *Wajin* and *Ainu* to distinguish between the two populations. This is also a usage that this study will adopt, since both are self-designations of identity widely used today. Wajin, which entered common usage with the advent of the Bakufu administration in the northern regions from the nineteenth century, literally means 'person of Wa (Yamato)', summing up the majority sense of identification for Self as opposed to the Ainu Other, whom the Wajin called barbarians – *ijin, iteki* or most commonly, *Ezo*. The Ainu, however, have their own terms for Self and Other; like many other groups around the world they call themselves 'humans' – *Ainu*. Besides man, or human being, Ainu is also used to designate the group in the sense of 'we, the people' or of 'real humans' as opposed to outsiders. Japanese are called *shisam* or *shamo*.

Japanese and modern Ainu names in this study are given following Japanese convention, with family name followed by given name. Macrons are used to indicate long vowels except for well-known place-names like Tokyo and Osaka. Unfamiliar terms are italicised. As for Ainu words, the phonological structure of Japanese has tended to distort them to fit the syllabic constraints of *katakana*. But where Ainu terms occur within everyday discourse, their standard Japanese transcriptions are given since these are generally used by most Ainu themselves as monolingual speakers of Japanese.

1 'Race', ethnicity and the Ainu

Despite the pervasive myth of Japan as a 'homogeneous nation', between 4–6 per cent of the Japanese population are members of minority groups, many of whom 'suffer considerable discrimination'.[1] Consideration of the historical formation and marginalisation of minority populations like the Koreans and Burakumin has stimulated a growing interest among historians and sociologists in the discourses of 'race' and 'nation' in Japanese society, and how these discourses have shaped constructs of Self and Other.[2] Scholarly interest in the Ainu, however, has been largely confined within the disciplines of anthropology and archaeology (and, to a lesser extent, history and linguistics) and has mainly concerned itself with the reconstruction of 'traditional' Ainu culture as part of wider investigations into Japanese origins. The few scholars who have attempted to assess the importance of 'race' and ethnicity within the context of Ainu–Wajin relations have foundered on inadequate or anachronistic formulations of these notoriously slippery analytical concepts. Most fail to identify either the social and economic bases of 'racial' discrimination, or the historical process through which images of the Ainu as an excluded and subordinated Other have been reproduced.

A few examples will suffice. While the work of the American scholars Peng and Geiser in the 1960s, for instance, represented a great advance over the Ainu as a 'vanishing people' paradigm exemplified by anthropologists like Hilger, their explanation of the exclusion of the Ainu from 'full admittance to Japanese society' as merely the operation of 'informal social processes' ignored the centrality of racism in the formation of colonial relations of domination over the Ainu.[3] In contrast, other scholars like Baba and Emori have actively sought the roots of discrimination in the colonial encounter, but their analyses have ultimately foundered on the lack of a clear theoretical conceptualisation of 'race' and a failure to consider the wider social and historical contexts in which the discourse of 'race' gained acceptance as a common-sense explanation of Japanese superiority and Ainu subordination.[4] Work on Ainu ethnicity displays similar weaknesses. Both premodern and modern Ainu identity have been little studied and understood, even though Ainu identity is now more strongly emphasised and celebrated by the Ainu themselves than in any other period of their recent history. With the exception of Sjöberg, scholars have displayed little interest in the analysis of the present Ainu movement as a creative attempt to fuse culture and politics in a new discourse of ethnicity.[5]

A systematic analysis of the interplay between 'race' and ethnicity within the context of the creation of the modern Japanese nation-state is critical to an understanding of Ainu–Wajin relations, both past and present. Under specific historical and material conditions, two competing discourses of 'natural difference' – the 'dying race' and the 'Ainu nation' – have served to shape Ainu–Wajin relations in a dynamic and continuing process. Since 'race' and ethnicity represent the modes in which the Ainu have been marginalised, and have responded to that marginalisation, during the incorporation of Hokkaidō into the modern Japanese state, this chapter explores both the nature of these concepts and the historical contexts in which they have been articulated.

'RACE' AND NATION IN MODERN JAPAN

As a biological concept, 'race', in the sense of the taxonomic classification of *Homo sapiens* into subspecies on the basis of phenotype, has been outdated by the development of genetics.[6] The notion, however, is employed by many social scientists in the guise of a 'social race', 'a group of people who are *socially* defined in a given society as belonging together because of *physical markers* such as skin pigmentation, hair texture, facial features, stature, and the like'.[7] 'Race' is therefore conceived of as a socially constructed notion of biological difference used by one group to categorise another in the context of unequal power relations.[8] Miles, in particular, argues strongly against tendencies to reify 'race':

> There are no 'races' and therefore no 'race relations'. There is only a belief that there are such things, a belief that is used by some social groups to construct an Other (and therefore the Self) in thought as a prelude to exclusion and domination, and by other social groups to define Self (and so to construct an Other) as a means of resisting that exclusion.[9]

The object of study, argues Miles, should be racism, an ideology that 'constructs (real or imagined) difference as natural not only in order to exclude, but additionally, in order to marginalise a social collectivity within a particular constellation of relations of domination'.[10] Within a context of unequal power relations, real or imagined biological difference can become the definitive criterion for categorisation, exclusion and domination. It is not only populations that share distinct phenotypical characteristics (like black skin) that are categorised as 'naturally different' in this way; Miles points to the Irish, Jews and Gypsies as examples of culturally distinct European populations 'racialised' on the basis of imagined biological difference.[11] Such ideas do not result from inherent human propensities to discriminate but are articulated in certain historical contexts by groups located within specific material and power relations:

> In certain historical conjunctures and under specific material conditions, human beings attribute certain biological characteristics with meaning in order to differentiate, to exclude, and to dominate: reproducing the idea of 'race', they create a racialised Other and simultaneously they racialise themselves.[12]

The historical and material context in which the Ainu became a racialised and subordinated population was one of colonialism. Although relations between the indigenous inhabitants of Hokkaidō and their southern neighbours predate the production of historical records, archaeological sites in Hokkaidō provide evidence of trade dating back to the early centuries of the Christian era. By the seventeenth century trade relations had taken on an increasingly unequal nature as the Japanese extended control over the region and its 'barbarian' inhabitants. The process of establishing Japanese domination greatly accelerated after the Meiji Restoration of 1868 when the modernising Japanese state established a colonial order in the newly acquired territory of Hokkaidō. While Hokkaidō is not recognised by most Japanese today as a colony, the material and ideological relations of domination established over the original inhabitants of the region after 1868 clearly fall within the bounds of what Beckett terms a colonial order:

> A colonial order arises when the state that has annexed a territory formally and systematically discriminates between the conquering invaders and the subject indigenes in such a way as to entrench the differences between them and to foster their economic, political, and cultural inequality. This discrimination is sustained by some form of ideology that justifies the domination of the indigenous population in terms of differences of race, mentality, moral qualities, cultural advancement, religion, or historic destiny.[13]

Modernisation, mass immigration, and capitalist development in the new territory of Hokkaidō drastically altered Ainu–Wajin relations, transforming pre-Restoration Confucian and folk images of barbarian Ainu in the process. As the Tokugawa (1603–1868) world-view gave way under the impact of rapid political, economic and social change and the import of Western knowledge, Ainu dispossession and subordination came to be explained and legitimised in the language of 'race'. In other words, the Ainu became a 'racialised' population.

As Japan underwent the transition to its own version of modernity during the late nineteenth and early twentieth centuries, the notion of 'race' became accepted by both scholar and layman alike as one of the 'common-sense' categories that served to distinguish human populations. Such views were also widespread in late nineteenth century Europe and America, where 'races' were perceived to exist objectively as natural communities that reproduced themselves in time and space and possessed innate and immutable characteristics. These ideas developed within the context of advances in scientific knowledge and technology that greatly facilitated industrial and imperial expansion. With much of the globe ruled by a handful of European nation-states after the 'scramble for Africa' at the end of the nineteenth century, the cultural and technological differences between colonial elites and subject populations were increasingly explained in terms of 'racial' difference and such scientific 'truths' as Darwin's paradigm of evolution. Although there were differences in approach between and within Empires, for most of the citizens of the imperial nation-states it was self-evident that relations of domination were a result of the natural propensity for 'superior races' to conquer and rule 'inferior' ones. This common-sense explanation also served to justify colonial domination and render that domination inevitable.[14] Seen in these terms, social and economic inequality was no more than an expression of 'natural' difference.

Racialised subject populations like the Ainu were thus perceived as innately inferior precisely because they were subordinated. The circularity of such an argument is obvious, but logical consistency is not essential to common-sense understanding, a concept first developed by Gramsci in an attempt to explain the social processes of ideology – the ways in which dominant ideologies arise, are reproduced, and achieve 'hegemony'. As explained by Miles:

> [Commonsense] refers to the complex of ideas and perceptions, organized without coherence, which are a consequence of both historical tradition and direct experience and by which people negotiate their daily life . . . the internally contradictory and incoherent set of ideas through which daily lives are lived.[15]

The naturalisation of 'race' as a common-sense category of difference in

Japan did not happen overnight, but was part of a much larger process of reinterpretation of meaning in the face of widespread social disruption after the Meiji Restoration. During the late nineteenth century, Japanese constructs of Self and Other underwent a radical transformation as the new leadership steered Japan towards industrial development and a place on the world stage as a modern 'nation'. The rapid social change that ensued undermined the common-sense frameworks of understanding by which individuals had negotiated their daily lives under the Tokugawa. For those who lived through such changes, like the novelist Natsume Sōseki, such mental dislocation was akin to waging 'war against oneself'.[16] Not only did old certainties dissolve but new knowledge entered Japan. The leadership of Japan embarked upon a conscious policy of modernisation along Western lines, motivated by the need to build a 'prosperous country and a strong army' (*fukoku kyōhei*) in the face of Western power, exemplified in the so-called 'unequal treaties'. Many foreigners were hired to introduce Western knowledge and technology to Japan. As Dower has pointed out, during this initial period in which the Japanese turned to the West for education, both natural and social sciences in Europe and the United States were dominated by the evolutionary paradigms of 'race' inspired by the work of Darwin.[17] The introduction of Darwinian thought in the early Meiji period (1868–1912) was the beginning of a process which, by the end of the period, would see common-sense Japanese notions of national Self and Other increasingly influenced by the idea of 'race'.

While both 'race' and 'nation' were new constructs for Meiji period Japanese, they built on deeply rooted notions of difference that had been present at all levels of Tokugawa society. For the elites, it was the essentially Confucian distinction between civilised and barbarian that served to mark the outsider. As Japan redefined its identity *vis-à-vis* China during the Tokugawa period, nativist scholars like Motoori Norinaga attempted to challenge Confucian orthodoxy by stressing that civilisation and moral purity actually originated in Japan. Initially only a minor current in Tokugawa intellectual life, nativist ideas began to reach a wider audience as the Bakufu atrophied in the face of internal change and a new foreign threat in the early nineteenth century. Strident ideologues like Hirata Atsutane attributed animal qualities to Europeans while extolling Japanese uniqueness and superiority:

> Japanese differ completely from and are superior to the peoples of China, India, Russia, Holland, Siam, Cambodia, and all other countries of the world, and for us to have called our country the Land of the Gods was not mere vainglory.[18]

A widening geographical knowledge among intellectual elites like those involved in *rangaku* (Dutch Studies) had also resulted in an increasing awareness of peoples of colour. Nevertheless, while early curiosity and admiration for African sailors had given way by the eighteenth century to more derogatory beliefs, civilised and barbarian remained the overriding categories for the classification of the peoples of the world.[19]

In contrast, commoners held an image of the outsider that was tied less to Confucianism and more to the worlds of folklore and everyday social experience in what remained a largely rural society. Complex patterns of identification included those based on kinship and the stratified caste system imposed by the Tokugawa, while groups of outcastes, perceived as polluted and non-human, existed as marginalised social pariahs in both town and country. Commoner attitudes were also influenced by pervasive folk beliefs that populated the netherworld of rural Japan with numerous goblins, ghosts and demons. However, as Dikötter has noted with regard to China, 'the coexistence of a more or less naive mythology at a popular level with a more sophisticated cosmology among the elite often serves to maintain the *same* symbolic universe'.[20] As Dower has argued, notions of pure Self in contrast to demonic and non-human Other were common to Japanese of all backgrounds.[21] When Darwinian ideas of evolution and natural selection began to enter Japan after the 1870s, such categories of difference and inferiority were not completely superseded but coexisted with, or were adapted and transformed within, the discourse of 'race'.

The initial conduit for Darwinian ideas was Edward Morse, a staunch Darwinist regarded as the father of archaeology and zoology in Japan, who lectured on evolution at Tokyo University in 1877. Darwin's ideas first reached a reading public in Thomas Huxley's *Lectures on the Origin of Species*, translated in 1879, and became widely known after the publication in 1881 of Morse's lectures.[22] The same year also saw the first of Darwin's own works to be translated and published, *The Descent of Man*, which appeared as *Jinsoron*. In this book Darwin commented on the decline in native populations around the world, and noted that 'extinction follows chiefly from the competition of tribe with tribe, and race with race', and also that when 'civilised nations come into contact with barbarians the struggle is short'.[23] Although not available in Japanese until later, the recapitulation theory of Haeckel and Lamarck's linear theories of evolution were also known to some Japanese intellectuals.

The practice of applying the concept of evolution to explain social phenomena, which was widespread in late nineteenth century Europe and America and has been labelled Social Darwinism, also reached a wide audience in Japan when popularised through the writings of Herbert Spencer.[24] Spencer's evolutionary theory was translated in 1884, and in all around thirty translations of his works appeared between 1877 and 1900. Part of the reason for his popularity in Japan was probably due to the simplicity with which 'he reduced the universe to a simple system' that provided explanations and strategies for success in a hostile social and international environment.[25] Against a background of widespread social change brought about by policies of industrialisation, national and social conflict were increasingly presented in terms of the 'survival of the fittest' (*yūshō reppai*) in the 'struggle for survival' (*seizon kyōsō*) in the journals and newspapers that proliferated between 1890 and 1920.[26] Such ideas permeated to all levels and persuasions in society; some socialists, for instance, including Ōsugi Sakae who translated *Origin of Species* in 1914, equated the struggle for survival with class struggle.[27] From the 1890s, school textbooks also helped to spread stereotyped racial images and related ideas such as environmental determinism, in which the characteristics of 'races' and nations were attributed to geographical and climatic factors. This latter school of thought is associated with the historian Thomas Buckle, whose *History of Civilisation in England* was widely read in Meiji Japan.[28]

But what, above all, facilitated the rise of racial thinking in Japan was the parallel discourse of nationalism.[29] The Meiji period was marked by the strenuous efforts of Japanese political leaders and intellectuals to create a 'sense of nation' from among the social turmoil, in response to what they perceived as an imminent threat to the country. As to the actual nature of this threat, however, they often disagreed. The immediate issue, for some, was national security, while others were concerned with social disorder; for yet others the problem was the maintenance of power in the face of the People's Rights (*jiyū minken*) movement of the 1880s, the influence of socialism and the forthcoming political franchise. The oligarch Yamagata Aritomo worried about all of these.[30] For although the Japanese shared certain broad cultural and linguistic traits, the Meiji political and intellectual elites of the late 1880s saw only an unenlightened and disparate population that needed to be forged into a 'nation'.

The process of building the 'imagined community' of the nation, of turning passive peasants into self-conscious Japanese, involved the redrawing of symbolic boundaries to include all Japanese in a sense of belonging to a naturally occurring community.[31] By the end of the Meiji period, this had been achieved by the identification of the nation with the Yamato *minzoku*. The essence of the *minzoku*, that linked all members in the imagined community, was not just shared culture or language but lay also in the ties of common ancestry. For many, the Japanese were a 'race'. To borrow from Miles, the notions of 'race' and 'nation' had become overlapping categories of inclusion and exclusion:

> [U]se of the idea of 'race' for the purpose of self-identification and differentiation can function to define the parameters of a 'nation'. In other words, the ideas of 'race' and 'nation' can be overlapping categories, each functioning to define the parameters of the other.[32]

This does not imply a rigid, one-on-one correlation between biology and national identity. Indeed, the scientific word for biological 'race' in Japan, *jinshu*, while often used to define the national community, came to be overshadowed around the turn of the century by the term *minzoku*, a far more fluid and encompassing notion of both cultural and ancestral community. Despite a superficial distinction between the two terms, however, at the common-sense level of understanding this was largely irrelevant. Although there was no one historical moment after which it can be said that the two terms came to possess a functional equivalency, and there were some, mostly scholars, who continued to maintain a distinction, the historical record shows a gradual but increasing tendency for *jinshu* and *minzoku* to be used interchangeably at the level of common-sense understanding, blurring any real distinction between them. In the later stages of this process in the Taishō (1912–1926) and early Shōwa (1926–1989) periods, the word *jinshu* appears less often in non-scientific discourse as it becomes subsumed within the semantic boundaries delineated by *minzoku*. The Japanese 'nation' was increasingly defined not merely by cultural criteria but by 'blood'. The essence of Japanese identity lay in the ties of common ancestry. *Minzoku* encompassed this notion of consanguinity and, indeed, was frequently translated as 'race' by Japanese of the time. But, as Shimazu has noted, both scientific and nationalist concepts could still exist side by side in an apparently contradictory fashion in a 'two-tiered' conception of 'race'. This juxtaposed a broad East–West racial divide of 'yellow' and 'white' with a narrower identification of 'race' with nation, a conception of 'race' that made 'a clear differentiation between the Japanese on one hand, and the Koreans and Chinese on the other'.[33]

The term *minzoku* (race/nation) that was employed in such contexts was first popularised by Shiga Shigetaka, Kuga Katsunan and Miyake Setsurei, young intellectuals associated with the popular journal *Nihonjin* and newspaper *Nihon*.[34] Concerned with the nature of Japanese identity, these young men wrote on issues of the 'national essence' (*kokusui*) and 'nationalism' (*kokuminshugi*) in reaction to what they criticised as unrestrained Westernisation. Whereas in the early days of the Meiji period, the definition of Japanese in official documents had been couched in Confucian terms as 'subjects' (*okuchō, banmin, jinmin*) in a moral and political hierarchy, meaning those persons under the control of the territorial Japanese state, for Shiga and his fellow popular nationalists the *kokusui* was contained in the *minzoku*. The *minzoku* was the expression of the inherited and unique historical, environmental and cultural characteristics of a country in its human population. According to Kuga, writing in 1890, this meant that such a *minzoku* could be found in each country. For these writers, cultural unity strengthened by political control was the basis for the 'sense of nation' (*kokuminteki kannen*). Moreover, they often disagreed among themselves and used *minzoku* in an unsystematic way, occasionally substituting other expressions, indicating that the term itself had yet to become an accepted part of everyday usage.

Their notion of *minzoku*, however, was soon taken up and developed further by constitutional scholars debating the 'national polity' (*kokutai*) in the context of the new constitution (1889) and civil code (1898). Particularly influential was Hozumi Yatsuka of Tokyo Imperial University, who argued throughout the 1890s and 1900s that sovereignty lay in the Emperor, and that Japan's unique *kokutai* was founded on the unbroken imperial line and customs of ancestor worship (*sosenkyō*). For Hozumi, and others like the staunch Social Darwinist Katō Hiroyuki, the essence of the Japanese *minzoku* lay primarily not in shared culture but in ties of blood due to common ancestry, an ancestry rooted in the divine origins of the imperial line. According to Hozumi: 'The State is a great family; the family is a small state: this is the great basis of the founding of our racial state, and here is the source of our *Kokutai*.'[35] To sustain the sense of nation, Hozumi asserted, it was necessary for the individual citizen to become aware (*jikaku*) of the common bonds of blood. Not all agreed. A certain Ōnishi Iwao, for instance, expressed the resistance of many intellectuals to such ideological manipulation when he asked in 1897: 'In what sense can our citizens (*waga kokumin*) be said to be the same as a race (*jinshu*), or the descendants of a common ancestor?' But in the heightened nationalist atmosphere that surrounded the Sino–Japanese and Russo–Japanese Wars, the question of Japanese identity subsided and this concept of the *minzoku* spread rapidly to gain increasing acceptance as common-sense.[36] Although scientific theories about various migrations to and mixings within the Japanese archipelago were widely known and discussed, these were considered to be so ancient that the resulting groups had long since fused into a single 'race' and culture.[37]

The notion of the Yamato *minzoku* as a political community of common ancestry and blood sharing unique historical and cultural characteristics was part of the ideological drive of the 1890s to establish the Emperor at the pinnacle of the nation. The new sense of nation was constructed around the notion of the Imperial family-state as a primordial consanguineous community. Such 'natural' ties were reinforced, or invented, as in

European nation-states during the same period, by idealised narratives of historical continuity and the 'invention of tradition'.[38] As industrialisation advanced, vastly improved networks of transportation and communication helped knit the population together. A growing newspaper industry, a nationwide system of standardised and controlled primary education, and military conscription all helped raise levels of literacy, standardise the language, and spread ideals of loyalty and sacrifice on behalf of the nation; although predominantly among the male half of the population and with varying degrees of success.

Hozumi Yatsuka himself was a major actor on the ideological stage, concerned with the manipulation of 'meaning in the service of power'.[39] In 1908, Hozumi became chairman of the committee entrusted with the task of revising ethics textbooks for schools, and in 1910 he helped Yamagata Aritomo draft his notorious memorandum against socialism entitled *Shakaihakaishugi* (Social Destructionism).[40] This ideological effort to establish the family-state, of course, did not go uncontested, and was especially opposed by those intellectuals associated with socialist groups like the Heiminsha. For many individuals and communities in the Meiji period, the good of the nation was of secondary importance at best; driven by personal or local interests they subscribed instead to an ethic of striving and success. The ideological terrain of late Meiji Japan displayed considerable heterogeneity, as Gluck has pointed out:

> [There] were a number of other versions of reality as it was and ought to be. Some of these, like socialism, were excluded from the dominant view as unacceptable, and were suppressed. But most coexisted, overlapped, or interacted with one another, so that rather than a single ideology, there were several ideologies, each in a constant process of mutual adjustment and change.[41]

But these competing versions of reality gradually came to be articulated within overarching common-sense notions of nation and society which defined that ideological terrain itself. What Gluck calls the 'ideological attempt to pin things down', combined with improved mechanisms of social control and the suppression of contestatory discourses in the public domain, led to the boundaries of the discourses conceptualising nation and society achieving relative stability by the second decade of the twentieth century. Despite widely differing views as to the national interest or the means to achieve it, the existence of the nation itself was not in doubt. Although socially conceived and transmitted, such notions as civilisation, progress, citizenship and nation had become self-evident to ordinary Japanese. These social constructions were themselves subject to renewal and modification, but once established, such commonsensical categories provided the parameters within which both actual events and ideological expressions made sense.

Although usually overlooked by historians, relations with the Ainu were an important dynamic in this larger process of redefinition. The Meiji period saw the establishment and consolidation of a colonial order in Hokkaidō under the Colonisation Commission (Kaitakushi) between 1869 and 1882, and the Hokkaidō government (Dōchō) established in 1886. To exploit the strategic and economic potential of the region for the benefit of the centre, the Meiji government established specific administrative and economic mechanisms quite different from those of the mainland (*naichi*). Besides the rich fisheries, the main resource of Hokkaidō was land. This land, which belonged to the Ainu through a system of both communal and private rights of use, was unilaterally annexed by the state. Dispossessed of their resources, the Ainu were forced into chronic destitution. For both the officials and educators concerned with Ainu policy, and the bulk of impoverished Wajin immigrants who moved into the ancestral lands of the Ainu, the facts of Ainu destitution and social breakdown were plain to see; but these were attributed not to specific colonial policies but to the innate inferiority of the 'natives' (*dojin*) themselves. It made sense to most that the Ainu were losing the 'struggle for survival' as an 'inferior race', especially since such notions as 'survival of the fittest' enjoyed the status of scientific truth. Conversely, the speed with which Japan embraced Western ideas and embarked upon expansion and development in Hokkaidō proved the superiority of the 'Japanese race'. The innate inferiority of the Ainu as a 'dying race' therefore justified as well as explained their subordination. By 1918, for one high-ranking former government official it also sanctioned their exclusion from the national community, as the boundaries of 'race' and nation had become one:

> Our country is proud of the purity of our ancient race, and the long-term preservation of this racial purity (*shuzoku junsui*) is our nationalism . . . If interbreeding with Ainu introduces Ainu blood into Japanese it will violate the movement to preserve our national essence (*kokusui*).[42]

These concepts were not limited merely to 'foreign' Others. Social and economic relations within Japan were also viewed through the same deterministic framework of 'natural' difference and the 'struggle for survival' rather than as a result of the social upheavals consequent on industrialisation and capitalist development. Images of savagery and barbarism were therefore applied to the slum dwellers of the rapidly expanding cities. As for peasants, noted one refined urbanite, 'just as domestic animals have an odor peculiar to them, peasants have a peculiar physiognomy. One can easily recognize a peasant'.[43] Again, links can be drawn both across time, to the images of commoners held by Japanese elites in the premodern period, and across space to the similar imagery used against the lower orders (and women) both in America and the industrialising nation-states of Europe in the same period.[44]

The discourses of 'race' and nation within which the Ainu were enmeshed were further nurtured and sustained among the general population by Japan's increasing ability to flex its muscles as an expansionist regional power. Driven by a sense of vulnerability, Japan strove to establish itself in Korea and Manchuria and displace the influence of China and Russia. Victory over China in 1895 aroused widespread patriotic fervour; Tokutomi Sohō probably summed up the mood of those times when he commented that 'knowing ourselves was knowing our power and knowing our mission'.[45] With the victory over Russia in 1905 (popularly regarded in Europe as the first major defeat by a 'yellow race' of a 'white' power), the acquisition of territory in China and the annexation of Korea in 1910, Japan rose to prominence as a colonial power in East Asia. These victories swelled patriotic pride and feelings of superiority among ordinary Japanese. Letters from the front in Manchuria during the Russo-Japanese War, for instance, clearly display the contempt that Japanese conscripts felt for the local Chinese population.[46] Despite a waning in enthusiasm for the military once the conflicts were over, the superiority of the Yamato *minzoku* was widely accepted as underlying Japanese success. This linkage of 'race' and national superiority was characteristic of other imperialistic nations at the time; the British Empire was sustained by a similar conviction in the superiority of the 'English race'.[47] Despite such successes, many Japanese leaders remained insecure and increasingly viewed international relations as possessing a 'racial' dimension. In 1914, for instance, Yamagata Aritomo displayed considerable anxiety over the 'rivalry between the white and the non-white races' in the context of China policy and the outbreak of war in Europe.[48] At the end of the war, popular national pride was insulted by the failure to have a clause relating to 'racial equality' inserted in the Treaty of Versailles in 1919, and was further inflamed by 'yellow peril' sentiment and racist immigration laws in the USA and Australia.

Nevertheless, as Kawamura has noted, by the 1930s a 'mass orientalism' had developed among the general public in which stereotyped images of colonial 'natives' (*dojin*) served to highlight Japan's own civilisation and modernity.[49] Such images were widespread in novels and children's comic strips, in particular the immensely popular *Bōken Dankichi* (The Adventurer Dankichi) which portrayed the adventures of a Tintin-like character in the South Seas, and the serialised adventures of a common soldier nicknamed *Nora-kura* (Black Mutt) in which Chinese enemies were depicted as pigs.[50] Drawing increasingly upon nativist and folk traditions celebrated in the work of folklorists like Yanagita Kunio, conceptions of the Japanese nation, the Yamato *minzoku*, resonated with both cultural and biological connotations as a people or 'volk' rather than a strictly biological 'race'. Even approaching the mid-point of the twentieth century, Tokugawa notions of the civilised centre and the outer world of, at best, semi-human barbarians enjoyed widespread currency in the ideological representations of the West; the 'demonic Other' was a mainstay of Japanese wartime propaganda.[51] Nevertheless, Japan's colonial mission was cast primarily in terms of Yamato 'racial' supremacy – as Dower has indicated, 'blood told'.[52] All outsiders were classified in 'racial' terms – inferiority was due to being non-Yamato, not part of the great blood-related Imperial family-state. Both national Self and Other were, in effect, defined as hierarchically ordered 'racial' communities.

By the 1930s this overlap between 'race' and nation was firmly established in the official view of the nation as possessing 'consanguineous unity' since 'the imperial blood may be said to run in the veins of all Japanese, who have thus become kinsmen with one another, descended from a common ancestor' – none other than Amaterasu Omikami, the Sun Goddess.[53] This notion of the divine ancestry, and therefore superiority, of the Japanese 'race' was enshrined in such ideological texts as the *Kokutai no Hongi* (Cardinal Principles of the National Polity, 1937) and taught as fact to Japanese schoolchildren. While promoting national pride and loyalty, such beliefs sanctioned far more sinister actions; among the conscripts of the Imperial Japanese Army, for instance, a widespread conviction in the racial inferiority of their enemies played a large part in the perpetration of atrocities in China and the Pacific.[54]

But despite the prominence of such discourse, historians must be constantly alert to the danger of assuming the effects of an ideology from its content (what Thompson calls the 'fallacy of internalism') and assigning to human beings the role of mere passive recipients for the symbolic forms of ideologies.[55] By the end of the war, for instance, a widespread cynicism existed among the Japanese population. In early Shōwa Japan, however, ideological activity was accompanied by the tightening of social control and overt political repression so that it was increasingly difficult to challenge the official version of reality in public – 3,195 books alone were banned between 1926 and 1944, as well as numerous newspapers, magazines, pamphlets and advertisements.[56]

Although Japan suffered comprehensive military defeat and occupation in 1945, the dominant official ideology of the consanguineous family-state continued, somewhat transformed, in hegemonic narratives of Japanese uniqueness as a *tan'itsu minzoku* or homogeneous nation. The late 1940s and 1950s witnessed an 'introspection boom' of popular literature on Japaneseness, known generically as *Nihonjinron* (Discussions on the Japanese), which by the 1970s had become far more self-congratulatory in tone.[57] One strand of such popular theorising on Japanese uniqueness, promoted in the best-sellers of the early 1970s by Nomi Masahiko and Suzuki Yoshimasa, focused specifically on the links between character and blood-type that had been prominent in scientific discourse of the 1920s and 1930s. In *Nihonjinron* in general, common-sense Japanese concepts of a unique culture and society were, and are, still ultimately predicated upon a racialised understanding of Self. Yoshino, for instance, notes in his discussion of contemporary *Nihonjinron* that:

> A Japanese expresses the 'immutable' or 'natural' aspect of Japanese identity through the imagined concept of 'Japanese blood'. Since a scientifically founded 'racial' classification of the Japanese and non-Japanese is meaningless, 'Japanese blood' is, first and foremost, a case of social construction of difference.[58]

Not only difference, but also inequality. Common-sense notions of Japanese uniqueness and homogeneity contribute to the continued marginalisation of the Ainu population. While much has changed in rural Hokkaidō over the last few decades due to economic change and increased social mobility, the Ainu are still perceived as inferior within the deterministic parameters of this latest manifestation of the Japanese discourse of 'race'. The racialisation of the Ainu as immutably or naturally Other remains a feature of Japanese society in the 1990s.

INDIGENOUS PEOPLES, INVENTED INDIANS: COMPETING HISTORIES

During most of the period described above, the Ainu remained a marginalised and powerless population. By the second decade of the twentieth century a self-help movement had begun among a small group of educated Ainu, but this was essentially a movement that aimed to further the assimilation of the Ainu into Wajin society. After the dissolution of the formal Japanese Empire following defeat in 1945, the marginal economic and social position of most Ainu remained largely unchanged, and seemed to justify the stereotypical images of a 'dying race'. But this is no longer the case; Ainu–Wajin relations have been substantially transformed by an 'ethnic revival' among the Ainu since the late 1960s.[59]

The Ainu activation of ethnicity has taken place within the context of a worldwide movement of 'indigenous peoples' against the governments of the states into which they have been incorporated through colonisation.

While imperialist ambitions were driven by a variety of economic and strategic factors, the lives of certain populations, usually perceived as 'natives' or 'tribals' by their conquerors, were shaped in similar ways by their common experiences of dispossession and marginalisation under colonial orders. Despite the postwar wave of decolonisation that broke up overseas empires, many such 'internally' colonised populations only became politicised relatively recently. From the 1960s sub-national 'native' peoples in Australia, North America, the Pacific states, New Zealand, Scandinavia – and Japan – began to mobilise in an attempt to challenge colonial structures of domination and regain control over their lives. In the process, supratribal alliances were often formed that cut across historical rivalries. From the 1970s activists became increasingly aware of each other and their commonalities and began to forge alliances across national borders. Such commonalities were encapsulated within the new concept of 'indigenous peoples'. As Macdonald explains:

> Indigenous is not, of course, a newly coined word. What is new is this specific use to characterise people who originated within the area in which they continue to live but who are subordinated within a nation state which has been constituted through the appropriation of their material, human and other resources, and the consequent loss of the political, economic and other rights they formerly possessed.[60]

While such a neat definition serves to clarify 'indigenous' for academics, in practice the 'meaning is constantly changing to accommodate new alliances – it is not just a semantic construct but a political strategy for attaining collective rights to territories and cultural respect'.[61] Indeed, many of these groups, especially those in Asia, have only recently come to define themselves in such terms, so that 'indigenous peoples' is still 'a political category whose definition is in the making'.[62]

Political mobilisation among indigenous peoples has been accompanied by a dramatic cultural renaissance. This fusion of culture and politics has generated a new 'ethnicity' among previously diverse groups. Ethnicity, like 'race', remains a scientifically imprecise concept, usually referring to an identity based on shared culture or descent. A widely held view is that ethnic bonds are remnants of 'primordial' attachments, what Geertz calls the 'givens' of kinship, language, religion and social practices.[63] Using such a static concept, traditional anthropology tended to reify ethnicity, especially among non-Western societies, as 'an autonomous subject suspended in an ahistorical void' until such 'orientalist' discourse became discredited.[64] With a shift in emphasis from the primordial to the historical, ethnicity is now seen more in terms of subjective consciousness, or identity, than as objective fact.

Ethnic identities are not essential, static, primordial remnants but are socially constructed and articulated within specific junctures of historical, material and power relations. The possession by a population of shared objective cultural or linguistic traits is not sufficient in itself to constitute an ethnic group or *ethnie*.[65] Primordial attachments, while they may be valued aspects of lived individual experience, only become 'ethnic', and of significance to the historian or sociologist, when they become the primary criteria of self-definition for a group involved in competition over resources and power in a modern society; in the broadest sense of the term, a *political* community. In this sense, ethnicity is a strategic choice, and the activation of ethnicity is a creative and dynamic process that can be termed ethnic mobilisation. Cultural, linguistic or religious symbols, often in combination, are recast or manipulated to define the boundaries of an imagined 'natural' or primordial community. Control over collective social memory – history – and the invention of tradition play an important part in this process.

Although their ideological content may be fluid, internally inconsistent and malleable enough to be redrawn to accommodate altered material or historical circumstances, the notions of 'nation' and 'people' have proved extraordinarily powerful. Ethnic bonds, once created, can be extremely effective in uniting populations otherwise divided along socio-economic, generational or gender lines. Nineteenth century Europe, for instance, witnessed an explosion of 'peoples' forged out of populations that previously existed, not as self-conscious groups, but as bureaucratic, linguistic or cultural categories.[66] With the development of complex modern industrial societies, sub-national groups have also increasingly come to define themselves in ethnic terms. These include diverse populations categorised and subordinated in terms of 'race' who mobilise for political purposes around the very identity imposed upon them; the experience of American Blacks provides perhaps the best example of this. Australian Aborigines have adopted a similar strategy, as Tonkinson points out:

> There is no question that, for Aborigines, the activation of ethnicity, via a stress on pan-Aboriginal identity and cultural distinctiveness, is simultaneously a consciousness-raising and a political strategy, not a return to 'primordial sentiments' . . . What is notable is the way in which Aboriginal leaders are building on the notion of an Aboriginal ethnicity which their colonial masters originally imposed upon them.[67]

Ethnic identity among indigenous populations has been promoted both within groups, as divisions of age, wealth, status or opinion are accommodated through identification with the 'people', and, more loosely, among groups linked by the perceived common experience of being indigenous. In North America, for instance, some aboriginal peoples of the continent have adopted cultural manifestations of 'Indianness', based mainly on Plains Indian culture, as symbols of Indian solidarity.[68] In Australia, a pan-aboriginal 'Aboriginality' has emerged as a basis for political action, with urban, coastal or other more acculturated groups adopting aspects of desert culture as symbols of identity and distinctiveness.[69] Although Aboriginality is itself a fluid and often contradictory notion, there is a tendency for such 'nativism' to become an inversion of an ascribed, deterministic, 'racialised' identity. Among Native Americans, as Clifton points out, innate Indianness is often attributed to notions of 'Indian blood'.[70] But as Said warns:

> [T]o accept nativism is to accept the consequences of imperialism, the racial, religious, and political divisions imposed by imperialism itself. To leave the historical world for the metaphysics of essences like *négritude*, Irishness, Islam, or Catholicism is to abandon history for essentializations that have the power to turn human beings against each other.[71]

While the new identities of indigenous groups, especially a population as acculturated as the Ainu, often have little root in the 'traditional' past and owe much to the creation of new historical and cultural narratives such as the 'myth of Mother Earth', they provide a powerful focal point in the struggle for access to power and resources.[72] Ethnic identification can also nourish a renewed sense of identity for indigenous individuals who have previously been denied both resources and identity as members of a 'dying race'. As Cornell notes:

> The symbols of Indianness, from bumper-sticker slogans to religious fetishes, are becoming more visible, not less. Much of this trend reflects a movement by some individuals to locate their own roots, to touch base with some identity more substantial than the dominant culture seems able to provide, an attempt to put thicker flesh on the bones of the self-concept.[73]

Indigenous peoples have also been engaged in the 'politics of memory', challenging the official versions of the past that promote widespread historical amnesia when it comes to their dispossession. In official narratives, the colonisation process is obfuscated through the use of stirring images of pioneer struggles against the forces of nature, as the spirit of progress opens up 'virgin lands' to the forces of civilisation. Historical agency is obscured as the 'natural' forces of development and progress, made manifest in individual pioneers, spread out over empty geographical space. Where natives appear they are silent figures, uncomprehending and incomprehensible, doomed to engage in futile resistance before fading from the scene. The violence of colonisation for 'them' is suppressed in the narrative of development, or is even glorified in public memory as something that happened to 'us' by epics of heroism like Little Big Horn. As Said, quoting Richard Slotkin, points out:

> [T]he shaping experience of American history was the extended wars with the native American Indians; this in turn produced an image of Americans not as plain killers (as D.H. Lawrence said of them) but as 'a new race of people, independent of the sin-darkened heritage of man, seeking a totally new and original relationship to pure nature as hunters, explorers, pioneers, and seekers'.[74]

Such triumphalist foundation myths receive their fullest expression in public celebrations like those occasioned by the Australian Bicentennial of 1988 and, more recently, the five hundredth anniversary of the 'discovery' of America by Columbus. In the final irony, newer settler colonies like Australia also attempt to redefine their identity in terms of the culture of the dispossessed, now safely preserved in museums:

> Meanwhile, having separated Aboriginal culture from living people – or all but a few very old individuals who would 'soon die out' – Anglo-Australians could enshrine it in museums and libraries as part of the national heritage they were 'discovering' in the process of differentiating the Australian nation from that of the 'Mother Country'.[75]

Indigenous peoples, including the Ainu, are challenging the official histories of the coloniser with counter-narratives that provide them with a coherent and usable past, a collective memory that helps mediate their present experience of marginalisation and struggle. To borrow from Yoneyama's study of Hiroshima, Hokkaidō has become the site of a struggle over the 'politics of memory',

> a field on which differing opinions about not only the past but also the present social order and the future trajectories are contested and interfaced . . . a site of struggles over various historical representations, a terrain on which conflicting ideas about history, identity and the meanings of existence are fought out.[76]

In North America, Clifton has provided a succinct, though hostile, outline of the new Indian narrative.[77] Yet in labelling this a 'cultural fiction' Clifton raises, but does not satisfactorily address, the question of the nature of 'truth' – cultural, scientific or historical – and who may be said to possess it. While many Native Americans themselves have also questioned the tendency of the young to become 'New Age Indians', critiques of new cultural and historical narratives – 'invented Indians' – mainly come from those endangered by indigenous political resurgence. This includes those anthropologists whose role as the acknowledged 'interpreters' of 'traditional cultures', a role dependent upon their positions within established structures of power, is under threat.

By the 1980s Ainu activists had become part of a global network of indigenous organisations representing an estimated population of more than two hundred million indigenous people from the Arctic to the South Pacific.[78] These groups share a sense of distinct cultural and historical identity and a political agenda of self-determination. Within this indigenous movement, ethnicity has become equated with nationhood; that is, the idea that a 'people' – understood as an ethnic rather than a civic community – should determine its own political institutions within an ancestral territory. The rhetoric of indigenous activists stresses that before the invaders arrived their peoples were already territorial 'nations'. This reaffirmation of the indigenous as 'first nations' is more than mere nostalgia but carries a clear political message; in current international law, as reflected in international human rights instruments, 'peoples' (left undefined by the United Nations) have the right to self-determination, while minorities do not.[79] International gatherings such as the annual United Nations Working Group on Indigenous Populations have become the forums for the articulation and further development of these ideas, extending their influence to other indigenous peoples from around the world. Those who never had the opportunity to enter into treaty arrangements have adopted the concept of a 'nationhood' that is now being denied, leading to activism being focused on issues of territorial land rights and political self-determination. Although Ainu activists did not participate in any large international indigenous gatherings until 1981, the leadership now clearly identifies with this international movement for indigenous self-determination. In their eyes, the Ainu are also an indigenous nation.

In this way, the dominant view of the Ainu as a 'dying race' has come to be challenged by the rhetoric and symbolism of an 'Ainu nation'. In reacting to marginalisation, Ainu activists in the postwar period are engaged in 'ethnopolitics' – what Stavenhagen summarises as 'not the expression of some form of primordial attachments, but an instrument in the struggle for power, directly linked to the process of modernisation'.[80]

Such an instrumental view of ethnicity, however, is not meant as a denial of the affective value of ethnic identity and cultural practice as part of everyday lived experience, what some analysts have referred to as 'private' as opposed to 'public' ethnicity.[81] The need for identity is probably an essential human need. 'Private' ethnicity is without doubt extremely important for many individual Ainu, fostering feelings of self-worth in the face of prejudice, discrimination, and the denial of identity. But this study is primarily concerned with 'public' ethnicity, and its role in inter-group conflicts over the distribution of resources and power. This carries the possible danger inherent in discussions of ethnicity at the macro-level to reify ethnic identity so that it becomes an either/or distinction. This is not necessarily the case. For the individual, ethnic identity is only one aspect of overall personal identity which contains gender, occupational, familial and socio-economic elements as well.[82] Ethnic identities themselves can operate at different levels; an Ainu can be simultaneously a member of a local community, an Ainu, a Japanese citizen, and an 'indigenous person' as part of the transnational indigenous movement. In situations of acculturation and assimilation, individuals can have experience of dual socialisation at home and in the wider community, or consider themselves bicultural.[83] Identity can change over the course of a lifetime as individuals move between assimilationist and isolationist tendencies. Some indigenous individuals have been able to pass back and forth between ethnic groups where boundaries are unstable, depending on where they perceive their interests to lie.[84] All these aspects of the relationship between individual self-concept – itself a multi-faceted realm of gender, socio-economic, or familial status mediated by experience and memory – and a group identity defined in terms of an imagined primordial community are relevant to an analysis of the experiences of Ainu today; but they are beyond the immediate scope of this study.

2 Barbarians and demons

The origins of the Ainu remain a subject of debate. While human beings have inhabited Hokkaidō since the retreat of the last Ice Age, it is virtually impossible to reconstruct the movements of populations throughout northeast Asia until well into the historical period. All that can realistically be said is that the indigenous population of the island were almost continually in contact with populations and cultures to both the north and south. By the ninth century, two distinct cultures flourished in Hokkaidō, named by archaeologists as the Satsumon and Okhotsk. The bearers of the Okhotsk culture lived along the north and northeast coastlines of Hokkaidō while the Satsumon, regarded as the direct ancestors of the Ainu, occupied the rest of the island and perhaps the northernmost tip of Honshū. What is now regarded as Ainu culture developed out of the Satsumon culture around the thirteenth century, by which time the inhabitants of southern Hokkaidō were engaged in regular trade with Honshū.[1]

A population of perhaps forty thousand Ainu lived throughout Hokkaidō, the Kuriles and Sakhalin, mainly in the southern half of that island.[2] The Ainu occupied an area rich in natural resources, Hokkaidō in particular having abundant deer and salmon. Ainu culture was characterised by hunting, fishing, and the gathering of edible plants, and a complex spiritual relationship with the phenomena of the natural world (personified as *kamuy*, deities) on which the Ainu depended.[3] The Ainu also developed a rich oral tradition including long heroic epics or *yukar*. The main religious rite was the *iyomante* ceremony, in which local communities came together to 'send back' the spirit of a deity (usually a bear) to the land of the gods, although when the ceremony developed to its present form is a matter of debate.[4] Economic activities were conducted in clear hunting and fishing territories (*iwor*) based on river systems, and could exceed subsistence requirements to produce a surplus for trade. Trade networks extended both to the south and to the Asian continent through Sakhalin and the Kuriles, as evidenced by the discovery of Japanese coins and objects in Kamchatka. Social organisation was based on patrilineal and matrilineal kin groups with clearly demarcated distinctions in status. The communities were ruled by a leader (*kotankorokur*), selected on the basis of both inheritance and ability, who took a leading role in trade and mediated disputes based on customary law. As trade with the Japanese developed, in some areas powerful leaders came to exert control over surrounding communities within a river system. While the Ainu shared broad cultural and linguistic similarities, regional variations in dialect and culture were evident, especially in Sakhalin and the Kuriles where the Ainu were in close contact with other northern peoples. Overall, early Ainu culture supported a way of life that was spiritually complex and, in most years, materially comfortable. Nevertheless, in the eyes of their southern neighbours they were no more than savages and barbarians.

EARLY IMAGES

The peoples who inhabited the regions beyond the northeastern borders of the early Yamato kingdom were referred to as *Emishi* or *Ebisu* in its earliest chronicles. Emishi meant barbarian and was written incorporating the Chinese ideograph for 'eastern barbarians' (different ideographs were used for the barbarians of the other three directions). The notion of the barbarian had entered Japan as part of the massive importation of Chinese culture and ways of thought that occurred between the sixth and eighth centuries. In classical Chinese terms, barbarians were hairy, non-human, flesh-eating savages who dressed in skins and lived in holes.[5] The section of the *Nihonshoki* (compiled around AD 720) dealing with the reign of Emperor Keikō (71–131) contains one of the earliest descriptions of the inhabitants of the lands to the east of Yamato:

> Amongst these Eastern savages the Yemishi are the most powerful, their men and women live together promiscuously, there is no distinction of father or child. In winter they dwell in holes, in summer they live in nests. Their clothing consists of furs, and they drink blood . . . In ascending mountains they are like flying birds; in going through the grass they are like fleet quadrupeds . . . Sometimes they draw together their fellows and make inroads on the frontier. At other times they take the opportunity of the harvest to plunder the people . . . ever since antiquity they have not been steeped in the kingly civilising influences.[6]

These 'kingly civilising influences' that linked the civilised community, and distinguished its members from barbarians, consisted of the common possession of written language and a moral superiority sanctioned by Heaven. This moral order, derived from Confucianism, was reflected in the customs of civilisation such as the consumption of the 'five kinds of grain'. Customs that differed, such as ways of dress, hairstyles, or the eating of meat (which came to be regarded as taboo after the introduction of Buddhism in the sixth century), were despised as backward and morally inferior. Equally important, barbarians were people not subject to the direct control of the central authorities – 'those who do not obey' (*matsurowanu hito*) – and thus outside the moral order.[7] In this way politics, culture and morality were fused in the categorisation of the Other as barbarian.

This dichotomous distinction between civilised Self and barbarian Other is known to Japanese historians as *ka-i* thought (*ka-i shisō*). It provided the ideological foundation of the Chinese tribute system, in which barbarians submitted to Imperial authority and presented goods as tribute. In fact, this 'tribute' and the gifts presented in return often possessed an economic dimension as a disguised trade relationship. This system was emulated by the Yamato authorities as they consolidated the *ritsuryō* state along Chinese lines after the Taika Reforms of 646. Such Sinocentric interpretations of the world were, however, the province of the literate elite. To what extent these concepts were shared, however vaguely, by those peasants and conscripts who fought, defeated and finally assimilated the peoples on the borderlands will never be known.

Apart from some early references to *mōjin* (hairy people) in Chinese records dealing with the land of Wa, what is generally considered to be the first substantial account of the peoples living to the north of the Yamato court appeared in the *Saimeiki* section of the *Nihonshoki*.[8] In 659 or 663 envoys from Yamato visited the T'ang court (618–907) accompanied by a male and female Emishi. The *Saimeiki* also reported the adventures of Prince Abe no Omi, who encountered various regional groups of people called Emishi while leading three expeditions to the north between 658 and 660. It is likely that one of the areas he visited, Watari(no)shima, was the island now known as Hokkaidō. From this time on, Watarishima looms on the outer limits of Japanese geographical consciousness. The Watarishima Emishi appear in occasional references between 658 and 893 and seem to have been somewhat different from other Emishi, providing 'tribute' (more likely trade) of furs and skins in contrast to the horses of the Tōhoku Emishi. They managed to preserve a separate identity while other Emishi groups were disintegrating under the pressure of Japanese expansion, leading some scholars to link them to the distinct Satsumon culture bearers of north Tōhoku and Hokkaidō.[9]

Suppressing the fierce barbarians of the frontier was a high priority of the ritsuryō regime as it sought to expand landholdings and divert potentially troublesome leaders from the capital. The years 789 and 878 saw the outbreak of major Emishi wars in north Tōhoku as political control expanded northwards. The Abe and Kiyohara families became the rulers of the Ōu region of Tōhoku from the eleventh century, marking the final pacification of the area and the furthest expansion of ritsuryō authority. This authority was not absolute, however; the rulers of these powerful clans were also called Emishi to underline their tenuous links with the Heian (794–1185) court, using the word in its political sense as 'those who do not obey'. This appellation was also favoured by the Fujiwara of Hiraizumi, who later controlled the whole area until they were destroyed by Minamoto Yoritomo shortly after the establishment of the Kamakura shōgunate, or Bakufu, in 1185.[10] With the Kamakura Bakufu, the first administration to bring all of Honshū under its nominal control, the term Emishi faded from usage to be replaced by *Ezo*. Thereafter, the ambiguity inherent in the use of Emishi also faded as Ezo came clearly to refer to the 'foreign' inhabitants of the islands across the Tsugaru Straits, the islands of Ezoga(chi)shima. While the Ezo differed both culturally and linguistically from the Emishi, the connotations of barbarism inherent in the term continued intact.[11] Indeed, Ezo was simply a new pronunciation of the same ideographs used to write Emishi.[12] Besides Ezo, the inhabitants of this region were also known as *ijin* or *iteki*, written incorporating the Chinese reading of the second ideograph of Ezo (*i* – barbarian).

By this time Japanese had begun to cross over to Ezogashima. Some of the first arrivals were murderers deported from the capital in the early twelfth century. Others fled across the straits after defeat in the internecine warfare endemic in Tōhoku at the time. According to legend, the most famous refugee was Minamoto Yoshitsune, who, having survived the massacres at Hiraizumi and in flight from his vengeful brother, crossed over and lived with the Ainu for a time, teaching them how to grow crops.[13] The Kamakura Bakufu appointed the Andō family rulers (*Ezo Kanrei*) of the Tsugaru area, from where they extended their influence over the straits to Hokkaidō. The origins of the Andō family, later Lords of Akita, are a subject of debate with some scholars maintaining that they were local Ezo or Satsumon leaders.[14] The Andō seat was Tosaminato in Tsugaru, an important port on the Japan Sea trade route, and the Satsumon/Ainu inhabitants of Hokkaidō came here to trade salmon, *konbu* (tangle), furs and Manchurian goods which then made their way to central Honshū.[15] A document of 1356 mentions what appears to be a mixed group of Japanese and Ainu called Wataritō (hereafter Wajin), who were living on the Oshima peninsula in southern Hokkaidō and trading with

Tsugaru. By the early Muromachi Period (1333–1568) Tosaminato was a thriving port with many Ainu *uimamchip* trade boats calling there. When the Andō temporarily lost control of Tsugaru in a struggle with the neighbouring Nanbu clan in the mid-fifteenth century, they too crossed over to Hokkaidō before re-establishing themselves in Akita, from where they continued to control the Wajin settlements on Hokkaidō.

The Ainu of this period were barbarians to be reckoned with, although contemporary accounts are fragmentary and it is impossible to reconstruct the Wajin image of the Ainu with any certainty. The overall impression, however, is that Ezogashima was a fearful place 'haunted by demons'.[16] In the *Heike Monogatari* (compiled between 1190 and 1218) defeated warriors pleading for their 'worthless lives' mention that they would even accept exile there if only they were spared.[17] The *Suwa Daimyōjin Ekotoba* (Pictorial Account of the Great Deity of Suwa) of 1356 divides the inhabitants of Ezogashima into three groups, those belonging to the outer 'foreign' groups having the appearance of demons, flesh-eating habits, no knowledge of the five kinds of grain and a strange tongue. The members of the Wataritō, traders with Tsugaru, although they speak a semi-comprehensible language and appear similar to 'men of the land of Wa', nevertheless grow hair all over their bodies.[18] Kaiho has pointed out that this description is very similar to that of the inhabitants of Kikaigashima (Devil Island, off Satsuma) in the *Heike Monogatari*.[19] Both areas were used for the transportation of felons, and similar descriptions of hairy, flesh-eating savages reflect what seems to be a stereotyped image of the lands bordering Kamakura territory at its eastern and western extremities.

Painted scrolls from this period offer further confirmation of these stereotypes. One of the earliest, dating from the late Kamakura period (1185–1333), portrays a group of Emishi paying homage to the seventh century Regent, Shōtoku Taishi. Probably based on images of the contemporary Ezo, the men are bearded and carry short bows similar to those later used by the Ainu, but their faces bear striking resemblances to the demons that appear in religious art of the period.[20] A whole series of these paintings based on legends of Shōtoku Taishi appeared in the late Kamakura and early Muromachi periods and are all very similar, indicating that the tendency to exaggerate the Otherness and subordination of the Ainu in art was already established.[21] By the early sixteenth century, this tendency towards demonising the Ainu is even more pronounced, illustrated by one work of 1517 that makes no attempt to portray reality.[22]

Despite the demonic character of the inhabitants of Ezogashima, they controlled natural resources that the Wajin desired, and as time passed a flourishing trade developed. Increasing numbers of Wajin began to cross the Tsugaru Straits undeterred by the images of a savage land; and with them the historical record becomes clearer. By the fifteenth century, Wajin trading settlements were dotted around the southern tip of Ezogashima and engaged in trade with powerful Ainu leaders in the vicinity. Both sides had come to rely on the trade; the Wajin settlements existed primarily for this purpose, while the Ainu not only depended on Wajin for iron tools, weapons, utensils and other necessities but valued trade goods as symbols of wealth and status, enabling local Ainu leaders who controlled trade to amass wealth and power.[23] In 1456 friction between the indigenes and newcomers flared into open warfare after a Wajin blacksmith murdered an Ainu in a quarrel over a blunt knife. The following year, Ainu led by Koshamain destroyed all but two of the settlements and almost drove the Wajin out of Hokkaidō altogether, initiating a century of intermittent warfare. The Wajin response to many of the Ainu attacks was to invite the leaders to peace negotiations and feasting, then cut them down during the banquet. The use of treachery (*damashi uchi*) is a common feature of this period, and was not seen as dishonourable among the Wajin leaders who employed it against each other in their own power struggles; but it was directly opposed to the Ainu custom of settling disputes through *charanke* or discussion.[24] In 1514 the Kakizaki family emerged as the leader of the Wajin in Oshima, subject to the Andō in Tsugaru. In 1551, Kakizaki Suehiro, convinced that continued warfare was not beneficial for trade, sought an accommodation with the local Ainu. The resulting agreement split the profits of trade between Ainu and Wajin leaders, but it gave Kakizaki monopolistic control over trade and established Japanese territorial control over the land between Kaminokuni and Shiriuchi. While this was only a very small area, it represented the first physical incorporation of part of Ezogashima into the political system of the 'mainland'.

Although these events took place at a considerable distance from the power struggle inaugurated by Oda Nobunaga and continued by his successors Toyotomi Hideyoshi and Tokugawa Ieyasu that eventually resulted in a unified regime at the start of the seventeenth century, evidence suggests that knowledge of Ezogashima and its strange inhabitants was fairly widespread among the elites of the mainland. In 1548 a Japanese from Kagoshima, a thousand miles from Ezogashima, made his way to Goa, where he informed Jesuit priests that to the north of Japan was a land called 'Gsoo' (Yezo) inhabited by huge, bearded natives who fought courageously with no fear of death.[25] This was the first time that Europeans heard of the existence of the Ainu. In 1591, another Jesuit, Ignacio Morera, visited the palace of Hideyoshi in Kyoto where he met an Ainu accompanying a Kakizaki delegation. This man informed the Father that he was from an island called Ainomoxori (Ainu moshir), the term used by the Ainu for the area where they live.[26] Somewhat later, as more consistent information concerning the Ainu began to reach the major urban centres of Honshū after the Shakushain War of 1669, often in the form of lurid and fantastic reports by travellers, the great popular playwright Chikamatsu Monzaemon described Ezogashima in *Kenjo no Tenarai* (A Wise Woman's Learning, 1685):

> This so-called Ezo island is located more than one thousand *ri* away. Whoever is born on this island possesses a great natural power. The hair grows upward and the light of the eyes is like the golden morning sun. Their angry shouting frightens the animals. They hunt and eat animals of the mountains and fields as well as fish. They indulge in fine wines and beautiful women and live lavishly. It is a strange country of no law and dissolute habits.[27]

In popular consciousness, as in political reality, Ainu territory was 'foreign' land.

THE MATSUMAE DOMAIN

In 1599 the Kakizaki family took the name of Matsumae, and in 1604 their small domain (*han*) was incorporated into the Tokugawa regime as a minor fief. The black seal edict of Tokugawa Ieyasu that legitimised the Matsumae *han*, following an earlier edict of Hideyoshi in 1593, confirmed Matsumae political authority within the territorial confines of the domain. The Matsumae were also granted a trade monopoly and the authority to regulate Wajin travel to Ainu territory. This territory encompassed most of the island and surrounding areas and was known as Ezochi (Ainu-land) in contrast to the Matsumae domain which was called Shamochi, Matsumaeryō or (later) Wajinchi. Borders were demarcated after a Bakufu inspection in 1633. While the Matsumae domain possessed rich fishing grounds there was little agricultural potential and the mainstay of the *han* economy was the Ainu trade, so it was imperative for the Matsumae to gain control of this process. Ezochi was therefore vital to Matsumae interests. Bakufu concerns, on the other hand, were based on the mistaken belief that Ezochi bordered on Korea and the Jurchen kingdom of Tatary (Manchuria).[28]

Trade largely took the form of *uimam*, whereby Ainu would travel to Matsumae to pay 'tribute' and receive gifts in return in the presence of Honshū traders. Ainu traders still visited Tōhoku as well as Sakhalin and the Amur region to the north. As it was up to Ainu communities to produce a trade surplus and take the decision to travel, the trading initiative was firmly in their hands. To reverse this situation and impose control on trade, during the early seventeenth century the Matsumae set up a series of trading posts in Ainu territory known as *akinaiba* and discouraged Ainu from trading at Matsumae. Matsumae was a poor domain, and while minor retainers received stipends in rice the most important were granted monopoly trading rights in these trading posts and the trading territories that went with them. These major retainers were known as *chigyōnushi*. Products from the *akinaiba* were exchanged with Honshū traders who were limited to the port of Matsumae where they were subject to control and taxation. This system increased trade volume and therefore domain profits from the taxes levied on cargoes, and later Esashi and Hakodate were also opened with similar restrictions. After 1644 Ainu boats were no longer to be seen in Tōhoku ports, an indication of the success of Matsumae attempts to monopolise trade. Although the Matsumae initially operated their own shipping fleet of seven small vessels, the *han* was becoming increasingly dependent on traders from Honshū, especially those of Ōmi (modern Shiga Prefecture), who brought in all the necessities of life that could not be produced in Matsumae. The domain, for instance, required some 55,000 bales of rice annually, of which the Matsumae and their retainers took 20 per cent.[29] Ōmi trading houses such as Ryōhamagumi and Yawatagumi began setting up branch offices in Matsumae from the 1630s and lending money to both the *chigyōnushi* and the ruling family itself. As debts increased the trading houses were able to take over the running of the trade with the Ainu. Motivated by risk and profit, the traders began to exploit the Ainu. For instance, the size of the *ezotawara*, the special small rice bales used in the Ezo trade for convenience of transportation, was reduced, in effect raising prices for one of the staple Wajin goods on which Ainu society had become dependent. As the leader of the Ainu in Shirafuka explained:

> During the time of the Lord of the Island (probably [Kakizaki] Yoshihiro) trading conditions were one sack of rice containing two *to* for five bundles of dried salmon. Recently they have started to give us only seven or eight *sho* of rice for the same amount of fish. Since we people have no power of refusal we are obliged to do as they please.[30]

The Wajin were also beginning to exploit the resources of Ainu territory (Ezochi) directly by fishing in Ainu waters near Matsumae, using nets to take large catches of salmon in the rivermouths and directly affecting the livelihood of the upstream Ainu. The discovery of gold brought thousands of Wajin miners into Ezochi from the 1620s, while hawk hunters also ranged through the hunting territories of the Ainu territorial groups. These incursions had a drastic affect on Ainu subsistence activities and lifeways.

Discontent among Ainu led by Henauke immediately to the north of the Matsumae domain flared in 1643 into a brief armed confrontation that was suppressed by Matsumae troops.

While the absence of Ainu records has led historians to focus on the dynamics of Japanese expansion, Ainu society itself was neither static nor passive. Under the influence of trade, Ainu communities along some river systems were coalescing into larger groups led by powerful chieftains capable of raising raiding parties to fight each other; some probably possessed firearms.[31] Ainu population density was heaviest in what is now the Hidaka region of South Hokkaidō due to lower snowfall and an abundance of deer. This area was roughly bisected by the boundary between two Ainu regional groups, the Shum(un)kur led by Onibishi and the Menash(un)kur under Kamoktain. In 1648 a feud arose between the two groups over a series of territorial violations, a matter taken very seriously in Ainu society.[32] While fearful for their trade and gold-panning interests in the area, the Matsumae were powerless to do more than offer to mediate. When Kamoktain was killed in 1653, Shakushain became leader of the Menashunkur. In 1655 both leaders accepted the Matsumae offer of mediation, but incidents continued to occur sporadically until Shakushain's men ambushed and killed Onibishi in 1668 while he was conferring with the leader of the Wajin miners in the area. The Shumunkur suffered further reverses and begged the Matsumae for assistance, but the Matsumae refused to intervene, saying they never interfered in Ainu wars. In reality, the Matsumae domain was small and militarily weak. A census in 1777, for instance, revealed that the population of the domain was 26,500, with only 170 samurai families including foot soldiers.[33]

By this time, discontent among the Ainu over merchant exploitation was running extremely high, and historical sources indicate that Shakushain was able to effect a reconciliation with the Shumunkur and send out envoys to other nearby Ainu groups in preparation for war against the Matsumae. In mid-1669 Ainu from many communities began attacking traders, miners and hawk hunters. In all, nineteen vessels were attacked and between two hundred and four hundred Wajin were killed. As the news began to trickle through to Matsumae panic gripped the commoners, but the Matsumae began to construct defences and sent a force of samurai, miners and fishermen to Kunnui to intercept Shakushain, then advancing west with several hundred men towards the Matsumae domain. The Matsumae, although normally resentful of any outside interference in their affairs, realised that they could not hide the facts from the Bakufu and sent a report to Edo. Still jittery after the Shimabara Uprising of 1637–1638 and concerned over the imagined proximity to Tatary, the Bakufu ordered Tsugaru and Nanbu domains to send troops and equipment to Matsumae.

When battle was finally joined Ainu weapons proved no match for samurai firearms. Later in the year Shakushain was treacherously assassinated during feigned peace negotiations. Tensions remained high, and pacification campaigns were sent against the Yoichi Ainu in 1670, to Shiraoi in 1671, and Kunnui in 1672, although the Matsumae were able to continue trade with Ainu in the far north and east who had not taken part in the fighting.

This war is commonly interpreted today as a straightforward 'ethnic' conflict, Ainu against Wajin. The imposition of twentieth century perspectives on the events of the mid-seventeeth century, however, can lead to serious distortion. The evidence suggests a far more complex picture. The repeated mention of Ainu regional groupings in the contemporary sources indicates that there is some basis for believing that Ainu society was undergoing a form of political consolidation. This, however, is not the same as nation-building and the formation of an overarching Ainu 'ethnic' identity. Inter-Ainu warfare shows that these groups often saw each other as rivals and enemies. The Matsumae were one among several powerful forces and allegiances were fluid; Ainu soldiers, for instance, had previously fought among Kakizaki troops in Tōhoku to put down the rebellion of Kunohe Masazane against Hideyoshi in 1591.[34] Even the Matsumae, in the tradition of peripheral warlords, did not always perceive themselves as unequivocably Japanese; in 1618 the daimyō Matsumae Kimihiro asserted to the visiting missionary Geronimo de Angelis that 'Matsumae is not Japan'.[35] Contemporary accounts also mention that among Shakushain's allies were four Wajin. It is possible that they were Christians, as were many of the miners who had fled from persecution on Honshū after the Shimabara Uprising. Another view is that they were traders from other domains along the Japan Sea coast, eager to break the Matsumae monopoly on the Ainu trade and share in the profits, and were supported by Shakushain who wished to be able to re-establish direct trade links with Honshū. One of the Wajin was the son-in-law of Shakushain, an indication that certain Wajin allies and traders may have been incorporated within the Ainu kinship system.[36]

Nevertheless, within a few years independent Ainu power had been broken. Even proud leaders like Haukase of the Ishikari Ainu, who had refused to take sides on the pretext that he and the Matsumae had nothing to do with each other, were now forced to swear allegiance to the Matsumae and promise to observe certain regulations.[37] These included reporting plotters and refraining from harming any Wajin. Another regulation stipulated that the Ainu were not to trade with any other region. This has been variously interpreted either as indicating that Ainu interest in establishing relations with other *han* and breaking the Matsumae monopoly had been an underlying cause of the war, or that Ainu from different areas were no longer to trade with each other.[38] Either way, it indicates that the Matsumae now had firm control over trade. Ainu in the outlying areas to the north and east, however, still remained independent or maintained a *uimam* or tribute relationship with Matsumae. But with the rise in Matsumae dominance, the trading posts and trade vessels gradually began to penetrate into their territories as well, reaching Karafuto (Sakhalin) in 1679, and the island of Kunashiri in 1754. In 1774 Kunashiri became the trading territory of the merchant Hidaya Kyūbei, although the establishment of permanent commercial operations in this area was impossible until 1782 due to the intransigence and power of the local Ainu leaders.

From the early eighteenth century the trading territories, now numbering around seventy and known as *basho*, gradually came under the direct control of mainland traders. There were a number of underlying reasons for this. From the point of view of the Matsumae, a decrease in *han* income from other traditional sources such as lumber, gold mining and the capture of hawks (these resources were exhausted by around 1720) led to strong pressure to expand trade. Moreover, expenses were increasing. The Matsumae had been granted full daimyō status in 1716 and even though obligations to the Bakufu were limited to visiting Edo once every three or five years, rather than residing alternate years in the capital, this put a severe strain on *han* finances. Before long the Matsumae were deeply in debt to the mainland merchants. The Matsumae hoped that letting merchant contractors operate the *basho* after paying a fee (*unjōkin*) would increase trade volume and profits, and therefore tax receipts. This arrangement gradually developed over the course of the eighteenth century and has come to be known as the *basho ukeoi* (subcontracted trading post) system. By 1804, *han* income from contractors' fees alone stood at 7,000 *ryō*, whereas income in 1739 from all taxes levied on trade had only come to 3,200 *ryō*.[39] Conversely, to pay these taxes and *unjōkin* (along with forced 'loans' to the Matsumae of which there was little chance of repayment), the traders began to move away from barter trade to a more rationalised system designed to increase trade volume. This was aided by the development of mainland agriculture which increased demand for fish fertiliser and stimulated interest in the fisheries of Ezochi. By 1740, according to a contemporary observer, half the rice paddies in western Japan were using fish-meal fertiliser from Ezochi.[40] Goods from the region also entered international trade routes via Nagasaki. These developments were made possible by the systematic exploitation of fishing grounds using merchant capital, technology and management, and Ainu labour. This was a gradual process that did not reach full development until the nineteenth century. Contractors introduced advanced fishing methods and equipment, built processing facilities and barracks for the Ainu labourers, and shipped the products directly to markets in the Kinai region. Risks were high, and high fees and forced loans to the Matsumae put pressure on the contractors to make the highest profits possible. While conditions varied between *basho*, in some areas this resulted in cruel treatment of the Ainu.[41]

Emphasis had shifted from obtaining the products of Ainu labour through trade to the direct exploitation of that labour itself. Ainu communities around the *basho*, heavily dependent on Wajin trade goods and whose leaders also derived authority from their involvement with the *basho*, were coerced into providing labour in return for rations or goods. Conditions were often harsh. In 1789, after some years of suffering an exceptionally cruel regime, Ainu attacked and killed seventy-one Wajin on Kunashiri and in the Nemuro area. This final act of armed resistance was eventually suppressed by the Matsumae with the help of local Ainu leaders under their political control. After an investigation thirty-seven Ainu were sentenced to death at Nokkamappu. The condemned Ainu refused to be quietly beheaded one by one in front of their fellows, forcing Japanese troops to rush the stockade and slaughter them there.

The development of trading posts and fishing stations had significant effects on Ainu–Wajin relations, which in turn led to changes in Wajin perceptions of the Ainu. Contacts with the Ainu increased in both duration and intensity accompanied by an increasing systematisation of economic and political relations. Such changing relations were still interpreted within the overarching *ka-i* world-view – whose stock of images ranged from the ancient bestial Emishi to the fantastic apparitions of Chikamatsu – but as relations evolved these images themselves came to be modified. This is not to imply that these images and stereotypes were mere epiphenomena that passively reflected material relations; on the contrary, since they both explained and justified reality they influenced those relations themselves in an ongoing dialectical process. Cruel exploitation of the Ainu, for instance, driven by the need for high profits, was initially facilitated by the fact that they were already regarded as inhuman and inferior, and the consequent spectacle of Ainu degradation encouraged the myth that they were descended from dogs. This belief then justified further inhuman treatment and exploitation.

But wider political developments in northeast Asia were now beginning to make themselves felt in Ezochi. By the mid-eighteenth century, the adventurers and fur traders who operated on the eastern limits of the Russian Empire had begun to penetrate into the Kurile Islands. The northern frontier became a matter of urgent concern to the Bakufu. One aspect of the Tokugawa response to the perceived Russian threat was a discourse of moral obligation towards the barbarians of Ezochi. In stark contrast to the beliefs prevalent in the *basho*, the Bakufu viewed the natives as potential allies to be won over with kindness and the benefits of civilisation.

These contradictory images can be clearly seen in the increasing number of historical documents concerning the Ainu that appeared in the eighteenth and nineteenth centuries. These records fall into two broad categories. First there are the accounts left by those who were outsiders to the region: the explorers, travellers and officials visiting Ezochi on what were often official Bakufu missions. The attitudes of these men were informed by Tokugawa concerns, which they in turn influenced, with military security and the development of the region. They transcended the bounds of immediate local political and economic relations and perceived the Ainu in terms of a broader geopolitical reality. In contrast are the accounts of the local Wajin inhabitants of Matsumae and Ezochi. These men – traders, itinerant workers and Matsumae officials – saw the Ainu in a different light, one which reflected the actual everyday experience of subjugation and exploitation for profit. While both groups viewed the Ainu as barbarians, their differing experiences and priorities led them to emphasise different aspects of the barbarian image.

CIVILISING THE BARBARIANS: THE BAKUFU IN EZOCHI

As the Bakufu consolidated internal rule in the early seventeenth century it also made a systematic attempt to regulate diplomatic and commercial contacts with neighbouring countries, leading to a transformation in the notions of civilised and barbarian. Tokugawa attempts to construct a 'Japan-centered *ka'i* order' in foreign relations included a deliberate rebuff of China in 1621, and with the fall of the Ming dynasty to the 'barbarian' Ch'ing in 1644 the orthodoxy of civilised China and barbarian Japan no longer matched the reality of Tokugawa ascendancy.[42] By 1715 the Chinese at Nagasaki had been relegated to 'barbarian' status in trading regulations. Yamazaki Ansai (1618–1682) and Yamaga Sokō (1622–1685) were among the scholars who debated how to justify Japan replacing China as the Middle Kingdom, and therefore as the repository of civilised values in the world. This theme was given new direction by Motoori Norinaga (1730–1801) and others associated with the *Kokugaku* (Native Learning) movement, which arose as a reaction to attempts to justify Japanese civilisation in Chinese terms. Motoori repudiated Confucianism, and based his teaching on the largely ignored classical texts of ancient Japan, the *Nihonshoki, Kojiki* and *Manyōshū*, in which he found that the true Way and innate superiority of pre-Confucian Japan were revealed.

The unbroken Imperial line was taken as living proof of this moral superiority; all other peoples were therefore inferior. For the nativists, Japanese culture and customs were the basis of Japanese superiority. While *Kokugaku* was initially only a minor and subversive current in Tokugawa intellectual life, these ideas were later incorporated into a regenerated Confucianism by the xenophobic Mito School, concerned by increasing incursions by foreigners in the late eighteenth and early nineteenth centuries. The appearance of Russians in the north meant that Ezogashima and the Ainu were now a matter of utmost concern in Tokugawa political circles.[43]

Russian explorers and traders had become increasingly active in the Kuriles at about the same time that Japanese influence was extending to the southern islands of the chain.[44] Shumushu, the most northerly of the Kuriles, was first colonised by Russians in the 1730s, and by 1749 most of the mixed indigenous population of Ainu and Kamchadal had been baptised as Orthodox Christians. As they penetrated further south, Russian imposition and occasionally brutal enforcement of the fur tax (*iasak*) in the southern Kurile islands angered the local Ainu, and in 1771 they massacred a Russian party on Uruppu (Urup) and removed Russian influence from the area for a brief period. But the Russians soon returned, and in 1792 Adam Laxman landed at Nemuro requesting the opening of trade relations with Japan. Permission was refused. In Edo arguments for the annexation of Ezochi, stimulated primarily by the perceived Russian threat, had become increasingly influential. Agents and explorers were dispatched by the Bakufu (and by other interested parties like the powerful Mito *han*) to survey the northern regions and spy on both the Russians and the Matsumae. These men were aware of the importance of the Ainu, not just as a source of labour, but as potential allies. In 1798 the Bakufu sent a large expedition to Ezochi, including Sakhalin and the Kuriles, and in 1799 overrode Matsumae objections by annexing part of the region. By 1807 all Ezochi had been placed under direct Bakufu control through offices established in Hakodate. An official was stationed at the former Matsumae trading post in Karafuto to control directly the trade between the local Ainu and the northern peoples of the Amur river (known as the Santan trade). In most respects, however, Ezochi retained the nature of a foreign land (*iiki*) since it was too vast and rugged to administer in the same way as other Tokugawa lands. The Bakufu stationed garrisons around the coast, reinforcing these after Russian marauders raided Karafuto and Etorofu (Iturup) in 1806 and 1807, but most Wajin still lived in the narrow bounds of the Matsumae domain or at the fishing stations.

For those who urged the annexation and administration of Ezochi by the

Bakufu, and for most of the Bakufu officials who implemented it after 1799, the Ainu were childish and backward barbarians. As morally and culturally inferior they needed to be brought into the fold of civilisation under the benevolent guidance of the Bakufu. Barbarians could become civilised with the adoption of the customs of 'ritual and righteousness', interpreted as Japanese customs, and indeed, this was seen as morally desirable by some thinkers.[45] Hayashi Shihei (1738–1793) noted that 'to educate the Ezo, to teach them humanity, and to help them cultivate the land [are the] wishes of the Gods'.[46] Honda Toshiaki (1744–1821) argued in 1798 that:

> By helping the natives and giving them everything they desire, one will inspire a feeling of affection and obedience in them, like the love of children for their parents. This is true because they are moved by the same feelings that pervade the rest of the world, barbarians though they may be considered.[47]

The Bakufu heeded this advice after taking control by introducing a policy of 'enlightening' or 'civilising' (*kyōka*) the Ainu in conjunction with welfare measures and the elimination of unjust trading practices.[48] Enlightenment meant assimilation through 'Japanising customs' (*kizoku* or *kaizoku*). The instructions issued to officials in charge of the new administration clearly reveal how the ideological rhetoric of bringing civilisation to the natives only thinly disguised political motives:

> The reasons for bringing Ezochi under the rule of the central authorities are that the island is undeveloped, and the barbarians (*ijin*) have poor clothing, food and housing and do not know the moral way. Officials sent there will enlighten and educate them, gradually bring them to adopt Japanese customs (*Nihon fūzoku ni ki shi*), and make them gratefully submit to us and not be won over by foreign countries.[49]

These objectives were echoed in the *Kyūmei Kōki*, a record of the early years of Bakufu control. Stating that 'the natives in Ezo, although they are human beings, are a very ignorant people', the author went on to note that the best course was to pursue a policy of assimilation and 'treat the natives with kindness'. It was also pointed out that the Tōhoku Emishi had been successfully assimilated:

> In the early days the Ezo occupied what is now Miyagi-gun in Sendai and it has, over the years come into its present condition . . . so with the passage of years it would not be an impossible task to achieve the same with Ezo. And the gain to our country would be immeasurable.[50]

That Japanising the Ainu was feasible was pointed out throughout the first half of the nineteenth century by travellers and explorers from Ezochi. Referring to the barbaric custom of fastening garments on the left, a taboo associated with death as well as Confucianism, one account noted:

> In lands where learning has not penetrated, the inhabitants are no different from children. Those who find their left hand convenient tie on the left; those who find their right hand convenient tie on the right. Among the Ezo there are even a rare few who tie their garments on the right without having been taught. If they were exposed to the light of learning is there any doubt that they would be equal to our countrymen?[51]

Similar sentiments were expressed by the explorer Mogami Tokunai (1754–1836) who appears to have regarded the enlightenment of the Ainu as something of a personal mission.[52] To buttress their support for assimilation, these writers went out of their way to stress the 'common origins' (*Wa-i dōso*) of the Ainu and the Japanese, based largely on superficial cultural and linguistic comparisons.[53]

In its implementation of the policy of Japanisation, the Bakufu administration attempted to compel the Ainu to adopt Japanese dress, hairstyle, eating habits, law, religion and lifestyle. Beards were shaved, often forcibly, and *iyomante* (bear festivals) were banned. Most Ainu resisted this policy, fearing the punishment of the gods that was sure to come if they abandoned their cultural traditions, and immediately reverted to their usual customs when it was dropped. The military and political concerns that informed the Japanisation policy are highlighted by the fact that it was most aggressively pursued on Etorofu island where the Russian threat was greatest and the Bakufu were devoting considerable manpower and resources to establishing a Japanese presence. Even here, however, only 44 per cent of the men and 27 per cent of the women adopted Japanese customs.[54]

Ultimately, whatever its influence in Edo, the rhetoric of 'Japanisation' had little effect in Ezochi. The assimilation policy was resisted not only by the Ainu themselves, but also by Matsumae officials and the local operators of the *basho*. Nominally, this was because it made the Ainu harder to control, but another reason was that the idea of assimilation was incompatible with the deeply prejudicial attitudes of those Japanese in everyday contact with the Ainu. Reports and writings from Ezochi in the Tokugawa period clearly reflect the alternative view of Ainu society held by local Wajin.

DOGS AND HUMANS

Most of the early visitors to Ezochi used the classical Emishi stereotype to describe their encounters with the Ainu. In the *Ezo Dan Hikki* of 1710, for instance, little had changed in the thousand years since the *Nihonshoki*:

> They know not the moral way, so fathers and children marry indiscriminately. They do not have the five kinds of grain and eat the flesh of birds, beasts and fish. They gallop around the hills and dive into the sea and are just like some kind of beast.[55]

One over-sensitive traveller recorded that his first sight of the Ainu made him 'feel sick, until my eyes got used to it'.[56] The unfamiliar customs of the Ainu were also singled out as proof of barbarism. Besides such obviously barbarian customs as ear-rings and female tattoos, the absence of civilisation was also indicated by the eating of flesh, unkempt hair, clothing fastened on the left and the lack of a written language.[57] The hairy and dirty appearance of the Ainu was emphasised: 'When you walk past an Ezo they are extremely smelly, to the point that you have to hold your nose.'[58] 'Their bodies are most hairy and their eyebrows a single line; some even grow body hair like bears.'[59] In character, the Ainu were seen as ignorant and childish, easy to deceive but capable of violent emotion. It was also believed that they could only count with difficulty, and did not know their own ages since they had no calendar and no sense of time.[60]

As noted above, the establishment of the Tokugawa Bakufu, followed a few years later by that of the Matsumae *han*, had initiated a new stage in Ainu–Wajin relations. The clear delineation of Wajin and Ainu territory was a local variation on what has retrospectively, and somewhat misleadingly, been termed *sakoku* (closed country), the Bakufu policy of controlled contact on its borders that was also evident in the Ryūkyū islands, with the Dutch and Chinese in Nagasaki, and the Koreans through Tsushima.[61] In conjunction with geographical barriers, Wajin in Ezochi went to great lengths to prohibit the Ainu from using Japanese language, hairstyles, clothing and raingear. As Honda Toshiaki reported:

> It is forbidden to carry . . . seeds for the five cereals or edged tools for use in building houses. It is forbidden to teach Japanese to any natives. These lamentable prohibitions are supplemented by a host of others, all designed to keep barbarians forever in their present condition.[62]

The extent to which these measures were a systematic policy of the Matsumae authorities to maintain a distinct barbarian identity for the Ainu remains unclear.[63] Certainly, outsiders like the explorer Mogami Tokunai regarded them as such. Mogami, however, was no friend of the Matsumae, who had treated him harshly after he had taught his Ainu companion Japanese on a surveying expedition in 1786.[64] There is certainly evidence to suggest that the Matsumae actively discouraged agriculture since it would deprive the fishing stations of labour (the Bakufu also realised this, and quietly dropped its own plans for agriculturisation in 1802).[65] Under the terms of the Bakufu edicts, however, Ezochi was outside domain borders and the Ainu were not subject to political control, although the Matsumae became increasingly inclined to regard Ezochi as Matsumae territory and exercise direct authority in exceptional circumstances, as illustrated by the executions at Nokkamappu in 1789. In the *basho* Ainu were generally controlled indirectly through leaders (*otona, kozukai*) appointed or recognised by the contractors, but who exercised real authority within their communities. It is equally likely, therefore, as Takakura has noted, that 'many of the oppressive acts recorded as being rules of the Matsumae were, in actuality, regulations set up by the merchant contractors for their own benefit'.[66] The Matsumae appointed officials (*uwanoriyaku*) to supervise the *basho*, but these men were often in the business of personal enrichment and turned a blind eye to the activities of the traders, who were essentially a law unto themselves in Ezochi.[67]

Be this as it may, at the local level the Otherness of the Ainu was rigorously reinforced by such prohibitions. It is probably no coincidence that these regulations were similar to those enforced on the *eta:hinin* outcastes of Tokugawa society; both Ainu and outcastes were regarded as non-human and outside the status system. The two groups were consciously linked in the minds of some. The unbound hair of the Ainu reminded a few travellers of the outcastes, perhaps prompted by a current theory that the outcastes were originally of Emishi origin since both ate meat and were therefore ritually polluted. Hoashi Banri, for instance, put forward this view in 1844 in support of his suggestion that *eta* be sent to colonize Ezochi.[68]

The often severe exploitation of Ainu labour in the *basho* was facilitated by these existing images of barbarians that denied humanity to the Ainu while emphasising bestial and demonic traits. When not describing themselves in their economic roles as contractors or overseers (*ukeoinin, shihainin, bannin*), Wajin referred to themselves, echoing ancient Chinese convention, as 'humans' (*ningen*) in contrast to the 'barbarians' (*Ezo, ijin*).[69] The Japanese language became 'human language' (*ningen kotoba*).[70] Ainu who attempted to learn *katakana* or agriculture were mocked for 'mimicking the ways of humans' (*ningen no mane*).[71] Besides emphasising their own 'humanity', the local Wajin denied that of the Ainu by attributing to them animalistic qualities or origins. The most notorious, and persistent, example of this was the notion that the Ainu were descended from a dog.[72] This legend is attributed to the Ainu themselves in contemporary records such as *Ezogashima Kikan* (Strange Views of Ezo, 1799) although this type of legend also has parallels in China.[73] Mogami Tokunai had his own theory for the origins of this belief, speculating that it was a story initiated by the Matsumae 'to show that the Ainu are a different kind of human'.[74] Whatever its origins, there is little doubt that the generation of this myth paralleled and justified the dehumanisation of the Ainu as exploited labour on the fishing stations and the callous cruelty with which they were treated. Western travellers who began to arrive in the area in the late nineteenth century also reported the widespread belief in the canine origins of the Ainu. One related being told by a grinning Japanese companion that the Ainu were 'remarkably like dogs'.[75] The intrepid British traveller Isabella Bird, visiting in 1878, records her Wajin manservant exclaiming 'the Aino are just dogs; they had a dog for a father', an allusion to 'their own legend of their origin'.[76]

Most of the Wajin in closest contact with the Ainu were not the officials and merchants of Honshū and Matsumae but illiterate and itinerant *dekasegi* (seasonal migrant workers) from Matsumae and the poor northern fiefs of Ōu (Tōhoku). These men (and they were all men until the final years of the Bakufu) filled positions as overseers, translators and sailors. As the scale of the fisheries increased from the late eighteenth century they also came to be employed as labourers alongside the Ainu, although wage differentials were rigorously applied. In 1855, for example, the contractor at the Tokachi *basho* paid a Wajin *dekasegi* 240 *mon* for a bundle of twenty dried cod while an Ainu received 80 *mon* for the same amount.[77] These *dekasegi* were typically uneducated second or third sons of struggling Tōhoku farmers with no chance of inheriting land or forming a branch family; in short, the lowest stratum of rural society. Of the eighty-seven migrant workers at the Etorofu *basho* in 1860, for example, by far the largest number, thirty-two, were from Miyako in Morioka *han* (now Iwate Prefecture). Twelve came from Hakodate and three from Matsumae, the rest originating from other areas of Tōhoku.[78]

The *dekasegi* themselves left no written records of how they perceived their relations with the Ainu. How they behaved, however, is recorded in contemporary accounts. The *Tōyuki* (Record of a Journey to the East, 1783) noted that the crews of vessels trading in Ezochi were 'mostly men of poor education and morals who took it for granted that all Ezo were ignorant and cheating and stealing were very common'.[79] The *Tōkai Santan* (Three Stories of the Eastern Seas, 1806) describes most of the *dekasegi* as 'outlaws, refugees or persons denounced by their kinsfolk'.[80] Cruelty and rape were commonplace. The main cause of the fighting in 1789 in Kunashiri was a brutal regime in which at least one Ainu woman was beaten to death.[81] Mogami Tokunai noted that the Wajin plundered, cheated and 'treated [the natives] like animals'.[82] One observer at Oshamanbe in 1808, watching Ainu labourers clad only in thin garments working in the bitter cold while being beaten by the overseers, neatly reversed current demonic stereotypes in his image of 'the demon torturers at the court of the fiery king punishing sinners'.[83] Besides the belief in the Ainu as dogs, it is likely that the superstitions and images of demons and outsiders that were a vital part of the folklore of village Japan also influenced the way Ainu were perceived by the *dekasegi*.[84]

Despite such attitudes and behaviour, and the prohibitions on Japanese customs that served to clearly demarcate the two groups and preserve status distinctions, it was next to impossible for the contractors to regulate the carnal desires of single men working for long periods in a foreign land. Before long, liaisons began to arise between the Wajin migrant workers and Ainu women. There was an element of coercion in many instances, and some women died as a result of abuse while others committed suicide.[85] Nevertheless, although sexual impropriety was taboo in Ainu culture, under conditions in the *basho* many women, willingly or otherwise, did become mistresses of the *dekasegi*. With the possible exception of Etorofu island during the most urgent phase of the assimilation policy, these relationships were never legalised and the women were usually abandoned.

In general, the children of such liaisons were brought up as Ainu and treated as such by the local contractors and *dekasegi*, even those who were conscious of their Wajin inheritance. A certain Ichimatsu, for instance, the son of an Ainu woman of Shiranuka named Onhetsashi and a minor Bakufu official, attempted to retain a Japanised lifestyle after his father was sent back to the mainland on reversion to Matsumae rule. But the overseers confiscated his weapons and forbade him to use Japanese, and he was only able to adopt Japanese customs when the Bakufu resumed control over thirty years later.[86] Nevertheless, despite the rhetoric of assimilation the Bakufu, too, tended to regard these individuals as members of Ainu society.[87] This was certainly the view of the authorities during the early Kaitakushi (Colonisation Commission, 1869–1882) period. When a census of the Ainu of Shari was carried out in 1877, around one in five were of mixed descent, but were registered as Ainu with some such note as 'father Wajin of Nanbu'.[88] There is almost no evidence to indicate how such people were accommodated within Ainu society, although one Wajin official (perhaps not impartially) observed in 1856 that there were many offspring of Wajin men and Ainu women in the Saru and Mombetsu areas, and that they were called '*shamo-shu*' (*shamo*-kind) and respected by other Ainu. Some of them expressed pride in their mixed ancestry.[89]

Given the prevalence of strong negative attitudes among the local Wajin, it is unsurprising that Bakufu officials encountered considerable opposition from the *basho* when they attempted to enforce an assimilation policy as part of a broader strategy of employing the Ainu as allies against the Russians. With their strong antipathy towards the Ainu, the contractors and *dekasegi* were particularly resistant to the notion of the Ainu as equally human 'new Japanese' (*shin shamo*). Apart from their inability to accept as equals those whom they had despised for so long, there was concern that Japanisation would make the Ainu harder to control, thus jeopardising Wajin economic interests. When the Russian threat receded and Ezochi was handed back to the Matsumae in 1821, the first act of the contractors was to scrap the Japanisation policy and return to the *ka-i* status ante by reintroducing the regulations banning the use of Japanese language and customs.[90]

The gulf that separated the rhetoric of 'civilising the Ainu' from the actual conditions in Ezochi was reflected in the further economic exploitation and consequent degradation of the Ainu that occurred under the re-established Matsumae between 1821 and 1855. Traders, now subcontracting directly from the Matsumae, were given increased administrative and political control over the Ainu through seasonal ceremonies known as *omusha* at which regulations were read out to the assembled Ainu. Forced labour and resettlement became a feature of Ainu life. Ainu labour was used for roadbuilding, transportation and servicing the fisheries, in addition to direct economic production. Ainu were brought down from the mountains to work on the coast, or were transferred between *basho* run by the same trader. The recruitment of labour was accomplished by the use of physical coercion by armed Wajin if necessary, and the elderly and infirm were left behind in their villages to cope as best they could. The sexual exploitation of Ainu women increased. In the Kushiro *basho*, for instance, thirty-six out of the forty-one *dekasegi* had taken Ainu women after sending their husbands to work in the fisheries at Akkeshi.[91] Not all women succumbed:

> Uetematsu was twenty-two years old and extremely beautiful . . . One overseer desired her and sent her husband Sekkaushi to the fisheries. While Sekkaushi was away the overseer would repeatedly enter the room where Uetematsu slept and make lewd suggestions, but she gave not the slightest sign of assent. He continued to harrass her, taking her to the fisheries and threatening her if she did not do as he wished, but she would not give in. When he again entered her room and attempted to rape her she struggled and crushed his penis. I have forgotten the man's name, but in 1856 his penis was so painful that he could not work.[92]

Diseases inadvertently introduced by the *dekasegi* also contributed to the destruction of Ainu society; in 1817, for example, 833 out of 2,130 Ainu in the Ishikari *basho* died in an epidemic. The Ainu population of West Ezochi fell from 9,068 in 1798 to 4,384 in 1854.[93] As the Ainu ceased to be the main economic producers of Ezochi the movement of immigrants increased, encouraged by the easing of travel restrictions and tolls. As a result, by the 1850s the strict distinction that had previously been maintained between Wajinchi and Ezochi had begun to break down.

In response to a renewed threat from Russia and pressure to open Hakodate as a treaty port to Western powers, the Bakufu again moved into the Matsumae domain to take over Hakodate in 1854, extending control over all Ezochi the following year and Karafuto in 1856. Though an assimilation policy was reintroduced in this second and final period of Bakufu control, it met with only limited success. Contractors complained that the burden of paying for the associated 'welfare' (*buiku*) measures and the provision of rations for infirm and dependent Ainu fell upon their shoulders and that periodic inspections by Bakufu officials diverted the Ainu from work and lowered production. Some contractors resisted even to the point of open defiance of the authorities. In an effort to undermine assimilation policy, one disingenuous protest to the Bakufu argued that allowing the Ainu to cultivate fields and use 'human language' would make their native gods unhappy.[94]

Writings from this time display the conflicting images prevalent among the Wajin. On the one hand, sympathetic Japanese officials argued that:

> The Ezo are not to be thought pitiable due to their dishevelled hair or habit of tying their robes on the left, or for eating raw meat and living in holes. The reason they are to be pitied is that formerly no-one has taught them the way of humanity, the relationships between lord and subject, father and child, husband and wife, and older and younger. If they were to learn the way of humanity, then unkempt hair and left-tied kimono would not matter in the least.[95]

The feasibility and desirability of Japanisation were also echoed by Yoshida Shōin, who visited former Ainu villages in Tsugaru in 1852.[96] For most Wajin in Ezochi, however, the Otherness of the Ainu defied Japanisation. Local reports indicate that most Ainu, however willing to assimilate Japanese norms of dress and behaviour, could not escape their barbarian status. One official on an inspection trip to Karafuto in 1856–1857 noted that there were around thirty Japanised Ainu on the east coast of Sakhalin but only one in the west, and that 'although he dressed his hair, shaved his beard and tied his robe on the right he could not escape being an Ezo'.[97] Ainu who adopted Japanese ways were not referred to as Wajin, but as 'Japanised natives' (*kikoku Ezojin* or *kizoku dojin*). In a telling anecdote, the great explorer Matsuura Takeshirō (1818–1888) related the following incident concerning Ekashihashui, a boy from Abuta who adopted Japanese ways and changed his name to Ichisuke. Ichisuke mastered the Japanese writing system within a year and could use the language fluently in everyday life, learning much from Japanese maps and books. He approached Matsuura asking to be taken to Edo:

> I told him, 'I will take you after the Bakufu lift the ban on it'. To this he answered, 'That is a long time ago and is now irrelevant. I may have been Ainu once but I have now Japanised and become a Wajin. If you tell me that because I used to be Ainu so now I cannot do the same as Wajin then why did I go to the trouble to learn an unfamiliar language and shave my head so that I feel cold in this severe climate?'[98]

Matsuura was impressed by the boy, applied for travel permits to Bakufu officials in Hakodate, and took Ichisuke with him to Edo in 1855. But most Wajin were not so easily persuaded. In his travel journals and other works, Matsuura provided a wealth of examples of the inhumane treatment of Ainu by *basho* workers and officials, and the contempt in which they were held despite the official ideology of benevolence.[99]

NINETEENTH CENTURY IMAGES OF THE AINU

By the time of the Meiji Restoration a well-developed image of the barbarian and inferior Ainu paralleled their political and economic subjugation. This image survived intact into the subsequent Kaitakushi period, when, despite a programme of active colonisation by the Meiji authorities, conditions in most of Hokkaidō actually changed much less than is often assumed. The stereotypes first articulated under the *basho* system were to prove extremely durable and resurface in later periods and within different contexts; some can still be encountered today.

A prime example is the belief in Ainu incapacity for mathematics, expressed in the myth of *Ainu kanjō* (Ainu counting).[100] Stated simply, this is the belief that the Ainu could only count with difficulty, adding extra words for 'beginning' and 'end' during the counting process. It was also said that they did not know their own ages. In fact, the Ainu actually employed a highly developed counting system based on units of twenty, which indicates that it was not copied from the Japanese, and they used a variety of devices such as knots and carved marks to keep track of numbers and trade transactions.[101] The myth of *Ainu kanjō*, then, like other myths of Ainu inferiority, has its origins not in observed reality but in the dynamics of an unequal trading relationship in which the dependent and powerless Ainu were unable to avoid being cheated on most transactions. Another explanation, given to Matsuura Takeshirō by an Ainu elder named Kotonran, is that as Ainu society began to break up under forced migration and long periods of labour in the barracks of the fishing stations the traditional patterns of teaching and learning were disrupted, with the result that Ainu on the coast were unable to inherit traditional concepts of time and space.[102]

Graphic arts of the period also display the crystallisation of negative images of the Ainu. The *Ishū Retsuzō* of 1790, the paintings of the powerful leaders of the Akkeshi and Kunashiri Ainu, are a good example.[103] In these portraits, painted by Kakizaki Hakyō, a member of the Matsumae family, and circulated among the Tokugawa elite, the Otherness of the Ainu is highlighted by the exaggeration of physical characteristics, including hairiness. Eyebrows appear as a thick black line above fierce protruding eyes, while distorted, bestial features appear to parody humanity. The men wear fine embroidered Manchurian gowns obtained through trade. Both barbarity and strength are emphasised, implicitly glorifying the Matsumae who had subjugated these powerful leaders. It is no coincidence that these paintings appeared the year after the fighting in Kunashiri. In other illustrations, for example the finely executed drawings of Ainu everyday life from *Ezo Seikei Zusetsu*, the Ainu, again exaggeratedly hairy, all look alike with almost no trace of individuality while Wajin are portrayed quite normally.[104] This tendency to exaggerate the barbarian Otherness of non-Japanese is also evident in pictures of Westerners from the same period in which long noses, red hair and hairiness are emphasised. The few Africans or Javanese who worked as sailors on foreign ships are usually portrayed as devils. While not evident in art of the period, it was widely believed that the Dutch and the Russians had misshaped limbs and penises, and urinated like dogs.[105]

By the eve of the Meiji Restoration an ambivalent negative image of the Ainu – on the one hand ignorant and uncivilised but capable of being enlightened, on the other essentially demonic and non-human – was rooted deep in Tokugawa society. These images and their associated stereotypes were not artificial creations employed to justify Japanese domination, but had arisen during the long process of establishing military and economic hegemony over the Ainu. The ancient Chinese world-view and its dichotomous divisions into civilised and barbarian, human and non-human, had provided the initial framework for the interpretation of Ainu inferiority within the contexts of both trade and conflict. As the subordination and exploition of the Ainu increased in the *basho*, these negative images were reinforced and elaborated in a circular process that served to sustain relations of domination. The result was widespread contempt for the Ainu. The final word on Wajin attitudes should perhaps be left to the manservant of Isabella Bird, who, on being requested to be courteous to the Ainu, responded indignantly: 'Treat Ainos [sic] politely! They're just dogs, not men'.[106]

3 Former natives

Despite the tendency of late nineteenth century Japanese to refer unambiguously to 'colonisation' (*takushoku*), the history of post-Restoration Hokkaidō is usually interpreted today through a narrative of 'development' (*kaitaku*, a word that has the sense of 'opening up' or 'reclamation' of empty lands) and settlement. In his discussion of Japanese attitudes towards colonialism, for instance, Mark Peattie dismisses Hokkaidō as merely providing 'practical experience in the creation of a settlement colony' between 1873 and 1883, in which 'a government settles its own lands with its own peoples'. Peattie then excludes the area from any further discussion of Japanese colonialism.[1] The implication is that Hokkaidō was somehow an integral part of Japanese territory, or perhaps a 'natural' extension of it, an empty geographical region, that was speedily and painlessly incorporated after the Meiji Restoration.

In fact, the incorporation of Hokkaidō into the Japanese state was a long-term colonial project whose ramifications are still felt today; Hokkaidō, along with Okinawa, presently enjoys special status with a Ministerial level government agency (the Hokkaidō Kaihatsuchō) devoted to its development. Hokkaidō retains certain economic and political aspects of its colonial legacy. Colonialism is here understood as the conquest and direct control of other people's land, and the creation of political, economic and social structures designed to exploit that land for the benefit of the metropolitan centre. The island can be regarded as an 'internal colony' in the most general sense of a previously foreign region and its indigenous inhabitants incorporated within state borders by annexation, and then administered and exploited through colonial structures. The racialisation and subsequent treatment of the Ainu can then be placed within the broader historical process of colonisation and the creation of 'indigenous peoples' within other empires around the world in the nineteenth and twentieth centuries.

There is another reason for emphasising the colonial process in

Hokkaidō. In altering modes of production and relations between peoples, colonisation necessarily involves force. To naturalise conquest as development (*kaitaku*) is to obscure the violence associated with the economic, cultural and social marginalisation of conquered peoples to the fringes of colonial society. Even after the fact of physical dispossession, this violence towards the dispossessed takes new forms, often disguised as a movement for 'protection' and 'civilisation'. As Attwood has argued of such a movement to remake the Australian Aborigines, 'in the very nature of its practitioners' belief in their own cultural superiority, their assumption that they had a right to 'civilise', and their desire to regulate and control the colonised, it too was violent'.[2]

THE TRANSFORMATION OF EZOCHI: FROM FOREIGN LAND TO INTERNAL COLONY

Although some in Tokugawa circles argued otherwise, until the Treaty of Shimoda in 1855 Ezochi was officially seen, as Kaiho has noted, as 'politically clearly outside the Bakuhan state; to use the language of the time, it was a "foreign region" (*iiki*)'.[3] This is in contrast to the island kingdom of Ryūkyū, later Okinawa, which had been annexed by the powerful Satsuma domain in 1609 and provided a lucrative trade with China, and was recognised by the Bakufu as attached to the domain. In the north, however, the Matsumae were a much weaker and far less influential *han*. The territory of their domain only covered Wajinchi, and the vast area of Ezochi was perceived as a distinct and unincorporated region to the north, despite the economic importance of the fisheries to both the Matsumae and mainland merchants. Paying no heed to Matsumae protests, the Bakufu decided to intervene and annex Ezochi when perceived Russian aggression threatened the interests of the Bakuhan state.[4]

With the first period of direct Bakufu control from 1799, attempts were made to bring Ezochi within the borders of the state (*kaikoku*). Japanisation of the Ainu was one aspect of this policy of incorporation. But as the threat from Russia receded, the expenses involved in the coastal defence and administration of the region became too much of a burden and the Bakufu abandoned Ezochi to the Matsumae in 1821. The border situation consequently reverted to its previous ambiguity under the Matsumae. Later in the century, however, renewed Russian activity in Karafuto and a Western presence in the new treaty port of Hakodate led to a second period of direct Bakufu control after 1855. Both Russian and Japanese authorities in the region regarded the Ainu, where they considered them at all, only in terms of their relevance for the manoeuvrings of the two states. In Ezochi, Japanisation of the Ainu was reintroduced and the Ainu in most areas were entered in population registers (*ninbetsuchō*).[5] As for Karafuto, a convention was drawn up between the Bakufu and Russia in 1867 which allowed for joint jurisdiction and settlement on the island. Article Three of this convention gave some consideration to the indigenes; but it also gave either power the right to enslave a native for debt. Russian observers noted that the Japanese made good use of this provision. On the other hand, it was noted by Japanese (and some Ainu) that the Russians also treated the Ainu with cruelty. Both sides interpreted the situation of the Ainu as it suited them; when Russian officials pointed out during early negotiations that no Japanese, only Ainu, lived on Etorofu and so it could not be Japanese territory, their Japanese counterparts retorted that wherever Ainu lived was Japanese territory.[6]

The terminally weakened Bakufu regime finally expired with the Meiji Restoration of January 1868, although there was a brief and bloody finale provided by the suppression of the forces of Admiral Enomoto Takeaki at Hakodate in May and June 1869. On 8 July of the same year the Kaitakushi (Colonisation Commission, 1869–1882) was established. On 15 August Ezochi was renamed Hokkaidō (the North Sea Circuit) and divided into eleven major administrative districts (*kuni*) and eighty-six counties (*gun*). This renaming was in itself a symbolic Japanisation of the island; whereas previously it had been known by the simple description 'Ainu-land' (Ezochi), that is, as a foreign region, the legalistic and cultural symbolism of the new name contributed towards the legitimisation of Japanese rule. North Ezochi (now officially known as Karafuto) had already come under joint Russian and Japanese jurisdiction at Shimoda in 1855, while in the Kuriles the border had been fixed between Etorofu and Uruppu. The strategic importance of Hokkaidō was clearly realised by the new leadership. Kaitakushi officials about to leave for Hokkaidō in September 1869 were encouraged in language that echoed that of the Bakufu seventy years earlier:

> Hokkaidō is the most important place for the Northern Gate of the Empire. With regard to the proclaimed development, sincerely carry out the Imperial Will, and make efforts to spread welfare, education and morals with kindness. With the gradual immigration of mainlanders, make sincere efforts to encourage harmony with the natives and a prosperous livelihood.[7]

Russian policy in Karafuto became increasingly aggressive from 1869 as the garrisons were reinforced and the island turned into a penal colony for political prisoners. Russian interests in the mineral wealth of Karafuto were also combined with a strategic desire to exclude the British from the area. Russian and Japanese civilians clashed, sometimes fatally, and Russian troops harassed the Japanese population. The Russians were actually numerically weak, but opinion among the Meiji oligarchy was divided over whether to fight for Karafuto. Saigō Takamori and Etō Shinpei, both later to rebel against the government, favoured an aggressive policy while their opponents, led by Kuroda Kiyotaka, argued that Karafuto was not worth the effort required to retain it. In the end, political and financial instability, and a concurrent confrontation within the oligarchy over war with Korea (*seikanron*), led the Meiji government to seek a peaceful solution in the north. In 1875 the two states signed a treaty which gave Russia sole jurisdiction over Karafuto in exchange for Japanese sovereignty over all the Kurile Islands as far as Kamchatka. This treaty, while forcing Japan to relinquish all claims to Karafuto, provided a temporary settlement of the border issue and confirmed the incorporation of Hokkaidō within Japanese borders and under Imperial authority. The Emperor himself visited his new territory in 1876 and 1881. Russia was now perceived as less of a threat, but it was none the less imperative that the Japanese state consolidate the area within its new borders through the settlement and development of Hokkaidō.[8]

Although Hokkaidō was now within state borders, its special status as a frontier region was reflected in the introduction of specific administrative structures. Japan proper (*naichi*) had been organised into prefectures in 1871, but Hokkaidō continued to be governed by the Kaitakushi under Count Kuroda Kiyotaka until 1882. Kuroda, a forceful samurai from Satsuma who had distinguished himself against the Bakufu forces and defeated Enomoto's remnants at Hakodate, was an important member of the early ruling elite who rose to become Prime Minister in 1888. Kuroda based himself in Tokyo (where he also found time for armed diplomacy in Korea in 1876 and the suppression of his former clansman Saigō Takamori's rebel army in 1877), while in Hokkaidō the Kaitakushi headquarters were located in the newly constructed township of Sapporo. Under Kuroda's patronage the ranks of the Kaitakushi were swelled by officials of Satsuma origin, many of whom performed no useful function and whose salaries swallowed much of the budget.[9] Initially envisaged as a ten-year experiment, the Kaitakushi started development projects in earnest in 1872 after extensive preparations, but operations were hampered by waste and inefficiency. The Kaitakushi was eventually dismantled in 1882 after the government had become embroiled in the public scandal surrounding the proposed sale of Kaitakushi assets for an extremely low sum to a well-connected consortium led by a businessman of Satsuma origins. This scandal had far-reaching consequences; Ōkuma Shigenobu and others campaigning for representative government were able to exploit the public outrage over the deal to exact from the Meiji oligarchy a promise to introduce constitutional government within ten years.

Hokkaidō was then divided into three prefectures, Hakodate, Sapporo and Nemuro. While this implied that Hokkaidō would enjoy the same administrative status as other regions, there were no prefectural assemblies and the authorities were expected to continue the work of the Kaitakushi. The growing complexity of central government, coupled with communication difficulties, led to all Hokkaidō affairs being delegated to a special agency (*Hokkaidō Jigyō Kanrikyoku*) within the Nōshōmushō (Ministry of Agriculture and Commerce) from 1884. This arrangement was seen as inefficient by officials like Kaneko Kentarō, a protégé of Itō Hirobumi, who urged a new system of colonial government for Hokkaidō (*shokuminkyoku*) and development along Western lines. In 1885 central government was reorganised from the Dajōkan (Council of State) to a Cabinet system, whereupon Prime Minister Itō Hirobumi took the opportunity to reform Hokkaidō into a single administrative body under a Governor (*chōkan*). Formally established in 1886, the Hokkaidō government (Dōchō) was placed under the direct jurisdiction of the Prime Minister and the Home Ministry (Naimushō) but did not enjoy the same degree of independence as the Kaitakushi had done. With the acquisition of Taiwan in 1895, Hokkaidō was briefly moved to a new Colonial Office (Takushokumuchō) divided into Northern and Southern Bureaus, but was soon returned to Naimushō control. Although Hokkaidō maintained a separate police force, central ministries gradually took over their respective functions in Hokkaidō. The Sapporo Agricultural College, for instance, founded in 1876 and later to become Hokkaidō University, came under the jurisdiction of the Ministry of Education instead of the Dōchō in 1895. While the mainland (*naichi*) received an extremely limited franchise in 1890, Hokkaidō was seen as a backward area of low cultural development and therefore ineligible for political representation. Hokkaidō finally received a weak prefectural assembly in 1901, but the right to elect members to the National Diet was not extended until the following year, when three members were elected from Sapporo, Otaru and Hakodate. Hokkaidō had not been included in the local administrative system set up in 1888 and established its own system between 1897 and 1902, not to be brought into conformity with the *naichi* pattern until 1927.[10]

DEVELOPMENT AND IMMIGRATION POLICY

Integral to the consolidation of Japanese control and legitimacy was the settlement and development of the region. The Kaitakushi justified this policy by its own version of the 'virgin lands' argument used by colonisers elsewhere; namely, that the region 'for several hundred years had been in a state of undisturbed nature with only fishing operations conducted'.[11] It was also hoped that Hokkaidō could be developed as a source of food and other natural resources for the country, and generate enough exports to cover costs and finance further development. Seventy-six foreign advisers, under the leadership of a former US Commissioner of Agriculture, Horace Capron, were recruited at high cost by the Kaitakushi (Capron earned more than the Prime Minister) to advise on the economic development of the region. The emphasis was on agriculture, although Capron in particular also urged industrial development. Immigration was encouraged to provide manpower for both development and defence.

Whereas policy was subject to frequent change, in the early years it mainly took the form of direct recruitment and assisted immigration. Attempts were made to resettle peasants, former samurai and the soldiers of the domains defeated in the Restoration War. But life was hard and the settlers ill-prepared; with the exception of the members of the defeated domains, nearly all went back to *naichi* or to the fishing stations when government rations were exhausted. Another plan, instigated by Kuroda in 1874, was the recruitment of *tondenhei*, militia-colonisers who could be mobilised in the event of Russian aggression. Thirty-seven *tondenhei* villages, subdivided into numerous hamlets, were eventually established in the Ishikari Plain and other areas before the scheme was finally abandoned in 1899.

Various regulations were introduced to sell or grant land to prospective settlers. Although initially opposed by the Kaitakushi, at Capron's insistence private ownership of land was permitted in the Hokkaidō Tochi Baitai Kisoku (Regulation for the Lease and Sale of Hokkaidō Land) and Jisho Kisoku (Land Regulation Ordinance) of 1872. Article Seven of the latter regulation provides evidence for the assertion that the land policy of the Kaitakushi was grounded in a doctrine of Hokkaidō as *terra nullius*, in which indigenous land use was clearly not recognised as ownership:

> The mountains, forests, rivers and streams where formerly the natives fished, hunted and gathered wood shall be partitioned and be converted to private (*jinushi*) or collective (*murauke*) ownership.[12]

During the Kaitakushi period, however, the authorities were largely unsuccessful in initiating agricultural settlement and industrial development except in former Wajinchi and around the capital of Sapporo. The mainstay of the economy in this period remained the same as in former times, the fisheries. Although the *basho* were abolished in 1869, contractors still operated in many fishing stations exploiting the rich stocks of herring, salmon and trout. In 1880 the yield from fisheries totalled just over 7.3 million yen, while the total value of all agricultural production was just 786,922 yen.[13] The overwhelming bulk of the catch was destined for Honshū markets – one observer at Otaru port counted two hundred vessels load fish for Honshū in a single day.[14]

After the establishment of the Dōchō in 1886 there was also an increase in public interest in Hokkaidō. A proliferation of articles appeared in newspapers and journals concerned with the development of the area (*kaitakuron*). These focused on Hokkaidō as an area of renewed strategic importance (the Russians were constructing the Trans-Siberian railway), a source of raw materials for capitalist development, and as a destination for some of the excess population from the mainland. This public debate and criticism of current government policy encouraged the production of a series of official development plans that incorporated a review of existing immigration policy. Emphasis shifted from assisted immigration of the poor to the use of Honshū capital to exploit the potential of Hokkaidō resources. From this time on, agricultural development was to be pursued through cheap land grants to immigrants who were otherwise self-supporting, although certain types of incentives and assistance were maintained. While governors tended to come and go fairly rapidly, most were active in putting forward development plans. The fourth *chōkan* (1892–1896), Kitagaki Kunimichi, was a career Naimushō bureaucrat and close to the oligarch Inoue Kaoru. Under his administration work was begun on a transportation network of port facilities, railways, and roads built by convict labour. Inoue himself visited Hokkaidō during 1893 and his report the next year was influential in the formation of development policy.[15]

Large areas were surveyed and partitioned (*shokuminchi sentei*) for agricultural settlement. These surveys represent an important stage in the process of colonial legitimisation through the remaking of Hokkaidō in the image of the mainland (although with an American overlay). The physical landscape was mapped, named and claimed; although most of the place-names were actually of Ainu origin. (Sapporo, for example, comes from the Ainu *sat poro pet*, large dried-up river.) Order was imposed on the 'wilderness' in the form of grid-like blocks of land divided into plots for agricultural settlement. These were then advertised in the national press for prospective immigrants. Ironically, this process was greatly facilitated by Ainu labour on the survey teams; Ainu men were accustomed to travel in the interior as these areas formed important seasonal hunting territories, and working for the survey teams was therefore much more to their liking than farming. In this way the Ishikari plain was surveyed and partitioned from 1886–1887 (200,000 *chōbu* – one *chōbu* equals 0.99 of a hectare), Tokachi, Teshio and eastern lowland areas from 1888–1889 (750,000 *chōbu*), and the process was largely completed as 350,000 *chōbu* were partitioned in other smaller pockets between 1891 and 1900.[16] Large areas of land were also set aside as Imperial estates, notably in Niikappu where an Imperial Ranch was established in 1873.

As a result of the new immigration policies, population began to increase steadily from the 1890s. The Hokkaidō Tochi Haraisage Kisoku (Regulations for the Sale of Hokkaidō Land) of 1886 distributed 426,800 *chōbu* by 1896 for agricultural development.[17] This land was sold cheaply to the occupier if successfully developed within a ten-year period, but even this soon came to be seen as a disincentive. As a result, the 1897 Hokkaidō Kokuyū Mikaichi Shobunhō (Law for the Disposal of Undeveloped National Land in Hokkaidō) allocated larger tracts of land free of rent and tax for ten years; if successfully developed it was then given to the occupier. By 1908, 1.83 million hectares had been granted, much of it to members of the peerage, wealthy Honshū landlords and politicians.[18] This coincided with the rise of rural capitalism and the displacement of destitute farmers in many areas of Japan which fuelled emigration to Hokkaidō and abroad; many later immigrants were thus poorer farmers who became tenants. The number of full-time farming households cultivating only rented land rose twentyfold from 1886 to nearly thirty thousand in 1900, and after 1906 exceeded the number of owner-cultivators. The numbers of all farming households had reached 186,766 by 1920.[19] Group immigration of migrants originating from the same village or area was also encouraged throughout the 1890s and the first two decades of the twentieth century. The law was amended in 1908 to encourage immigrants with small amounts of capital to settle as owner-occupiers. By 1900, agricultural production, stimulated by the development of fast-maturing strains of rice as well as crops such as wheat, barley, maize and potatoes, had overtaken that of the fisheries. Whereas in 1890 the total area farmed was 23,952 *chōbu*, just ten years later agricultural land totalled 188,942 *chōbu* and the value of output had risen ten times to almost 13.4 million yen.[20] This trend was accelerated by the First World War which established Hokkaidō as a prosperous agricultural region, boosting immigration levels to a peak of 91,864 people in 1919. By 1920, however, the numbers of new arrivals intending to engage in non-agricultural occupations had caught up with those of agricultural migrants. From this time on, net immigration began to be overtaken by natural population increase.[21]

Industrial policy concentrated on local self-sufficiency, the development of coal and sulphur mining, and the processing of fish and agricultural products. Mining was developed through the use of convict labour, including defeated soldiers from the rebel army of Saigō Takamori as well

Table 3.1 Population of Hokkaidō (Wajin and Ainu)[22]

Year	*All Hokkaidō*	*Ainu*	*Ainu as % of total*
1873	111,196	16,272	14.63
1878	191,172	17,098	8.94
1883	239,632	17,232	7.19
1888	354,821	17,062	4.81
1893	559,959	17,280	3.09
1898	853,239	17,573	2.06
1903	1,077,280	17,783	1.65
1908	1,446,313	18,017	1.25
1913	1,803,181	18,543	1.03
1918	2,167,356	17,619	0.81
1923	2,401,056	15,272	0.64
1926	2,437,110	15,247	0.63
1931	2,746,042	15,969	0.58
1936	3,060,577	16,519	0.54

as ordinary criminals. Convicts played an important role in the development of Hokkaidō; as forced labour used for the extraction of raw materials and creation of infrastructure they performed a similar function in the new colony to that of the Ainu under the *basho* system. The use of convicts in the Horonai mines, where they provided 70–80 per cent of the labour force, did not end until 1894, and they continued to be used for roadbuilding for a number of years.[23] The scale of convict use and the extreme hardships they endured are illustrated by the deaths of over two hundred convicts during the construction of the road over the central mountains to Kitami in 1891. The initial efforts of the Kaitakushi to develop industrial self-sufficiency had not met with success, but the factories were sold to private entrepreneurs who continued to enjoy government support, and industry began to take off in the last years of the century. Capitalist development was encouraged by the establishment of a special Colonial Bank (Takushoku Ginkō). Some of the companies that later developed into the huge industrial and financial combines or *zaibatsu* were active in Hokkaidō from early on; Mitsui, for instance, were involved first with Kaitakushi finances and then coal mining, while Mitsubishi controlled shipping to and from Hokkaidō. Within a few decades Hokkaidō was well established as a colonial economy based on primary industry – coal, timber, marine and agricultural products – for export to the metropolitan centre, from which it imported manufactures; a pattern that continued well into the twentieth century.[24]

It was not just in its political and economic structures that Hokkaidō was colonial; local society clearly differed in composition and development from that of *naichi*. Until Japan regained Karafuto in 1905 Hokkaidō was the wild frontier of the nation. It also supported a considerable convict population. While the population had risen from close to 60,000 at the establishment of the Kaitakushi to reach nearly a million by the end of the century, men outnumbered women by a ratio of 100:85.[25] Prostitution was rife. The entertainment districts of Sapporo were notorious and alcoholism was a severe problem. Such social problems characteristic of a rough frontier society led to Hokkaidō becoming one of the first areas in Japan to see the rise of civic movements based around religious and women's organisations. The Hokkaidō Kinshūkai (Hokkaidō Temperance Society) was formed in 1887 to combat alcoholism. The Sapporo Fujin Kyōfukai, a Christian women's group, campaigned for women's welfare and proper relations between the sexes; in a newspaper advert in 1889 promoting moral behaviour in marriage the group claimed three hundred members.[26] The Sapporo Agricultural College was a centre of Christianity after the short sojourn there of Dr William Clark in 1876, producing a number of noted Christian intellectuals like Nitobe Inazō and Uchimura Kanzō.[27] One feature that Hokkaidō did share with *naichi* in the 1880s and 1890s was political activism. Groups in Sapporo, Otaru and Hakodate campaigned for the establishment of a prefectural assembly and the right to elect members to the National Diet. Such movements were distrusted by the authorities and harassed after the enaction of the Peace Regulations in 1887 and the Police Peace Law in 1900.

EARLY AINU POLICY AND FORCED RELOCATION

The transformation, outlined above, of Hokkaidō into an internal colony of Japan was to have drastic consequences for the original inhabitants. But this did not happen overnight; despite some attempts at reform, the patterns of production and unequal economic and social relations with the Ainu that had been formed in the Tokugawa period continued relatively unchanged into the early years of the Kaitakushi. During the period of the Kaitakushi administration much of Hokkaidō was, in Wajin eyes, still mountain and forest 'wilderness', although for the Ainu it was intimately known, named and travelled. Consider this description of Hokkaidō in 1878 by the British traveller Isabella Bird:

Very little is known of the interior except that it is covered with forest

> matted together by lianas, and with an undergrowth of scrub bamboo impenetrable except to the axe, varied by swamps equally impassable, which give rise to hundreds of rivers well stocked with fish. The glare of volcanoes is seen in different parts of the island. The forests are the hunting-grounds of the Ainos, who are complete savages in everything but their disposition. [28]

Even allowing for traveller's hyperbole, it is clear that the Kaitakushi faced an immense task and had made little progress in this period.

Early immigration was concentrated in former Wajinchi and around Sapporo where relatively few Ainu lived, while most Ainu communities maintained their traditional lifestyles or congregated around the fisheries as they had under the *basho* system. As the journals of Isabella Bird indicate, the Ainu continued to be perceived by Wajin in terms of the traditional barbarian stereotypes. Local attitudes towards the Ainu remained highly negative, even though they were now referred to more often as natives (*dojin*) than barbarians (*ijin*). Bird noted that Ainu lived apart from Wajin and were 'held in great contempt' by Wajin neighbours in southern Hokkaidō.[29] When the young British theological student and future missionary John Batchelor arrived in Hakodate in 1877, he was informed by some Japanese friends

> of a barbarous and fierce savage people living among the mountains and by the sea shores of Hokkaidō. They said they were not quite human because they had a common cur to their father and a woman to their mother. And they were a very hairy people because of this.[30]

Kaitakushi policy towards the Ainu was essentially informed by the same attitudes and images that had been behind the policy of the Bakufu in the periods of direct control. Kuroda Kiyotaka stated in his first official report after assuming control in 1870 his intention that 'the natives should be treated with affection, protected, and educated'.[31] One of the first manifestations of this policy was the banning in 1871 of Ainu customs such as tattooing, the wearing of ear-rings, and the burning of the dwellings of the deceased.[32] This order was repeated in 1876. Another was the sending of a group of Ainu to a school in Tokyo in 1872 to see if they were capable of being educated, since, wrote Kuroda, 'through development projects [Hokkaidō] will become a developed area like the mainland, so I want there to be no difference between them and us'.[33] Three Ainu men from the group were subsequently employed by the Kaitakushi and the school aroused some interest in Tokyo newspapers, but the experiment was not regarded as a success.

Although the fisheries continued to be run by contractors, the *basho* system was abolished in 1869. The Ainu were freed from coercive labour, and the associated 'welfare' (*buiku*) measures of distributing rations to the needy were also gradually dismantled. Officials of the new administration did not have time or resources to spend on the Ainu, who were now encouraged to labour under the same conditions as Wajin. As the *basho* were broken up, some coastal Ainu were given fishing and seaweed collection grounds alongside Wajin. Mirroring this equalisation of economic status came official equality in terms of citizenship. In 1871 the Kaitakushi announced that the Ainu had become *heimin*, or commoners, of the new Japanese state. Most Ainu were entered on family registers (*koseki*) from 1875–1876, some with Japanese names, others with their Ainu names transcribed in *katakana*. In the Hidaka area where the population was numerous, officials saved time and effort by giving whole communities the same surname. Ainu were also now subject to the same laws as Wajin, ending the practice of recognizing Ainu tribal law as the basis for settling Ainu disputes. This incorporation of the 'childish and ignorant' Ainu into the Kaitakushi legal system alarmed one leading official, Matsumoto Jūrō, who expressed his reservations and urged leniency in a letter to Kuroda in 1874.[34] Despite the equality implied by *heimin* registration, it was also Kaitakushi policy from the beginning to maintain separate population registers (*ninbetsuchō*) for the Ainu.[35] In other documents the Ainu were at first distinguished by such designations as *kyūezojin* (former Ezo), *komin* (ancient people), or *dojin* (native), but these were later standardised by Kaitakushi order to *Kyūdojin* – former native – in 1878.[36] All Ainu, regardless of regional or community loyalties, were regarded as a single homogeneous people, and for administrative purposes were subsumed under a single official category.

In the early years of the Kaitakushi, Ainu communities inland were relatively unaffected by the limited immigration and development. This did not remain the case for long as attention soon turned to the exploitation of the large deer herds, valued both for hides and meat which was canned for export. In 1876 prohibitions were enforced on spring-bow traps and poisoned arrows, the traditional means by which Ainu hunted deer, in view of the danger to Wajin hunters, although many Ainu ignored the ban and continued to hunt as before. What had a far more devastating impact on Ainu subsistence activities, however, was drastic overhunting by Wajin armed with rifles. Whereas during the Matsumae period the Tokachi *basho* had yielded around six or seven hundred hides annually, over 12,500 were produced there in 1878 alone. The total Hokkaidō yield in 1875 was 76,500 hides.[37] Even though the Ainu were exempted from the hunting restrictions that were belatedly imposed it did them little good as the deer herds were close to extinction after the severe winter of 1878–1879. Ainu, with a lifestyle previously well adapted to the conditions in their homeland, began dying of starvation. Periodic bans on fishing, the result of irresponsible over-fishing by Wajin which had reduced stocks to dangerously low levels, also contributed to the erosion of the independent economic base of the Ainu. After the 1883 prohibition on fishing in the Tokachi area widespread starvation was reported among the upstream Ainu the following year. An official described the Ainu as 'sitting waiting for death'.[38] Those Ainu who had received fishing and seaweed grounds or who hunted deer for commercial purposes were largely unable to compete on an equal footing in the new money economy and were frequently cheated, leading Kaitakushi officials to step in and oversee trade.

Not all Ainu were victims. Some Japanised Ainu were able to adjust to the new conditions; a handful even prospered and became landholders. One of these men was Ōta Monsuke (Ainu name Montereku), after whom the *tondenhei* village of Ōta near Akkeshi was named. Ōta was the son of a Wajin *dekasegi* and an Ainu woman. Orphaned as a young child, he had picked up some education from a friendly Wajin, and from the age of twenty turned his hand to farming and fishing. By 1886 he had become one of the leading pioneers in the Akkeshi area 'even though he is a native', as a local newspaper reported.[39] Kotoni Mataichi, an Ainu from Ishikari, became an official of the Kaitakushi in 1870.[40] Men like these who spoke Japanese and could therefore understand the bureaucratic procedures for obtaining land grants along with Wajin were unrepresentative, however, and the great majority of traditionally oriented Ainu slipped further into destitution.

The destruction of Ainu lifeways and economic livelihood was the direct result of Kaitakushi policies; but there were also some efforts to provide relief. These were the first of a series of policies that attempted to turn the Ainu into productive Japanese citizens, but actually served to emphasise their inequality and subordination to the state. Provisions in the Hokkaidō Jiken Hakkō Jōrei (Ordinance for Issuing Hokkaidō Land) of 1877 put Ainu residential land under bureaucratic control. Measures were taken to give Ainu small plots to cultivate, but by 1881 only 724 households, mostly around Sapporo, possessed the miserable average of 310 *tsubo* (approximately one-tenth of a hectare).[41]

The main Ainu issue of concern to the Kaitakushi, however, arose from the border settlement with Russia. As a result of the 1875 treaty between Japan and Russia exchanging Karafuto for the Kuriles, 841 Sakhalin Ainu were relocated to Sōya, then moved on again the following year to Tsuishikari, on the Ishikari River. These Ainu had been working under Japanese contractors in Sakhalin and their self-sufficient lifestyle had been largely destroyed. Although the terms of the treaty gave the indigenous inhabitants three years to choose which nationality to adopt, the Japanese authorities moved swiftly to transport these Ainu to Hokkaidō, claiming that 'although they are subordinate natives, as time goes on there is no difference in knowledge between them and mainlanders (*naichijin*) . . . and it is necessary to make them subjects of the Empire'.[42] The Ainu were not unwilling to avoid Russian rule, especially since they could see their old homeland just a few miles away across the La Perouse Strait from Sōya. Kuroda, however, reneged on his promise to let them settle there and had them forcibly removed to Tsuishikari. Matsumoto Jūrō, who had been supervising the Ainu in Sōya, was furious at the betrayal and resigned in protest, further incensed by a suggestion that the Ainu could provide labour in the Ishikari coal mines that Kuroda was planning to develop. It is unclear whether this idea originated from Kuroda or not; in any event it was not carried out and convicts were used there instead. The authorities set up a school in Tsuishikari and attempted to encourage self-sufficiency through agriculture and the development of fishing cooperatives, the former against Ainu opposition. The 'ignorant and stubborn women and children who cannot speak Japanese' were given training in cottage industry. The swampy land was poor and unhealthy, and around half of the original evacuees died in a series of cholera and smallpox epidemics in 1886 and 1887. Most of the survivors began to return home even before southern Sakhalin reverted to Japanese control after the Russo–Japanese war of 1904–1905.[43]

The failure of such attempts to transform the Ainu into useful and loyal subjects of the Emperor led to the conviction that a more systematic programme was required. After the dissolution of the Kaitakushi in 1882 the new prefectural authorities adopted a policy of turning the Ainu into farmers by providing agricultural tools, seeds and instruction. While in line with general development policy in Hokkaidō, conversion of the Ainu to agriculture had its antecedents in the Japanisation policies of the Bakufu, which had drawn the distinction between a 'barbarian' lifestyle based on the eating of flesh and the customs of a civilised, agricultural society. Nemuro Prefecture passed a Relief Law (*Kyūsaihō*) granting small plots of land in 1883, and Sapporo followed suit two years later. Small Ainu cooperatives were established, adding to the few set up by the Kaitakushi. The profits from these were held as communal property (*kyōyū zaisan*) along with funds granted by central ministries and the Emperor himself. These were managed by officials since the Ainu were not regarded as capable of administering the funds. In a communication to central ministries, the Nemuro authorities blamed Ainu destitution not on the development policies of the government, but on the Ainu themselves:

> They have brought this difficulty upon themselves since they lack the

> spirit of activity and progress. In their society in the past there was nothing they needed to record through writing, no stimulus to develop their knowledge through learning; when thirsty they drank, when hungry they ate. They are a purely primitive people.[44]

In 1884 ninety-six Northern Kurile Ainu were removed by force from Shumushu island near Kamchatka, which functioned as a base from where they ranged throughout the Kurile archipelago to hunt and fish. They were resettled on barren Shikotan island near Nemuro, where an attempt was made to turn them, many of whom spoke Russian and had been baptised into the Orthodox Church, into 'permanent subjects of the Empire' through a policy of agriculturalisation and education. Nearly half of the original group died within five years. Although this relocation was justified on grounds of Ainu welfare, as it was becoming increasingly costly to deliver rations to Shumushu, in actuality it had more to do with reasons of national security in a sensitive border zone.[45]

To facilitate the policy of agriculturalisation, free the land for immigrants, and increase control over the Ainu, the authorities forced scattered Ainu communities to combine and relocate to new settlements. Many of these were located on inferior or marshy land. This marked the beginning of what was to become a systematic, although never completely successful, policy of separation. The segregation of the Ainu meant that contacts between them and the later waves of settlers decreased in both frequency and intensity, increasing still further the psychological gulf between settler and native. The creation of these artificial settlements as 'native villages' also gave clear physical boundary to Otherness. Segregation of Ainu and Wajin communities was, in itself, nothing new; Bird had noted that in 'mixed villages' in southern Hokkaidō the Ainu were 'compelled to live at a respectful distance from the Japanese'.[46]

Ainu were also moved out of areas designated for new townships. In 1885 the Ainu in Kushiro were moved upstream out of town limits. The authorities advanced four reasons for the relocation. First, it was doubtful that the objective of welfare through agriculture could be met in the present location. Second, even if such a policy was possible it was unclear whether or not Ainu and Wajin could live side by side. Third, if Ainu lived in town any money they made was all spent on food and alcohol without consideration for the future. Finally, when they ran out of money, day labour was easily available; in all, these factors hindered the agriculturalisation policy. It was also pointed out that 'the natives tend to dislike *naichijin* and move away to avoid them', and that 'even in America, mixed residence with natives never actually occurs and the natives move to the depths of the mountains'.[47] In 1886 Ainu were relocated to make way for the establishment of what was to become Abashiri, a move again justified as making it easier to implement Ainu welfare policies. With the advent of the Dōchō, however, these welfare policies under the *Kyūsaihō* were largely abandoned, and by 1888 most of the Ainu had left the land to work as seasonal labourers for the fisheries, survey teams and growing lumber operations.

The policies of land grants and agricultural training were not a success. Hokkaidō Ainu had traditionally practised agriculture; but it was seen as women's work, and some agricultural practices such as manuring were contrary to their religious taboos on cleanliness. Moreover, seasonal work in the mountains and on the coasts was closer to traditional labour patterns for Ainu males. Most preferred to hunt or fish, a fact that Batchelor attributed to their 'untamed, wild nature'.[48] Some Ainu also became accomplished horsemen on the Imperial ranch and in other areas. In spite of this, official policy was that the Ainu must become farmers, so various local administrations began to set up small 'reservations' (*hogochi*) based on the 1877 regulation authorising bureaucratic control over Ainu residential land. The Ainu were only given the use of the land, not rights of ownership, as they were seen as incapable of grasping the concept of land ownership. In 1891, for example, the Asahikawa authorities set aside 500 hectares in Chikabumi, and moved thirty-six unwilling Ainu families to part of it three years later. From 1884, Ainu in the Tokachi region were resettled away from the rich farmlands set aside for the Wajin moving into the area; these communities were reorganised around small *hogochi* from 1894. Reservations were also established in Shintotsugawa (1889) and Chitose (1894). The land of the Shintotsugawa community soon became the object of Wajin desires, and in 1910 the Ainu were moved again to a remote mountain settlement at Wakkauenbetsu. (This name, meaning 'bad water river' in the Ainu language, itself illustrates the quality of the area thought suitable for Ainu by the authorities.) In 1888 Ainu had been moved into the vicinity of the Niikappu Imperial Ranch, established in 1873, to provide labour. When this was no longer required, the whole community was again forcibly relocated to a desolate inland area in 1916. Even small communities were not ignored. In the early 1890s the adventurer Henry Savage Landor described Tetcha (Teshikaga) as 'an Ainu village, near which a few Japanese houses have been built'.[49] Ten years later the Ainu had all gone; the eight families of Teshikaga were moved out to Kussharo in 1903 after the area was designated Imperial pastureland. In Karafuto, after reversion to Japanese control in 1905, the new authorities attempted to concentrate the Ainu there within 'designated settlements' (*shitei buraku*) after 1907. A few large Ainu settlements were created in this way at places like Tarandomari and Shirahama.[50]

Forced population transfers of this kind ensured that a large proportion of Ainu were segregated and excluded from the most productive land. In the final years of the century, increasing waves of settlers began moving into the newly partitioned areas. Whereas some early settlers appear to have lived amicably alongside Ainu – indeed, had sometimes relied upon them for assistance and knowledge to survive the bitter winters – these later immigrants overwhelmed the scattered Ainu communities.[51] The villages were ravaged by diseases introduced by the settlers, an aspect of the contact between settler and indigene that also decimated aboriginal populations in Australia and North America. Epidemic and infectious disease was not in itself a new phenomenon, but had been responsible for a large decline in Ainu population in the previous century, despite an inoculation campaign against smallpox by the Bakufu in 1858. Disease was prevalent in the fishing stations in the Kaitakushi period; in 1873, for instance, around ninety Ainu died of cholera in Horobetsu.[52] By the turn of the century, syphilis, trachoma, and, increasingly, tuberculosis had become commonplace in Ainu communities, although reliable statistics are not available until later.

Alcohol, an indispensable element of traditional religion, had been freely available since the time of the Kaitakushi, when Isabella Bird had observed 'strings of horses laden with *sake* going into the interior. The people of Yezo drink freely, and the poor Ainos outrageously.'[53] With the accelerated disintegration of traditional society, that had begun with the fishing stations of the *basho* and by the end of the century reached to even the most isolated communities, alcoholism became rife. Alcohol was also frequently used by unscrupulous Wajin to force Ainu into debt or cheat them out of property. The artificial nature of many of the larger relocated communities led to a loss of social cohesion which was occasionally manifested in acts of violence and suicide.[54] When he first arrived in Hokkaidō, John Batchelor 'could not help noting what a chilling air of depression [the Ainu] wore on their countenances'.[55] Half a century later, Neil Gordon Munro, a medical doctor and amateur ethnologist of Scottish origin, remarked that:

> Deliberate suicide is heard of. Within recent years this has increased. I have heard of half a dozen cases in this neighbourhood within twenty years or thereby, chiefly desperate women, who could not endure the wretched existence occasioned by present circumstances, a complex of alcoholism, abject poverty, surrounding detraction, psychic depression and demolition of the old social order.[56]

Within twenty years of the Meiji Restoration economic and social relations between Ainu and Wajin had been radically transformed.

Throughout the Tokugawa period, Ainu labour had been essential in the Japanese exploitation of the natural resources of the region. Prior to the eighteenth century the products of Ainu labour had been appropriated through an increasingly unequal trade relationship. With the consolidation of the *basho* system from the early eighteenth century this had been accompanied, and later superseded, by the direct exploitation of Ainu labour itself under the management of traders and itinerant workers for the purpose of harvesting natural resources. Along with their economic role, the Ainu were also perceived as allies, or pawns, to be used to counter Russian expansion in the region. With the establishment of direct colonial rule, large-scale Wajin immigration, and the integration of Hokkaidō as a settler colony with a market economy based on agriculture and other primary industry, these factors lost their relevance. Ainu labour was no longer essential. While some Ainu were mobilised to work on the Imperial ranch at Niikappu and others played an important early role on the teams that surveyed the largely unexplored interior, on the whole Ainu labour contributed little to Hokkaidō development. The function of exploited labour for the extraction of primary resources and the construction of infrastructure was now taken over by convicts.

THE HOKKAIDŌ FORMER NATIVES PROTECTION ACT OF 1899

By the last decade of the century, the growing immigrant population had founded settlements over most of the region. With them had come the apparatus and institutions of the modernising state: civic administration, a police force, schools (from 1880) and newspapers. The Kaitakushi published a bulletin from 1873, and in 1878 Hokkaidō saw the birth of its first privately owned newspaper, the *Hakodate Shinbun* (circulation over 2,000 by 1881), soon to be followed by others in Sapporo and Otaru. Circulation figures remained low until after the establishment of the Dōchō, when figures were boosted by increased population and the interest in politics generated by the movements for civic rights and the imminent establishment of the National Diet. Newspapers were founded in most of the other major townships around the turn of the century, many to be later taken over by the larger Hokkaidō newspapers.[57]

In 1895 a pamphlet entitled *Ainu Mondai* (The Ainu Problem) was published by Doi Katsumi, a journalist on a local newspaper. Doi pointed out the decrease in the Ainu population and made concrete proposals for welfare measures. These included action to protect against fraudulent attempts to gain control of Ainu lands in the *hogochi*; the construction of medical facilities and workshops at national expense; the appointment of officials in each village to prevent Ainu being cheated; and a thorough policy of education.[58] This pamphlet, and the occasional newspaper articles which highlighted the decline in Ainu numbers or criticised the authorities for the mishandling of Ainu communal property, were the manifestation of a growing perception among certain liberal and Christian intellectuals in Hokkaidō that an 'Ainu Problem' existed and demanded action. This view was supported by the noted liberal commentator Nakae Chōmin, who travelled around Hokkaidō in 1891 during a brief spell as editor of the *Hokumon Shinpō* in Otaru. Another issue of concern was that of Ainu education. In 1891 the Hokkaidō Society for Education (Hokkaidō Kyōikukai) was established and presented the Dōchō with a proposal for an Ainu education policy the following year. These views were not initially received with enthusiasm by the authorities. The Dōchō were suspicious of the activities of those concerned with Ainu welfare and education, in particular foreigners like John Batchelor and his companions of the Church Missionary Society who had founded a number of schools. Batchelor had even been prosecuted in 1885, officially for living outside the areas prescribed for foreign residence, but more likely because, as his prosecutor finally admitted, 'Mr. Batchelor is trying to make the Ainu language live while *we* desire it to die out.'[59] Another reason was that his efforts to eradicate alcoholism were not appreciated by Wajin traders who were making a living by selling *sake* to Ainu or using it to force them into debt.[60]

The liberals and missionaries concerned with the Ainu problem were determined to press for the enactment of a comprehensive Protection Act to replace the moribund *Kyūsaihō* and *hogochi* system. Social welfare had by then become an issue of national importance and the subject of debates in the Diet, since it was seen by oligarchs like Yamagata Aritomo as an antidote to socialism. There is also some evidence to suggest that those involved in calling for a Protection Act also had some knowledge of native policy in other colonial countries. Indeed, Batchelor himself had collected such information from New Zealand and the USA and presented it to the Dōchō in the early 1890s.[61] In 1894 the Sapporo Historical Society heard a speech by a visiting American on the General Allotment Act (Dawes Act) of 1887, an attempt to turn American Indians into propertied citizens through land grants. The speech was translated by his host, Nitobe Inazō, then an instructor at Sapporo Agricultural College and consultant to the Dōchō, who published it in the magazine of the Hokkaidō Temperance Society. Nitobe himself was involved in surveys of agricultural and tenancy conditions and thus had firsthand knowledge of the Ainu problem.

A Protection Act was first proposed as a private bill in the 5th Imperial Diet in 1893 by Katō Masanosuke of the Kaishintō (Progressive Party), who had earlier worked as a reporter in Hokkaidō. On a visit to the USA, Katō had noted that the natives had completely died out in Massachusetts and implored the government not to make the same mistake with the Ainu. The bill failed to gain enough support after revisions in committee. Another attempt was made in the 8th Imperial Diet in 1895 when it was proposed by a group of six Dietmen led by Suzuki Mitsumi. This second draft bill arose from a petition presented to them by Ozawa Sanrottee, a Saru Ainu leader who had travelled to Tokyo with a Hokkaidō journalist. Hastily put together, it could not withstand intensive questioning. By this time, the Dōchō itself was becoming convinced of the necessity for a Protection Act. Having failed to persuade the Home Ministry to issue such a law as an Imperial Ordinance, the Dōchō ensured that it was proposed instead as a government-sponsored bill in the 13th Diet in 1898. The Hokkaidō Former Natives Protection Act (Kyūdojin Hogohō) passed into law on 1 March 1899.

The Protection Act focused on three main areas of Ainu policy: agriculturalisation, education and welfare assistance, notably in the area of medical care. Ainu families engaged, or wishing to engage, in agriculture were to be granted up to five hectares of undeveloped land as an allotment (*kyūyochi*) without charge (Article One). This did not mean full rights of ownership; various restrictions were placed on the transfer of the allotments which could not be sold or used to secure a mortgage, although they were exempt from land registration fees, local tax and land tax for thirty years (Article Two). Land not developed within fifteen years, however, would be repossessed (Article Three). Agricultural tools and seeds were to be made available for needy families (Article Four). Education was to be provided through the medium of special Native Schools (*Kyūdojin gakkō*) to be constructed at national expense in Ainu villages (Article Nine). Financial assistance was available for school fees (Article Seven). For the destitute, sick, and people too old or too young to support themselves, medical fees would be paid. Funeral expenses were also covered (Articles Five and Six). Some of the money for these measures was to come from the profits of Ainu communal property, which was under bureaucratic control, the rest from the national treasury (Articles Eight and Ten). Article Eleven empowered the Governor to issue ‘police orders’ – fines and periods of imprisonment – with regard to protection matters.[62]

The Protection Act represented the systematisation of a policy of assimilation. Assimilation (*dōka*) meant, in this instance, the transformation of the Ainu into model Imperial subjects through the eradication of their former language, customs and values. While displaying superficial similarities to early Meiji cultural policies that prohibited ‘backward’ folk customs and suppressed local dialects at school in order to bring 'civilisation and enlightenment' to 'ignorant' Japanese peasants, Ainu policy was quite different in that it was a systematic policy designed for a subordinate and inferior native population under a colonial regime.[63] The continuing emphasis on agriculture as the way towards civilisation and participation in the market economy remained the primary means of denying occupational and residential freedom of choice to the Ainu. Since they were forbidden to sell their plots of land, many were forced to remain within the artificial communities that had been created by previous policies, although there were also a large number of hamlets with only a handful of Ainu households scattered among Wajin.[64] While over the next ten years most Ainu managed to obtain some land, the average was just over two hectares per household. This was only a fraction of the area allotted to Wajin settlers, and it fixed the Ainu on the lowest rung of rural society. Moreover, much of the land was of poor quality or unfit for cultivation; of 300 hectares allotted in Shiraoi, for instance, only twenty could be farmed.[65] As a result, 21.5 per cent of granted lands were later repossessed under the fifteen-year regulation.[66] Provision of seeds, tools and instruction was also limited and haphazard. While some Ainu received decent amounts of reasonable land and were able to succeed as farmers, the majority soon lost control of their plots to Wajin tenants, often through devious means. A typical strategy employed by Wajin neighbours was to force an Ainu into debt and then obtain perpetual lease to the allotments as repayment. Another was to persuade illiterate Ainu to lease their lands for minimal rents while drunk. Some Ainu even ended up as tenants on their own land. A survey of 1923 found that out of 7,633 *chōbu* granted in total under the Protection Act, 3,438 (45 per cent) was being cultivated. Of this area, 1,465 *chōbu* (43 per cent) was owner-cultivated, a mere 19 per cent of the total allotments granted.[67] In spite of this, in 1922 over 50 per cent of 2,354 Ainu households were engaged primarily in farming; 27 per cent had to undertake day or seasonal labour to make a living, while less than 13 per cent were engaged in fishing, by this time a declining occupation. Only ten households were classed as artisans and thirty were involved in commercial activities.[68]

Whereas agriculture was the means of physically transforming the Ainu into productive citizens and Japanising their lifestyle, education was the key to Japanising hearts and minds. A special system of Ainu education was established by the Protection Act and the Kyūdojin Jidō Kyōiku Kitei (Regulations for the Education of Former Native Children) of 1901. Under this system education was segregated; where large communities existed Native Schools were built under Article Nine of the Protection Act, or existing schools brought under the Act. Some twenty-four were established in all, although a small number lasted only a few years. In other areas with smaller Ainu populations, Ainu children attended Wajin schools but were taught in separate classes under the above Regulations. Attendance rates rose dramatically in just over a decade, from 17.9 per cent in 1895 to 84.2 per cent in 1907. By 1928, 99.2 per cent of Ainu children were attending elementary school.[69] The education these children received was of inferior quality and duration. The first year was almost totally devoted to learning Japanese, and there were also non-academic subjects such as farming and sewing. From 1916 the curriculum was fixed at four years, starting at age seven, in contrast to Wajin children who started at age six and continued for six years. Such inferior education was justified as appropriate given the 'backwardness' of Ainu children and implied that they were not expected to continue on to further education.

Most importantly, education was assimilationist. The Ainu language was actively discouraged and love for the Emperor and nation was stressed, a doctrine enshrined in the Imperial Rescript on Education of 1890 and elevated to quasi-sacred status after the Russo–Japanese War of 1904–1905. Use of the Ainu language began to decline sharply. 'Among those [Ainu] who have received education', noted a report in 1922, 'there are many who speak a comparatively high level of Japanese . . . these days the number of those who do not understand Japanese has become extremely small.'[70] Success was reported from all districts; in Asahikawa, for instance, the only non-Japanese speakers were three Ainu over seventy years old. The schoolmaster was an important figure in the *kotan* (group settlement), often the first Wajin to live there and the only official trusted by the Ainu, while the school itself functioned as a focal point during national holidays and other imperial celebrations which adult Ainu were required to attend. The school also promoted programmes aimed at improving sanitation and living habits in the community. The inferior curriculum was dropped in 1922 and separate Ainu schooling was finally abandoned in 1937.[71]

In addition to assimilation, the other main objective of the Protection Act was welfare. In matters of health, the medical provisions of the Protection Act only paid bills for medicine; no attempt was made to provide facilities in Ainu areas. These were desperately needed, for one of the gifts of civilisation the Wajin had brought with them was tuberculosis. In the five-year period 1912–1916, tuberculosis accounted for 25.3 per cent of Ainu deaths, compared to 7.5 per cent for Wajin. In Kasai (Tokachi) District the figure was as high as 48 per cent; in Urakawa District, the area of highest Ainu population, tuberculosis accounted for a full third of all recorded deaths.[72] Child mortality rates were also high and the average age of for death Ainu ranged from ten in Sorachi to thirty-seven in Rumoi.[73] A Dōchō medical study attributed the high rates of tuberculosis to lack of resistance, mixed-blood, interbreeding within communities, syphilis, alcohol, the change in diet, unsanitary habits and poverty.[74] The medical welfare situation was partially improved with the first revision of the Protection Act in 1919, and by supplementary measures which provided medical expenses and established native hospitals and clinics (before long also attended by Wajin patients). But tuberculosis continued to cause tragedy among the Ainu until the arrival of penicillin after the Second World War.

The lack of agricultural success and high rates of Wajin tenancy on Ainu allotments led in 1923 to the appointment at the community level of Native Welfare and Guidance Commissioners (Dojin Hodō Iin). These officials, of whom there were 112 in 1925, were local notables, often teachers or policemen.[75] In 1924 the Dōchō introduced cooperatives (*gojokumiai*). These were ostensibly to try and regain control of allotments and encourage Ainu owner-cultivation, and indeed, by 1933 the proportion of Ainu owner-cultivated allotments had increased to 60.7 per cent throughout Hokkaidō. Of the remaining 1,997 *chōbu* leased to Wajin, 1,556 (78 per cent) were rented through the thirty-six cooperatives.[76] Before long, however, these bodies were running Ainu affairs as the Ainu were seen as incapable of managing for themselves. The cooperative managers and the Commissioners made detailed investigations of the financial situation and personal habits of the Ainu under their charge, information that found its way to the Dōchō. The assimilation process was furthered by military conscription and the incorporation of Ainu into the many youth, women's and other community-level organisations that had sprung up under the guidance of the authorities. These organisations facilitated the adoption of important Wajin social customs. Marriages and funerals, for instance, were increasingly conducted along Wajin lines, depriving male Ainu of opportunities to make orations and develop their skills of eloquence, highly prized in traditional Ainu society.[77]

The Protection Act extended to the survivors of the Kurile Ainu on Shikotan Island, but not to the Karafuto Ainu. In 1905 Japanese forces overran Karafuto during the final stages of the Russo–Japanese War, and the subsequent Treaty of Portsmouth gave Japan sovereignty of the island south of the 50th parallel. The island was soon transformed to a settler colony with nearly 11,000 Japanese residents in the first year after the war. Total population grew rapidly to 20,469 in 1907, 66,280 in 1916, 189,036 in 1925, and 447,967 by 1944, while the indigenous population remained consistently below 2,000.[78] In 1907 the legal system of the mainland was extended to Karafuto and it became a colony under a civilian or military Governor (*chōkan*). Colonial development proceeded along similar lines to Hokkaidō, with surveys, assisted immigration, and the wholesale exploitation of natural resources (fish, forests and coal deposits) by private capital in close association with the government or military. The Navy, for instance, was heavily involved in the activities of the companies working the oil concessions in North Sakhalin, extracted from the Soviets after the Japanese occupation of the Russian half of the island between 1920 and 1925. Due to the harsh climate, however, agriculture never assumed any major importance in the Karafuto economy, and although immigrants from Hokkaidō boosted production after 1928 under settlement schemes similar to those of late nineteenth century Hokkaidō, self-sufficiency was never attained.[79]

Of the Karafuto Ainu relocated to Tsuishikari, those who had not obtained visas and returned home during the period of Russian control went back after 1905. Those Ainu who had remained under Russian sovereignty, however, were denied Japanese citizenship along with the other indigenous peoples of the island. In 1907 the authorities set up the first designated 'native villages' (*dojin buraku, shitei buraku*). Although some communities later amalgamated or divided and new settlements were created, there were around ten such 'native villages'. Agents were appointed to market fish and other produce, while outside traders were forbidden to deal with the Ainu and Wajin were banned from living in the designated areas. In July 1909 this was followed by the designation of ten native fishing grounds. Legal rights to the fishing grounds, however, rested with the Governor who leased the grounds to outside contractors and used the profits for Ainu welfare. While boats and equipment were provided for Ainu engaged in fishing, Ainu were regarded as incapable of managing the fishing grounds for themselves. Six Native Schools (*Dojin Kyōikusho*) were established between 1909 and 1930. In 1930 there were 1,485 Ainu in Karafuto, of whom 935 were descendants of returnees from Hokkaidō. A further 80 Ainu lived in the Shikuka (now Poronaisk) area along with 324 Orok (Uilta), 121 Nikubun (Nivkh, known in the West as Gilyak), 20 Keerin, 9 Sanda and 2 Yakutsk. These other indigenous peoples, mainly nomadic reindeer herders, had been relocated to Otasu no Mori just outside the town of Shikuka. Little is known about the history of Otasu no Mori, but the relocations seem to have taken place after 1926. A school was established there in 1930 and operated until 1945, although the other Native Schools were disbanded in 1933.[80]

The dispossession of the Ainu, which had largely been accomplished by 1890 through the expropriation of Ainu land (and fishing grounds) as the primary economic resource on which colonial development was based, was institutionalised by the enactment of the Protection Act of 1899. The Ainu were constituted as second-class citizens: legally, they were 'protected' wards of the state; economically, they occupied the lowest socio-economic stratum as marginal farmers or labourers; and socially, they were distanced from the rest of colonial society through the *hogochi* system. These institutional and material changes were accompanied by a change in how the Ainu were perceived. The Tokugawa world-view, including the image of the barbarian, had not survived intact under the impact of widespread social and economic change brought about by the drive for modernisation. Part of that process was the importation of the new knowledge and ideas which underlay modernity itself. As the next chapter will argue, although Tokugawa stereotypes of the barbarian Other were adapted or transformed in the process, the subordination of the Ainu to the Japanese state now came to be interpreted and justified almost entirely within the discourse of 'race'.

4 The dying race

> According to the principle of the survival of the fittest, as civilisation advances superior races succeed while inferior races die out . . . This can clearly be seen these days in the case of the Aino, that is to say, the natives.
>
> *Hakodate Shinbun*, 3 September 1886

This chapter examines the racialisation of the Ainu – how the Ainu came to be perceived through the lens of 'race', and how these perceptions served to structure relations of inequality. This was not something that happened just to the Ainu; as cultural, historical and social boundaries between populations came to be understood as a reflection of deeper, immutable 'natural' difference, all Japan's subject peoples were to be similarly constructed as 'racial' Others in a discourse that served to legitimise and sustain Japanese superiority. But colonial relations with the Ainu and their construction as primitive 'natives' provided an important initial context in which notions of native inferiority and Japanese modernity were articulated and gained acceptance as common-sense.

As the Ainu began to attract public attention from the 1890s, the ideas and language of 'race' and nation were gaining increasing currency as intellectuals debated Japanese identity and the nature of the state. By the early twentieth century, these categories had become effectively coterminous for many Japanese in the common-sense perception of the consanguineous Yamato *minzoku*, or 'Japanese race', that developed in the context of the ideological drive to establish the Emperor at the head of the family-state. The destitution and marginalisation of the Ainu that was a result of the colonisation and economic development of Hokkaidō after 1868 were interpreted almost exclusively within the confines of these complementary discourses. Inequality was attributed to innate inferiority that marked the Ainu as among those destined to lose in the 'struggle for survival'. Besides providing an explanation, the discourse of 'race' also justified relations of domination and the further exclusion of the Ainu from participation in the economic and political life of the nation. While opinions and ideas differed, often widely, among the bureaucrats, academics, educators, officials and journalists who concerned themselves with the 'Ainu Problem', few disputed the notion of the superiority of Japanese civilisation, and increasingly, of the 'Japanese race' itself. On the level of day-to-day interaction, the conflation of the Yamato 'race' with the imagined community of the nation that was part of the common-sense view of the world broadly shared (if rarely articulated) by the majority of Wajin immigrants ensured the subordination of the Ainu within colonial society through the social processes of discrimination.

Racialised understanding thus took root in Japanese society and shaped specific policy measures that furthered the subordination of the Ainu to the state. While the consciousness of the colonial elites of Hokkaidō was directly shaped by 'racial' stereotypes, a wider perception of the Ainu as a 'dying race' was also propagated and reproduced among the public at large through such channels as newspapers and the public education system. By the 1920s it was a rare voice that prefaced any article on the Ainu without the seemingly obligatory reference to the 'dying race'. Japanese modernity and power contrasted all too sharply with Ainu destitution and despair.

SCHOLARS

The growth of Ainu Studies

It is no exaggeration to state that the disciplines of anthropology, archaeology and linguistics in Japan owe their formation and early development to the presence of a 'primitive' people, under control and easily accessible, as their object of study. Many historians recognise the link between Ainu Studies and the development of these disciplines in Japan, and the role that they played in spreading awareness of the Ainu and the problems they faced.[1] Less has been said, however, on how power relations and narratives of civilisation and progress shaped and informed Ainu Studies. Since the scientific paradigms of these disciplines were overwhelmingly those of scientific racism, obsessed with hierarchical classification and the explanation of 'natural' difference between primitive and civilised societies, the Ainu were tailor-made material for research. For a modernising society seeking acceptance as a civilised country, and later, as a Great Power, the Ainu, in the guise of the primitive Other, served also as a yardstick against which the civilisation and progress of Japan could be measured.

While Japanese travellers, officials and explorers had produced accounts of the Ainu during the late Tokugawa and early Kaitakushi periods, even those most sympathetic to the Ainu, Mogami Tokunai, Matsuura Takeshirō and Matsumoto Jūrō, had viewed them through the *ka-i* images of civilised and barbarian. Western scientific thought was not unknown in Japan during this time, having actually entered Japan from the mid-eighteenth century through the medium of Dutch Studies (*rangaku*), but this knowledge was limited to a small circle of elite scholars and did not influence descriptions of the Ainu. The first accounts to view the Ainu within the framework of Western scientific thought were those generated by Europeans and Americans travelling, working, or in the case of Bronislaw Pilsudski and other opponents of Tsarist Russia, exiled in the region.

Many of the foreign travellers and employees of the Kaitakushi were enthusiastic amateur anthropologists who took a keen interest in the Ainu. Benjamin Lyman, for instance, hired in 1874 to undertake a geological survey of Hokkaidō, took comprehensive physical measurements of the Ainu labourers on his team, and impressed Kaitakushi officials with his arguments on environmental determinism.[2] Another early Kaitakushi employee who examined the Ainu was the botanist Louis Boehmer. John Milne, introducing seismology to Japan at Tokyo Imperial University, recorded the life of the Kurile Ainu in 1875. Edward Morse, the founder of zoology and archaeology in Japan, visited Hokkaidō for research in 1878, the same year as Heinrich von Siebold and Isabella Bird. The role of resident expert was adopted by the British missionary John Batchelor, who translated the Bible into Ainu and produced many works on Ainu language, customs and folklore in the course of a long career in Hokkaidō from 1877 to 1939. On the other side of the border, Bronislaw Pilsudski, brother of the famous Marshal, spent the years 1887 to 1899 as a political exile in Russian Sakhalin, where he 'married' an Ainu woman, fathered two children, and recorded Ainu customs and oral literature. He later returned to the island to continue his work. Few workers and travellers from the West seemed to be free of the positivistic spirit of the age; even adventurers like Isabella Bird and the ironically named Henry Savage Landor could not resist the temptation to record, measure and classify.

Many of the European travellers and explorers in the eighteenth and early nineteenth centuries had been favourably impressed by the Ainu they encountered, deeming them 'noble and hardy full grown men as opposed to their effeminate Japanese rulers', but also courteous and gentle; an ideal personification of the noble savage.[3] Most of the later visitors, however, and those who were to influence the Japanese most, took a more negative view. For these men and women, the Ainu fitted into the hierarchical classification of humanity on its lowest rungs as a race of primitive savages. Certain themes and images run consistently through their writings. The Ainu were incapable of progress: 'after a century of contact with the Japanese, they have learned no arts, adopted no improvements' (Hitchcock); 'so little have they profited from the opportunities offered to them during the last thousand or two thousand years, that there is no longer room for them in the world' (Chamberlain); 'incapable of improving themselves' (Landor); 'a harmless people without the instinct of progress' (Bird). As savages, they lived in the present, incapable of higher thought: 'they have no writings, no records of their past, no aspirations' (Hitchcock); 'like the monkeys, the Ainu cannot concentrate their attention, and they are easily wearied' (Landor); 'low unlettered savages without moral courage, lazy, and strongly given to drunkenness' (Morse); 'it is nonsense to write of the religious ideas of people who have none, and of beliefs among people who are merely adult children' (Bird). Individuals of mixed ancestry were often described in pejorative terms, especially by Landor; for him the 'half-breeds' were 'malformed, ill-natured, and often idiotic', or 'ill-tempered, lazy, and vindictive'. Chamberlain warned future visitors to Hokkaidō that 'the comparatively smooth half-breeds usually speak Aino, dress Aino fashion, and are accounted to be Ainos', thus misleading those seeking the real savage. As for hairiness, most accepted this as an Ainu characteristic, although Bird thought reports on this 'much exaggerated', while Landor, for his part, encouraged such exaggeration with sketches of extremely furry Ainu. There was general agreement that the Ainu were doomed to extinction: 'the race is rapidly dying out, destroyed by consumption, lunacy, and poverty of blood' (Landor); 'doomed to extinction from the face of the earth' (Hitchcock); 'descending to that vast tomb of conquered and unknown races which has opened to receive so many before them' (Bird). Chamberlain refused to mourn 'the probable speedy extinction of the race' since 'the existence of this race has been as aimless, as fruitless, as is the perpetual dashing of the breakers on the shore of Horobetsu'. A few observers also picked up some of the earlier stereotypes widely held by Japanese. Landor, for instance, noted that Ainu experienced 'extreme difficulty . . . in counting even up to ten', and did not know how old they were, while Morse remarked that they 'do not have any knowledge of the simplest arithmetic'. Bird also mentioned that the Ainu 'have no method of computing time, and do not know their own ages'.[4]

Landor made explicit the theoretical background to his observations when he noted that his 'readers will probably have noticed certain facts which strongly support Darwin's theory of evolution, and the hairy arboreal ancestor with pointed ears from which the races of men are descended'.[5] Even those like Isabella Bird who were drawn to the Ainu and found much to admire in this meeting of 'eastern savagery and western civilisation' were unable, in the end, to escape the confines of the discourse:

> They have no history, their traditions are scarcely worthy the name, they claim descent from a dog, their houses and persons swarm with vermin, they are sunk in the grossest ignorance, they have no letters or any numbers above a thousand, they are clothed in the bark of trees and the untanned skins of beasts, they worship the bear, the sun, moon, fire, water, and I know not what, they are uncivilisable and altogether irreclaimable savages, yet they are attractive, and in some ways fascinating, and I hope I shall never forget the music of their low, sweet voices, the soft light of their mild, brown eyes, and the wonderful sweetness of their smile.[6]

By this stage of her visit, 'the glamour that at first disguises the inherent barrenness of savage life has had time to pass away', although she considered Ainu life 'considerably higher and better than that of thousands of the lapsed masses of our own great cities', displaying the Victorian tendency to view the lower orders of their own societies in the same deterministic terms.[7] For those, however, tempted to indulge in romantic images of the noble savage, Hitchcock had the following warning in his description of the Ainu:

> Few who read these lines have ever seen the lower stages of human savagery and barbarism, still less have they an adequate conception of the physical and moral condition, or the manner of life, which characterizes the lower types of human existence . . . To know how miserably a savage lives, one must see him in his house.[8]

These men and women, and their ideas, directly influenced the first generation of Japanese scholars trained in the Western scientific disciplines at Tokyo Imperial University in the 1880s. Edward Morse was instrumental in introducing the ideas of Darwin to Japan. In November 1884 he also helped establish the Tokyo Anthropological Society (Tokyo Jinruigakkai) which began publishing a journal, the *Tokyo Jinruigakkai Zasshi* (later *Jinruigaku Zasshi*), two years later. Between 1886 and 1890, Basil Hall Chamberlain, already well established in Japan, inaugurated the study of linguistics while Professor of Japanese and Philology at Tokyo University. Other disciplines were soon established at the University. Interest in Western scientific historiography was stimulated by Ludwig Riess; in 1889, the Historical Society began publishing the *Shigakkai Zasshi*. A work by Heinrich von Siebold had become the first book on archaeology to be published in Japanese in 1879, although an Archeological Society of Japan was not founded until 1895, starting publication of the *Kōkogakkai Zasshi* the following year.[9]

The main question that occupied these Western scholars and their young Japanese students was the 'racial' origins of the Japanese, a debate that was also underway among historians such as Inoue Tetsujirō and Kume Kunitake.[10] 'Race' in the language of science was translated by the Japanese word *jinshu* or, less often, *shuzoku*. While Western scholars were fascinated by the idea of a race of lost Europeans, Japanese scholars were more concerned with establishing Japanese identity. In the Tokugawa period, the official view on Japanese origins was that the country had been continuously inhabited by the descendants of the Sun Goddess since the Age of the Gods, although some scholars like Arai Hakuseki speculated that Stone Age remains were of human, not supernatural, origin. However, it was Philipp-Franz von Siebold, resident physician in the Dutch settlement at Nagasaki and father of Heinrich, who first postulated, on the basis of archaeological evidence, that the Ainu were the original inhabitants of the archipelago. In contrast, Edward Morse argued on the basis of evidence from his excavations of the Ōmori shell mound near Tokyo in 1877 that the Stone Age (Jōmon) inhabitants were not Ainu since they also produced pottery, which the Ainu did not. One of Morse's students was Tsuboi Shōgorō, a founder member of the Anthropological Society and later Professor of Anthropology at Tokyo Imperial University. Tsuboi unearthed an Ainu legend about a dwarf-like people who had occupied the area when their ancestors arrived, the *kor-pok-un-kur* (*koropokkuru* in Japanese transcription), which he used to back up the theory of a non-Ainu indigenous neolithic people. Tsuboi's theory was opposed by Koganei Yoshikiyo, the first Professor of Anatomy at Tokyo University, who argued, based on skeletal remains, that the Jōmon people were Ainu. Koganei was a follower of Erwin von Baelz, who introduced physical anthropology to Japan and with Wilhelm Dönitz of the Faculty of Medicine at Tokyo Imperial University stimulated interest in the racial (*jinshuteki*) classification of the Japanese and the Ainu. Torii Ryūzō, known for his studies on the Kurile Ainu, proposed a variation on the theory with his argument of a later migration of an iron-using people (later known as the Yayoi) from the Asian continent. The debate was fought out in the *Jinruigaku Zasshi* until the death of Tsuboi in 1913, Koganei and his supporters gradually gaining the upper hand. Both men visited Hokkaidō to undertake research – Tsuboi in 1887 and Koganei in 1887–1888. Ainu Studies were also stimulated in Hokkaidō, especially among the students of the Sapporo Agricultural College, leading to the formation of a Sapporo Historical Society in 1892 and the Hokkaidō Anthropological Society three years later. The development and topics of scientific interest in the colony can be judged from the eighteenth meeting of the Sapporo Anthropological Society in 1897, where the agenda consisted of presentations on Ainu funerals, Karafuto Ainu skulls, and Landor's *Alone with the Hairy Ainu*, published four years previously.[11]

With the growth of literacy in the late Meiji period (already higher than in most European countries even before the Restoration), the debate over racial origins began to reach a wider audience. Most educated Japanese of the day, keen to absorb scientific knowledge and understanding, were familiar with the main propositions. Over two hundred articles on *koropokkuru* and other Ainu topics appeared in the *Tokyo Jinruigakkai Zasshi* and its successor alone during the last twenty-five years of the Meiji period, and the debate spilled over into other journals such as the *Chigaku Zasshi* (Journal of Geology) and the *Tōyō Gakugei Zasshi* (Journal of Oriental Art and Science), as well as the popular press. There was widespread interest in Japanese origins among intellectuals in the context of the increasing discursive activity devoted to establishing, or inventing, a Japanese 'sense of nation', activity that was eventually to locate Japan's national essence in the national polity (*kokutai*) and the *minzoku*.[12]

The image of the 'Ainu race' (*Ainu jinshu*) that this debate promoted from the 1890s was that of the ignorant, primitive savage; an image that dressed the Tokugawa barbarian in scientific clothing. Implicit in this categorisation was the obverse image of Japan as civilised, progressive and modern. Since both Ainu and elephants had large heads, noted Miyake Setsurei in 1891, large heads could not signify intelligence.[13] A similar view was expressed by the historian and philosopher, Inoue Tetsujirō, who argued that the absence of the Mongolian spot in European babies did not imply physical superiority since it was lacking in inferior Ainu babies as well.[14] Nitobe Inazō, then Professor of Colonial Studies at the University of Tokyo after a period spent in the colonial administration of Taiwan, published *The Japanese Nation* for an American audience in 1912. In the chapter on 'Race and National Characteristics' he provided a brief summary of the *koropokkuru* debate, describing the 'hirsute Ainu' as 'not yet emerged from the Stone Age, possessing no art beyond a primitive form of horticulture, being ignorant even of the rudest pottery'. The distinction between a modern, civilised Japan and 'primitive people' was even more explicitly drawn in the chapter on 'Japan as Coloniser' which dwelt on the benefits of Japanese colonial rule in Taiwan.[15]

In keeping with their scientific theories of savagery, these scholars saw the Ainu as doomed to extinction. Most of them felt no obligation to try to alter the course of Nature. Their attitude towards the people who were providing them with income and reputation was at best cavalier, and at worst extremely callous. This is clear in the way they went about their work, although research methods and attitudes were largely inherited from their Western teachers. For instance, one of the first desecrations of Ainu graves in the name of science, at the village of Mori in 1865, was the work of a certain Captain Vyse, the British Consul at Hakodate. In this case, however, subsequent events took a somewhat unusual turn. Ainu from the village protested strongly to Bakufu officials in Hakodate, who in turn demanded the return of the remains. An international incident ensued eventually involving Sir Harry Parkes, the British envoy to Japan. Seventeen bodies were returned and the original culprits disciplined by the British.[16] Unfortunately, such an understanding attitude on the part of the Japanese authorities probably had some relation to underlying anti-foreign sentiment and was not destined to be repeated. Similar 'excavations' soon became an important method of data collection for the anthropologists and archaeologists of Japan's newly established universities. Koganei Yoshikiyo was typical in this respect. In a retrospective article in 1935, Koganei provided anecdotes from the early days of Ainu Studies and his research trip to Hokkaidō in the 1880s. In a tone of engagingly schoolboyish enthusiasm, he described secretly excavating Ainu graves by night to avoid discovery while joking with his labourers about ghosts. When confronted by distraught Ainu on another occasion, Koganei hastily constructed a makeshift altar and went through the motions of appeasing the dead. At one site the remains had only been recently buried and had to be washed clean of flesh and skin in a nearby stream. To obtain physical measurements from living Ainu, Koganei lied to them, explaining that he was a medical doctor come from Tokyo to set about finding a cure for their people for the many infectious diseases, introduced by Wajin, that assailed them. Some thanked him profusely and even offered him tiny sums of money.[17]

Not all scholars ignored the plight of the Ainu in such cynical fashion. Lectures on the Ainu language were given at Tokyo University by Jinbo Kotora, who had worked for five years as a surveyor in Hokkaidō from 1888 and studied Ainu to communicate with the Ainu labourers on his teams. Together with Kanazawa Shōsaburō he produced an Ainu conversation dictionary in 1898. In order to learn the language both these men had spent long periods of time with the Ainu. Aware of the destitution to which the colonisation of Hokkaidō had reduced the indigenes they spoke out about the need for welfare measures.[18] Another scholar who campaigned for Ainu welfare and education was John Batchelor, now established as a leading authority on Ainu language and folklore, who took the Ainu Piripita with him on a lecture tour of the Tokyo and Kansai areas in 1892. Batchelor was consistently critical of Wajin prejudice, especially the widely held belief in the Ainu as half-human, half-dog, stating that 'to say the myth is in any way of Ainu origin is a purely gratuitous assertion, without the least foundation in fact'.[19] As a result, Batchelor favoured the adoption of 'Ainu' over 'Aino' as the name of the people, since the latter was often taken as an abbreviation of *ainoko* (half-breed).[20] Scholars were also involved with the Hokkaidō Kyūdojin Kyōikukai (Hokkaidō Former Natives Education Society) established by the Christian educator Oyabe Zenichirō in 1900. 'The existence of ignorant and lazy people', proclaimed the founding document of the Society, 'is the shame of our citizens.'[21] In a 1906 article that echoed this language, Tsuboi Shōgorō called for more welfare projects for the Ainu, arguing that although most of them were ignorant, they were not foreigners, but 'Japanese citizens (*Nihon shinmin*) the same as us'. It was therefore the duty of the enlightened to teach and to guide them.[22]

The activities of these early scholars achieved two results. First, since the origins of the Japanese was a popular subject of discussion the scientific discourse of 'race' was introduced to an increasingly wide intellectual audience, although elements of Spencerian thought that emphasised the 'struggle for survival' were already popularised to the extent that they permeated late Meiji society. Second, since the Ainu were the primary raw material out of which this discourse was constructed, they ensured that the Ainu would be perceived within these parameters. Increasing awareness of the Ainu meant increasing awareness of them as a backward race (*rettō no jinshu*) of primitive savages. These images were then further propagated among the public at large through the active involvement of academics like Tsuboi in the preparation of school textbooks and expositions (*hakurankai*), both of which will be discussed below.

Blood, smell and character: Ainu Studies, 1912–1945

By the early Taishō period a new generation of scholars were involved in Ainu Studies. Alongside continued research into racial origins there was a growing interest in the preservation, or salvage, of the material and spiritual culture of the 'dying Ainu' (*horobiyuku Ainu*). Kindaichi Kyōsuke emerged as perhaps the leading Ainu scholar in this period, conducting extensive research on the Ainu language and oral traditions, publishing widely in these fields after 1911. Ainu Studies was now a field that attracted international interest; besides the early involvement of foreign scholars, Ainu had been displayed in 'native villages' at the Louisiana Purchase Exposition (St Louis, 1904) and the Anglo-Japanese Exhibition of 1910, and it was widely believed that they belonged to a lost 'white race'. Kodama Sakuzaemon, an anatomist at the Medical Faculty of

Hokkaidō Imperial University after 1929 and a mass excavator of Ainu graves, remembered being exhorted in various countries while on a trip overseas to carry out research on the Ainu after his return.[23]

Overarching narratives of progress and civilisation, of which scholarly discourse was an essential component, legitimised the colonisation of Hokkaidō and the subordination of the Ainu. According to the first official history of Hokkaidō, edited by noted Ainu scholar Kōno Tsunekichi and published in 1918, responsibility for colonisation of Hokkaidō had fallen to the Japanese as 'no other superior race' (*yūtō jinshu*) was in contact with the Ainu.[24] The scientific 'objectivity' of scholars was therefore not in any sense 'neutral' but was embedded within these structures of power. Colonial domination ensured that Ainu could not protect their ancestral and sacred grave sites from widespread destruction, or prevent scholars from entering their communities and homes with impunity. Any action could be justified in the name of science. Scholars were leading members of society, closely linked to structures of authority. After Kodama, for instance, was once questioned by an 'arrogant' junior police officer at the Dōchō over his excavations, he immediately went up the corridor to pay his respects to the senior detective. This man criticised his junior for overstepping the mark and promised to inform Kodama if any Ainu bones turned up in future at construction sites around Hokkaidō.[25] Ainu scholars also began turning their expertise to investigation of the colonised in Japan's other overseas possessions. Yoshida Iwao, a Native School teacher in Hokkaidō and prolific ethnologist and linguist, visited Taiwan to study the indigenous hill peoples. Dr Fujii Tamotsu, a leading parasitologist from Hokkaidō Imperial University who had undertaken research among the Ainu, was sent by the colonial authorities in Micronesia in the late 1920s to investigate the causes of population decline in Yap.[26] This became a wider trend in 1930s Japan when many scholars joined research bodies like the Tōa Kenkyūjo (East Asia Research Institute), a supposedly neutral establishment whose research contributed to government policies towards colonised peoples.[27] Those with Socialist inclinations, and this included some noted Ainu scholars, were forced either to recant (*tenkō*) or keep silent.

Within this framework of domination, scholars began refining their classification of Ainu inferiority. A major trend of the 1920s and 1930s was the increasing interest in such pseudo-scientific disciplines as eugenics and serology which were mobilised in the search for unique Japanese origins. Two scholars instrumental in initiating and popularising research into blood-types from the 1920s were Furuhata Tanemoto and Furukawa Takeji. Furukawa in particular argued that 'it is possible to determine the fundamental basis of [racial] temperament (*minzoku kishitsu*) by analyzing the distribution of the blood types for each [race]'.[28] This notion that racial identities (*minzokusei*) existed and were inheritable encouraged scholars to search for the characteristics carried by Ainu blood. Furukawa himself participated in this research, contributing an article on the racial characters of Ainu and Taiwanese aborigines to the journal *Hanzaigaku Zasshi* (Journal of Criminology) in 1931. Identifying two broad character types, an active type (blood groups O and B) and a passive type (A and AB), he then turned to an analysis of the 'violent and cruel' Taiwanese aborigines (the Musha Rebellion in which 134 Japanese had died had occurred only a few months before). Their 'stubborn' and energetic natures were due to a high proportion of O blood type, which meant that 'it will be necessary to exert an enormous amount of energy to civilise them'. The Ainu, on the other hand, 'not far from extinction', were predominantly B type, happy to live in the present 'with little care for the past or future'. In his conclusion, he suggested that a concrete proposal for pacification of the Taiwanese aborigines would be to let them intermarry with Japanese and so reduce the prevalence of O type, something that education alone could not accomplish.[29] Over a decade later a Hokkaidō Imperial University team also carried out a survey on Ainu character; although based this time on a psychological questionnaire, it did not question the underlying assumption that racial character was objectively quantifiable. Their results agreed with observations by Kindaichi that the Ainu 'were strong of body, but weak in spirit', although they were capable of perseverance. Ainu were also introverted, jealous and suspicious of each other's success, and backward in such social feelings as public justice.[30]

Besides detailed research of such topics as blood-types, hairiness and ear-wax, there was also an investigation into the 'unpleasant' and 'unbearable' body odour of the Ainu.[31] This was an attempt to link the Ainu with the 'white race', who 'as a race possess a strong body odour'. The research found that 'the Ainu are a smelly race' (*nioi jinshu*) as had been noted by Kindaichi. This was not due to uncleanliness but was a racial characteristic. The scientific research method involved was the placing of the nostrils close to the half-naked body of an Ainu in a room overheated by a roaring stove; one of a series of experiences with Ainu odour that led the researcher to muse that 'it's tough for those engaged in ethnology (*jinshugaku*)'.[32]

Studies were also carried out on the intelligence of Ainu children. In 1926, research on Ainu and Japanese children in Karafuto found that Ainu children were inferior to Japanese children on virtually all the tests carried out.[33] A detailed survey was conducted in wartime Hokkaidō by a Hokkaidō Imperial University team, some of whom later went on to study Ainu character. To a certain extent, their report in *Minzoku Eisei* (a eugenics journal, official English title *Race Hygiene*) acknowledged that deterministic notions of 'race' were not universal among scholars by bringing forward two theories of Ainu inferiority. On the one hand, there were those who thought that Ainu backwardness was due to adverse factors in the social environment such as disease and discrimination in education. The opposing view stressed that Ainu inferiority was due instead to 'innate' (*sententeki*) and 'characteristic' (*sōshitsuteki*) difference. The report stressed, however, that this latter view was the correct one. On intelligence tests, Wajin children performed best, followed by 'mixed-blood children' (*konketsu jidō*); 'full-blood children' (*junketsu jidō*) were consistently at the bottom in all tests. The report commented on the influence of mixed blood:

> Mental ability clearly displays a racial (*jinshuteki*) difference, and this difference is reduced by the mixing of blood. Through mixing of blood, superior ability is lowered, while inferior ability is raised . . . If our race (*waga minzoku*) has no choice but to mix blood, we should choose a race (*shuzoku*) that has a mental ability not inferior to ours, or at least a race possessing some special mental characteristic.[34]

The net result of such scholarly activity was that popular myths and stereotypes, dating from Tokugawa times and already in widespread circulation, were now backed up by modern scientific authority. It was already common knowledge, for instance, that the Ainu were fetid and stupid, could not count, lived only in the present, and were indisputably inferior to Japanese. By casting socially constructed cultural difference as 'natural' and inevitable, such scientific research reconciled popular images of Ainu inferiority with theoretical science, and located both within a wider common-sense understanding in which the categories of 'race' and nation overlapped. Even in scientific discourse, the distinction between *jinshu* and *minzoku* often was not clearly drawn, as can be seen in the passage above. Conversely, the discourse of scientific knowledge itself was proof of Japan's status as a modern nation of superior attributes. The power relations that underlay this ability to classify the primitive were seen, if they were acknowledged at all, as the workings of the scientific principle of the survival of the fittest.

OFFICIALS AND EDUCATORS

While scholars were instrumental in fixing the Ainu within the discourse of 'race' and spreading this awareness among the intellectual elites, those who were actually in closest contact with the Ainu were the colonial officials in charge of their welfare. In the early days of colonial administration the Ainu were perceived broadly through the inherited stereotypes of the Tokugawa period as ignorant, half-human barbarians. By the 1890s, Confucian stereotypes of civilised and barbarian were undergoing transformation to conform to the new paradigms for the explanation of difference and inequality; 'race' and the 'survival of the fittest'. The widespread acceptance of these ideas by government officials can be clearly seen in the parliamentary debates that accompanied the various attempts to introduce a Protection Act. Although Wajin exploitation was occasionally discussed, it was generally seen as a natural result of the laws of nature; in effect, the Ainu themselves were to blame.

Protection and education, 1890–1930

Individual attitudes and behaviour, of course, varied widely among officials. On a visit to the Tsuishikari Ainu in 1883, so one story goes, Saigō Tsugumichi, brother of Takamori and a leading figure in the government, joined wholeheartedly with the Ainu drinking and dancing, to the disgust of future Governor Nagayama Takeshirō.[35] And not all agreed with the increasing tendency to apply Darwinian 'laws of nature' to the Ainu. The first proposal in the Diet for a Protection Act came from Katō Masanosuke in the 5th Imperial Diet in 1893. In his opening statement, Katō referred to the argument put forward by some that:

> The survival of the fittest is a natural feature of the world. The Ainu race (*Aino jinshu*) is an inferior race, while our Japanese race (*naichi jinshu*) is a superior race. The superior race say that the inferior Ainu race will naturally die out . . . and that there is no need to protect them.[36]

Katō argued that the Ainu were not an inferior race, since, for instance, 'if you look at the results of those who go to school, there are some who now know how to count well and can do commercial calculations'. Other Dietmen, however, were worried that 'because they are innately stupid they will spend any money they are given on alcohol and other things', or would eat any seeds given to them instead of planting them. The bill failed.[37]

After failing again in 1896, a draft Protection Act was put forward by the government in the 13th Imperial Diet in 1898. In an opening statement, the government spokesman Matsudaira Masanao put forward the reasons for proposing the legislation:

> The natives of Hokkaidō, that is to say, the Ainu race (*Ainu jinshu*) have been from olden times part of the people of the Japanese Empire, but as a result of the survival of the fittest the race is in decline. They have no

> means of livelihood, no way to protect property. As for making a living, most are tending to fall into extreme destitution . . . From the standpoint that it is the duty of the government to protect them we have proposed this bill. Since we have proposed the protection of the Hokkaidō natives for the above reasons and from a spirit of universal benevolence (*isshi dōjin*) we request your cooperation and understanding.[38]

The bill moved into its committee stage. One member expressed his hope for unanimous adoption of the legislation for the protection of the 'Ainu race', those 'infants living under the universal benevolence of our Emperor'. When asked about education, the leading government member, Shirani Takeshi, argued that while the 'inferior race' (*rettō no jinshu*) could not compete with the Japanese race, basic education would alleviate the present situation of natives 'unlearned, illiterate and living for the moment'. Whereas Ainu children were equal to Wajin children at reading, they were inferior at mathematics and could never attain the scores of *naichijin* children. One member asked how half-breeds (*ainoko*) were identified. Admitting that it was sometimes difficult to tell, Shirani replied that they were recorded as Ainu if ancestry was known. If this was unclear, phenotypical criteria were employed; 'only those whom anyone can clearly recognise [as Ainu] are treated as Ainu, Former Natives'.[39] This became official policy in the by-laws enforced after the Protection Act became law and a system of Ainu land grants introduced.[40] Shirani was well placed to argue for the legislation; in a previous appointment as an educator and Dōchō official he had been active in the original movement for a Protection Act. During this period he had made clear his underlying rationale for Ainu welfare policy, arguing in a speech in 1894 that Ainu extinction could not be avoided, but that welfare was necessary since 'it is against human nature not to extend a helping hand to our neighbours', although 'we must definitely not undertake the preservation of the race'.[41]

The Protection Act was duly enacted, and the Imperial Diet only occasionally considered the Ainu thereafter, usually when the Protection Act was being amended or Ainu welfare and education were under consideration during budget deliberations. One exception to this trend was the 1907 debate on the extension of the *naichi* legal system to the new colony of Karafuto. Special consideration had to be given to the status of the indigenous inhabitants, including Ainu, who had not been granted Japanese citizenship (although the relocated Ainu who had returned home from Hokkaidō were Japanese citizens). Giving details of the natives, the committee member representing the government pointed out that 'the term natives means Ainu, and besides them the most inferior races, Gilyak, Orochon, Tungus and Yakutsk'. Since they were such 'extremely inferior races' (*goku rettō no jinshu*) the application of domestic law to them was clearly inappropriate.[42] Racial inferiority justified legal inequality.

Besides legislators and bureaucrats, educators were also prominent in the campaign for a Protection Act. There had been some sporadic interest in Ainu education on the part of the authorities in the early decades. Schools had been established, for instance, for the evacuees of Tsuishikari and Shikotan. In these earlier years, arguments for Ainu education were still largely couched within a Confucianist framework. After being granted some money for Ainu education in 1883, Sapporo prefecture commented:

> From olden times the Former Natives have not known Confucius and have no knowledge of time. If they see snow they know that winter has come; if they see flowers they realise that spring has arrived; herrings mean it must be summer; when the salmon come they think it is autumn. They have no fixed place, when they go out they wander aimlessly . . . they have no writing, no methods of teaching, no inherited sensibility.[43]

As elementary education began to spread throughout Hokkaidō after 1880 some Ainu children began to attend school alongside Wajin children. In a few communities like Hiroo, Ainu children were in the majority, although this situation was rarely seen after 1890 due to increased immigration. Those most concerned with Ainu education, however, were not the authorities but John Batchelor and his associates in the Church Missionary Society (CMS), who founded around a dozen schools in southern and eastern Hokkaidō between 1888 and 1900. Children in these schools received religious education in their own language and were taught to write Ainu in the Roman alphabet. In 1891 the Hokkaidō Education Society was formed, publishing a journal, the *Hokkaidō Kyoiku(kai) Zasshi*, one of the few local journals available for an intellectual readership. These educators began to turn their attention to the issue of Ainu education since it was seen as 'a disgrace to the state' that only foreigners were undertaking this work.[44] In 1892 a committee was formed to look into Ainu education, and it presented a report to the Dōchō the following year. Since the notion of 'race' was increasingly becoming an accepted element of common-sense understanding among educated elites, it comes as no surprise to find that the 'racial' discourse of the Protection debate also characterised the education movement. Iwaya Eitarō, for instance, one of the committee members, was well within mainstream opinion when he argued in 1891 that the decrease in Ainu numbers was the result of the 'principle of the survival of the fittest' since the Ainu were an 'inferior race' (*rettō naru jinshu*).[45]

The influence of these ideas on Iwaya are also evident in a 1901 article in which he compared the Protection Act with the Dawes Act of the United

States. 'The character of the North American natives', Iwaya noted, 'is violent, coarse, and loves revenge . . . while the Ainu are mild and servile.' Referring again to the survival of the fittest, he argued that it was the duty of the 'Yamato race' (*Yamato jinshu*) to extend their sympathy and compassion to protect the Ainu.[46] In 1903 Iwaya again addressed the topic of Ainu education in two articles, the first of which attacked alcoholism as the 'harbinger of a dying race'. The second article focused more directly on policy. Recollecting that at the time the issue had arisen back in 1889 and 1890 there had been 'some who in their hearts were not pleased about the spread of Former Native education, but who were happy to see [their] speedy extinction', he then outlined three approaches to Ainu education: Westernisation (*ōkashugi*), preservationism (*hozonshugi*), and assimilationism (*dōkashugi*). Iwaya rejected the first approach as inappropriate for the Ainu since they were Japanese citizens, implicitly criticising the work of the 'zealous' Batchelor. As for preservationism, the proposals to preserve the Ainu through segregation in semi-autonomous areas, he noted, were mainly put forward by scholars who argued that protection was necessary from unscrupulous Wajin but who were possibly more interested in preserving the raw materials for their own research. Assimilation, concluded Iwaya, was the 'safest and most appropriate doctrine'. This was to be carried out in two stages, hybridisation (*konwa*) and fusion (*yūgō*). As 'intercourse between the Former Natives and the Wajin becomes intimate', Wajin would stop cheating the Ainu, mutual trust would develop, and Wajin would teach them Japanese customs. Sympathy and education would then lead to fusion, although assimilation of this 'different race' was not something that would happen in only ten or twenty years.[47]

As these articles indicate, although the Protection Act was now law, Ainu were receiving land grants, and schools were being constructed in the native villages, the debate on Ainu welfare and education was far from over. It was also not limited only to supporters of these policies arguing as to the best means to carry them out, or discussing the merits of segregated over 'mixed' education. There were those who considered the whole idea a waste of time and money. In a 1918 essay entitled *Ainu Jinshu Shobun Ron* (On the Management of the Ainu Race), the arguments for and against protection of the Ainu were put forward by a former Governor of Karafuto, Hiraoka Sadatarō.[48] Hiraoka was clearly influenced by the new pseudo-science of eugenics. Opening with a discussion on 'racial rebuilding' (*jinshu no kaizō*) and its importance for national survival, Hiraoka presented the arguments for leaving the Ainu to fend for themselves. For Hiraoka and those whose views he articulated, 'race' and nation had clearly become coterminous:

> The world is a stage upon which the strong devour the weak . . . As Darwin wrote in *Origin of Species*, the so-called idea of the survival of the fittest is a principle that rules the whole world of nature. From the phrase 'survival of the fittest' it follows that those unadapted for life are oppressed. The Ainu are unadapted members of humanity . . . The Ainu today have nothing to contribute to the happiness of humanity; consequently their survival or extinction should be left to nature. In particular, artificial preservation through human agency is unnecessary, and moreover, is said to be impossible. Another view [for letting the Ainu die out] argues from the standpoint of the Yamato race [*Yamato minzoku*]. Our country is proud of the purity of our ancient race, and the long-term preservation of this racial purity [*shuzoku junsui*] is our nationalism . . . If interbreeding with Ainu introduces Ainu blood into Japanese it will violate the movement to preserve our national essence [*kokusui*].[49]

A shorter following section put the arguments for preservation, both humanitarian and practical; the Ainu must be preserved as living specimens with a unique language and culture for the benefit of anthropologists and historians of early Japan. Hiraoka then moved on to consider whether allowing interbreeding with Japanese would physically and mentally improve the Japanese race. Mentally, he concluded, the Ainu were clearly an inferior race, and although physically robust, had been weakened by alcoholism and an insanitary lifestyle. Recent eugenics, he noted, now paid attention not only to physical improvement but also to mental improvement. Physical size mattered less than health. In his final recommendations for Ainu policy, which was 'a duty of the nation, indeed, of all mankind', Hiraoka proposed that the Ainu race live within a prescribed area under Japanese jurisdiction, making a living from agriculture or livestock but not allowed to work for Japanese. They should also be exempted from military conscription but ought to be civilised through programmes of agriculturisation. However, Ainu should be forbidden to intermarry with, or be adopted by, Japanese.

In the same year as this article appeared, the prominent educator and Native School teacher Yoshida Iwao called for a similar policy of segregation and education on reservations in Hokkaidō.[50] Interbreeding between Ainu and Wajin, however, was already occurring in Hokkaidō. In 1916 the Dōchō used racial categories to classify the Ainu population into 13,557 'recognised full-bloods', 4,550 'recognised mixed-bloods', and 714 'Yamato race' (*wajinshu*), primarily Wajin children who had been adopted as infants and brought up by Ainu.[51]

In the background to such discussions on protection was the widespread realisation that Ainu policy was not producing the desired results. Whereas in Karafuto actual policy at the time closely followed Hiraoka's model, with Ainu segregated in native villages and fishing grounds and dealing only with appointed Wajin traders, in Hokkaidō it was becoming evident that the policies of converting the Ainu to agriculture under the Protection Act were not working. Many Ainu had lost control of their lands which were held in perpetual lease by Wajin. In some cases under earlier legislation, as the authorities later admitted, Ainu lands had even been incorporated into state lands or assigned to Wajin immigrants by 'forgetful' officials.[52] In an attempt to remedy the situation, the Dōchō appointed Welfare Commissioners in 1923 and set up cooperatives the following year. In instructions to local officials about the cooperatives, the Dōchō justified the decision by pointing out that Ainu 'are almost all dissolute and lacking in managerial sense'.[53] These measures had some beneficial effect, but served also to perpetuate the image of the Ainu as inferior and dependent wards of the state and so ensure their continued subordination. The real reasons for the problems of Ainu land, fraudulent Wajin behaviour and careless officials, were not seriously addressed.

Just in case the Ainu or their sympathisers harboured any doubts about their subordinate position, the authority of the colonial state was symbolically reinforced through visits by members of the Imperial family to Ainu villages.[54] The most important visits were those of the Crown Prince, later Emperor Taishō, in 1911, and the future Emperor Shōwa who toured Hokkaidō as Crown Prince in 1922. On both occasions the future Emperors were taken on tours of Native Schools and villages, and in each place they were greeted by enthusiastic crowds of children mobilised for the occasion. Adult Ainu, many trying dutifully to assimilate and improve themselves, were organised to appear in traditional dress and perform traditional ceremonies in front of the Crown Prince. Instead of emphasis on the modern and progressive which were the supposed objectives of the assimilation policy, Ainu were cast again in their role of primitive barbarian. Besides emphasising differences these occasions also represented a symbolic re-enaction of the oldest form of political tie between state and barbarian, the tribute relationship or *uimam*. They further proved useful in the attempts to indoctrinate Ainu children into the ideology of the imperial family-state with its emphasis on loyalty and sacrifice. The extent of the success of this indoctrination can be seen in the poems and essays Ainu children were made to compose during these visits.[55]

Besides members of the royal family, other dignitaries made frequent visits to the Native Schools, underlining the importance of the education system as a means of perpetuating the subordination of the Ainu. In its inequality, in both content and length of curriculum until 1922, the system itself was a concrete manifestation of the inferior status of the Ainu. Fushiko Second (Nisshin) Elementary School was run for many years by Yoshida Iwao and was one of those Native Schools most frequently visited by dignitaries. Between 1904 and 1931 the school entertained a total of 4,074 visitors, including thirty-two foreigners.[56] These visitors observed Ainu children being trained in 'diligence, order and cleanliness' to 'improve their personalities' since they suffered from 'idleness, no sense of hygiene, untidiness and disorderliness'.[57] Visitors also included scholars undertaking research on Ainu physical, mental or cultural characteristics, and tourists curious to see how the Ainu were being civilised.[58]

Fusion and the mixing of blood, 1930–1945

By the early 1930s, Ainu leaders had become active in a movement for self-help and the revision of the Protection Act, in particular the system of discriminatory education that was now viewed as an obstacle to assimilation. An Ainu organisation, the Ainu Kyōkai, had been formed in 1930 in cooperation with officials of the Social Section (*Shakaika*) of the Dōchō to further these aims. These officials took it upon themselves to encourage the movement: 'The Ainu are not racially (*jinshuteki*) inferior in any way; merely culturally backward having been separated by the Tsugaru Straits', opined the Director for Social Welfare Projects at the Dōchō in 1931.[59] He opened his article in the Ainu newsletter, *Ezo no Hikari* (The Light of Yezo) with a short lecture on race and discrimination:

> No discrimination between races (*jinshu*) is a worldwide [ideal] trend and few would deny this. But what is the situation in reality? Do not Orientals suffer discriminatory treatment by Europeans and Americans as a yellow race? We Japanese are always indignant about this. But Japanese citizens, who have these bitter experiences, within our own country treat people of the *buraku* who follow certain occupations as outcastes, despite no racial difference whatsoever.[60]

Wajin prejudice against Ainu, he argued, was also not 'racial' and would be alleviated by increased assimilation as Ainu furthered their knowledge and social standing. Another attempt to challenge the dominant discourse of Ainu 'racial' inferiority current in educated circles (but not the idea of 'race' itself) was made by Kita Masaaki, the official most involved in Ainu welfare. Like Hiraoka, Kita employed eugenics to make his case, but for entirely opposite purposes: 'Based on the principles of eugenics, mixed-blood children take after the superior race, and are born almost as Wajin.'[61]

For those involved in this movement, one of the primary means of assimilation was seen to be intermarriage and subsequent miscegenation. To overcome the negative image of the 'inferior race' and widespread distaste for interbreeding, some officials used the imagery of Ainu blood merging and 'fusing' (*yūgō*) with that of the 'Yamato race'. At the same time, this image could be used to deny the assertion of a 'dying race'. Ainu blood was not dying out, but would continue to flow in the veins of the 'Yamato race'. This represented progress for the Ainu.

> The natives are being gradually Japanised. Assimilation and intermarriage – for these two reasons the natives are gradually losing their primitive appearance. The volume of their blood is swiftly fusing into the Yamato race and increasing . . . As time goes by the Hokkaidō natives are assimilating. Assimilation (*dōka*), that is, the transformation of customs and appearance, is not the so-called extinction that people believe, rather, we can say that they are a race that is developing and progressing, uniting and fusing with the Yamato race.[62]

The author of the above, and the main proponent of this view, was Kita Masaaki. In another typical article, one of the many he wrote in the journal devoted to social welfare in Hokkaidō, *Hokkaidō Shakai Jigyō*, Kita discussed intermarriage (*zakkon*) between Ainu and 'the general public' (*ippanjin*). Pointing out that there were historical precedents for this in Tōhoku, he introduced the results of a 1936 survey which showed 756 Wajin in Ainu households, and 695 Ainu in Wajin households.

> Ainu women hope to marry Wajin men, and this tendency is increasing every year. So the children inherit the influence from this environment and in strength resemble the superior side. In other words, since they inherit many Wajin physical features the special Ainu characteristics are gradually fading out . . . Although statistically the Ainu are showing a decline, in fact this is not extinction in the absolute sense of the word. Through the mixing of blood and assimilation they are fusing into the broader Yamato race and can be said to be developing.[63]

Another to take up this theme was the Chief of the Dōchō Social Section, Okabe Shirō, although in a more cautionary tone. In an article investigating Ainu population statistics and intermarriage, Okabe concluded:

> Year by year, through the mixing of blood between the two parties, reconciliation (*yūwa*) is taking place, which while we are unaware of it is forming the superior Yamato race of which we are so proud. Even if, for instance, the pure Ainu race dies out, should we feel sadness at the extinction of a race? Ah, what is the meaning of racial preservation? In

> the present century the policies in Nazi Germany for the preservation of the blood of the pure German race are moving racial problems forward into a new area, although I do not have time to refer to this now.[64]

Others writing in the same journal also had doubts. Sonoda Kunihiko, an official in Tokachi, asked rhetorically why, despite some cultural improvement, were Ainu still looked down upon by Wajin? The tendency to cling to old customs, he concluded, retarded intelligence and this was further affected by insanitary living conditions and disease. Another major problem was alcoholism among both men and women; any money gained through the cooperatives was soon spent on alcohol. Ainu were also unable to manage their own affairs and lacked the mental ability to count, which was exploited by Wajin to defraud them. Therefore, Sonoda concluded, the Protection Act was flawed and officials had to increase their supervision of the Ainu.[65]

The Protection Act itself was revised in 1937. The Ainu movement and their Dōchō sympathisers had mustered strong support and the debate focused on assimilation, education and progress. For this reason, and also because by this time it had become self-evident and part of common-sense understanding, the overt discourse of Ainu 'racial' inferiority was more muted than in the debates decades before, although the 'struggle for survival' was brought up in the early stages of discussion. One Diet member attributed Ainu destitution to the following causes:

> Along with the progress of development in Hokkaidō, catches of game decreased in the hills and fishing was banned in the rivers. The lifestyle that they had grown used to over the ages was pushed aside on the tide of human evolution.[66]

In committee, another commented that 'the rate of assimilation is now extremely high, something we are very happy about'. In reply, the Governor of Hokkaidō, Ikeda Kiyoshi, agreed:

> The preservation and maintenance of the race is an extremely difficult thing. Moreover, from the viewpoint of the benefit to the Imperial realm I think that it is inappropriate, so I am completely in agreement that we should proceed with the ideal of assimilationism (*dōkashugi*).
>
> In the future even on the reservations (*shūdanchi*) they will gradually fuse with Wajin, and after several decades have passed it will be difficult to tell. This must be our ideal, I think, and if it occurs then this law, too, will become naturally extinct.[67]

The deterministic stereotypes of Ainu inferiority occasionally surfaced with reference to the past, but in the end, the arguments for assimilation and progress carried the day in the Diet. The Protection Act was duly amended to abolish the separate Native Schools (of which only eight remained, and of those seven were taking Wajin students) and ease restrictions on land ownership.

By this time, Japan was deeply involved in conflict with China and the country was being mobilised on a war footing. The sense of Japanese 'racial' uniqueness and superiority was firmly established, and efficient policing, censorship and social control ensured that the official line was rarely questioned in public. But although relations between Wajin and Ainu were now almost exclusively seen in racialised terms, the fluidity of racialised expression itself permitted contradictory and paradoxical attitudes to exist. Many officials of the Dōchō had now come to believe that assimilation would be eventually achieved not through policies of education and agriculture, but through intermarriage, miscegenation and fusion, and they aimed to encourage this. Among the public at large upon whom they relied for success, however, racialised common-sense in practice fostered prejudices that only exacerbated the exclusion and subordination of the Ainu.

IMAGES OF THE DYING RACE

As Thompson reminds us, it is a mistake to assume the effects of an ideology merely through an analysis of its contents. The discussion so far has concentrated on the images of Ainu 'racial' inferiority held by a relatively narrow circle of elite intellectuals and bureaucrats, observing how these informed policies towards the Ainu that served to perpetuate their subordinate status for all to see. But the discourse of 'race' and consequent categorisation of the Ainu in these terms also reached a far wider audience through such media as newspapers, popular journals, and school textbooks. These ideas combined with the widely held folk images of the Other to explain the reality of economic, political and social marginalisation of the Ainu to the 'average person' (*ippanjin*) who encountered them. The remainder of this chapter attempts to reconstruct the images held at the popular level, and show how they were translated into action in the form of prejudice and discrimination which served to further structure relations of inequality.

Newspapers and popular literature

The press was a major vehicle for the transmission of the discourse of 'race' from scholarly and official circles to a wider audience. In the early years of the press in Hokkaidō, readership was largely confined to intellectual circles, but began to broaden with the spread of mass education in the late Meiji period. Newspapers did not devote much column space to Ainu issues, although interest tended to increase around the time of revisions to the Protection Act. The Ainu were also predominantly a local issue taken up by newspapers in Hokkaidō and Karafuto. Reporting on the Ainu fell into three broad categories. First, there were reports on the failures, and occasional successes, of Ainu welfare policy. Related to this was continued interest in educational matters. Finally, there were general interest articles on Ainu culture or language, often written by academics or members of the local intelligentsia. All these categories of reporting were characterised by the use of the epithet 'dying race' (*metsubō naru jinshu, horobiyuku minzoku*). Moreover, they contributed to this image; welfare issues emphasised Ainu backwardness and dependence, a theme echoed in reports on education, while other articles lamented over, or attempted to salvage, the disappearing culture of the dying race.

Reports on the movement for a Protection Act that arose from the 1890s, and those on the policy implemented after the eventual enaction of the Act in 1899, clearly reflect the spread of the deterministic notions of 'the survival of the fittest' and the 'struggle for survival' among intellectuals of the time. Almost without fail, it was mentioned in the manner of a routine preamble that Ainu destitution and population decline were a result of these 'principles'. Although the report would then move on to its main objective of criticising government policy or mixed education, readers were left in no doubt that the Ainu were an 'inferior race' (*rettō no jinshu*) whose problems stemmed from losing out in competition with the superior Japanese.[68] Even 'native children' were seen in these terms; in an 1897 article under that headline one journalist described meeting some Ainu children on the road, including some of mixed ancestry about whom a fellow traveller laughingly commented '*ainoko*' (half-breed, also a pun on Ainu). Far from laughing, the writer remarked, it made him feel like crying, since the Ainu, 'a dying race on the battlefield of the struggle for survival', were vital for the research on Japan's 'racial problems' – in other words, the quest for racial origins.[69]

Within this Darwinian framework, a range of stereotypes existed to characterise the native. Rather than being the invention of journalists, these stereotypes owed their origins to both the 'primitive savage' of scholarly discourse and the images of the barbarian formed in the *basho*, and which still enjoyed widespread currency within rural Hokkaidō society. The Ainu were characterised as ignorant, alcoholic, disease ridden, dirty and lazy. These stereotypes frequently occurred with reference to the agriculturisation policies of the authorities. These were largely failing, the papers noted, because the Ainu were lazy and lacked the notion of accumulating for the future which was essential for agricultural activity, having lived on the bounty of nature virtually without effort.[70] In Tokachi, it was reported in a typical article in 1910, the natives still had not escaped from their old customs and relied on nature, lacking a sense of accumulation (*chōzōteki kannen*) and interest in agriculture. The men were lazy and loved alcohol, leaving their wives to earn a living.[71] A similar situation existed among the survivors of the Kurile Ainu on the barren island of Shikotan; reports on their plight sometimes managed to include all the above negative images in the space of a single article.[72] As for health, one report informing the public of the situation of the Ainu in 1918 ended with the words 'these days the natives themselves are a splendid congealed lump (*katamari*) of tuberculosis and syphilis'.[73]

Besides journalists, academics or visitors to Hokkaidō occasionally aired their views on the Ainu in the local press. One such observer was the writer Iwano Hōmei, whose travel journals of a tour around Hokkaidō in the company of a prefectural official and legislator were serialised in the *Hokkai Taimuzu* in 1910. Near the end of his tour he commented:

> Generally, our nation has a mistaken policy towards the Ainu. In particular, the plans of those directly concerned with the Ainu, the Dōchō, are mistaken. Since the Ainu are living creatures it is natural to give them some land and a means of livelihood, but after all, their fate is to die out. Are they not an inferior race begging for extinction? What is the point of educating them? Even if, for instance, a handful of men or women advance they will produce mixed-blood children with *shamo* which is nothing to be thankful for. In my opinion, it is enough to give them welfare to keep them alive as living creatures. Instead, we should preserve the things that the once flourishing Ainu race leave behind before they disappear. What should be left are not just rotten bear skins and utensils but the language and literature of the race. Although Greece and Rome perished, their literature survives permanently. The Ainu have a literature that should be preserved. Perhaps the central government and the Dōchō have not so far spent any money for the preservation and study of this.[74]

Academics also contributed learned opinion. In a series of three articles in 1919, a certain Professor Fujinami recorded his thoughts on the 'Ainu, who are important academic research material', but 'clearly approaching extinction' as a 'result of competition with Wajin, that is to say, the survival of the fittest'. As a medical specialist, he pointed out to the public that the main Ainu health problems were tuberculosis, trachoma and hereditary syphilis, but that they themselves had a 'filthy lifestyle' and were 'completely indifferent' to their health. In character Ainu were mild-natured, and despite ill-treatment from Wajin did not protest. Even when they did, they were much less aggressive than Koreans. In conclusion, he was saddened by the decline of pure Ainu as research material, adding that it was the duty of Japanese to preserve them.[75]

Other academic theories were popularised or introduced to the general public through the press. Jinbo Kotora, Nagata Hōsei, Torii Ryūzō, John Batchelor, Kōno Tsunekichi and Tsuboi Shōgorō all contributed articles in their time. The pseudo-scientific researches of the later generation of scholars also attracted attention. Reporting in 1939 on a study of the mental ability of schoolchildren in Asahikawa, the *Hokkai Taimuzu* ran a triumphant headline proclaiming 'Mixed Blood Ainu Display the Superiority of Japanese Blood'.[76] On the other hand, there were scholars like Kindaichi Kyōsuke who attempted to point out that the Ainu were not inferior since, for instance, they had produced a student of genius in his protégé Chiri Mashiho, later a Professor at Hokkaidō University. Kindaichi also expressed disquiet at the widespread use of the epithet 'dying race', saying in a lecture in the early 1930s that it suggested that the fate of the Ainu was extinction. While those who used it perhaps felt pity and sympathy, for the Ainu themselves it 'echoed cruelly like a sentence of death'. He himself supported the 'humane' colonial policy of biological assimilation.[77]

Newspapers and popular magazines like *Chūō Kōron* also occasionally serialised fiction that took the Ainu as its theme. Much of this dealt with love stories or the romantic past of legendary Ainu heroes like Shakushain, as in the first work of this kind, that of Kōda Rōhan in the *Yomiuri Shinbun* in 1889. But a handful of writers did attempt to tackle social issues directly. In 1914 *Chūō Kōron* ran a story called 'Ainu no Ko' (The Ainu Child) by Nagata Mikihiko, in which an Ainu boy was shot dead by a rancher after setting fire to the forest in retaliation for the persecution he had suffered at the hands of Wajin labourers. Miyamoto Yuriko, aroused by the sight of 'the Ainu being driven to racial extinction' and the 'tragic characters' of such men as Yamabe Yasunosuke, visited Batchelor and Kindaichi before writing a short story based on the relationship between an old Ainu man and his adopted Wajin son, *Kaze ni Notte kuru Koroppokuru* (Koroppokur Borne on the Wind). Originally written in 1918, it was cut short when the author left Japan for America and was not published until after her death. In 1935, the magazine *Bungei* serialised 'Hotchare Gyozoku' (The Dog Salmon) by Osami Gizō, which featured the oppressive lives of a young Ainu boy, his blind brother, and his sister who had been deserted by her Wajin lover. The next year, Tsuruta Tomoya won the Akutagawa prize for *Koshamain Ki* (The Story of Koshamain) which dealt with Wajin oppression and Ainu resistance, albeit in a romanticised fashion in the form of an oral legend inspired by the author's reading of the Bible and the Koran. In contrast, contemporary Ainu life was again realistically portrayed by Osami in *Ainu no Gakkō* (The Ainu School), published in 1942, which depicted the struggle of a group of Ainu to save their school from relocation. In keeping with the atmosphere of the times, however, there was no criticism of assimilationist education policy in the novel.[78]

In general, however, in both the issues they reported and the tone they used, newspapers and popular literature served to promote a negative image of the Ainu among the reading public. The emphasis on welfare issues emphasised the dependency and subordination of the Ainu as 'protected' or 'welfare people' (*hogomin*). This was linked to their lack of civilisation and progress which would ultimately doom them to extinction. This gave the Japanese public an opportunity to reflect, perhaps wistfully, on the modernity and progress of the nation. In the words of one official annoyed by this tendency, whenever 'journalism opens its mouth on the Former Natives it talks sorrowfully about the 'dying race' to tempt the reader to pathos'.[79]

Expositions

Another vehicle for the propagation of the image of the 'inferior race' among the general public was the exhibition or exposition (*hakurankai*). Expositions had developed in eighteenth century Europe and grew into great public spectaculars celebrating civilisation and modernity, and, increasingly, imperial glory after the success of the first international exposition at Crystal Palace in 1851. The concept of the exposition entered Japan soon after the opening of relations with the West, and the Bakufu participated in the Paris Exposition of 1867. With the Meiji Restoration, the new authorities continued to participate in World Fairs in Europe and the USA, and began to develop national expositions to promote industrialisation and showcase Japan's own emerging modernity. The first Domestic Industrial Promotion Exhibition (Naikoku Kangyō Hakurankai) ran for 102 days in 1877 at Ueno in Tokyo, and was attended by 45,400 people, who viewed the wares of 16,000 exhibitors. Further similar exhibitions were held at Ueno in 1881 and 1890, in Kyoto in 1895, and Osaka in 1903.[80]

Karafuto Ainu from Tsuishikari had displayed some goods from their cooperative at the 1881 exhibition and a small group had travelled down to Tokyo for the occasion. But the first display of Ainu in a 'native village' occurred at the notorious Hall of Mankind (Jinruikan) at the Fifth Industrial Exhibition at Osaka in 1903. The Jinruikan was the brainchild of Tsuboi Shōgorō, and took its cue from the native villages that had become a regular fixture in world fairs since the 1889 Paris Exposition. But Tsuboi's intention to display the 'races of the world' and their native customs for the education of the masses ran into strong public opposition from the Chinese, Koreans and Okinawans who objected to the humiliation of being portrayed as primitives. Tsuboi had to be content with Ainu, Taiwanese aborigines and some Malays, Javanese and others. Nobody, however, raised doubts about the primitive status of the Ainu. The Ainu group itself was led by Fushine Yasutarō (Kōzō, Ainu name Hotene) of Fushiko who participated in order to raise funds for the school he was attempting to build for Ainu children in his home village. Fushine himself thought that the spectacle of some Ainu walking around the grounds selling seal meat while shouting and singing in loud voices was a 'disgrace to the race', and persuaded them to work inside the Jinruikan.[81]

The image of the Ainu as primitive, subordinate colonial subjects was strikingly reinforced by their display at the Colonial Exposition (Takushoku Hakurankai) of 1912 in Tokyo, which featured a native village to display the 'natives of the new territories'. These included Ainu from both Karafuto and Hokkaidō. A commemorative book of photographs of the Exposition shows traditionally dressed and unhappy looking Ainu and Nivkh from Karafuto standing beside their native dwellings behind stout fences, surrounded by crowds of grinning onlookers dressed in the latest modern fashions.[82]

These native villages represent an early stage in the formation of what Kawamura has termed a 'mass orientalism' among the public at large. The contrast between subordinate and inferior natives, and the modern, civilised Japanese, and the power relations that underlay such a representation itself, were starkly represented in the clothes, buildings and fences within which the indigenous peoples of the Empire were enclosed. Whether expressly articulated or not, the discourse of 'race' and the Darwinian notions that underlay colonial expansion found concrete expression in these displays. These images were effectively conveyed to large numbers of ordinary Japanese; over 4.3 million people, for instance, visited the Osaka Exhibition during the five months it was open.[83]

On a much smaller scale, the colonial subjugation of the Ainu also found expression in the official version of the past presented in the Natural History Museum of the Sapporo Agricultural College. According to one foreign visitor in the early 1920s, the museum displayed a 'lifesize waxwork group' of Kuroda exploring the island in 1870. Kuroda was accompanied by two 'native bearers', while before him was a 'venerable native'.[84] Although 'native villages' are no more, such official representations of the past in museums and public art have continued to underscore the subjection of the Ainu until very recently.

School textbooks

Compulsory national education was established in Japan in 1872, in an ambitious plan that envisaged the establishment of 256 middle schools and 53,760 primary schools throughout the country. The burden of school fees, however, meant that attendance was still below 50 per cent in 1890, and it was not until schooling became free in 1900 that attendance increased, reaching 98 per cent in 1907. By the early 1920s literacy had spread throughout society.[85] At first, textbooks for the new schools were not regulated and private publications were the norm. From 1880, however, the government began to exercise control over textbooks, and after a series of bribery scandals in 1903 inaugurated a system of state compilation and regulation.

Geography was an important subject in Meiji Japanese schools. Early geography textbooks such as Fukuzawa Yukichi's *Sekai Kunizukushi* (World Geography, 1869) and Uchida Masao's *Yochi Shiryaku* (Short Description of the World, 1870) grouped countries into the evolutionary categories of barbarian, semi-civilised and civilised. Fukuzawa's book sold over a million copies in official and pirated editions. With the introduction of government supervision, textbooks underwent a change in the mid-1880s; from this time on environmental determinism and racial stereotyping become common in textbooks, particularly at the secondary level.[86] After the promulgation of the ideological Imperial Rescript on Education of 1890 an emphasis on national consciousness (*kokka ishiki*) became important in geography lessons.

Geography textbooks had already established a trend of describing the Ainu in sections on Hokkaidō. An 1887 textbook introduced them as the 'Ezo, or Aino, natives who have lived in Hokkaidō from ancient times', then described their hair and tattoos and how they lived off the flesh of fish and beasts, before concluding 'although they used to be a wild people, they now have a gentle character and are well mixed in with mainlanders'.[87] An 1892 description followed the standard justification for colonisation by stating that Hokkaidō was undeveloped land, and repeated the above description of the Ainu, deleting the passage on character but adding that they were partial to alcohol.[88] One of the last textbooks before the Ministry took over publication described the Ainu as an 'extremely tranquil and honest race' in the section on Hokkaidō, and included them again under 'Races' (*jinshu*) in the section on the Japanese Empire.[89] Another textbook informed pupils in 1903 that the Ainu did not dress their hair or wash, and could not read, write or count.[90] All these books included illustrations of Ainu in traditional dress beside their traditional dwellings.

With the introduction of the Ministry of Education textbooks from 1904 the appearance of the Ainu in sections on Hokkaidō and the Japanese Empire became a fixed pattern. Among the advisers to the Ministry on such matters were academics like Tsuboi. From 1910 the Elementary School Reader included a lesson on 'Ainu Customs'. The passage introduced exotic customs such as ear-rings and facial tattoos, then mentioned that these 'are now completely forbidden'. After a description of the bear festival and other customs the young reader was informed that:

> The Ainu language is completely different from Japanese. Although they originally did not know how to read and write, and lacked mathematical ability, there are now some who can read, write and do sums the same as Japanese. There are also some who have become elementary school teachers.[91]

When the Ministry issued a circular asking for opinions on the current textbooks, the Saitama Prefectural Women's Teacher Training College replied that this last sentence should be amended to 'there are *even* some who have become elementary school teachers', as otherwise it was an insult to the profession.[92]

This lesson in the Reader was seen by Ainu leaders and their supporters at the time as influential in spreading the image of the Ainu as a backward 'race' throughout the younger generations. Since this was part of a widespread tendency in elementary school textbooks to propagate the official ideology of Japanese 'racial' superiority and colonial mission, especially after 1910, the first encounter of most Japanese 'little citizens' (*shōkokumin*) with the Ainu through textbooks like these resulted in the formation of just such a stereotyped image.[93]

Tourism

Since the days of Isabella Bird, visitors to Hokkaidō usually took the time to pay a visit to an Ainu village. After all, as the *Hokkaidō Shakai Jigyō* noted in 1935: 'Along with snow and bears, it is the Ainu, regarded as a primitive race, that are thought of as the special characteristics of Hokkaidō.'[94] Although mass tourism had not yet developed, those with the money and inclination to travel were sufficient in number to turn at least two Ainu villages, Shiraoi and Chikabumi, into regular tourist attractions during the Taishō period.

Carving was a traditional male skill, and some Ainu had been selling 'toys and other articles' to travellers since the early nineteenth century, but the carving of bears for tourists was first systematically developed in Chikabumi after 1917 by Matsui Umetarō. This activity was encouraged by the Asahikawa authorities who formed a group that provided materials and conducted workshops for the Ainu. During the 1930s Ainu handicrafts from Chikabumi and other communities were displayed in department stores in Sapporo and Tokyo, usually against a prominent background of the *hinomaru* Japanese flag.[95]

Shiraoi, on the other hand, had been receiving visitors since the early Meiji period. *Terry's Japanese Empire*, a guidebook for the English-speaking tourist, devoted a section to Shiraoi in its 1914 edition redolent of Chamberlain and Bird. After giving detailed instructions on where to leave luggage and how much to pay the guide ('25 sen ample'), and advising the traveller to provide some 'candies, foreign knick-knacks' or 'anything that pleases children' for the 'gentle, submissive, courteous, and harmless' Ainu, directions were given to the village.

> Flanking the dirt lane are the wretchedly poor huts (60 or more) of the (approx. 200) people, each surrounded by a little garden in which men, women, and children delve diligently. Side lanes cross the main one at right angles, and are in turn flanked by other houses. The interiors vary with the habits or poverty of the owners. Some are as well furnished and comfortable as the poorest Japanese shack; others are mere styes where the blear-eyed inmates dwell amid vermin and destitution. The town straggles along the beach for a half M.; the deep cauldrons sunk in the sand are used for boiling fish for oil and manure. If the traveler has time to spare he should walk along the beach and inspect the curious *Ainu* boats drawn up there – long, narrow craft, rowed from the side by slender oars. On a foggy day the sea is of a beauty indescribable; gray as a gull's breast, and sometimes broken into great waves which sweep in from the California coast 4000 M. away vainly to thunder their message of civilisation at the very doors of the unheeding *Ainu*.[96]

By the 1930s, however, the village and nearby Noboribetsu had an organised tourist industry. The situation in 1941 was described in a book published in English by the Board of Tourist Industry of the Japanese Government Railways titled *Ainu Life and Legends*, authored by none other than Kindaichi Kyōsuke. In the final section, 'A Guide to the Ainu Villages for Foreign Tourists', Kindaichi warned that 'It is too late now to see the Ainu in their primitive state of life. We are sorry to have to say so.' Nevertheless, he goes on to describe arrangements for the tourist at Shiraoi and Chikabumi, pointing out that 'if you are prepared to pay money, you may perhaps be able to see a number of Ainu people dance and sing'. His final advice for the visitor gives a hint of attitudes encountered by the Ainu performing for tourists:

Money goes a long way here as well as elsewhere, it is true; but even here it is not omnipotent. Many thoughtful Ainu people are ashamed to perform the old manners of their ancestors for money amid the laughter of spectators. They consider it disrespectful to their forefathers. You are therefore requested, while looking at them, to refrain from laughing without any reason or assuming an attitude of mockery.[97]

The Native Schools were also on the itinerary of many a tourist, encouraged by the Dōchō which recommended to visitors in an official guide to Hokkaidō that they visit the villages of Shiraoi and Chikabumi and also a Native School, where they could observe the efforts being undertaken to civilise the Ainu.[98] Besides such organised tourism, traditional Ainu ceremonies also attracted large numbers of local sightseers; in one early bear festival in Otaru, a newspaper reported a huge crowd of 1,500 onlookers surrounding a few Ainu performing their sacred rite.[99] Photographs of such festivals from the late Meiji period onwards nearly always include large crowds of curious sightseers.

While tourism no doubt enabled some Ainu to make a reasonable living and provided them with an opportunity to explain aspects of their culture to Wajin, it mainly served as yet another means of contrasting the primitive with the civilised. Ainu destitution and the fringe-camp nature of the villages were displayed to the public, not as the direct result of the appropriation of Ainu land and resources for colonial development, but as a showcase of the primitive, which the casual visitor could fleetingly observe then leave confident in his or her own modernity and civilisation.

Popular attitudes

While it is a relatively straightforward matter to trace the means by which images of the 'dying race' were diffused among those whom Kita Masaaki termed the *ippanjin*, it is altogether more difficult to determine to what extent these notions were rejected or adopted within the common-sense categories that people employed to understand the everyday world around them. Those categories themselves underwent considerable change as the Tokugawa world-view collapsed during the social turmoil that followed the Meiji Restoration. But by the end of the Meiji period the notions of civilisation, progress and the nation had become self-evident to ordinary Japanese, and provided the overarching commonsensical categories within which individuals made sense of the world.

For the ideologues of this period, Japanese national identity was increasingly comprehended by reference to the colonial Other and a sense of national mission. Rising nationalist sentiment during and after the

Russo–Japanese war was accompanied by increased colonial expansion. Korea was formally annexed in 1910, and the former German colonies of Micronesia, occupied in 1914, came under Japanese trusteeship after the First World War. Attention now turned to mainland China. 'Incidents' occurred in Shanghai and other parts of China throughout the 1920s, and in 1931 the Guangdong Army engineered the takeover of Manchuria, establishing the puppet state of Manchukuo in the following year. From 1937 Japan was involved in full-scale war in China. This was accompanied at home by increased censorship and social repression, exemplified by the Peace Preservation Law of 1925, and indoctrination to the ideals of the Imperial family-state through education, conscription and the pervasive influence of such ideological texts as the *Kokutai no Hongi*. Both imperial expansion and social conformity were justified by reference to the destiny or essence of the Yamato *minzoku*, the 'Japanese race'.

Historians generally agree that the dominant discourses that constituted official ideology were firmly established by the early Shōwa period as alternative or competing discourses were suppressed in the public domain. One expression of such trends was the growth of a 'mass orientalism' through which the colonised were categorised in popular media as backward and uncivilised 'races' of inferior natives in contrast to a modern and civilised Japan. Individuals, of course, received the messages carried by symbolic forms in highly individual ways according to their own frameworks of understanding and complex social contexts. But on the surface, at least, little opposition to notions of Japanese superiority was evident. For the average inhabitant of Hokkaidō, this common-sense world-view both explained and justified Ainu inequality, and the extent to which it was held can be partially glimpsed through social practice and the behaviour of individual Wajin towards Ainu with whom they came into contact.

Most of the residents of the island who entered in the period of mass immigration after 1890 actually had little contact with the indigenes since government policy had confined most Ainu to the native villages and reservations, and what they did know about them would have been largely gathered from the sources mentioned above. This social distance and the depersonalisation it engendered is hinted at in a 1928 article about a rail journey through the Hidaka region. After a scene of some 'simple and honest countryfolk' struggling with large loads in the narrow carriage some Ainu passengers are described:

> Some Ainu got on. There was a *menoko* carrying a child, one that looked like its husband (*sono otto rashii no*) and one that looked like the mother, four in all. On the face of the old woman there was a large tattoo

> around the mouth that seemed to symbolise the loss of all happiness and hope in the world . . . Splendid horses turned loose to graze, Ainu; autumn was slowly deepening on the road to Hidaka and brought to mind the sparseness of human habitation.[100]

But there were also many Wajin who did live in close proximity to Ainu villages, and evidence suggests that intimate contact encouraged highly negative attitudes.

Contempt for the Ainu was, of course, nothing new. From Tokugawa times negative stereotypes had accompanied Ainu subordination, and these continued to be widely held among the rural lower classes. Life was hard for these men and women, too, especially during the famines that hit Hokkaidō in 1913 and 1931–1935, or as a result of frequent epidemics and floods. Many were struggling tenant farmers, and disputes were common with the large landlords who had established themselves in Hokkaidō as a result of official encouragement after 1890. Economic considerations motivated many farmers and small traders who lived around the native villages to employ unscrupulous methods to swindle Ainu out of their land, and it is likely that negative stereotypes served to justify such acts in the eyes of their perpetrators in many cases.[101] The memories of Ainu who grew up in the early twentieth century are full of incidents of cheating and manifestations of an overt prejudice that was rife among the rural poor. Although immigrant attitudes were complex and defy simplistic categorisation, it appears that many members of the professional classes, on the other hand, treated the Ainu considerately, perhaps motivated by feelings of pity.[102] As Sunazawa Kura recalled of life before the war:

> Those who mistreated us were somehow always those who had never received any education and were forced to do the most menial jobs. When I was a young woman working as a nurse at the clinic, those who abused me with the name 'Ainu' and bullied me were the illiterate labourers. School teachers, doctors, and those who had received education and were aware of things, respected us as being real Japanese.[103]

This generalisation does not always hold up under scrutiny; Sunazawa herself ran away from the clinic after the doctor had attempted to rape her. But among the less-educated Wajin immigrants, older stereotypes persisted. Besides the negative stereotypes common among their predecessors, the itinerant workers of the *basho*, immigrants from areas with considerable *eta* populations brought similar prejudicial notions of non-human Others. These negative folk images functioned as they had in the *basho* period to exclude the Ainu, however Japanised on the surface, from ever becoming Wajin, and in this respect they harmonised well with 'race' thinking. Beliefs in Ainu inhumanity persisted. As John Batchelor pointed out in 1919, while Japanese were polite among themselves and to Westerners, they treated the Ainu as 'outside the brotherhood of man', referring to the continued belief in the bestial origins of the Ainu.[104] One Wajin fisherman in Karafuto was recorded as saying around 1928: 'So what if the Karafuto Ainu have no registration, they are not counted as human so it makes no difference if you kill one or two of the animals.'[105] Those Ainu who were phenotypically distinct found that their features, in particular hairiness, marked their inferiority and singled them out for abuse. As one Ainu wrote in the 1940s:

> Why do we have to be ashamed of our hairiness? 'I just don't want to be thought of as Ainu.' Is not this inferiority complex based, consciously or unconsciously, on a mistaken sense of aesthetics in comparing our physical characteristics to *shamo*? . . . But is hairiness, from the standpoint of science, enough of a reason to give us this sense of inferiority? . . . *Shamo* are unhairy. Chinese are unhairy. Koreans are unhairy. Indonesians are unhairy. African negroes are unhairy too. But Whites are hairy. Looked at in this way, it is clear that hairiness or unhairiness has nothing to do in determining the superior attributes of a race.[106]

Outside Hokkaidō, ignorance of the Ainu was the norm; one of the oldest stereotypes, that of the wild Emishi, was encountered by an Ainu conscript during his wartime service. On reaching his unit in Manchuria he was questioned as to whether he could eat army rations instead of raw meat, and even had two NCOs assigned to teach him Japanese.[107]

Physical mistreatment was common in both military and civilian life, often stemming from Wajin perceptions that Ainu were forgetting their inferior status. One Ainu recalled a fight starting with the following exchange:

> [Wajin] 'What are you doing?'
> [Ainu] 'I can't find my *geta* (footwear).'
> 'You came in *geta*? Didn't you come barefoot?'
> 'I wore *geta*.'
> 'What are you talking about? Ainu go barefoot. Do you think you go around in *geta*?'
> 'No, I really wore *geta*.'
> 'Liar!'
> 'No, it's true.'
> 'You insolent.'

The Ainu was then set upon and severely beaten by a group of Wajin, encouraged by a crowd of drunken bystanders.[108] For Ainu children, school became a torment whenever they were a minority in numbers. This was a feature of Ainu life from the early days of mass immigration. One educator noted in 1892 that arguments and fights were common since Wajin children inherited negative attitudes from their parents:

> Because they are despised [Ainu children] tend to stay at home and hate starting school. Wajin complain that they are extremely dirty, terribly smelly, rude and incapable of speaking Japanese properly . . . Their parents, especially those of higher status, detest these things.[109]

That the situation had not improved thirty years later was illustrated by an official report from Kasai District in 1923, which found that Ainu children who attended mainly Wajin schools were 'clearly affected by racial (*jinruiteki*) prejudice', and that absenteeism was high.[110] The Ainu leader Kayano Shigeru, who grew up in the 1930s, recalls that Wajin parents would quieten crying children with the words 'We'll give you to an Ainu', or 'An Ainu has come to get you', and that 'Ainu' was used as an insult that frequently led to physical confrontation between workmen.[111]

With such attitudes widespread, it is no surprise that despite the official rhetoric of intermarriage and 'fusion', records of the time indicate that enthusiasm for this was not widely shared in rural Hokkaidō society. Social practice did not lead to the acceptance of those of mixed ancestry as Wajin. Relationships between Wajin men and Ainu women tended to follow the pattern of temporary liaisons set by the *dekasegi* migrant workers in the days of the *basho*, with the women often being abandoned after a winter of cohabitation. Nevertheless, one visitor to Hokkaidō noted in 1926 that:

> Recently marriages to Japanese have greatly increased. Usually the man is Japanese and the woman Ainu. Occasionally the opposite case is seen, but these are extremely few. Mixed-blood children are gradually taking root. Most are entered in the woman's family register, but this is not a phenomenon we should be happy about [as pure Ainu are decreasing].[112]

One official investigating Ainu family registers also noted that children of such liaisons were usually entered as illegitimate in the register of the Ainu woman. If the couple were married, he explained, the child could be registered as Wajin and would thus be ineligible for welfare under the Protection Act.[113] While such practical reasons obviously existed, the fact that those of mixed ancestry were overwhelmingly categorised as Ainu, or 'mixed-blood Ainu' (*konketsu Ainu*), but never as 'mixed-blood Wajin', indicates that identity was essentially determined by 'racial' notions of innate inferiority carried by blood. This was helped by the fact that 'race' thinking meshed easily with established social customs, in particular those that surrounded the institution of marriage and incorporated folk attitudes towards blood-lines and pollution.[114] Even the many *moraiko*, or adopted Wajin infants who were brought up by Ainu, were usually treated as Ainu unless they moved away; in the words of one character in Osami's novel *Ainu no Gakkō*, 'if brought up in a native household even a Wajin child ends up nativised'.[115]

In contrast to this bleak picture of social exclusion and prejudice, many Ainu autobiographies and oral histories concerned with this period include recollections of Wajin who helped and encouraged their Ainu neighbours with acts of great kindness. Conversely, some Ainu state they rarely, or never, encountered any discrimination and were able to succeed on their merits. Clearly, it is necessary to heed the warning that ideology is often more apparent in studies of the subject than it is in everyday life and to recognise that however hegemonic the dominant discourse of Ainu inferiority, individuals received and mediated such messages, and incorporated them into their everyday experience, in very different ways. Oral histories and other autobiographical sources can provide a corrective by showing the wide variety of individual experience. The personal histories of many Ainu women, for instance, reveal that the immediate source of the misery of their lives was not material and ideological marginalisation under a colonial order, but oppression by men, both Wajin and Ainu.[116] Ainu suffered at the hands of other Ainu as well as becoming victims of Wajin exploitation. But a general pattern of Ainu–Wajin relations emerges even from such diverse testimony. While the nature of oral sources as historical evidence can be problematic, depending as they do on an individual's construction of the past within the context of his or her own self-image, overall they provide overwhelming evidence that negative attitudes and discriminatory behaviour were widespread in pre-war rural Hokkaidō.[117]

From the 1880s onwards the Ainu had increasingly come to be perceived as a 'dying race', an image that encompassed both folk images of the Other and the deterministic notions of popular Social Darwinism. This in turn was part of a larger process in Japanese society in which the boundaries of 'race' and nation had overlapped in the context of modernisation and the expansion of a colonial empire inhabited by inferior 'racial' Others. While there were differences of opinion among both expert and layman on matters of domestic and foreign policy, it was a rare voice indeed that succeeded in transcending the boundaries of the master-narratives of Japanese superiority and modernity, or the right of the nation to develop and civilise nearby lands, including Hokkaidō. By the Shōwa period, the expression 'dying race' had become so commonly used whenever the Ainu were mentioned that it provoked extreme annoyance among those like Kita Masaaki who were attempting to promote the assimilation of the Ainu.

> Ainu! Whenever this word is written, it is attached without fail to the phrase 'dying race'. Ainu! Whenever the average person (*ippanjin*) hears this word, preconceptions of 'primitives, hairy men, simpletons' flash like lightning through his mind and echo there.[118]

For Kita, the problem was that the association of the Ainu with a primitive 'dying race', if not seen as actual scientific truth, was certainly part of the common-sense world-view of the 'average person'. Building on earlier notions of difference, premodern stereotypes of the barbarian had been adapted and reproduced within the discourse of 'race' alongside the language of Darwinism. Whether Ainu were consciously perceived by individual Wajin through the lens of 'race' or not, common-sense understanding ensured that an essential Otherness excluded the Ainu from membership in the superior 'Yamato race'. Although less explicitly stated than in the discourse of the scholars, educators and officials of the colonial administration, for the 'average person' too, Ainu subordination and inequality were in effect matters of 'blood'.

5 With shining eyes

Ainu protest and resistance, 1869–1945

Ainu military resistance to Japanese expansion ended with the executions at Nokkamappu in 1789. The Japanese state thereafter consolidated and refined its domination over the Ainu, a process that accelerated after the Meiji Restoration. Subordination and marginalisation were the fate of the 'dying race'. Having detailed the material and ideological structures in which the Ainu became enmeshed, the way that they were 'made' under a colonial order, the focus of this study now shifts to a consideration of Ainu response. The Ainu were not all docile and passive victims of progress. Once military resistance became futile, individual Ainu still attempted to influence the structures through which they were controlled or to accommodate themselves to changing circumstances. Whether by active campaigns against the Protection Act, or merely through passive resistance to assimilation policy, many Ainu attempted to exert a degree of control over their own lives. From around 1920, some educated young Ainu began an attempt to create a shared sense of identity and purpose among their scattered communities. The movement they formed produced the first all-Ainu organisation, the Ainu Kyōkai, in 1930. While largely conforming to the welfare agenda set by the authorities, the increased communication among like-minded Ainu and the growing realisation of a shared predicament, expressed in the newsletters and other publications of the movement, were to lay the foundations of a new unity and identity.

EARLY ACCOMMODATION AND OPPOSITION

Attempting to conceptualise Ainu identity in the premodern period, especially in terms of 'ethnicity', is fraught with difficulty. While the Ainu certainly shared a loosely defined sense of identity that was based on a broadly common set of symbolic beliefs, cultural practices and language, social organisation and authority had been located in autonomous local river groups. Contact and trade with the Wajin had transformed these bases of organisation into powerful regional groups under leaders like Shakushain that cooperated, competed, or occasionally fought each other for perceived advantage. Political allegiances were fluid. After Matsumae military power had destroyed these groupings, others had been formed as a result of labour requirements on the fishing stations. An Ainu sense of Self, however, perhaps reinforced by anti-assimilation policies in the *basho*, remained distinct enough to provoke widespread resistance to the subsequent Japanisation policies of the Bakufu and ensure their failure. Mogami Tokunai and other travellers noted that most Ainu opposed changing the ways of their ancestors since they believed that such acts would anger their gods.[1] When Hafura, the leader of the Saru Ainu, was ordered to cut his hair in the Japanese fashion, he retorted to Wajin officials that he was loyal whatever his hairstyle. Hafura then went on to warn that forcibly cutting the hair of the Ainu would make them hate the Wajin and lead them to offer no resistance to the various foreigners who were appearing off the shores of Ezochi in ever-increasing numbers. The Wajin would do better, Hafura added, to concentrate on helping the Ainu to survive rather than on forcing them to change their hairstyles. When the Russians had appeared in the past, he reminded the officials, although the Ainu were following their traditional customs they had not obeyed the intruders. The policy was subsequently dropped in the Saru region.[2]

As Ainu–Wajin relations entered a new phase with the policies of colonisation and development of the Meiji period, for everyday purposes the identities of most Ainu remained based in the local community. At first, local Ainu leaders continued to exercise real authority, despite being dependent to a certain extent on Wajin recognition of their position. In the large Ainu community of Biratori, visitors in the early days of the Kaitakushi usually commented on the iron grip with which 'Chief' Penriuk ruled the village, whatever they thought of his personal habits and alcoholic tendencies.[3] Most Ainu continued to follow their traditional lifestyles as long as the resources and activities that sustained their customary way of life remained untouched by colonial development. But from the 1880s these local groups began to undergo further change as forced relocation concentrated scattered Ainu in artificial communities that ignored traditional kin groupings, communal loyalties and settlement patterns. Traditional structures of authority were difficult to maintain under such circumstances, leading to a breakdown in social cohesion. With little contact between regions and accelerating social disintegration, while strangers from different communities would have recognised each other on the basis of a shared cultural identity as Ainu, the idea of the 'Ainu people' as a unified entity, an imagined community, had yet to develop.

But one Ainu, at least, already possessed this vision. This was a young man from Horobetsu, Kannari Tarō, who became the first Ainu to speak out on behalf of 'the Ainu people'.[4] Born in 1866 into a successful Ainu family that owned both agricultural land and fishing grounds, Kannari attended one of the first schools established in Hokkaidō in Muroran. Graduating with an excellent academic record, he continued his education at an institution for training teachers in Sapporo. In 1883, at the age of only seventeen, Kannari petitioned the authorities in vain to provide money for Ainu education. Soon after this he met John Batchelor, and following his baptism in Hakodate in 1885, Kannari became the main teacher at Batchelor's Ainu school in Horobetsu. Kannari also became active in local organisations devoted to improving the lot of the Ainu through agriculture and education. In 1886 Kannari travelled to Tokyo to visit the residence of Kuroda Kiyotaka and to make fundraising speeches, activities which were favourably reported in the press and the recently inaugurated journal *Kyōiku Jiron*. Two years later he visited Tokyo to speak again, but by this time he had become discouraged by lack of success and was drinking heavily. In 1888 Kannari was sacked from his position at the Horobetsu school by Batchelor, supposedly for alcoholism, but perhaps also because the Hokkaidō authorities were becoming increasingly suspicious of the liberal political circles in which Kannari moved. In 1894, for instance, publication of the newspaper *Hokkai Shinbun* was suspended after a report on a speech by a student of the Sapporo Agricultural College was judged to be inflammatory and against the interests of public order.[5] Kannari continued his activities, however, attempting to gain support for a petition on Ainu welfare to be presented to both Houses of the newly established Diet, but failed in the face of opposition from traditionally oriented Ainu elders. He continued to make speeches on politics and Ainu issues before dying of alcohol-related illness in 1897 at the age of thirty. The tragedy of his short life lies in the fact that in his education, political activism, and links with local liberal journalists like his schoolfriend Itō Shōzō of the *Hokumon Shinpō*, he was too far removed from the rest of his 'people' on whose behalf he campaigned.

Another twenty years would pass before other young Ainu men and women would begin to speak out for their people in the manner of Kannari Tarō. Overwhelmed by colonial development and waves of settlers, most Ainu were struggling to survive the drastic changes with which they were confronted. Rather than resist, many of the more acculturated sought to adjust to the new ways of life and their new status as Japanese citizens. The more successful occasionally achieved public recognition. In 1902 a small team of Ainu from Otoshibe, near Hakodate, led by Benkai Takojirō (Ainu name, Ikasuba) spent nearly ten weeks searching the Hakkōda mountains with dogs to recover bodies and equipment from an ill-fated training march that left 199 soldiers dead. Shortly after his return, Benkai and a local Wajin doctor sent an unsuccessful petition to the Army Minister urging the formation of a unit of Ainu soldiers for winter operations. The content and tone of this petition reflect the fact that the Ainu from this area closest to former Wajinchi were the most acculturated; as Benkai pointed out, 'with the exception of the twenty-three Ainu villages in Oshima and nearby, the rest are extremely undeveloped and lack a sense of the state (*kokkateki kannen*)'.[6] Another Ainu who proved his loyalty to the state was Kitakaze Isokichi, who was decorated for bravery in the Russo–Japanese war. Ainu were liable for conscription after 1895, and Kitakaze was drafted in 1904 into the 7th Division of the Imperial Army, based in Asahikawa and formed from ex-*tondenhei* militiamen and regular conscripts. He was then sent to the front in Manchuria, where he distinguished himself in battles that cost the 7th Division 6,206 men. After the war, Kitakaze's exploits appeared in such widely read youth magazines as *Chūgaku Sekai*. Kitakaze returned to his native Nayoro and took up farming, but ended his days in poverty.[7] Yamabe Yasunosuke, originally from Karafuto but relocated to Tsuishikari, had returned to Karafuto before the war broke out and immediately joined the Japanese army when it invaded Karafuto in the final stages of the conflict. After the war he devoted himself to Ainu education in Karafuto, and also participated in the Antarctic Expedition led by Shirase Nobu in 1910. With the aid of Kindaichi Kyōsuke, Yamabe published his memoirs in 1913, in Japanese with an Ainu translation appearing alongside the main text.[8]

In the main, these Ainu who had succeeded on Wajin terms, either to achieve public recognition like Kitakaze or Yamabe, or economic success like Ōta Monsuke or the Kannari and Chiri families, decried what they perceived as the backwardness of their people. The way forward for the Ainu lay in the path they themselves had taken, that of education and assimilation. At the same time, however, as Yamabe's memoirs and Benkai's attempt to turn Ainu cultural knowledge to the service of the state indicate, they remained proud of their Ainu heritage even while acknowledging that it belonged largely to a former age. In contrast, however, there was a small group of Ainu who were prepared to confront Wajin interests and the authorities that represented them. These were the Ainu of Chikabumi, who enagaged in a long-running land dispute with the municipality of Asahikawa and the Dōchō that was to last four decades and give the community a stubbornly independent outlook that continues to this day.

Wajin records indicate that the Ainu of Ishikari acted on the basis of a recognisable regional identity as early as the seventeenth century, when their leader, Haukase, refused to join in the Ainu campaign led by Shakushain in 1669, stating that it was no business of his. In 1869, before forced relocation became official policy, an attempt was made to move all the Ishikari Ainu down to the coastal fishing stations, but this had to be abandoned after the resistance of Ainu under their overall regional leader, Kuchinkore. But by the final decade of the nineteenth century they had been forced to leave their ancestral homes in the face of Wajin colonisation of the Ishikari region. In 1890 the village of Asahikawa was established as the intended hub of a large-scale development effort, which began in earnest with the opening and partitioning of the Chikabumi plain the following year and the arrival of 400 *tondenhei*. Along with the establishment of Asahikawa, the Dōchō set aside land as 'provisional allotments' (*kyūyo yoteichi*) for local Ainu under the 1877 regulation authorising bureaucratic control of Ainu residential land, although some of this was soon taken over by *tondenhei*. In 1894 around two hundred *chōbu* were allocated as individual allotments for use by thirty-six Ainu households. Although the Ainu leader, Kawamura Monokute, had argued strongly for the right to be allotted land under the same conditions as Wajin, this request was ignored and the Ainu were compelled to live as a segregated group in Chikabumi, away from the rest of the township. The Ainu had no rights of ownership, and in 1896 six households had their allotments repossessed during the construction of the railway to Asahikawa. This rail link was completed in 1898, and the immigrant population began to rise rapidly, from 5,865 in that year to 18,110 in 1903. The year 1899 saw the enactment of the Protection Act, under which the Ainu should have received limited rights of ownership to the allotments, but due to their strategic location the local authorities ignored the provisions of the Protection Act and retained control of the land. As a result, it soon became the target of Wajin speculators.[9]

That same year also saw the transfer of the recently created 7th Division of the Imperial Army to Asahikawa as part of the military build-up in Hokkaidō in preparation for conflict with Russia. This greatly stimulated the growth of the township and brought about a sharp increase in land values. Construction of the military base, which adjoined the Ainu lands at Chikabumi, was contracted out to Ōkuragumi, a large and well-connected Tokyo company used to working for the military. The company soon began manoeuvring to gain control of the Ainu allotments, and presented a petition to the Dōchō in January 1900 calling for the relocation of the Ainu for the following reasons:

1 Allowing the ignorant and filthy [Ainu] villagers to remain within city limits is extremely dangerous from the point of view of sanitation.

2 It is necessary that the Division and the township be closely connected, and this is hindered by the existence of this village.
3 The development of the township does not permit the existence of cultivated land.
4 Even if [the Ainu] are given the same rights as Wajin and allowed to live among them, they will be overcome in the struggle for survival (*seizon kyōsō*).
5 They will be much happier, and welfare better provided, if they are moved to suitable new lands.[10]

To back up this request the Ōkuragumi began efforts to influence the Chikabumi Ainu through a local merchant, Miura Ichitarō, who persuaded many of the illiterate Ainu to affix their seals to a document relinquishing the land to Ōkuragumi and requesting relocation to remote Teshio in the north. Within a month of the first request by the company, the Dōchō had decided to grant the land to Ōkuragumi and informed the Ainu leaders in February that the community must leave for Teshio. So began what is known as the First Chikabumi Land Dispute. Ainu leaders, aided by neighbouring Wajin who also feared that their interests would not be served by the granting of the land to the company and by local politicians who saw an opportunity to challenge the authorities, formed the Kyūdojin Ryūjū Dōmeikai (Alliance for Continued Former Native Residence) with the backing of the new Kenseitō (Constitutional Party). This group presented petitions to the Dōchō in February and May. Led by Amakawa Ezaburō, an Ainu of Hamamasu who had come to Chikabumi to support the movement, a delegation consisting of Kawakami Konusaainu and two Wajin allies travelled to Tokyo in April to visit Shirani Takeshi, head of the Hokkaidō Section of the Home Ministry, and to lobby the Home Minister and politicians of both houses of the Diet to reverse the decision. The group also visited the offices of all the major newspapers in the city. The central government, facing possible embarrassment after articles in *Jiji Shinpō*, *Hōchi Shinbun*, and the *Mainichi Shinbun* exposed the 'secret manoeuvres' of Miura and the Ōkuragumi and criticised the authorities, decided on 3 May 1900 after discussion with Shirani Takeshi and other officials to cancel the order for relocation and disposal of the land to Ōkuragumi.[11]

Although the Ainu had won the first round, the land in question remained the target of speculators since it was still not brought under the Protection Act, despite a request by Amakawa to the Dōchō that it now be granted to them. By 1905 many of the Ainu had been reduced to such destitution that they were forced to live on leftovers from the 7th Division kitchens. The Asahikawa authorities, increasingly aware of the strategic location of the land which was now officially within the municipal boundaries, began negotiations with the Dōchō to lease the *kyūyo yoteichi*. In January 1906 the Dōchō agreed to lease the land to the municipality for thirty years, under condition that Asahikawa grant each Ainu household one *chōbu* of agricultural land, construct a house for each family, and use the remaining land for a model farm. Any profits were to be used for Ainu welfare in accordance with the provisions of the Protection Act. The land grants, however, represented only a fifth of what the Ainu were eligible to receive under the Protection Act. Only a fraction of the remainder was actually used for a model farm, the rest being designated communal land and leased to Wajin at low rents or used for municipal development. Although Asahikawa claimed to be acting in the interests of the Ainu and used the income from the rents for Ainu welfare, it was the town and the Wajin tenants who benefited most. The Asahikawa Regulations for Former Native Welfare (Asahikawa-chō Kyūdojin Hogo Kitei) were introduced in June 1906 and a Native School was established, but this later became a tourist attraction with the children forced to produce Ainu handicrafts for sale. The Ainu community became deeply divided, many blaming Amakawa for their reversal of fortunes. This was the end of the Second Chikabumi Land Dispute. The Ainu had been subordinated to the power of officials and the police, but Chikabumi had acquired a reputation of active opposition and the problem was destined to erupt once more at the expiration of the lease in the 1930s.

TAISHŌ DEMOCRACY AND THE AINU

The decade of the 1920s is often referred to by historians as the period of 'Taishō democracy', a period when party politics and social movements gained a brief ascendancy over oligarchic cabinets and civil repression. The success of the 1917 Bolshevik revolution in Russia and the growing industrial and social unrest that culminated in the Rice Riots of 1918 led to a wave of labour and socialist activity after the First World War. In 1919 the previously conciliatory labour organisation, Yūaikai (Friendly Society) renamed itself Sōdōmei (General Federation of Labour) and began to take a radical, anarcho-syndicalist approach to trade unionism and industrial action. A loosely defined and faction-ridden 'left-wing' movement began to emerge, based on labour and student activism, and socialist ideas were embraced by many intellectuals. An underground Communist Party was founded in 1922. In the countryside, peasants unions were formed and tenant disputes escalated sharply from 408 disputes involving 34,605 tenants in 1920 to 1,680 incidents involving 145,898 tenants the following year, a level of activity maintained for much of the decade. By 1927,

365,000 farmers belonged to tenant unions. In 1925 all males over twenty-five received the right to vote and political activity was further stimulated. But this was offset by the draconian Peace Preservation Law that was passed at the same time.[12]

One important social movement that achieved public prominence during this period was that of the former outcastes of Tokugawa society, the *Burakumin* or *eta*. Despised as ritually polluted and forced to engage in restricted occupations and live in segregated settlements, the outcastes were viewed in much the same deterministic terms as the Ainu, to whom some believed they were related. While members of both groups were seen as only partially human, Burakumin were stereotyped as unruly and dangerous in contrast to the docile and submissive Ainu. In 1907, Mie prefecture officials described them thus:

> The people of this race in this prefecture . . . are ruthless and cruel. Not only do they steal and kill cats and dogs, but they also steal other property. They are immoral and unruly and often defy public officials. People of this group are usually paupers . . . This race of people stands outside society and knows nothing of morality. By and large they are lazy and addicted to gambling. Because of their perverse nature they have a strong inclination to unite for unjust purposes.[13]

In 1871 the outcastes had been elevated to *heimin* (commoner) status in the same way as the Ainu; but the unequal status of both groups in reality was apparent in the way that they were registered under separate designations. The Ainu became *kyūdojin*, while the Burakumin were usually distinguished as *shin heimin* (new commoners). Education policy for Burakumin was also conducted on the principle of separate schools until 1908. In 1922, influenced by both left-wing and Christian thought, a group of young Burakumin intellectuals formed the Suiheisha (Leveller's Society) to campaign forcibly against discrimination. Militants within the organisation forged links with radical socialist elements and it was soon regarded by the authorities as subversive, a view strengthened by confrontational Suiheisha tactics. In response, the authorities consolidated their hold over the alternative, and far less radical, Yūwa (Conciliation) movement established in 1903, merging all the groups in this movement into one organisation under the Home Ministry, and establishing the Chūō Yūwa Jigyō Kyōkai (Central Yūwa Project Council) in 1928.[14]

Some observers drew parallels between prejudice against the Burakumin and that suffered by the Ainu. The socialist Sakai Toshihiko, in an article in the early 1900s, linked Wajin treatment of the Ainu to discrimination against Burakumin and likened it to 'racial discrimination' in the West.[15] In 1918 the doctor Neil Gordon Munro conducted a survey of the Ainu on behalf of the Dōchō in which he described how Wajin despised the Ainu as dirty and ignorant, in a manner that resembled the 'class prejudice seen against the *eta*' in the south of Japan.[16]

This period saw the formation of another substantial 'racial' minority in Japan, the Korean community. The movement of Korean men to Japan as migrant labourers increased after the annexation of Korea in 1910, fuelled by both labour shortages in Japan's growing industrial sector and the dispossession of rural Koreans. The number of Koreans employed in the Hokkaidō coal mines increased so rapidly that John Batchelor began to learn Korean in order to undertake missionary work among the immigrant miners. Some Koreans were active after 1920 in the labour movement in the mines and elsewhere, and there was also opposition to Japanese colonial rule among the growing number of Korean students in Japan. While Koreans were subject to the same colonial ideology of assimilation (*dōka*) as the Ainu, similar popular perceptions of an inferior race of colonial 'natives' served to reinforce subordination and militate against assimilation in fact. Popular prejudice against Koreans, and the fear of a link between their perceived violent natures and radical labour activism, were factors behind the massacre of thousands of Korean men and women after the Great Kantō Earthquake in 1923.[17]

The 1920s also witnessed a growth in social movements among the Ainu. Ultimately, however, the Ainu were unable either to form an organisation like the Suiheisha that was able to confront the authorities, or to link up with the labour and left-wing movements in the manner of Korean activists and students. The reasons for this lie in the scattered, rural nature of Ainu communities, which were largely isolated, self-contained, and unable to come together to forge a broad sense of common unity and purpose. By contrast, the early Burakumin and labour movements thrived in the growing urban areas where modern communications enabled ideas to be efficiently diffused to large numbers of people who could be mobilised for meetings and rallies. An urban milieu also favoured the mobilisation of financial resources; most worked for wages, and some urban Burakumin owned small businesses. The 17,000 Ainu, on the other hand, were overwhelmingly rural and on the periphery of the money economy. The Ainu were also distributed over a wide area; only in the Hidaka and Iburi districts were they present in any numbers. Given these constraints, links with organised labour were unlikely; as for student movements, only one Ainu, Chiri Mashiho, attended university during this period. One route for organisation was agrarian activism; but although tenant unrest was rife in Hokkaidō since many large landlords had profited from the land distribution policies of the Dōchō, strong negative attitudes among Wajin and disputes over Ainu land usually ensured that there was little likelihood of cooperation between marginal Ainu and Wajin farmers against 'class enemies'. In this respect, the First Chikabumi Land Dispute was an exception. On the other hand, few Ainu had the opportunities to gain a close acquaintance with socialist thought that could have led them to embrace their Wajin counterparts as allies in a larger class struggle. With the exception of one small group, the short-lived Kaiheisha that was formed in Chikabumi in 1926 and affiliated to the Nihon Nōmintō (Japan Peasant Party), there is little evidence to suggest Ainu involvement in agrarian activism. At the same time, Wajin allies of the Ainu tended to be members of the educated elite, often Christian educators and officials driven by a sense of pity rather than class struggle; for them the Ainu still needed to be managed and controlled. Even noted Ainu scholars with Socialist sympathies, including Takakura Shinichirō and Kōno Hiromichi, subscribed to this view. Again, Chikabumi was an exception in that a handful of local politicians in Asahikawa took up the Ainu cause against the bureaucrats. But the handicaps to organisation faced by the Ainu were seen in different terms by most Wajin, and attributed instead to their innate inferiority. For one journalist who visited Shiraoi in 1922, the Ainu were simply too backward, disease ridden and alcoholic to possess the energy to undertake a Suihei-type movement.[18]

Despite these constraints, a loose movement of educated young Ainu united by a commitment to work for their people began to emerge in the 1920s. The expressions of identity and solidarity that come out of the writings of these men and women are the manifestation of a refusal to accept their categorisation by the colonists as a 'dying race'. This refusal was grounded in a resistance that was more widespread than the majority image of the docile Ainu assumed. Many Ainu had their own explanations for the situation in which they found themselves, explanations that were not grounded in a discourse of 'racial' inferiority. One Ainu elder, for instance, told a local newspaper in 1918 that Ainu social problems, widely seen at the time as a result of losing the 'struggle for survival', had more to do with the breakdown in the traditional authority of the community leaders.[19] Since most Ainu activists, however, were more directly influenced by Wajin philanthropists and Christianity than radical or socialist thought they tended not to question their incorporation into the Japanese state or their loyalty to the Emperor. Most, too, did not question their eventual assimilation.

While no formal institutional links were formed with labour and social movements, some younger Ainu were nevertheless inspired by reports of their activities. Influenced by what little they knew of the Suiheisha and, in the case of some, their own Christian beliefs, these young Ainu came to understand the marginalisation of the Ainu as the product of colonialism and discrimination, and not as the result of the innate inferiority of a 'dying race'. This understanding led not to radical activism, however, but to renewed efforts aimed at the incorporation of the Ainu into Wajin society. The onus was on the Ainu to improve themselves. Inferior education, in particular, was seen by Ainu leaders and their supporters as perpetuating Ainu subordination and thus hampering the efforts of the Ainu to become loyal and useful subjects of the Emperor. Efforts to have this system abolished, combined with movements at the community level to eradicate alcoholism, improve social and economic conditions, and remove the legal inequality enshrined in the Protection Act, were the axes around which the Ainu social movements of the 1920s and 1930s revolved.

TEACHERS, POETS AND CHRISTIANS: AINU SOCIAL MOVEMENTS, 1918–1930

The appearance of a new generation of young Ainu determined to work for an improvement in the situation of their people was heralded by the publication in 1918 of *Ainu Monogatari* (Ainu Tales) by a young schoolteacher, Takekuma Tokusaburō. Takekuma was one of a handful of Ainu, who, despite the handicap of the Native Schools, had received an education with support from concerned Wajin and John Batchelor.

Since Batchelor was a key figure in the early movement for Ainu education and welfare and was a major influence on virtually all the young Ainu activists of this period, and therefore on the nature of Ainu activism itself, his career warrants some consideration.[20] John Batchelor was born in Sussex in 1854, and he arrived in Hakodate in 1877 as a young theological student recovering from a bout of malaria contracted in Hong Kong. The resident Anglican priest, Walter Dening, took Batchelor with him to the Ainu village of Biratori. Batchelor decided his lifework lay among the Ainu and began to study the language in preparation for his work as a lay missionary for the CMS in 1879. In 1884 he married Louisa Andrews, the sister of a fellow missionary. Batchelor's first missionary efforts were concentrated around Biratori, but he was forced to abandon work there after being prosecuted for living outside the zone prescribed for foreigners. He next turned his attention to the Ainu villages of Usu and Horobetsu on the Pacific coast near Muroran and his first convert, Kannari Tarō, was baptised in 1885. Batchelor was ordained as a priest in 1888, the year his establishment for Ainu children in Horobetsu formally opened as a school. In 1891 he and other CMS colleagues established three Ainu schools in the Kushiro area, followed by a clinic in Sapporo a year later and a school in Hakodate in 1893. From 1895 he resumed missionary and educational work in the Biratori area with some success, later delegating this area to another CMS missionary. He also became active in the movement against alcoholism conducted by the Temperance Society. After 1898, apart from trips overseas and a few years in Usu, Batchelor lived permanently in Sapporo, turning part of his house into an Ainu Girls Home. In 1906 he adopted Mukai Yaeko, from a prominent Ainu family of Usu, as his foster-daughter.

In addition to his CMS activities, Batchelor established a reputation as an Ainu scholar in the fields of both linguistics and ethnology. During his career he published some forty articles, dictionaries and monographs on Ainu language, folklore and customs, as well as an Ainu translation of the New Testament in 1897. Modern linguists and ethnologists have criticised Batchelor's work as severely flawed by his amateurish approach, Eurocentric bias and rigid Christian beliefs, but there is no doubt that he was acknowledged as the leading European expert on the Ainu during his lifetime.[21] Batchelor gradually became a respected figure in Japanese circles as well, earning the friendship and patronage of influential figures including a member of the now aristocratic Tokugawa family, Marquis Tokugawa Yoshichika. In 1909 Batchelor received the Order of the Sacred Treasure (4th Class) from the Emperor Meiji. He also lectured on Ainu customs to members of the Imperial family when they periodically visited Hokkaidō. Despite his undoubted sympathy and affection for the Ainu, however, Batchelor too saw the Ainu as a 'dying race', believing that such a fate was in God's plans.[22] In a 1927 book, significantly subtitled *Echoes of a Departing Race*, Batchelor wrote:

> But nothing now can avert their doom. They must soon be quite of the past. And they will depart without having left any history or having made any perceptible mark in the world. One feels very sorry for them, but the laws of nature are inexorable and must take their course.[23]

By the Taishō period, the efforts of Batchelor and the other CMS missionaries under his authority to educate promising Ainu students had begun to bear fruit in the form of talented youths like Takekuma. Born in Fushiko *kotan* near Obihiro, Takekuma had gained the elementary school teacher's qualification in 1914 and taken up a teaching post at the Native School in Otofuke.

Batchelor wrote a preface for *Ainu Monogatari* in which he congratulated 'my Friend Takekuma Tokusaburo' as 'the first native Ainu known to have written any book about this, his own race'.[24] While *Ainu Monogatari* provided simple descriptions of Ainu life and customs, Takekuma also took the opportunity to point out that the Ainu were loyal citizens of the Japanese Empire who wished to 'assimilate to Wajin and become splendid Japanese citizens'. He also challenged the 'dying race' image:

> Although some scholars and intellectuals feel sad about the decline of the Ainu race, the Ainu will definitely not become extinct. Even if appearance and customs gradually lose their previous form, the quantity of Ainu blood will certainly not decrease. As a result, the writer believes that the Ainu race in future will not die out but should assimilate to the Yamato race (*Yamato jinshu*).[25]

Takekuma then described and criticised the current system of inferior education for Ainu, a result of the second (1916) Regulations for the Education of Former Native Children that gave Ainu schoolchildren a four-year curriculum starting at age seven. He then proposed some plans for improving Ainu life that involved eradicating 'bad habits' and alcoholism, and improving sanitation and economic conditions. He also called for an end to Wajin prejudice that in deterministic fashion laid all blame on innate Ainu inferiority and engendered a corresponding defeatism among the Ainu:

> Up till now, the average person uses the expression 'it's because you are Ainu' against the Ainu if anything happens. If this hurts Ainu feelings and becomes the basis for inviting mutual misunderstanding we must banish it and further discourage, as natives, a defeatist sense of 'because we are Ainu'.[26]

Finally, Takekuma appealed for an end to the system of discriminatory education, the removal of the lesson on 'Ainu Customs' from the Elementary Reader to encourage mutual understanding among Wajin and Ainu children, and for more financial support for the Native Schools and for Ainu students who wished to continue to higher education.

In this way Takekuma laid out the concerns and agenda of the emerging Ainu movement. Heavily influenced by Christian values, Ainu efforts were directed towards self-improvement and not against the state. Takekuma's campaign against the discriminatory curriculum was supported by another Ainu schoolteacher, Ega Torazō (Ainu name, Shianreki). Ega, an Ainu from Oshamanbe, qualified as a schoolteacher in 1913 and taught at a number of schools in the Hidaka district. After encountering discrimination from his colleagues he began drinking heavily, but his life was transformed when he converted to Christianity after meeting John Batchelor. Another leading figure in the movement was Fushine Kōzō, an elder from Tokachi, who shared Ega's Christianity, his commitment to expand educational opportunities for Ainu (which extended to appearing at the 1903 Osaka Exposition to raise funds), and his determination to eradicate the evils of alcoholism. After a survey which revealed the extent of Ainu opposition to the Regulations and also that many Native Schools were not actually implementing the inferior curriculum, the Dōchō abolished the Regulations in April 1922. Thereafter, Ainu children received more or less the same education as their Wajin counterparts, but they continued to do so in separate institutions as opposition from Wajin educators to 'mixed education' remained strong. Abolition of the Native Schools now became the object of the reformers who continued to believe that it was mainly due to a lack of equal educational opportunities that Ainu were ridiculed and oppressed. As for Ega and Takekuma, however, both resigned as teachers soon after; Takekuma to work as a railway employee in Karafuto, Ega to become a lay preacher among the Ainu in Hokkaidō and Karafuto, first as a member of Batchelor's Ainu Dendōdan (Ainu Mission), then independently after his withdrawal from the group in 1925.[27]

The movement for educational reform was accompanied by the emergence of a small but articulate group of educated young Ainu who expressed themselves through poetry and essays. The Ainu had a long tradition of storytelling, ranging from folktales (*wepeker*) to long heroic epics (*yukar, oina*) relating the deeds of both humans and gods. As Pilsudski noted early in the century:

> The Ainu folk-lore is, by the admission of the Far Eastern tribes, exceedingly abundant. The proportion of Ainus acquainted with either one kind or another of these primitive tales is – to my own knowledge – greater than with the Ghilyaks. Their lore of eloquence, of speeches, and of song, is quite astonishing.[28]

Some of these traditional literary forms were adapted to become vehicles of Ainu pride and resistance in more recent times. Kindaichi Kyōsuke's unpublished field notes, for instance, include a fascinating epic taken down by hand in Karafuto in 1915 which relates the story of an attack by Ainu on the old imperial capital of Kyoto (*kyoto moshir*) and the abduction of some imperial maidens (*kyoto menoko*).[29] Songs transcribed by Kindaichi in the Hidaka district expressed the anger and sadness of Ainu women forcibly parted from their husbands in the *basho*, while stories of earlier resistance to the assimilation policies of the Tokugawa period were also handed down.[30] There is also some evidence that as traditional Ainu culture began to disintegrate rapidly in the late nineteenth century, a few Ainu elders may have passed on their knowledge to selected individuals in order to preserve the stories and traditions of the past.[31] This was part of a wider picture of passive resistance to acculturation. Although the mode of life that underlay the traditional animistic belief systems had been destroyed, Ainu were loath to abandon their customary spiritual practices. In a 1931 survey, the Dōchō reported that nearly half of all Ainu households still adhered to 'natural religion' (1,648 out of 3,417; of the remainder 1,189 were Buddhist, 355 Shintō, and 189 Christian – a low number given their disproportionate influence).[32] By this time, it is likely that most of these beliefs survived only as fragments of a formerly coherent world-view or had been adapted to the new circumstances in which the Ainu found themselves. Important ritual events such as the *iyomante* (bear festival), for instance, began to be celebrated less often from the 1920s, but the underlying spiritual belief of 'sending back' the souls of deities to the realm of the gods was maintained through children's games with sparrows, and rituals with household objects.[33] In the more isolated communities like Kussharo *kotan*, customs and traditions were maintained for considerably longer than in regions of heavy Wajin immigration. Ainu in Kussharo, for instance, were largely able to ignore the authority of the policeman in Teshikaga, ten miles away, and fish in the traditional manner right through to the pre-war years.[34]

These attempts to preserve indigenous pride in the face of cultural change are hinted at in a small collection of *yukar* translated by Chiri Yukie, a young Ainu woman from Noboribetsu. Chiri had spent much of her childhood living with her aunt Kannari Matsu (Ainu name, Imekano) in Chikabumi, a Christian convert who had attended Batchelor's mission school in Hakodate and learned how to write the Ainu language in the Roman alphabet. After meeting Kindaichi in 1920, Kannari began transferring her vast repertoire of *yukar* and other oral forms to a series of notebooks. While working with Kannari, Kindaichi met Chiri Yukie and invited her to Tokyo to study and assist him with his work. Chiri began collecting and transcribing oral literature to send to Kindaichi, and in 1922 she travelled to Tokyo to stay with the Kindaichi family. After only a short time, Chiri was taken ill and died of heart failure. She was nineteen.

Just before she died, Chiri had finished revising the manuscript of *Ainu Shinyōshū* (Collected Songs of the Ainu Gods), which was published in 1923. In the preface of the book she evoked a nostalgic vision of a happy Ainu past in harmony with nature, lamenting that the 'beautiful spirit' (*utsukushii tamashii*) of those days had been lost – 'Ah, those doomed to die (*horobiyuku mono*) – that is our name now, how sad a name we have.'[35] The songs themselves, however, have recently been interpreted in a different light. The most famous of the stories in the collection, the Song of the Owl God, concerns a boy 'who was once rich but is now poor', whose noble bearing is recognised by the Owl God despite his ragged clothing. The Owl God restores him to his rightful place above 'those who used to be poor but are now rich'. For some modern Ainu, this is seen as Yukie's allegory of the dispossession and spiritual resistance of the Ainu.[36]

Chiri Yukie's book was one of a series of publications by young Ainu poets that attempted to restore a sense of pride and worth in Ainu identity among those they saw as Utari, fellow Ainu. In 1920, the members of Batchelor's Ainu Dendōdan, including Kannari Matsu and Ega Torazō, began publication of a small magazine entitled *Utari Kusu* that featured poems by Batchelor's adopted daughter, Yaeko. One member of the group was a young Ainu from Yoichi, Iboshi Tatsujirō (pen name Hokuto), who had decided to devote himself to the cause of his people after reading Chiri Yukie's *Ainu Shinyōshū*. A close friend of Yaeko, Iboshi occasionally assisted with the magazine and in the Ainu kindergarten that Batchelor had established in Biratori. Another member of their circle was Chiri Yukie's younger brother Mashiho, a highly intelligent youth who entered Tokyo Imperial University in 1933. While motivated by a common cause, the members of this group were not immune from occasional friendly rivalry, especially where it concerned the favour of influential patrons. In a letter to Kindaichi in August 1930, Yaeko pointedly noted that three poems published by Iboshi as his own had actually been jointly composed with Yaeko and Chiri.[37]

The collection of Iboshi Hokuto's verse and essays to which Yaeko referred was published in 1930, a year after the author's death from tuberculosis at the age of twenty-seven. Iboshi was an angry young man in the mould of Kannari Tarō. Born in Yoichi in 1902, he worked as a labourer after graduating from elementary school, contracting tuberculosis in Abashiri in 1918. Dogged by recurrent illness Iboshi continued to work as a labourer until moving to Tokyo in 1925, where he met Kindaichi and others who supported Batchelor's work among the Ainu. On Kindaichi's invitation, Iboshi gave a speech to the Tokyo Ainu Gakkai (Ainu Study Group) in March 1925. The Okinawan scholar Iha Fuyū was present and took down the gist of Iboshi's address. Iboshi began by describing his early life and schooldays in Yoichi, and how the sight of the poverty and despair of his fellow Ainu had aroused him to anger. This was not a result of innate Ainu inferiority but was due to their dispossession by Wajin immigrants and the ravages of imported disease, and Iboshi drew parallels with the extinction of the Tasmanian aborigines. Stressing the need for Ainu to regain pride in their identity, he commented:

> While I respect the Suihei movement that has the eyes and ears of the nation these days, I can fully understand how they hate the name *eta*. But I think it would be braver of them to to use the name *eta* just as it is.[38]

In his concluding remarks, perhaps tailored for his audience, Iboshi remarked that since he had come to understand that there were also sympathetic Japanese and that the prejudiced Wajin immigrants of Hokkaidō did not represent the Japanese as a whole, 'my radical ideas completely disappeared, and now I've become a good Japanese and want to do something for both the Ainu and Japan'.[39] Iha enthusiastically applauded Iboshi and told him that, as an Okinawan, 'I understand your feelings better than anyone else.'[40]

The following year Iboshi decided to give up his relatively easy life and job in the capital to return to Hokkaidō to work for his people. Together with two other young Ainu, Pete (pronounced Pehteh) Warō of Mukawa and Yoshida Kikutarō of Tokachi, he formed the Ainu Ikkan Dōshikai (The Association of Staunch Ainu Comrades) and travelled round various *kotan* to investigate Ainu conditions at first hand. Pete later recalled that in these activities he and Iboshi were inspired by the example of the Suiheisha.[41] While helping out at Batchelor's kindergarten in Biratori in 1927, Iboshi also studied Ainu history and culture, and composed poetry depicting the sufferings of the Ainu. Some of his poems were published in the *Otaru Shinbun* and elsewhere. In the same year he formed another small group with a fellow Ainu youth from Yoichi, Nakasato Tokuji, and published the first and only issue of a small magazine, *Kotan*, containing many of his poems and essays. In 1928 Iboshi became a travelling medicinal salesman, the better to be able to move about and meet other Ainu. All this activity had taken an increasing toll on his health, however, and he suffered a relapse of tuberculosis and died in early 1929. His writings were collected by a Yoichi schoolteacher and published by Gotō Seikō, a patron of Batchelor's, the following year.

Iboshi's hundreds of poems, mainly written in *tanka* form, and his essays cover the whole range of emotions and issues faced by young Ainu of his time. In particular, he was sharply critical of the material and ideological structures of colonialism to which the Ainu were subordinated – the 'dying race' stereotype, tourism, Ainu Studies, alcoholism, Wajin exploitation, and the destitution and desperate desire to assimilate into which the Ainu had been forced:

Making profit out of Ainu
Only the stores grow big
And rust the *kotan*.

To people who ask me
If I study the Ainu will I make money?
You will make money, I used to reply.

Again the Shiraoi Ainu
Have gone to the Exposition as exhibits
What?! What?!

Even in the loneliest mountain *kotan*
I find empty *sake* bottles.

The Ainu have produced no great men
But more shameful than this
Is a single beggar.

It is just those Ainu who appear as exhibits
Who will die under the label of the dying race.

These are the days
When the birth of an atavistic *shamo* child
Brings joy among the Ainu.[42]

Other poems expressed the pride he felt in his Ainu identity and his determination to fight on despite the ultimate futility of attempting to overcome 'racial' barriers to assimilation:

Standing up for the dying Ainu
With shining eyes –
Iboshi Hokuto, Ainu.

Adjusting my necktie, I glance at my face
The mirror tells me
You are Ainu, after all.[43]

Perhaps the essay that best summarises Iboshi Hokuto's views appeared in the first issue of *Kotan*. Entitled 'Ainu no Sugata' (The Condition of the Ainu) it opens with a description of the victims of 'twentieth century civilisation' in Hokkaidō, 'fettered under the euphemism of protection, robbed of their land of freedom and forced to become loyal slaves'. Assimilation was 'not simply a matter of time or blood', since Ainu could only ever become imitations of *shamo*. The Ainu were 'oppressed by the *shamo* sense of superiority' that was based on widespread social preconceptions of the Ainu as 'primitive'. In conclusion, Iboshi called for a pluralistic society in which all peoples could be equal and respected citizens of the Empire. Now was the time, he stated, to assert Ainu identity, recall the 'pride of an indigenous race' (*senjū minzoku*) and 'kick aside the social feelings of irrational prejudice and manifest our purity as a race (*minzoku*)'.[44]

Iboshi clearly regarded the Ainu as a unified group linked by common ancestral and cultural bonds and sharing common political aspirations – in short, an 'imagined community' or nation. He also saw the Ainu as an indigenous people, dispossessed of their ancestral land and resources by settlers of a colonial regime. While by calling for pluralism and equality between the peoples of the Empire Iboshi challenged the official assimilationist ideology that was rapidly gaining ground among the colonial authorities, he stopped short of attacking the colonial framework itself. Despite the stimulus that Iboshi received from reports of Suiheisha activities, it is unclear how much he actually knew about the political agenda of that organisation. His writings, while sharply critical of Wajin prejudice and Ainu defeatism, are conspicuously lacking in overt left-wing rhetoric and criticism of the state. This places Iboshi in stark contrast to the Suiheisha, which in 1923 had appealed to all Burakumin 'who are fighting valiantly the final class war against bloodthirsty capitalism' to 'fight side by side . . . in our common battlefront of world revolution'.[45] Iboshi, although driven by a sense of injustice and anger, was not a revolutionary.

The plans of the Ainu Ikkan Dōshikai for social and political action were frustrated by the conscription of Pete and the death of Iboshi. A handful of Ainu influenced by left-wing thought, however, did manage to form a short-lived organisation. This was the Kaiheisha (a name that played on the meanings of liberation [*kai*] and equality [*hei*] while echoing the Suiheisha) devoted to the 'realisation of the liberation of the Ainu race' that would 'borrow the strength of the Suiheisha and the Nōmintō' (Japan Peasant Party).[46] The leaders of this group were young Ainu from Chikabumi, Sunazawa Ichitarō, Matsui Kunisaburō, Kobayashi Shikazō and Monno Hautomutei. The organisation was linked to the Nōmintō through an agrarian activist and local politician, Kinoshita Gengō, who had been prominent in a local tenant dispute in 1922. Apart from a handful of articles in newspapers and a Yūwa journal announcing its formation, no other records of the activities and political agenda of the Kaiheisha exist, although it is likely that it was formed in connection with the land disputes in Chikabumi. Sunazawa put up some hand-written posters for a public meeting in Sapporo soon after the formation of the Kaiheisha, but it is unclear how many people attended, or even if any meetings actually took place.[47] The Kaiheisha did succeed, however, in attracting the attention of other Ainu like Moritake Takeichi of Shiraoi who praised its efforts to liberate the Ainu from social discrimination.[48] One exaggerated report of its scale of activity was even provided by a Wajin traveller in Karafuto who mentioned that 'influenced by the modern spirit, the twenty thousand Ainu of Hokkaidō who live in primitive villages raised a notable cry for liberation in the Kaiheisha movement'.[49]

The Kaiheisha, it appears, soon ceased to be active. Whether it was actually suppressed or not is unclear, but in any event it was unrepresentative of most Ainu organisational activity which was still concerned mainly with education and self-help. Most Ainu were already members of the various community-level groups, often led or influenced by the local schoolteacher, that had been established as part of the nationwide growth in such citizen-level organisation after the Russo–Japanese War. By 1920 Abuta *kotan*, for instance, had a Dojin Kumiai (Native Association), a Kyūdojin Fujinkai (Former Natives Women's Society), and the Abuta Second Elementary School Dōsōkai (Alumni Association), this latter group founded in 1905 and engaged in night classes, regular discussion meetings, and cooperative agricultural activities. With neighbouring Usu, Abuta shared the Ryōyūkai (Good Friends' Society), based on the Native Schools of the communities, which published a small magazine. Fushiko and Shiraoi had a similar set of organisations by the 1920s. The women's organisations concentrated on agricultural instruction and the improvement of sanitation, and attempted to turn Ainu women into model Japanese housewives through the promotion of Japanese 'womanly virtues' (*futoku*). Ainu youth groups (*seinendan*) were set up in the Biratori township in Nibutani (1907), Nioi (1909), and also Kaminukibetsu, while in other areas Ainu attended Wajin youth groups.[50] In addition, there were the thirty-six *gojokumiai* (agricultural cooperatives) established by the authorities in 1924 and run by local Wajin officials, and further groups associated with the small local churches established by the CMS under John Batchelor. Batchelor himself was still active despite retirement from the CMS in 1923, drawing a pension from the Dōchō and acting as an adviser to its Social Section (*Shakaika*). In 1927 he founded the Bachira Gakuen (Batchelor Academy) in Sapporo as a boarding facility for bright Ainu students to continue in higher education, and devoted much effort to fundraising activities. In 1930, for instance, the Imperial Ministry donated 2,000 yen to the Academy.[51]

While much of this activity was controlled by local officials, there was some scope for Ainu to meet and create organisations with similar aims. On 8 May 1927 Ainu from the Tokachi region gathered in Obihiro to launch the Tokachi Kyokumeisha (Tokachi Clear Dawn Society) with Fushine Kōzō, the Ainu elder, educator and veteran campaigner against alcohol, as the first President. Also involved in the establishment of the Kyokumeisha were John Batchelor and Kita Masaaki, the Wajin official who supervised the cooperatives in the Tokachi district. The stated goals of the organisation were the 'management and promotion of the culture and economy of the Ainu race'. Under this general heading came eleven specific objectives, including increased food production through agricultural guidance, help in seeking employment, provision for small loans, improvement in housing, and the general raising of Ainu living standards and social education (*shakai kyōka*). Funding was to come from donations, income from projects, and members' annual dues of five yen or more.[52] Although the establishment of the Kyokumeisha was linked to the Suiheisha movement in the popular press, it was essentially a non-radical, self-improvement organisation, closer in character to the Yūwa movement.[53] Its basic aims were to facilitate the incorporation of the Ainu into the state, and it did not question the legitimacy of the state itself. Between 1927 and 1930 the Kyokumeisha concentrated on agricultural programmes, in particular the encouragement of self-cultivation and the renegotiation or nullification of long-term leases held by Wajin on Ainu allotments, and on improving Ainu housing. While it inspired the formation of a number of Ainu community organisations in the area, the activities of the Kyokumeisha were soon to be overshadowed by the formation, three years later, of the first organisation that claimed to represent all the Ainu of Hokkaidō.

THE AINU KYŌKAI AND THE COOPTATION OF THE AINU MOVEMENT

While the Chikabumi Kaiheisha can be tenuously linked to agrarian activism through its connection with the Nōmintō, most of the efforts by Ainu and their Wajin allies to improve social and economic conditions can hardly be described as radical. Nevertheless, there is evidence that the authorities were concerned about Ainu activism. As early as 1921 an article in *Utari Kusu*, the magazine of Batchelor's Ainu Mission, had been criticised by the Police Bureau (Keihokyoku) of the Home Ministry. In 1927 Kaizawa Hisanosuke of Biratori was marked out as a potential subversive after petitioning the Dōchō the previous year for support to attend the Ajia Minzoku Taikai (Convention of Asian Peoples) in Nagasaki as an Ainu representative.[54]

By 1930 the liberal era of Taishō democracy was all but over. The illegal Communist Party and other left-wing organisations had been stifled by a series of mass arrests in March 1928 and April 1929, and those popular parties that were permitted to remain in existence increasingly adopted the official line on domestic and foreign policy as the influence of the right and the military increased. By the early 1930s even militant labour unions had begun to be penetrated by a right-wing 'Japanist' labour movement.[55] After the crises provoked by the Manchurian Incident of 1931 and the assassination of Prime Minister Inukai Tsuyoshi the following year, power became increasingly concentrated in the hands of the ruling civil and military elites. Against this general background of increasing civil repression, and given the dual constraints of rural isolation and lack of resources, the emerging Ainu movement was only able to develop along the lines sanctioned by the authorities.

On 10 March 1930 the Kyokumeisha met in Obihiro to discuss tactics for a campaign for revision of the Protection Act. The Ainu delegates, led by John Batchelor and Kita Masaaki, the latter now an official of the Social Section of the Dōchō, called for substantial revisions including an extension of its provisions to Ainu engaged in occupations outside agriculture, an easing of restrictions on the sale of allotments, increased financial support for the destitute and the abolition of the Native Schools. This proposal was presented to the Dōchō, but triggered a disagreement between the Social and Education Sections. Moreover, as the head of the Social Section, Takeya Gentarō, pointed out, the proposal came only from Tokachi Ainu, whereas the issue was one that concerned all Ainu. Accordingly, on 18 July 1930, at a kindergarten in Sapporo, 130 leading Ainu representatives from all over Hokkaidō attended a Former Natives Convention (Kyūdojin Taikai) organised by the Kyokumeisha to discuss revision of the Protection Act. To facilitate this movement, one agenda item called for a vote on the establishment of an organisation to represent all Ainu in Hokkaidō. Amid applause the motion was carried unanimously and the Hokkai Ainu Kyōkai (soon to become the Hokkaidō Ainu Kyōkai – Hokkaidō Ainu Association) was born, with Kita Masaaki as its first Chairman. Vice-chairmen included Fushine Kōzō and Yoshida Kikutarō of Tokachi, while Iburi was represented by Samo Kikuzō and Mukai Yamao, the latter an ordained priest from Usu and the brother of Batchelor Yaeko. There was also one representative each from Hidaka and Kitami.[56]

From its inception, the first organisation for all Ainu was therefore partially controlled by the Dōchō through the leadership of the Social Section bureaucrat Kita Masaaki. Kita, as seen in the previous chapter, was a champion of Ainu assimilation through the 'fusion' of blood and ensured that the agenda was largely confined to issues of social welfare. Moreover, despite its claims to speak for all Ainu, the Ainu Kyōkai was dominated by the Tokachi Ainu of its parent organisation, the Kyokumeisha. Nevertheless, it provided the first forum in which the previously isolated Ainu communities could come together to discuss their common predicament and build a sense of common purpose. Over the next few years, more Ainu from other areas began to participate in the movement and contribute articles to the journal of the Association, *Ezo no Hikari* (The Light of Yezo).

Many of the leaders of the Ainu Kyōkai were Ainu who had succeeded in Wajin society to become influential and, occasionally, wealthy. A Dōchō survey in 1936, for instance, noted that two Ainu households each had assets worth over 200,000 yen (around five times the average annual expenditure by the Dōchō on Ainu education and welfare), while five Ainu had an annual income of over 5,000 yen at a time when over 80 per cent earned less than 500 yen.[57] A few Ainu were elected to serve as municipal councillors in their communities; Ōgawahara Kobisantoku and Niida Shusankuru in Mukawa in 1933 ('As their names eloquently relate', a newspaper reported, 'both of them are Former Natives, treated as an inferior race'), Yoshida Kikutarō (Makubetsu, 1932), and Moritake Takeichi (Shiraoi, 1937).[58] It has been argued that this elite group, by urging assimilation to a society in which their own position would be furthered, were acting out of their perceived class interests and not from a sense of pride as Ainu.[59] While this cannot be entirely disregarded, it represents an oversimplification of the motives of the Ainu leadership. Whereas the Dōchō viewed assimilation as the way to rid itself of its 'Ainu problem' and remove the embarrassing human wreckage left by the colonial enterprise in Hokkaidō, the Ainu leaders perceived assimilation in a different light. Although only a tiny proportion of the Ainu population, they saw themselves as pioneers to be emulated, since assimilation as loyal citizens of the Emperor was the only practical way to alleviate the suffering and destitution of their fellow Utari. This view was reinforced by the reality of subordination and the lack of effective resources to mobilise in opposition to the state. Within these parameters, these men and women were actively responding to their subordination with a determination not to be beaten by Wajin (*Wajin ni makenai yō ni*), and an attempt to create a better life for themselves and their compatriots. The fact that their views on the means of Ainu progress coincided with those of the Dōchō bureaucrats does not mean that both acted out of the same motives. As the articles in *Ezo no Hikari* show, there was still pride in the Ainu heritage and regret at its passing, as well as anger directed against the institutions and attitudes of majority society.

Ezo no Hikari first appeared in November 1930 and ran for four issues before ceasing publication in 1933. For the most part, it featured articles concerned with education and welfare issues, the dangers of alcoholism, and the revision of the Protection Act, many of them penned by Kita himself. The magazine also carried regional news and introduced leading members of the movement. But some Ainu also used the magazine as a forum to attack stereotypes and injustice. In the first issue, Onobu Shōtarō of Shiranuka complained that 'if *naichijin* say Hokkaidō, they immediately imagine bears and Ainu', and went on to condemn Wajin preconceptions of 'barbarian Ainu' and the myth of Ainu counting (*Ainu kanjō*).[60] In the next issue, Onobu again spoke out against the exploitation of the Ainu, this time by scholars, who treated the Ainu merely as 'physical research specimens'.[61] Kaizawa Hisanosuke, after exhorting Wajin not to forget the help extended by Ainu to the early explorers and immigrants, expressed similar anger against the stereotyped image of an 'innately inferior race' (*sentensei teinō jinshu*):

> Our social existence weakens day by day. Ainu, welfare people; not only do we receive treatment equal to that of animals, recently even our shadows have faded. Moreover, whether we are mistaken for antiques and preserved as anthropological specimens, or have our blood sampled, the fact that we have become research materials for scholars is unbearable for a human being with the slightest degree of personality. Of course, because there are those of us who turn themselves into exhibits to make a living, I cannot very well blame them.[62]

Another article asked, 'Do we live as Ainu or assimilate to *shamo*?' Displaying the conflicting emotions of most Ainu in his position, the author condemned the old religious customs and their reliance on alcohol as holding the Ainu back, but concluded:

> The yellow race, the white race, the black race and the Ainu are all equal before God. We have no need to despise ourselves. Despising ourselves is taboo for us. Rather, we must come to have pride in ourselves as Ainu.[63]

In the third issue, Ogawa Sasuke of Urakawa made a strong attack on 'racial prejudice' (*jinshuteki henken*) and the stereotypes of the 'dying race' and 'welfare people'. Addressing young Ainu like himself, he asked:

> Who has not been weakened by racial prejudice, despised and insulted, or wept with rage as a result of social discrimination? In the enterprises we undertake in order to engage in society and fight in the struggle for survival, in the education of our children, the many tragedies that arise because we are natives, have they not brought us all to tears? Have they not stirred us to action?[64]

The Ainu must awaken, he urged, abolish the Protection Act and raise their standards of living to eliminate such prejudice and discrimination.

Although not a stated objective of the Ainu Kyōkai, which aimed, after all, at eventual assimilation, the movement it represented was thus helping to foster a growing awareness of Ainu identity and common purpose. This was furthered by the opening of the Ainu Seinen Taikai (Convention of Ainu Youth) in Sapporo on 2 August 1931. Organised by John Batchelor, the Convention provided an opportunity for seventy young Ainu to come together, exchange views, and commit themselves to improving the position of their people. While this was again publicly expressed in terms of revision of the Protection Act, the young men and women themselves were fired with anger and a sense of injustice. As one participant, Kaizawa Tōzō, recalled soon thereafter:

> Although we did not raise quite the bitter voices and vehement curses of

the Suiheisha Convention that we had read about in the papers, we raised a call for justice filled with passion and strength. Rather than directing this towards society, it was more in the nature of an alarm bell to waken our sleeping comrades.[65]

Although *Ezo no Hikari* folded after four issues, intellectual activity continued to flourish. In 1931, Batchelor Yaeko published an anthology of verse with the help of Kindaichi Kyōsuke entitled *Wakaki Utari ni* (For the Young Ainu), in which she called for an end to alcoholism and despair. The Batchelor Academy began publication of a small magazine, *Utari no Tomo* (The Ainu's Friend) in Sapporo from 1933, the same year in which John Batchelor was awarded the Order of the Sacred Treasure (3rd Class) by the Emperor to add to his previous decoration. Other Ainu intellectuals also founded small groups. In 1932 Pete Warō set up the Chin Seinendan (Chin Youth Group) in his home *kotan* near Mukawa, and began publishing a small magazine called *Utari no Hikari* (Light of the Ainu). Nukishio Hōchin (Yoshizō) of Shiranuka formed the Hokkai Shōgun Kōseidan (North Seas Regeneration Group) in 1933 to promote self-development and loyal citizenship. Nukishio, who had encountered former Karafuto Governor Hiraoka's Darwinist musings in *Ainu Jinshu Shobun Ron*, launched a vigorous attack on this racial stereotyping of the Ainu as inferior and ill-equipped for the struggle for survival. After quoting Hiraoka at length in his 1934 book *Ainu no Dōka to Senchō* (Ainu Assimilation and Its Examples), Nukishio commented:

> When I saw the above passage I felt extremely annoyed. I did not shed tears over the stupid words that the Ainu are unfit members of humanity. Rather, I felt that the person who uttered these words is a pitiful idiot. I think that such a shallow view is a matter of regret. However, regardless of whether he believes that the Ainu are an inferior people and therefore a lower race (*rettō minzoku de aru katō jinshu nari*), thus defining them as unfitted for the world of humanity while Wajin are a superior people and well adapted members of humanity, to publish such notions publicly causes confusion in the spirits of our sound citizens, and leads to the creation of various human animals. When I consider such matter-of-fact pseudo-scholarship among our citizens it makes me shudder, and I cannot help but weep.[66]

Moritake Takeichi of Shiraoi had a distinguished career in the National Railways until resigning in 1935 after the company began promoting Ainu tourism, after which he set up the Kōsei Dōshikai (Reborn Comrades Society) in his home community. He was also active in the Ainu Kyōkai and involved in the movement to end discriminatory education and revise the Protection Act, a fact that is reflected in many of his poems, collected and published as *Genshirin* (Primeval Forest) in 1937.

The activities of this emerging Ainu movement, and the growing sense of Ainu identity that it fostered, were confined to a relatively small group of people. While it is likely that a small number of better educated or self-made Ainu from each main community were involved in the Ainu Kyōkai or other aspects of the movement, it is difficult to judge the levels of support it enjoyed among the Ainu population at large during this period. Certainly, in the period after Japan's defeat in the Second World War it became clear that class antagonisms were not absent from Ainu communities, and many of the poorest Ainu resented the stance and leadership role taken by the acculturated elites.[67] Divisions within Ainu communities clearly existed in the Taishō and early Shōwa periods, but it is unclear to what extent these were related to economic differentials between rich and poor Ainu. It is also unclear to what extent the ideals and aims of the movement were diffused throughout the rural Ainu communities, although some like Chikabumi were already politicised and most other settlements had numerous other organisations where Ainu gathered on a regular basis. Even so, *Ezo no Hikari* and most of the other literature produced by Ainu involved in the movement would have been read only by fellow Ainu or their Wajin allies in the Dōchō and elsewhere; it is unlikely that it made much impact outside this narrow circle.

One attempt to overcome this limitation and reach a wider audience was made by Kawamura Saito of Chikabumi, who attacked the popular stereotypes of the Ainu through a series of speeches and newspaper columns. Saito was the younger brother of Kawamura Kaneto, by lineage the leader of the Chikabumi Ainu and a successful surveyor who had been responsible for the construction of the railway through the Tenryū Gorge in Nagano Prefecture. Kawamura Saito himself had saved enough money by his early thirties to build himself a new two-storey house at a cost of 2,000 yen. In 1934 Kawamura gave a series of lectures at elementary and middle schools in Sapporo, reasoning that although the negative stereotypes held by *naichijin* could not be helped, he wanted the inhabitants of Hokkaidō at least to overcome their ignorance of Ainu life. Kawamura also gave a similar series of lectures at schools in Toyohara, the capital of Karafuto, in 1937. It is likely that these speeches were similar in tone and content to a series of four columns he wrote for the *Hokkai Taimuzu* in December 1934 in which he scathingly attacked the popularly held negative images of his people.

The Ainu were children of the Emperor like everyone else, Kawamura argued, but 'Ainu elders and women have been used, taken to various parts of Japan as exhibition artifacts; a dying race'. This 'cruel and miserable spectacle' was compounded, he added, by school textbooks that always portrayed the Ainu as primitives in traditional dress beside grass huts. Why did discrimination exist, asked Kawamura, when in reality Ainu soldiers were serving the Emperor in Manchuria? In the second instalment Kawamura attacked the actions and misconceptions of tourists, and the stereotype of lazy, alcoholic Ainu men, pointing out that Ainu men relaxed with alcohol in the company of friends after returning from many months of economic activity away from home. Assimilation was taking place, but this did not mean the extinction of the Ainu but only the adoption of Japanese customs and identity. Nevertheless, Kawamura expressed his pride in his Ainu heritage by vigorously defending Ainu women and customs in the next article. Ainu women were more loyal and mature than modern urban women, he stated, wondering if the latter 'could really become mothers of children'. There were also more beauties among Ainu women. As for hairiness, all humans had the same number of hair follicles, but Ainu had naturally developed thicker hairs as a result of a cold climate and a diet of meat. Discussing the bear festival, Kawamura pointed out that although Wajin regarded it as cruel, they worked domestic animals to exhaustion then slaughtered them for meat. In the final essay, he boldly stated that the real Yamato spirit was lacking in Japan; although the ideographs of 'Yamato' stood for 'great harmony' among peoples, 'even in *naichi* there is discrimination against *eta* and the Suiheisha'. He recalled the words of a schoolteacher who had praised his Japanese and asked him if he really was Ainu. 'Who would lie about it?' he asked bitterly. The fact that such ignorant people taught the younger generations was a cause for regret. In conclusion, Kawamura argued that since the Japanese were a mongrel race that incorporated Ainu, Taiwanese and Korean blood, there should be no distinctions and all should treat each other as brothers.[68]

Perhaps because of activities like this, the Ainu movement was still subject to police suspicion despite the quasi-official status of the Ainu Kyōkai and repeated expressions of loyalty to the Emperor. In 1934 a Justice Ministry report entitled *Ainu no Hanzai ni tsuite* (On Ainu Criminality) pointed out that nearly all the victims of Ainu crime were *naichijin*. The report explained that this resulted from Ainu feelings of being a defeated race, Ainu envy of Wajin life, and a desire, based on 'racial consciousness' (*minzoku ishiki*), to avoid hurting their own people.[69] Moritake Takeichi came under police investigation after publishing an article in Pete's *Utari no Hikari* in 1934. This short piece referred to the renewed Chikabumi land dispute and portrayed the Ainu as 'an indigenous race (*senjū minzoku*) who, year by year, have been robbed and pushed from the broad lands that were expressly given to us by the gods, to be given only a fraction of land under the Protection Act'.

Moritake then called for all Ainu in Hokkaidō to raise the cry, 'Give us back our land!'[70] There is also anecdotal evidence that Ainu villagers occasionally aided Koreans who were on the run after escaping from their harsh conditions of forced labour in the wartime mines.[71] But what attracted the most attention from the authorities in the early 1930s was the resumption of the land dispute in Chikabumi, a struggle against the Dōchō and Asahikawa city that had little to do with the Ainu Kyōkai.

OTHER AINU MOVEMENTS: CHIKABUMI AND KARAFUTO

Although originally granted for thirty years, the lease held by the municipality of Asahikawa on the Ainu lands at Chikabumi had been renegotiated in 1922 and actually expired on 31 October 1932. The municipal authorities wanted to take over the land for industrial development in the expanding urban centre, officially designated a city in 1922. Both Ainu and their Wajin tenants, on the other hand, had begun separate and antagonistic movements with the intention of gaining rights of ownership over the land they farmed. In July 1931 an Ainu group sent a petition to the Home Minister for the land to be unconditionally granted to the Ainu, while in November another group distributed a pamphlet outlining Ainu history and the Protection Act and criticising the widely held belief that the Ainu were incapable of managing land. In February 1932, Maeno Yosakichi and three other Asahikawa assembly-men sympathetic to the Ainu cause put forward a resolution proposing rights of ownership for the Ainu residents of Chikabumi. Since city bureaucrats were already in contact with the Dōchō and central ministries with a view to appropriating the land, the city assembly became the scene of bitter dispute. In April, the ageing Amakawa Ezaburō travelled to Tokyo in the company of Maeno and Matsui Kunisaburō to petition the Home and Finance Ministries for the land to be returned to the Ainu.[72]

As the date for the expiry of the lease approached a sense of urgency began to spread among the Ainu. Two more petitions were sent to the Home Minister in April and May. On 15 May a meeting of Ainu, including some from other regions, was held at the house of Arai Genjirō, an Ainu employee of the Asahikawa judiciary. The meeting concluded with a resolution calling for the abolition of the Protection Act and the unconditional return of the Chikabumi lands. But this meant that there were now two Ainu factions actively engaged in the Chikabumi dispute, a group of younger activists led by Arai who demanded the return of all the land, including that occupied by Wajin tenants (but not their eviction), and a more conservative group who limited their demands of ownership to the one *chōbu* granted in 1906.

In June 1932, Arai, his wife Michie, Sunazawa Ichitarō and his wife Peramonkoro, and Ogawara Kamegorō travelled to Tokyo to campaign directly at the centre of power. Supported by the women who raised funds by making and selling Ainu handicrafts in front of the Asakusa Kannon temple, Arai and his companions embarked on a three-week round of lobbying that took in the Home, Finance and Justice Ministries, the Governor of Hokkaidō who was in town on business, and Diet members representing Hokkaidō and the State Property Survey Agency (Kokuyū Zaisan Chōsa Kikan), as well as the presentation of a petition to the House of Representatives through a sympathetic politician, Tsuchiya Kiyosaburō. Less sympathetic officials included three members of the Tokubetsu Kōtō Keisatsu (Special Higher Police) who forcibly searched and questioned Arai and the others in their lodgings on suspicion that they were Communists. The visit had to be cut short due to the tragic death of the Arai's young son who had been left in the care of relatives, but it had succeeded in bringing the issue to the attention of the authorities. As in the first dispute thirty years previously, Tokyo media coverage and the support of some Diet members led the central government to reconsider the matter, which had developed into a difference of opinion between the Dōchō and the Ministry of Finance over who held jurisdiction over disposal of the land. An investigation was begun and the Asahikawa city lease was extended for a further year.

Arai and the other Ainu group continued their activity with more petitions, and Arai again visited Tokyo in November for two weeks to continue the work of his earlier trip. In March 1934 the Asahikawa-shi Kyūdojin Hogochi Shobunhō (Act for the Disposal of the Former Native Reservation in Asahikawa City) was enacted by the Diet, a law applicable to just forty-nine Ainu households. But the contents fell far short of Ainu expectations; instead of the five *chōbu* other Ainu had received under the Protection Act they received only one *chōbu*, and this was subject to the same restrictions on ownership as under the Protection Act. The remaining land was designated communal property under the management of the Dōchō. Arai and his small group continued to meet but were suspected of being 'Reds' (*aka*), and were questioned by the *tokkō* police and kept under surveillance by the community agricultural instructor, an ex-policeman who acted as an informer.[73] Sunazawa Biki later recalled how his father Ichitarō often began to sing the Internationale when drunk, leading Peramonkoro to smother her husband in bedding to avoid him being overheard.[74]

There was another group of Ainu besides those in Chikabumi who were not subject to the Protection Act; in fact they were not even Japanese citizens. These were the Ainu of Karafuto who were not descended from the returnees from Tsuishikari. There was some tension between these two Ainu groups; a newspaper reported in 1910 that the 'simple Karafuto natives cannot endure the struggle for survival with the Japanised Ishikari natives' and were moving away from their designated 'native village' to form a new settlement.[75] Nevertheless, by the 1920s a handful of educated local Ainu were making efforts to improve education and living standards in their communities. There was also a movement for the granting of citizenship to all Ainu and the transfer of the state controlled fishing grounds to Ainu ownership. This had hitherto been denied on the grounds that the Ainu were 'lacking in the spirit of self-reliance and self-management'.[76] Kawamura Saburō, a young Ainu from Tarandomari and one of the founders of the Karafuto Senjūmin Rengō Seinenkai (League of Youth Societies of Karafuto Indigenous People), was inspired by the actions of the Chikabumi Ainu to petition the Karafuto-chō and also travel to Tokyo to petition the central authorities on these issues.[77] It was probably a member of one of the Youth Groups who replied under the guise of an 'Ainu youth' to a 1930 newspaper article in which *menoko* (Ainu women) were stereotyped as desiring only to marry *shamo* men. The reasons for this, the article stated, were that Ainu men were dirty, and the women would only be able to wear cotton clothes and eat white rice if they married *shamo*. In reply, the young man from Ochibo village stated that these stereotypes were all lies, and such irresponsible articles would damage the efforts of young Ainu to improve themselves.[78] In July 1932 two high-ranking officials from the Justice and Colonial Ministries visited Karafuto to tour the native villages and investigate the conditions of stateless Ainu. After consultation between the two Ministries, an Imperial Ordinance on 14 December granted citizenship to the Karafuto Ainu from 1 January 1933. At the same time the Ainu became liable for conscription and subject to Japanese criminal and civil law. The other indigenous peoples of the island, the Nikubun and Orokko (Nivkh and Uilta), were not granted citizenship (apparently because they had not asked for it) and were subject to Japanese criminal law only.[79]

Ultimately, this elevation to citizenship and equality was largely cosmetic and did little to rectify Ainu marginalisation. While the papers reported an enthusiastic display of thoughtfully provided Japanese flags in the native village of Shirahama, and Ainu celebrations and 'extreme happiness' at their new status, the fact that they were still less than equal was underlined by a petition from Ainu in Ochibo to let their children attend Wajin schools.[80] On the other hand, when this was rectified with the disbanding of the native schools (*Dojin Kyōikusho*) in April 1933, Ainu in Niitoi expressed opposition on the grounds, according to their teacher, that they would encounter problems due to their backwardness.[81] Economically, the Ainu remained disadvantaged and the Karafuto government continued to manage the native fishing grounds.

THE REVISION OF THE PROTECTION ACT

The main motive for the formation of the Ainu Kyōkai had been to gain revision of the Protection Act, and it was to this end that much of its activity was directed. Since the Ainu Kyōkai was actually an appendage of the Social Section and headed by a Dōchō bureaucrat with the support of the long-lived and increasingly influential John Batchelor, in 1931 the Dōchō began consideration of revision. A survey was undertaken of the conditions in Ainu villages and a draft revision was finally presented to the Home Ministry in September 1933. Most officials in Tokyo were almost entirely ignorant of Ainu conditions and policy, and by the time visits to Hokkaidō to tour the Ainu villages had been made and other concerned Ministries consulted, another year had passed. Little further progress was made during the next two years despite petitions and appeals.[82]

A snapshot of the activities of the Ainu movement during this period, and the resources mobilised in its cause, is provided by the Symposium on the Improvement of Welfare Facilities for the Former Natives (Kyūdojin Hogo Shisetsu Kaizen Zadankai), held at the Sapporo Grand Hotel on 7 July 1935. The thirty-six participants in this event included the Heads of the Social and Education Sections of the Dōchō; Kita Masaaki and John Batchelor, also of the Social Section; four scholars from Hokkaidō Imperial University including Takakura Shinichirō; Native School educators such as Yoshida Iwao; local Mayors; and against this formidable line-up of state officials, ten Ainu 'pioneers' including Yoshida Kikutarō, Moritake Takeichi, Ogawa Sasuke, Mukai Yamao and Ega Torazō. The meeting was convened by the Dōchō to discuss the revision of the Protection Act, since 'the Ainu villages, formerly hidden in the forests, have become villages, towns, even neon-lined streets', and the Ainu themselves have 'remarkably raised their level of assimilation' to the point where 'they even have to be taught the Ainu language by Wajin scholars'.[83] The conference proceedings were recorded in their entirety in the October issue of *Hokkaidō Shakai Jigyō*. The discussions focused mainly on concrete welfare issues, discriminatory education and Ainu efforts to become 'splendid Japanese'. But as the transcript shows, even those concerned with Ainu assimilation could not shake the habit of regarding them as Other and non-Japanese. In the early stages of the discussion, some of the Wajin participants repeatedly referred to themselves as *futsu no Nihonjin* (normal Japanese) until the Head of the Education Section thought it well to advise the participants thus 'I think it would be better to drop the label "normal Japanese" and talk about Wajin and Ainu as it is unreasonable for this meeting to imply they are not Japanese.'[84] Some Ainu delegates spoke out against the negative images held by Wajin. Complaining of streams of tourists, Mori Kyūkichi of Shiraoi explained:

> I think the responsibility for this lies with the Ministry of Education . . . When Hokkaidō is mentioned in textbooks, the materials lead one to associate it with an image of Ainu struggling with bears.[85]

Such events managed to keep the issues alive, and the draft revision of the Protection Act was finally submitted for consideration to the Diet in 1936. On 12 March 1937 it was accepted by the Diet. A group of twelve Ainu had travelled down to Tokyo with Kita Masaaki for the proceedings, and were present in the spectator's gallery in the House of Peers when the draft was passed, whereupon they joined hands and wept with joy.[86] The next day the party reaffirmed its loyalty to the state with a visit to the Imperial shrines at Ise. More 'emotional tears' were shed in front of the sacred buildings, while Kita rather patronisingly reflected on the violent and savage Emishi and their role in ancient Japanese history, and how 'their descendants, this group of the Hokkaidō Ainu race, will completely assimilate as citizens of the Empire; the sight of them making obeisance before the Gods and expressing their sincerity forbade such thoughts of the past'.[87]

Under the revised Act the Native Schools were abolished, although there were actually only a handful still operating and all except one were already taking Wajin students. Restrictions on ownership were eased so that it was now possible to sell the *kyūyochi* allotments with the permission of the Governor. Welfare measures were extended to those engaged in occupations outside agriculture, and funds were made available for housing reconstruction. The original objective of the Protection Act, the Japanisation of the Ainu, was seen as having been largely accomplished, and the revised Act now took on the nature of a straightforward welfare policy.[88] The *Hokkai Taimuzu* enthusiastically congratulated the Ainu on their 'liberation' – 'the spring sun rises for the Ainu along with the song of racial liberation', was how their journalist phrased it.[89]

The organised Ainu movement had now achieved its main aims. In the same year as the revised Protection Act was enacted, Japan plunged into open war with China. Over the next few years many Ainu were conscripted to serve in China and the Pacific where some succumbed to disease and others were killed in action; an estimated thirty-nine Ainu soldiers died on Okinawa.[90] Ainu issues largely disappeared from the newspapers. With increasing social control under a wartime regime, there was no opportunity for Ainu activists to consolidate their gains and move ahead, and there is little record of any activity during this time. Isolated voices, however, did occasionally speak out. One was Yanagi Sōetsu, the leader of the Mingei folkcrafts movement, who was interested in Ainu crafts and had encouraged the Ainu self-help movements. In 1941 he held a special two-month long exhibition of Ainu folkcrafts in Tokyo and wrote two articles in his journal *Kōgei* critical of fellow folkcraft specialists who looked down on the 'cultureless existence' of the Ainu and wished to let them die out. Although he compared the situation of the Ainu to that of Okinawans and Koreans, Yanagi stopped short of questioning their colonial status, in the same way as he criticised the excesses of colonial rule in Korea but not the notion of colonial rule itself.[91] It is also known that the Burakumin leader and politician Matsumoto Jiichirō criticised references to 'natives' (*dojin*) in the Diet and visited Chikabumi in 1942.[92] But these were exceptions. Even academics had their wings clipped, as Takakura Shinichirō later explained:

> There was in World War Two an intensified Japanese ideology that all people in the country were the Emperor's subjects, so that the study of the Ainu as a race distinct from the Japanese was frowned upon by the government.[93]

Official interest in the Ainu, however, cropped up from an unusual source. On 30 January 1940, the Head of the Legal Bureau of the colonial Government General of Korea sent an official request to the Hokkaidō and Karafuto governments for information on their policies on Japanising Ainu names (legislation to the same effect had recently been introduced in Korea). Karafuto replied on 7 February, while Hokkaidō sent a detailed reply two weeks later. The assimilation policies applied to Japan's first colonial subjects were now informing policies of forced assimilation in the more recent parts of the Empire.[94]

Although the Ainu movement was to remain dormant for nearly ten years before resurfacing in 1946, the activities of the young men and women of the 1920s and 1930s had brought the Hokkaidō Ainu together in important ways. Racialisation had resulted in a widespread perception among Wajin of the Ainu as an inferior Other, an Other constructed through a set of deterministic stereotypes in which all Ainu were essentially alike. In material terms, colonisation and development had forced Ainu throughout Hokkaidō into a common predicament which was then institutionalised by the Protection Act of 1899. Most Ainu thus found their lives shaped in similar ways by the ideological and economic structures of colonialism. This enforced homogenisation of regional variation and identity was mirrored by a coming together among the Ainu themselves. Young men and women like Kannari Tarō, Chiri Yukie and Iboshi Hokuto – sensitive, educated and articulate but ultimately unable to escape categorisation as 'natives' – reacted to their marginalisation by attempting to create a new sense of pride and worth in being Ainu. The formation of the Ainu Kyōkai in 1930 ended rural isolation and physically brought people together, and the Ainu were able to exchange ideas among themselves in the meetings and journals that the movement spawned. In their opposition to the Protection Act and the negative images that explained and justified their subordination in the eyes of Wajin, those involved shared a unity of purpose and a sense of belonging to an 'imagined community' rooted not in the local village but in their common experience of being Ainu. And it was from within this identity that they spoke out on behalf of all Utari; their brethren, the Ainu people. It is one of the ironies of Ainu history that this assertion of Ainu identity grew out of a movement that had as its ultimate aim the eventual disappearance of the Ainu within dominant Wajin society.

6 Ainu liberation and welfare colonialism

The new Ainu politics and the state's response

The history of postwar Japan is dominated by the 'economic miracle' that transformed a defeated and devastated country into a leading industrial and financial power. Despite the opportunities afforded by a newly democratised and demilitarised Japan, however, the Ainu failed to improve significantly on their pre-war position as an excluded 'dying race'. Continued marginalisation resulted in the Ainu being left even further behind in Japan's postwar economic recovery. It was not until the 1970s and 1980s that a strong resurgence in 'ethnic' identity among the Ainu began to challenge the *status quo*. Many Ainu became engaged in an active reconstruction of 'Ainuness' in response to racialisation, marginalisation and inequality as part of a political struggle for a more equitable distribution of resources. Originating in social movements of the late 1960s, new forms of Ainu political activity emerged that recast the Ainu agenda in terms of 'liberation' and struggle in contrast to the continued emphasis placed on assimilation and welfare by the Ainu elites. But this is to anticipate events. In the immediate postwar period, organised Ainu activity was oriented towards essentially the same goals and activities that had characterised the pre-war movement.

REBIRTH OF THE AINU KYŌKAI

Japan surrendered on 15 August 1945, although fighting continued for some days between Japanese troops and the Soviet forces that had launched a massive invasion of Manchuria, Karafuto and the Kuriles in the last week of the war. The Japanese populations of these areas were repatriated after the end of hostilities, including most of the Sakhalin Ainu, many of whom settled in the far north of Hokkaidō near Wakkanai. As a result of having been finally granted Japanese citizenship in 1933, they now had to leave their ancestral homeland for ever. Hokkaidō, like the rest of Japan, was reduced to levels perilously close to starvation.

Ironically, in the months after defeat the Ainu were closer than they had ever been to economic parity with Wajin, since the war had reduced most Japanese to levels of poverty formerly the preserve of the Ainu. In the early stage of the occupation, Supreme Commander Allied Powers (SCAP) moved quickly to dismantle the military machine, release imprisoned socialists, remove restrictions on labour and political organisation, and in general encourage *demokurashii* (democracy).

Encouraged by the liberal atmosphere of the times, Ainu leaders began to reorganise the movement that had been largely dormant since 1937. After a preliminary meeting in Sapporo attended by Ogawa Sasuke, Pete Warō and others, around two hundred Ainu men and women gathered in Shizunai on 24 February 1946 to attend the Zendō Ainu Taikai (Hokkaidō Ainu Convention). As a result of this Convention, the Hokkaidō Ainu Kyōkai was relaunched the following month as an incorporated organisation with Mukai Yamao as Chairman and Yoshida Kikutarō as one of two vice-chairmen. Directors included Ogawa, Pete, Mori Kyūkichi, Nukishio Yoshizō, Ega Torazō and Chiri Takao, while Moritake Takeichi acted as Secretary. Members paid five yen annual dues, and the stated aims of the organisation were welfare and the 'improvement of the Ainu people' through projects to improve education, agriculture, fishing, management of communal resources and access to welfare facilities. The organisation, with 2,000 members and a budget of 29,000 yen, was based in Sapporo with branches (*shibu*) throughout the regions. In reality, the Ainu Kyōkai operated out of an office within the Dōchō and was largely run in its early days by Ogawa Sasuke.[1] In character, personnel and attitudes, the organisation was clearly an extension of the pre-war movement, as a curious incident soon made clear. According to anecdotal evidence provided by Ainu leaders, the officer in command of SCAP in Sapporo, Major Joseph M. Swing, is supposed to have offered the Ainu independence at a meeting in June 1946. The Ainu leaders refused on the basis that they were good Japanese, although they later came to regret the missed opportunity to create an 'Ainu Republic'.[2] Consideration of American policy towards their own indigenous Indian population, however, leaves it difficult to imagine how anything more than a glorified reservation could have resulted.

Between 1946 and 1948 the Ainu Kyōkai was kept busy on a number of fronts. Revisions to the Protection Act were undertaken in 1946 and 1947 as part of sweeping reforms in welfare and tax-related legislation. In 1946, Articles Four, Five and Six were deleted, ending provision of agricultural inputs and medical and other welfare measures. The 1947 revision abolished tax exemptions on the allotments. But of more immediate importance to the Ainu was the prospective loss of around 40 per cent of their arable land (some 2,000 hectares) under the Land Reform legislation of 1946.

Land reform was one of the top priorities of SCAP as part of the sweeping programme of demilitarisation and democratisation. SCAP desired the creation of a prosperous and stable rural sector of small owner-occupiers and the removal of powerful rural interests. In Hokkaidō, for instance, holdings over fifty *chōbu* accounted for 20.5 per cent of total cultivated area, but were concentrated in the hands of 1,118 landowners, less than 1 per cent of the total. In 1945, 43 per cent of the total cultivated area of Hokkaidō was worked by tenant farmers. Tenant farmers had played an important role in the agricultural development of Hokkaidō, and 43.9 per cent of farming households owned no land at all, in contrast to the overall national average of 26.8 per cent in 1940.[3] In 1946 the authorities enacted the Nōchi Chōsei Hō (Agricultural Land Readjustment Law) and the Jisaku Nōsō Tokubetsu Sochi Hō (Special Law for the Creation of Freeholders) providing for compulsory purchase of the lands of absentee landowners and their redistribution to tenants at minimal prices. Since many of the Ainu allotments were rented to Wajin tenants through the cooperatives or private arrangements, and many Ainu worked away from home as *dekasegi*, much of the land granted under the Protection Act fell into the category of land for redistribution.

In May 1946 the Ainu Kyōkai began lobbying the Dōchō, Nōrinshō (Ministry of Agriculture and Forestry) and the Kunaishō (Imperial Household Ministry) for the exemption of the allotments from the land reform and the release of former Imperial lands (the Niikappu Ranch and a stud farm in Hidaka) to Ainu tenants. In early 1947 Ogawa put together two petitions to be presented to the Diet through the good offices of Diet man Bandō Kōtarō, the first called for national expenditure on Ainu welfare while the second outlined the history and dire situation of Ainu landholding and called for exemption from the land reform laws.[4] Ogawa, Mori Kyūkichi and another Ainu also travelled to Tokyo to visit the Imperial Ministry and were granted an audience with Prince Takamatsu of the Imperial family. Originally scheduled to last for only five minutes, the conversation went on for three hours while Ogawa earnestly explained the Ainu situation and asked for special consideration.[5]

Although the Dōchō initially expressed the view that it would be difficult to exempt Ainu lands, by late 1947 the Governor was actively siding with the Ainu Kyōkai, expressing to the Ministers of the Nōrinshō and the Kōseishō (Ministry of Welfare) his opinion that the Protection Act should take precedence over the Land Reform legislation. Bureaucratic attitudes, however, had not changed despite defeat. In the eyes of the Governor it was still imperative to exercise control over the Ainu, since, although they showed improvement, they were 'lacking in economic sense, especially the idea of saving for the future'.

> But if from now on they become subject to the Land Reform Laws and lose rights of tenancy and rights of ownership, the *kotan* (group settlement) that is the basis of their livelihood will be scattered in all directions and they will be cast adrift. As a natural consequence they will lose their social and economic confidence and it is clear that they will gradually move down the path of self-destruction.[6]

In November 1947 the Ainu Kyōkai began a last-ditch lobbying effort in Tokyo.[7] In meetings with officials of the Nōrinshō and Kōseishō, Ogawa Sasuke, Pete Warō and Samō Kikuzō explained the Ainu landholding situation. In reply, they were told that the Ministries could not decide this matter and it would have to be referred to the Occupation authorities at GHQ, but that the Dōchō proposals could be redrafted as a Nōrinshō plan and presented to the Agricultural Section at GHQ. A series of discussions and meetings over the following week resulted in a draft that shifted emphasis away from exemption from compulsory purchase towards provisions in the legislation for absentee landlords to go back to farming the land. Included was a proposal for Ainu land to be sold to a cooperative of Ainu farmers for five years as a temporary measure, at the end of this period to be sold either to the original owners or the present cultivators. This draft was also flatly rejected by GHQ. Increasingly desperate, the Ainu resorted to petitioning General Douglas MacArthur, the Supreme Commander. After another busy round of meetings with Ministry and Occupation officials both Pete and Ogawa, the latter acting for Ainu Kyōkai chairman Mukai Yamao, drew up draft petitions and had them translated into English. Both outlined the history and situation of the Ainu allotments, and how Ainu had come to lose control of their land to Wajin tenants. As Ogawa explained:

> However, since the termination of the recent war, some of the Ainu people awoke to the miserable state of their fellow compatriots, and they tried to get their farms back from the Japanese tenants so they could engage in improved farming on their own account. But it so happened that just about this time the Farmland Readjustment Law and the Special Law for Creating Freeholders began to be enforced, the result being that the Ainus cannot get their farms back from the more influencial [*sic*] and wily Japanese tenants. Under the present situation, there seems to be nothing left for the Ainu people but to stand aside and look on while the more wily Japanese people appropriate as much as one-fourths or 1,968 'chobu' 5 'tan' 3 'se' of Ainu land.[8]

Pete took a similar line, pointing out that most Ainu absentee landlords were actually living in dire poverty and existing as labourers, while their tenants were 'rich and prosperous'. Mentioning that the Ministries involved were sympathetic but unwilling to undertake 'specially favourable action', Pete concluded by asking for the land to be returned to the Ainu absentee landlords to cultivate themselves, as provided for by certain articles in both laws.[9] Although Ogawa was not completely satisfied with the final drafts, Pete posted them on 10 December.

It was all in vain. The authorities, busily pressing forward with ambitious programmes of national scope, had no time for minority interests. At a national meeting of the heads of the prefectural Agricultural Land Departments in January 1948, it was decided that the Ainu could not be exempted. On 10 February, the Agricultural Administration Bureau of the Nōrinshō informed the Dōchō of the decision, but added that Agricultural Land Committees supervising the reforms should take care not to be unfair to Ainu, instructions that the Dōchō passed on to local officials.[10] But in the end, 1,271 Ainu farmers lost their holdings, representing a loss of 34 per cent of total arable lands. Some areas suffered more than others; the Kushiro Ainu, for instance, lost 68 per cent of total arable land, while the figures for Tokachi, Hidaka and Iburi were 43 per cent, 32 per cent and 28 per cent respectively.[11] The communal lands of the Chikabumi Ainu were sold to Wajin in 1949. It seems that the Ainu Kyōkai never recovered from this defeat. A single issue of *Kita no Hikari* (Light of the North) was published in October 1948 and a sanitorium, the Hokuseiryō, was constructed at Noboribetsu Hot Springs in the same year, but there is almost no record of any further activity by the organisation until 1960.

In character, the Ainu Kyōkai represented a continuation of the assimilationist movement of the pre-war years. Its leaders were earnest, serious men, proud of their success and integration into dominant society. Yoshida Kikutarō, for instance, referring in all probability to the Ainu Kyōkai leadership to which he belonged, felt that 'since there are only a handful of self-awakened people (*jikakusha*) among the 17,000 Utari, the Protection Act which was put in place for those 17,000 should not be abolished'.[12] Yoshida also put out a booklet in 1958 in which he reproduced the rhetoric of the pre-war Ainu Kyōkai (including Kita's thoughts on fusion and the word 'Ainu') and presented photographs of smartly dressed and groomed 'modern Ainu' (*gendai no Ainu*).[13] In the early years of the Occupation, Herbert Passin encountered some of these young Ainu on a visit to the 'seedy little hamlet' of Usu. Passin and his research team found some elderly Ainu to sing and dance and encouraged them with liberal quantities of alcohol. The visitors were enjoying the party atmosphere when suddenly they were interrupted. Three young Ainu men dressed in jackets and ties took Passin into an adjoining room. As later recorded by Passin:

> 'We are here to protest your making a spectacle of these old people', the young man who had tapped my shoulder said immediately.'I don't understand', I started, confused by the sudden change of pace.'You are deliberately getting them drunk to make them do those barbaric songs and dances. We would like you to stop immediately. It's an insult to us. You are making a spectacle of us, treating us like barbarians . . . It's because of people like you, keeping these old things alive just to satisfy your curiosity, that discrimination continues.' (This was the first time I had ever heard the word 'discrimination', much as it would have been used about American Blacks.) 'I am as good a Japanese as anyone else here. I served in the army and several of my friends, from this very village, were killed in the war. The only difference is that my ancestors spoke a different language. But that doesn't make me different from other Japanese.'[14]

The party was ruined, but after meetings with the young Ainu over the next few days Passin came to understand the agony of the 'dilemma that all despised minority groups [face], especially those not strong enough to control their own destinies: assimilation or preservation of their identity'.[15]

Besides the Ainu Kyōkai leadership, some other Ainu were participating in the newly found democratic freedoms of the immediate postwar years. In April 1946 three Ainu stood in the first national elections held under the Occupation. Among the seventy-one candidates who stood for election in Hokkaidō No.1 Constituency were Ōgawahara Tokuzaemon (Kobisantoku) who represented the Nihon Jiyūtō (Japan Freedom Party) and polled 5,709 votes to come in 61st; Pete Warō (Independent – 5,254 votes, 63rd); and Kawamura Saburō, formerly of Karafuto (Independent – 1,258 votes, 70th).[16] Other Ainu candidates in this period include Samo Kikuzō who ran in the 1947 elections for Governor, and Ogawa Sasuke who stood for the Hokkaidō Assembly. Another young Ainu keen to enter mainstream politics was Takahashi Makoto, although he too failed in a bid to be elected to the Hokkaidō Assembly. Takahashi was a reporter for the Kushiro branch of the *Hokkai Taimuzu*, and in March 1946 he put this experience to good use by founding the Ainu Mondai Kenkyūsho (Centre for Ainu Issues), which published a small newsletter, the *Ainu Shinbun* (Ainu News). Strongly in favour of political participation, Takahashi urged the leaders of the Ainu Kyōkai to reflect on their role and transform the organisation from an 'Imperial Association' (*goyō kyōkai*) into a protest movement opposed to the 'Emperor system', pointing out that the formation of other small groups like Kawamura Saburō's Ainu Heiwa Renmei (Ainu Peace League) and the plans for an Ainu Seinen Dōmei (Ainu Youth League) in Nayoro demonstrated the 'iron solidarity' of the Ainu.[17] Takahashi incurred the wrath of some conservative Ainu by proclaiming that 'the Japan Communist Party are the allies of the Ainu'. He also pointed to some potential links with organised labour, noting that the *Hokkaidō Rōdō Shinbun* (Hokkaidō Labour News) had stated 'we must help the Ainu who were driven out by Emperor Jimmu. The Ainu are our comrades too'. Takahashi himself attended a meeting in Sapporo organised by Korean activists, where he made a short but impassioned speech congratulating Koreans on their liberation from their 'long period of oppression and discrimination by Japanese' and declaring that 'we Ainu, too, want to go forward as your true friends'.[18]

The brief honeymoon with socialism in postwar Japan, however, did not last in the face of Cold War realities and the rapid collapse of Japan's first socialist government in under a year. The *Ainu Shinbun* soon folded, and no other evidence exists of the organisations to which Takahashi referred, or of any substantial links with Korean or labour organisations. Austerity prevailed, and people were preoccupied with survival and the black market until the Korean War brought windfall gains to the economy with the boom in special procurements (*tokujū*) for the UN forces. By the 1960s Japan had embarked upon the well-documented period of high economic growth, with average growth in real GNP nudging 11 per cent throughout the decade.[19] Despite the dismantling of the rest of the Japanese Empire, however, Hokkaidō continued to be administered through quasi-colonial structures. In 1950 the Hokkaidō Kaihatsuchō (Hokkaidō Development Agency) was established in Tokyo with a branch bureau in Sapporo. In 1951 the Agency announced an ambitious five-year plan to improve infrastructure and boost agricultural, mineral and industrial production. Only a fraction of the plan was actually implemented, but considerable progress was made in certain areas such as electric power generation, and population increased from 3.5 million in 1945 to nearly 5 million in 1956.[20]

During this period very little was heard of the Ainu. This does not mean, however, that the Ainu were sharing equally in the social and economic advances enjoyed by the majority of the population. The continuation of both material and ideological structures of domination ensured that most Ainu remained on the margins of society. But the Ainu were not completely isolated from the social and economic changes that occurred over these two decades, and the tensions they provoked were to stimulate a new wave of activism from the late 1960s.

THE AINU IN THE PERIOD OF HIGH ECONOMIC GROWTH

Just how far the Ainu were falling behind the national average was revealed by a comprehensive survey of the socio-economic conditions of Ainu in the Hidaka region undertaken by the local authorities in 1962 and published in 1965. This survey was carried out in connection with the Furyō Kankyō Chiku Kaizen Shisetsu Seibi Jigyō (Project for the Improvement of Facilities in Districts with Unsatisfactory Environments), a five-year programme inaugurated in 1961 and funded by the national treasury, the Dōchō, and local municipalities. In keeping with official attitudes on Ainu identity, the survey focused on *Ainu kei jūmin* or 'residents of Ainu descent'. Admitting that this was 'an extremely delicate issue', the authorities nevertheless identified these people on the basis of family registers and other records, and by physical appearance, as those who had Ainu ancestry. Also important was whether those concerned recognised this fact, and were recognised as Ainu by local society. Statistics were compiled from census results and interviews with a sample of 105 Ainu households.[21]

The survey revealed a number of broad trends. First, it exposed the precarious economic position of the Ainu on the margins of society, and the host of social problems associated with such levels of poverty. The great majority of Ainu were poor farmers or day labourers subsisting in inferior housing, and educational achievement was extremely low. To illustrate: 38.2 per cent of Ainu households were hovering around the poverty line[22] and 17.5 per cent were on welfare, this latter representing 159 persons per thousand – six times higher than the overall figure for the Hidaka region.[23] Second, although the origins of Ainu marginality were not specifically addressed, findings pointed to the continuation of prejudice and discrimination in schools and within rural Hokkaidō society despite increasing intermarriage. Just over half of the sample stated that they had been discriminated against for being Ainu.[24] Significantly, 10.4 per cent of elementary school pupils and 15.6 per cent of those attending middle school were absent for long periods, although this probably had an economic dimension as well.[25] Third, it was evident that economic and social differentials were widening within Ainu communities, with an almost destitute class of unemployed and day labourers constituting around a third of all Ainu, in contrast to a small affluent elite of successful farmers or small businessmen. Finally, it exposed the increasing tendency for younger Ainu, especially those of mixed ancestry, to move away from the old 'native villages' to find work and, often more importantly, to lose their Ainu identity by 'passing' in majority society. Many left Hokkaidō altogether for the cities of the mainland, together with a number of middle-aged migrant workers destined for the day-labourer ghettos of Tokyo or Osaka.

These findings were backed up by the work of a number of other researchers, both academics and journalists, during the late 1960s. Baba, for instance, investigated class stratification and power relations among the Ainu as well as between Ainu and Wajin. Her fieldwork in one community in Hidaka with a substantial Ainu population found a small but significant elite group of Ainu who had been better placed to benefit from the general increase in prosperity. This group consisted of elected assembly-men, members of agricultural committees, directors of agricultural cooperatives, or small shopkeepers, who owned more than ten hectares of land and paid more than 40,000 yen in local property tax. She also concluded that 'racial prejudice' was an important factor in structuring Ainu–Wajin relations, pointing out that although intermarriage was increasing (one-third of marriages between 1945 and 1965), Wajin spouses all came from outside the community, and in the case of Wajin wives, mostly from Honshū. Moreover, 'the assignment of racial labels for those born of Ainu–Wajin unions has been simple; all are considered 'Ainu' regardless of how physically similar they are to Wajin'.[26] Another study of intermarriage in a rural community found that whereas in the pre-war period it was overwhelmingly Ainu women who intermarried, this pattern had finally begun to change. Although never seen before 1935, after 1957 marriages between Ainu men and Wajin women began to outnumber those where both spouses were Ainu.[27] Two American researchers, Peng and Geiser, found the Ainu community to be 'sharply divided within itself' along class and generational lines, as well as maintaining that there was 'in-group prejudice' between those of 'mixed' and 'pure' ancestry. A Japanese contributor to their volume analysed the links between poverty, social instability and divisions between Ainu of 'traditional orientation' and those of 'contemporary orientation' in a Tokachi Ainu community.[28] On a less academic note, Sugawara Kōsuke, a journalist of the *Asahi Shinbun*, published a book based on his coverage of Ainu issues in the 1950s and early 1960s. Sugawara looked closely at contemporary Ainu life, including the continuation of the predatory activities and attitudes of the pre-war Ainu scholars, the growth in tourism and the tensions it provoked, discrimination in education and employment, and the migration of numbers of younger Ainu to urban areas.[29]

'RACE' AND THE AINU IN POSTWAR JAPAN

While it is clear that much was changing in Ainu society as increased social mobility enabled some Ainu to move away from the land and the 'native villages', and divisions among the Ainu began to widen, much also remained the same. For one, the 'native villages' themselves remained largely intact although populated by a higher proportion of the elderly or those physically unable to 'pass' in wider society. Another continuation from the pre-war era, and one that underlay the economic and social marginalisation revealed in the statistics, was the categorisation of Ainu within the discourse of 'race'. The Ainu were still a 'racialised' group; marginalised and denied equal access to rights and resources on the basis of 'natural' difference.

Although the dominant pre-war official ideology of the consanguineous family-state was officially discredited after 1945, it continued, somewhat transformed, in hegemonic narratives of Japanese uniqueness, often reflected in notions of the *tan'itsu minzoku kokka* or homogeneous nation-state. Popular literature on Japaneseness (*Nihonjinron*) began appearing in the late 1940s and 1950s, and had reached boom proportions by the 1970s. As Yoshino has noted, the common-sense notions of a unique Japanese culture and society that were expressed in the genre were, and are, ultimately dependent upon a racialised understanding of Self, since 'a Japanese expresses the "immutable" or "natural" aspect of Japanese identity through the imagined concept of "Japanese blood"'.[30]

Conversely, Others are categorised on the basis of their non-Japanese blood, regardless of quantity. Irrespective of how Ainu perceived themselves, the determining factor of Ainu identity among Wajin in local society was whether an individual possessed Ainu blood (*Ainu no chi o hiku*). Educators in Hidaka, for instance, still referred to those of mixed ancestry as 'mixed-blood Ainu' (*konketsu Ainu*) and in the early 1950s undertook exhaustive investigations into differences of physique and character between 'full-blood', 'mixed-blood' and Wajin children.[31] Even if an individual was able to conceal his or her ancestry, they might still be marked by physical appearance. As one Ainu expressed it:

> If only half-*shamo*, or even only quarter-*shamo*, even when Ainu blood is only a small proportion of your actual blood, if you have an Ainu face you will surely be treated in general as Ainu. Where can we go, we Ainu who have been left hanging in mid-air?[32]

Such 'racial' categorisation ensured that many people of Ainu descent trying to divest themselves of Ainu identity and merge into the mainstream were thus unable to do so unless they physically resembled Wajin and could move away from their home area. Even if they succeeded in passing they often lived in fear of discovery. On the other hand, as a group the Ainu no longer existed in both the official and the popular imagination. With the dismantling of the Empire the subordination and control of 'native' populations was not an issue for the central authorities of postwar Japan; with national priorities cast in terms of economic growth the Ainu were at best an irrelevance. Typical of such an attitude was the Japanese government's report to the International Labour Organisation (ILO) in 1953 regarding Convention No.50 (Concerning the Regulation of Certain Special Systems of Recruiting Workers):

> In the course of the second world war, Japan lost all its dependent territories. As a result there no longer exist in Japan either workers belonging to or assimilated to the indigenous populations of the dependent territories, or to the dependent indigenous populations of the home territories. The Convention is therefore no longer applicable.[33]

The notions of 'Japanese' homogeneity prominent in such official discourse, and in the popular versions of *Nihonjinron* that also reflected a widespread amnesia concerning Japan's recent colonial past, denied the existence of the Ainu as a distinct population with a right to a separate identity. The resulting paradox was only awkwardly addressed officially at the local level in the category of *Ainu-kei jūmin*, residents of Ainu descent.

Ascribed a negative, essentially 'racial' identity as 'Ainu' that overrode socio-economic, occupational or gender roles, but denied under the notion of homogeneity any possibility of a positive 'Ainu' self-identification, most individuals existed in an identity-less void that could only be escaped by passing. As a result, many Ainu themselves had come to believe, along the lines advocated by pre-war officials like Kita Masaaki, that the only way to escape prejudice was by the thorough dilution of blood through intermarriage. In the words of Kaizawa Matsutarō, an Ainu of Biratori interviewed in 1972:

> The tendency to hide the fact that one is Ainu and try hard to assimilate to Wajin is certainly strong. But is it right that even while with our mouths we say that we have not experienced discrimination, we should spend our whole lives unceasingly conscious of the Ainu blood that flows in our bodies? I know far too many examples around here of the dangers of trying to assimilate at any cost. There are women who think that as long as a man is from *naichi*, anyone will do if only Ainu blood can be diluted (*Ainu no chi sae usumerarereba*), so they produce illegitimate offspring with the labourers who drift into Hokkaidō. There are also some who have married for such humiliating reasons and suffered many years of unhappy married life.[34]

'Racial' categorisation of the Ainu was accompanied by the continuation of the negative images associated with the subordination of the Ainu as colonised and inferior. Negative stereotypes and discrimination were rife in the integrated schools that the Ainu leaders of the pre-war period had fought so hard for, including the continued identification of Ainu with dogs; most children of this period were taunted with the words '*Aaa – inu*' (Ah – a dog).[35] It was at school that many Ainu children became aware for the first time of an ascribed identity that their parents had tried to suppress.[36] In some schools, mainly in Biratori where Ainu children were numerous, a 'progressive' outlook among the staff consisted of denial or avoidance of the Ainu 'problem' altogether. When Ainu children left the cosy circle of the school and entered into the adult world of employment and marriage, they were often shattered by the prejudice they encountered.[37] In response, many young Ainu turned their backs on their Ainu heritage and attempted to disassociate themselves from anything Ainu, in particular the activities of the tourist Ainu (*kankō Ainu*) or those working with scholars to preserve Ainu culture.[38]

Many of those Ainu working in tourism, however, did so out of necessity rather than choice. As affluence increased, so did tourism, boosted by improved transportation and infrastructure in rural areas, offering some Ainu their first opportunity to escape from destitution. As in the pre-war period, images of Hokkaidō still revolved around nature, bears, and Ainu. While a few Ainu, usually those already relatively successful as farmers or small businessmen, were able to prosper and develop carving or restaurant businesses, many merely ended up working for Wajin entrepreneurs as dancers or photographers' models dressed in traditional clothes. Some photographers refused to employ any male Ainu without a flowing white beard. In this way, commercial tourism contributed to the perpetuation of images of primitive barbarians. For many postwar visitors to Hokkaidō, knowledge of the Ainu was confined to stereotyped images derived from the media, school textbooks and the tourist villages themselves. A survey of 810 Tokyo schoolchildren and university students in 1975, for instance, reported that all age groups regarded the Ainu as non-Japanese and associated them with American Indians. Images clustered around tourist stereotypes of bearded elders, dancing, woodcarving and bears, while children of secondary school age and above also mentioned hairiness as an Ainu characteristic.[39] Many tourist Ainu were left aghast at the ignorance of such visitors.[40] One Ainu critic of the commercialisation of his culture, Hatozawa Samio, warned that 'all Ainu will just end up in the image created for them by Wajin'.[41]

Against this background of poverty and division, the Ainu Kyōkai was virtually powerless to take any kind of real leadership role. Most of its members continued to be drawn from among the elites of both the pre-war and postwar eras; indeed some, like Ogawa Sasuke or Sasaki Tarō, had become successful in the world of horse-racing and breeding, and had risen to positions of wealth and prominence. After its defeat over the land reform the Ainu Kyōkai appeared to hibernate until around 1957 when it again began to lobby Diet members and the Welfare Ministry over issues of Ainu welfare. At a meeting in Sapporo in April 1960, the Association was reorganised with Mori Kyūkichi as Chairman, and began to receive financial assistance from the Dōchō the following year. In 1961 the Ainu Kyōkai was renamed the Utari Kyōkai due to a widespread dislike among Ainu of the word 'Ainu', largely because Wajin used the word as a pejorative term. This cosmetic improvement did little to attract new members, whose numbers in 1963 stood at about 770.[42] In 1963 the Utari Kyōkai began to publish a newsletter, *Senkusha no Tsudoi* (Pioneers' Meeting). The first issue was reminiscent of previous publications, with articles on various subjects from welfare to hair, many written by Dōchō welfare officials; even Kita Masaaki came out of retirement to contribute. From 1964 the Association again operated from within the Social Section (*Shakaika*) of the Dōchō with a full-time clerical officer. The aims of the Association remained the raising of living standards and the elimination of prejudice, geared towards the eventual assimilation of the Ainu into mainstream society. To this end, tentative links were formed with Burakumin organisations in the early 1960s since Ainu leaders perceived that government-funded *Dōwa* (harmony) projects shared similar goals. One prominent Ainu, Kaizawa Tadashi of Nibutani, travelled to Osaka to attend the Buraku Kaihō Zenkoku Taikai (National Convention on Buraku Liberation).[43] But many poorer Ainu remained suspicious of the motives of the leaders, while others, attempting to divest themselves of any Ainu identity, criticised the Utari Kyōkai for perpetuating the illusion that an Ainu people existed, or simply ignored the organisation.[44]

The Utari Kyōkai was not, however, entirely ineffective. In 1959, the Welfare Section of the Dōchō announced that a survey of Ainu socio-economic conditions would be undertaken in response to the many reports of acute poverty from Ainu communities around Hokkaidō.[45] The following year the Dōchō put forward under the aegis of the Protection Act a five-year plan for improvement of areas with unsatisfactory living conditions. Projects included the construction of twenty communal bath houses, twenty communal halls, five communal workshops, and the provision of electric lighting in five areas and the improvement of 1,690 dwellings at an overall cost of 143.9 million yen. The Welfare Ministry, however, was initially unwilling to release funds from the national treasury, claiming that the existing welfare laws covered the same areas as the Protection Act.[46] In 1961, a compromise was reached that provided a special budget for the above mentioned Furyō Kankyō Chiku Kaizen Shisetsu Seibi Jigyō with a 200 million yen budget divided between the

Treasury, the Dōchō, and local municipalities. Fifty-one communities with over twenty Ainu households were targeted for improvements, and thirty-two communities with over thirty households received new communal bath houses and new ferro-concrete blocks of public housing. Sixteen communal halls were also constructed.[47] The project was administered with the help of the Utari Kyōkai and drew that organisation further into a corporatist relationship with the authorities. In effect, the Association functioned as an arm of the government from which it received both financial and personnel assistance.[48] The Dōchō, however, still found it necessary to study ways to 'plant the spirit of self reliance' (*jiritsushin*) among those it appeared to consider its charges, including consideration of a scholarship fund.[49]

The Ainu welfare project illustrates that although Japanese society was undergoing transformation, the Ainu were still enmeshed within power structures reminiscent of the pre-war period. The Ainu remained powerless wards of the state under the Protection Act, and were controlled by the Dōchō through channels established in the 1930s. Despite increased social mobility, the authorities could still trace those of Ainu descent through family or land registers.[50] Older attitudes persisted in new forms. In 1955, in a move redolent of the Kaitakushi, the Dōchō issued an administrative order to local authorities banning the bear festival as 'barbaric' in response to protests by animal lovers.[51] Ainu scholars also made use of their positions within the structures of institutional power. Kodama Sakuzaemon of Hokkaidō University, driven by a sense of scientific mission, resumed his quest for Ainu bones after the war. In 1956 a team of scientists looking for skeletal remains began digging in the cemetery of an Ainu village near Shizunai. Appalled, younger Ainu chased them away, but they returned the next day with local government officials and policemen and proceeded with their excavations. The eventual haul from the area was 132 skeletons, to bring the collection of Ainu remains at Hokkaidō University to a total of 1,004 individuals.[52] Hatozawa Samio, an Ainu essayist who died tragically young of tuberculosis in 1971, related how during his hospitalisation a group of Ainu patients were singled out for 'free treatment' by a visiting University 'doctor'.[53] In another example, which illustrates the links between universities and the authorities, the Hokkaidō Prefectural Government formally instructed a local municipality to assist a university survey after Ainu in the area had refused to give blood samples. Pressure was duly applied to the refusers, although with little success, and the researchers had to resort to buying blood from poor Ainu in other areas.[54] Scholars worked hard to ensure the separation of Ainu culture from living human beings by labelling it 'traditional' and of the past; even sympathetic scholars believed that 'the happiness of the Ainu lies in complete assimilation to the Wajin', though Ainu culture would of course be 'preserved' in museums.[55]

On occasion, such links in the overall structure of domination were laid bare for all to see. In 1964, the authorities in Asahikawa came up with a scheme for an Ainu Matsuri (Festival), an extravagant five-day spectacle to 'preserve the culture of the dying race and attract large numbers of tourists from inside and outside Hokkaidō to Asahikawa, which is said to lack any real tourist resources'.[56] Despite opposition from Ainu youth and others disgusted by the commercialisation of Ainu culture, Ainu from all over Hokkaidō gathered for the event, many for the 1,000 yen a day they were offered. On the opening day, 200 Ainu sat before a crowded gallery of 800 spectators to perform ceremonies and listen to speeches by academics Kindaichi Kyōsuke and Kodama Sakuzaemon.[57]

In general, then, the continuation of colonial structures of domination during this period ensured that the circumstances of most Ainu did little to offset the image of the 'dying race'. Indeed, this characterisation of the Ainu continued to be used in various guises by both Japanese and foreigners alike.[58] Ainu communities were deeply divided, and it seemed that the fragile flame of common identity and purpose kindled by the pre-war Ainu movement had been all but extinguished. But, at the end of the 1960s, dormant tensions within Ainu communities were brought to the surface by the convergence of a number of seemingly unrelated events. In many ways, 1968 was a pivotal year. Hokkaidō was caught up in the celebrations of a hundred years of Hokkaidō 'history' with ceremonies in Sapporo, attended by the Emperor, and various events around Hokkaidō from which the Ainu were largely excluded. In the same year the Protection Act was again revised as part of a government rationalisation. The following year saw the enactment of major welfare legislation for the Burakumin, the Dōwa Taisaku Jigyō Tokubetsu Sochi Hō (Special Measures Law for Dōwa Countermeasure Projects). Society at large was convulsed by various large-scale movements and demonstrations against the Vietnam War and for the reversion of Okinawa, and a vigorous and occasionally violent student movement. Affected by this mood of social and political activism, some young urban Ainu had begun to band together and form small groups. The Utari Kyōkai had also re-emerged to lobby actively for improved welfare measures. When the issues that formed the 'Ainu problem' were brought sharply into focus by the events of the late 1960s, a political regrouping was taking place among the Ainu that was soon to initiate a radically different style of Ainu politics.

THE NEW AINU POLITICS AND THE STATE'S RESPONSE

The new Ainu politics which developed from this period posed a direct threat to the prevailing pattern of Ainu–Wajin relations. As the Ainu resurgence gained momentum in the late 1960s and early 1970s, groups of young Ainu activists emerged who were sharply critical of the Ainu establishment and its links with the Dōchō, as represented by the Utari Kyōkai. Taking their cue from more radical currents in Japanese society, they bypassed the administrative structure of previous relations and sought instead to confront the social and administrative mechanisms that underlay Ainu marginalisation. In a reversal of the flight of Ainu youth from Ainu identity, these young men and women rejected assimilation. Asserting pride in their Ainuness, they actively undertook a search for their roots.

During the early postwar decades, many Ainu had moved out of their home communities and migrated to Sapporo or the cities of the mainland. Although there are no precise figures for this period, by 1975 there were nearly seven hundred Ainu residing in metropolitan Tokyo, and there were no doubt more in the neighbouring prefectures that make up the Kantō conurbation, as well as substantial numbers of temporary Ainu migrant labourers.[59] In 1963 some younger Ainu students came together with Wajin friends in Tokyo to form the Ainu Mondai Kenkyūkai (Society for the Study of Ainu Issues). Most of the Ainu members, however, soon drifted away and the group became dominated by more radically inclined Wajin. A more socially oriented Ainu group called the Peure Utari no Kai (Young Utari Society) also came into existence in Tokyo around the same time. Some of the members of these groups spent their summer holidays touring Hokkaidō to investigate conditions in the *kotan*.[60]

Younger Ainu who had remained behind in Hokkaidō had also occasionally been active. In Shizunai in 1962, for instance, fifty young Ainu had expressed their anger at the commercialisation of the Shakushain Festival, supposedly held in honour of the Ainu hero of 1669. Although they did not succeed in stopping it that year after the local Tourist Association which organised the festival agreed to negotiate with the Utari Kyōkai, it was discontinued thereafter. Small groups also began to appear in other communities. In Akan, young Ainu involved in the production of Ainu crafts began experimenting with contemporary Ainu art, while in Biratori, Hatozawa Samio was active in local literary circles after 1960.[61]

Although representing diverse interests and lacking a clear political agenda, when provided with a cause these younger Ainu were able to respond independently of the Utari Kyōkai, drawing inspiration from mainland movements. These were not inconsiderable; besides a widespread campaign against the Vietnam War in the latter half of the decade and agitation for the return of Okinawa, Japanese students at a number of elite universities were engaged in what they regarded as an aggressive class struggle against the state. In January 1969, 8,500 riot police were mobilised to control disturbances at Tokyo University. These disturbances soon spread to Hokkaidō, where twenty-eight people, including professors, were injured in a student assault at Hokkaidō University on Okinawa Day, 28 April. In July of the same year, 500 anti-Vietnam demonstrators burned Japanese flags in Sapporo, while 3,000 riot police broke up a blockade of Hokkaidō University in November.[62]

Between 1968 and 1970, various events occurred which highlighted the marginal status of the Ainu and stimulated activity among the emerging Ainu groups. The centennial of the Meiji Restoration, 1968, was also the hundredth year of Hokkaidō 'history'. Considerable sums were spent on celebrations, including public ceremonies at Maruyama Stadium in Sapporo attended by the Emperor on 2 September, and on the first stages of construction of a large memorial park with a tower, Museum of Development (Kaitaku Kinenkan), and 'pioneer village' outside Sapporo. Almost no mention was made of Ainu history or their role in the colonisation of Hokkaidō. This was not mere oversight; such historical amnesia was integral to the legitimising narrative of Hokkaidō kaitaku that served to mask the violence of the colonial enterprise by casting it in terms of the application of the beneficial effects of 'progress' to a 'natural' extension of Japanese territory. Hokkaidō, in effect, had been and remained merely geographical space to be claimed and Japanised for civilisation. The Ainu were largely excluded from this narrative, or given marginal roles as guides or coolies for the early explorers, since as a 'dying race' of primitives they had claim to neither land nor civilisation. Postwar social studies textbooks used in elementary school, for instance, made no mention at all of the Ainu until 1961, after which they printed extremely simplistic descriptions: 'A long time ago, the place known as Yezo (Hokkaidō) was covered in dense forest, and only a few people lived there besides the Ainu', one fourth grade text informed its young readers.[63] The official narrative of Hokkaidō *kaitaku* that the 1968 celebrations enshrined was that of Hokkaidō as the last frontier, a wonderland of 'nature' (*shizen*) with a unique and enduring pioneer spirit.

This denial of their existence aroused much resentment among Ainu of all generations. In a letter to the *Hokkaidō Shinbun*, one young Ainu from Kushiro called for Wajin not to forget that the ground under the commemorative tower was 'soaked with Ainu blood'.[64] A campaign which incorporated Ainu of all backgrounds raised funds to erect a large statue in Shizunai to commemorate the seventeenth century hero Shakushain, a project completed in 1970. Although the Shakushain story had long been part of the local tourist industry and the statue itself was incorporated into the centenary projects, nevertheless this represented one of the first attempts by Ainu activists to challenge the master-narrative of *kaitaku* and its implications of peaceful and orderly progress with their own narrative of invasion, dispossession and heroic resistance.

Another issue that provoked discussion among the Ainu was the revision of the Protection Act in June 1968 as part of a government initiative to streamline bureaucracy. The Welfare Ministry initially proposed its abolition, arguing that existing welfare laws now covered the financial provisions in the Protection Act for housing and education. In the face of opposition from Dōchō officials, who argued in reply that this law had historical precedents and had already helped the Ainu considerably, the inevitable compromise resulted in the deletion of items in Articles Seven and Eight covering housing and education, leaving only the restrictions on the sale of allotments.[65] Meanwhile, the central authorities had been considering a large-scale welfare programme aimed at raising living standards and encouraging assimilation among the Burakumin, later incorporated in the Dōwa Taisaku Jigyō Tokubetsu Sochi Hō or Special Measures Law. In 1969 the Chairman of the Utari Kyōkai, Nomura Giichi, was summoned to Tokyo by Akita Daisuke, head of the ruling Jimintō (Liberal Democratic Party or LDP) Special Committee on Dōwa Countermeasures, to be asked whether the Ainu would like to be included in this policy. Nomura consulted the Governor of Hokkaidō, Machimura Kingō, who was then in Tokyo, and rejected the offer after Machimura asserted that Ainu were different from Burakumin.[66] On 5 June 1970, the debate over the future of the Protection Act was further stimulated by the unanimous acceptance at a conference of the Mayors of Hokkaidō of a motion for the abolition of the Act. This had been put forward by Igarashi Kōzō, the Socialist Mayor of Asahikawa, in response to initiatives by local Ainu. In response, on 17 June the Utari Kyōkai voted overwhelmingly for the Act's continued existence on the grounds that it could be used as a convenient umbrella for special welfare policies, as in the Furyō Kankyō Chiku Kaizen Shisetsu Seibi Jigyō of the early 1960s. This attitude drew considerable opposition from other Ainu, especially in Asahikawa, who saw the Protection Act as the institutional expression of discrimination and inferiority – perhaps because they had never benefited from it.[67] Such attitudes were reinforced when in August 1970 Asahikawa celebrated eighty years since foundation with the unveiling of a statue, the Fūsetsu no Gunzo (Wind and Snow Group), depicting four young Wajin colonisers surrounding an elderly Ainu. Even though the pose of the lone Ainu had been altered after protest from a kneeling to a sitting position, Sunazawa Biki (the son of Ichitarō of the Kaiheisha) handed out leaflets during the inauguration ceremonies to protest this symbolisation of Ainu subordination.[68]

Stimulated by these developments, a proliferation of small groups began to appear, many with overlapping membership. Ironically, the growth of the movement was facilitated by the Utari Kyōkai since the existence of a network of over thirty branches throughout Hokkaidō enabled ideas to spread rapidly. Many Utari Kyōkai members joined or formed these new groups. Urban Ainu also moved to find a voice within the Utari Kyōkai, from which they had been largely excluded. In late 1971 the Ishikari, later Sapporo, Branch (*shibu*) was formed in Sapporo with Ogawa Ryūkichi as first Chairman. Ogawa was also a member of a Communist-influenced group of Wajin and Ainu from rural Hidaka known as the Hoppō Gun (Northern Regions Group). In February 1972, the Tokyo Utari Kai (Tokyo Ainu Association) was formed, with the support of the Ishikari Branch, after two Ainu women called in an *Asahi Shinbun* column for Ainu in the capital to 'join hands'. In the same year, two Ainu originally from Kushiro but now resident in Sapporo set up separate activist organisations. The Ainu Kaihō Dōmei (Ainu Liberation League) was the brainchild of a young Director of the Utari Kyōkai, Yūki Shōji, while the Yai Yukara Kenkyūkai (Yai Yukara Research Group) was formed and led by Narita Tokuhei. In Biratori, Hiramura Yoshimi formed the Ashi no Kai (Reed Society). From late 1972 the movement received added impetus from the fall-out generated by a terrorist campaign by Wajin radicals in the name of Ainu Liberation, inaugurated with the detonation of two bombs on 23 October, one of which blew apart the Asahikawa statue. Three days later, forty Ainu from Asahikawa met to protest the incident and deny any involvement, and formed the strongly local Ainu Kyōgikai (Ainu Council). On 21 January 1973, 150 Ainu gathered in Sapporo for the Zenkoku Ainu no Kataru Kai (National Ainu Discussion Meeting) organised by younger Ainu but open to all. Conservative leaders and those engaged in tourism were suspicious of the motives of the younger activists, who insisted, for their part, that it was a 'people's meeting' to discuss issues faced by all Ainu.[69]

During the next few years, the 'Ainu Problem' received considerable national attention as terrorist incidents continued. Besides numerous defacements of monuments with paint and graffiti, more serious incidents included arson attacks on the Hokkaidō Shrine and a tourist company in Shiraoi which operated the Ainu tourist village there. An attempt was also made to murder the Mayor of Shiraoi in protest against Ainu exploitation; although stabbed in the throat, he survived. The worst incident was the bombing of the Dōchō on 2 March 1976, on the anniversary of the promulgation of the Protection Act (the bombers were actually a day late), in which two people were killed and over ninety injured. With the exception of a single case involving the erasure of the name of the Governor of Hokkaidō from the statue of Shakushain, there is no proof of Ainu involvement in any of these incidents. Instead, the bombings were the work of the 'Wolf' cell of a terrorist group known as the Higashi Ajia Han-nichi Busō Sensen (East Asia Anti-Japan Armed Front), some of whom were arrested in April 1975. This group were also linked to bombings of large companies like Mitsui and Mitsubishi. Their leader, who later received the death sentence, was Daidōji Masashi, who came from Kushiro and had gone to school with many Ainu children.[70] But police suspicion of radical Ainu activism led to the arrests in October 1974 of Yūki Shōji and his Wajin allies over the statue vandalism, although Yūki was later released without being charged. Ainu activists and supporters complained of police harassment and physical mistreatment, a charge again highlighted during the 1976 court proceedings against a leading member of Ainu Kaihō Dōmei for alleged theft.[71]

Despite the lack of involvement in terrorism, Ainu throughout Hokkaidō could not ignore events so widely reported in the media. These incidents contributed to the increasing politicisation of the communities as the issues that underlay continued Ainu marginalisation were brought to the surface. Most Ainu were stunned by the violence carried out in their name and felt that they were being used. Such feelings were articulated by Kaibazawa Hiroshi:

> Although the attempted murder of the Mayor of Shiraoi and the erasure of Governor Machimura's name from the Shakushain statue have been tied to the Ainu through various arguments, how do they contribute to Ainu liberation? I think not at all. Rather, I wish to say that they are an unwanted interference.[72]

As Kaibazawa implied, the new Ainu groups were quite capable of acting on their own account. Their tactics generally differed radically from previous Ainu activity, which had been conducted through institutional channels such as the Ainu/Utari Kyōkai. Yūki Shōji's Ainu Kaihō Dōmei, for instance, adopted forceful extrainstitutional tactics of confrontation and denunciation. For Yūki, emphasis was not on the promotion of welfare and assimilation, but on exposing and censuring the structures and institutions to which the Ainu were subordinated. As the name of his group itself suggests, tactics were borrowed from the struggles of the Burakumin. Yūki employed the 'denunciation struggle' (*kyūdan tōsō*) developed by the Buraku Liberation League (Buraku Kaihō Dōmei) and its predecessor, the Suiheisha, that takes the form of forceful confrontation of alleged perpetrators of discrimination with demands for public apology and self-criticism, often in a tense atmosphere of potential violence.[73] Yūki was particularly active against scholars after forming his organisation in 1972. On 25 August of that year, in the company of Wajin activists, Yūki stormed the podium of the Joint Conference of the Anthropological and Ethnological Societies of Japan at Sapporo Medical University, where he read a list of criticisms to the assembled scholars and invited them to respond to the charges. No answers were forthcoming, although the chairman of the conference, who had criticised these 'childish' actions in a newspaper article on 1 September, was confronted a few days later in his study at Meiji University and induced to write a formal apology. Yūki's most effective campaign, however, was his denunciation of Professor Hayashi Yoshishige of Hokkaidō University between July 1977 and January 1978 in which Hayashi was eventually forced to offer a public apology after making allegedly 'racist' remarks about the Ainu in lectures.[74]

Protests were also made against media companies which conveyed discriminatory stereotypes of the Ainu. In March 1972 Ogawa Ryūkichi of the Sapporo branch of the Utari Kyōkai forced the cancellation of a TV programme put out by the Hokkaidō Broadcasting Company. This event caused much excitement among activists since, in the words of a participant, it was the first widely reported success in 'the movement to protect the human rights of the Utari that up to then had never won a victory'.[75] In May 1973 Narita Tokuhei protested against an episode of the popular TV series *Mito Kōmon*, leading to the screening of an apology during the broadcast.[76] The following year Ogawa forced the removal of an offensive promotional poster advertising Hokkaidō goods from a major Tokyo department store.[77] On another occasion, a Wajin tourist operator died suddenly the day after being confronted by Ogawa, leaving the activist feeling rather remorseful.[78] Another successful denunciation was a campaign by Ainu Kaihō Dōmei and Tokyo Ainu in 1978 against the magazine *Pureiboi* for publishing a discriminatory cartoon, which resulted in the recall of 6,300 copies and a public apology.[79] In 1981 Narita organised the denunciation of the Nihon Kōtsu Kōsha (Japan Travel Bureau) in response to advertisements in the English daily *The Japan Times* in 1979 and 1981 inviting foreign residents to visit a 'real Ainu village' to see 'the ancient customs and culture of the famed hairy Ainu'.[80]

In contrast to such direct action, other Ainu activists and their allies attempted to pursue the struggle within the institutions of the state, in particular the courts. In March 1973, for instance, the trial of Hashine Naohiko, an Ainu migrant worker in the notorious Tokyo district of Sanya who had killed a fellow worker in a fight, was turned into a showcase of discrimination and publicity for the Ainu cause by Wajin radicals.[81] In

July 1974 the lawyers defending an Ainu accused of murder in Shizunai asserted that the defendant was not Japanese and therefore not subject to Japanese law, an action that drew angry protests from the Utari Kyōkai, the Asahikawa Ainu Kyōgikai, and others.[82] The same assertion was made by defence lawyers, with the same lack of success, in a similar trial the following year.[83] In October 1974 an elderly Ainu woman from Shizunai and her supporters launched a court action to regain her Protection Act lands which had allegedly been obtained by a Wajin neighbour through illegal means, emerging victorious in October 1979 despite an appeal by the Wajin farmer.[84] An unsuccessful attempt to gain national political representation was made in the Upper House elections of July 1977, when Narita Tokuhei stood in Tokyo as an independent in the national constituency, gaining a respectable 53,682 votes.[85]

The impact of these activities on the Utari Kyōkai was mixed. On the one hand, many of the younger radicals were also members, or even, as in the case of Yūki, officials of the Association. The authority and assimilationist orientation of the more elderly and conservative leaders was therefore threatened by the divisions within the Association, and by further differences between the Association and other Ainu groups. While it resisted the regular proposals of younger activists to revert back to the former title of Ainu Kyōkai, the Association moved to distance itself from the state and transferred from a desk in the Welfare Section of the Dōchō to an 'independent' office in May 1974. It still received an annual subsidy from the Dōchō, however, as well as administrative expertise from Dōchō personnel. On the other hand, the publicity surrounding the 'Ainu problem' (*Ainu mondai*) was instrumental in eliciting a political response from the authorities. This response received added impetus from the interest in the issue among opposition political parties, in particular the Nihon Shakaitō (Japan Socialist Party – JSP) and the Nihon Kyōsantō (Japan Communist Party – JCP) which established Special Committees for Ainu Issues with similar agendas to the Utari Kyōkai.[86] As a result, the position of the Utari Kyōkai as the established institutional channel for Ainu negotiation with the state was strengthened.

This began to bear fruit with the establishment of another large-scale welfare project for the Ainu in the early 1970s. Spurred on by the debate in 1970 over the abolition of the Protection Act, the Utari Kyōkai began work on a proposal for the establishment of a special fund of 300 million yen for Ainu 'self-reliance' (*jiritsu*). In May 1971 this was presented to the cabinet of Satō Eisaku and the Liberal Democratic Party. From November 1971 the Dōchō began to consider the issue and undertook a survey of Ainu socio-economic conditions. This was released late the next year and illustrated that the situation of the Ainu had changed little since the 1965

Hidaka survey. As a result, in August 1973 the authorities drew up the Hokkaidō Utari Fukushi Taisaku (Hokkaidō Utari Welfare Counter-measures), a package of welfare measures – grants, subsidies, scholarships and low-interest loans – which were implemented from fiscal 1974. In May 1974 the Hokkaidō Utari Taisaku Kankei Shōchō Renraku Kaigi (Liaison Council of Ministries and Agencies Concerned with the Utari Counter-measures), was formed in Tokyo to oversee Ainu welfare policy. Based within the Hokkaidō Development Agency (Hokkaidō Kaihatsuchō), the Liaison Council consisted of representatives from the Prime Minister's Office and eight concerned Ministries. The initiatives of the Liaison Council, however, were largely modelled on the 1969 Dōwa Special Measures Law despite Dōchō requests that the issues be kept separate. The first Utari Taisaku policy ran for seven years with a budget of almost 12 billion yen, 41 per cent from the national treasury.[87] Following the corporatist pattern established in the 1960s, the policy was administered largely through the Utari Kyōkai, and the membership and influence of the Association began to revive. By 1976, 2,103 households (8,540 people) belonged to the organisation, nearly half of the total identified Hokkaidō Ainu population.[88]

The Utari Taisaku represented the state's response to the 'Ainu problem' by attempting to manage it through the structures of what Beckett terms 'welfare colonialism':

> the state's strategy for managing the political problem posed by the presence of a depressed and disenfranchised indigenous population in an affluent and liberal democratic society. At the practical level, it engages in economic expenditure well in excess of what the minority produces. At the political level, it sets up machinery for the articulation and manipulation of minority opinion. At the ideological level, the 'native' who once stood in opposition to the 'settler' and outside the pale of society undergoes an apotheosis to emerge as its original citizen.[89]

This final aspect of welfare colonialism, however, the incorporation of the Ainu into the master-narrative of nation-building, was not present in the Utari Taisaku, which aimed to bring the problem firmly back within the sphere of social welfare. Hokkaidō had been 'developed', not colonised; there was no indigenous minority to challenge comfortable beliefs in a seamless and harmonious homogeneity. As Yūki Shōji complained:

> Even now there are many Japanese who deliberately avoid a clear consciousness of the Ainu as a 'people' (*minzoku*), calling us Japanese of Ainu descent (*Ainu kei Nihonjin*), citizens of Ainu descent (*Ainu kei*

> *kokumin*) or residents of Ainu descent (*Ainu kei jūmin*). Besides being assimilationism, this way of thinking attempts to turn the Ainu into Imperial subjects.[90]

The government's adherence to such attitudes, although cloaked in legalistic argument, was made clear by Welfare Minister Saitō Kuniyoshi, in response to questioning in the Diet by Okada Haruo, a member of the JSP committee on Ainu issues, in March 1973. According to Saitō:

> Our basic attitude towards Ainu persons, or Utari, is that we definitely do not take the standpoint that the Ainu are a separate people (*minzoku*) within the citizenry of Japan. We strictly adhere to the view that they are equal Japanese citizens under the law.[91]

For the state, the contradictions inherent in having a separate welfare policy for a group defined as being of Ainu descent, and separate and discriminatory legislation in the form of the Protection Act, while simultaneously expounding doctrines of homogeneity and equality under the law, were obscured by renewed assertions of assimilation in progress. As another State Minister put it:

> Talking of assimilation, both the government and regional groups are making efforts that [the Ainu] will be self-awakened as Japanese. Therefore, I find it difficult to determine whether the term minority ethnic group (*shōsu minzoku*), especially the term ethnic group, is appropriate . . . It would appear that they are conscious of themselves as a minority group of different race (*jinshu*), but we sincerely hope that they will be conscious of themselves as Japanese the same as everybody else.[92]

But contrary to government wishes, it was this very consciousness of being a separate people, indeed, a nation, that was gaining strength among Ainu leaders, whether radical or moderate. One of the main motivations for the construction of a counter-narrative of Ainu nationhood was precisely the denial of Ainu existence that historical amnesia and the master-narrative of homogeneity made possible.

7 Beginning to walk for ourselves

The emergence of the Ainu nation

Perhaps the most important development of the new Ainu politics was the mobilisation of Ainu identity alongside political action. This, of course, was not a completely new phenomenon, and its roots can be traced back to the pre-war Ainu movement. Many Ainu had retained a genuine pride in their heritage despite Wajin attempts to denigrate it as primitive, a pride that can be seen, for instance, in the writings of the leaders of the Ainu Kyōkai even as they urged assimilation. Moreover, the notion of the Ainu as an 'indigenous people' had been clearly anticipated in the writings of Iboshi Hokuto and others in the 1920s. What was new, however, was the manipulation of the symbols of Ainu identity by activists in the service of a new political agenda that aimed to regain both a measure of control over their own lives and a larger share of the resources of society. In doing this, Ainu activists turned ascriptive 'racial' categorisation on its head. Previously subordinated on the basis of a supposed inherited 'racial' inferiority that was reflected in a backward culture, Ainu activists now transformed these same categories of culture and descent into means of positive identification and empowerment.

This use of 'Ainuness' for political ends operated in a number of ways. First, in an attempt to overcome Ainu powerlessness, it served to create a sense of community that could overcome differing interests and divisions of class, gender or generation to enable the presention of a unified front in negotiations with the state. Second, as an assertion of difference it challenged the assimilation policies that aimed at the eventual extinction of the 'Ainu problem' through complete absorption of all Ainu into majority society. Finally, through identification with emerging indigenous movements in other states, the politics of Ainuness represented an attempt to redefine the relationship of the Ainu to the state in terms of a culturally and historically unique group with distinct rights. The Ainu, as an indigenous people, were not just another disadvantaged social group in need of state welfare but a 'nation' desirous of decolonisation.

THE STIRRING OF AINU NATIONHOOD

The fact that little sense of unity existed among Ainu was self-evident to many Ainu activists in the early days. In an article in 1972, Narita Tokuhei called for the creation of a movement 'free from ideology and doctrine' to include 'young Utari of all backgrounds'.[1] The need 'to create a forum for Ainu to participate and discuss freely' the divisive issues that made up the Ainu problem was the main motivation for the young Ainu, led by Sunazawa Biki, who organised the Zenkoku Ainu no Kataru Kai in January 1973.[2] This role was then taken up by a bimonthly Ainu newspaper that appeared between June 1973 and March 1976, entitled *Anutari Ainu* (We Ainu), produced by a group of young Ainu from Hidaka. The editors made clear their aims and understanding of the forces that shaped Ainu lives in the first issue:

> What we are facing now is not the 'Ainu' as a race (*jinshu*), or the 'Ainu' as a people (*minzoku*), but 'Ainu' as a condition, a set of circumstances (*jōkyō*) – by this I refer to the meaning behind the word when people call us 'Ainu', which is a force that constrains our lives. It is precisely this 'Ainu' as a condition, and associated oppression, that is our problem.[3]

The divisions among Ainu activists were reflected in the variety of political ideologies they espoused. Many of the activists disagreed not only with the elderly rural-based elite of the Utari Kyōkai, but also among themselves. Yūki Shōji, despite severe criticism from fellow Ainu including Narita Tokuhei, drew much early inspiration from his association with the ultra-left Wajin revolutionary Ōta Ryū, who argued that mass revolution would begin with the Ainu.[4] This partnership did not last long, however, and Yūki and Ōta were soon to part company on acrimonious terms. Links were also formed with Burakumin, and in 1974 the 29th Convention of the strongly left-wing Buraku Kaihō Dōmei (Buraku Liberation League) formally included the Ainu in its United Front against Discrimination.[5] In Tokyo, Sakai Mamoru, an Ainu from Tokachi, was involved in radical left-wing activism among the day labourers of Sanya. When Sakai helped set up the Ainu Kaihō Kenkyūkai (Ainu Liberation Study Group) in Tokyo in 1978, Yūki encouraged the group with a message that displayed his left-wing credentials:

> The peoples and masses of the world are seeking liberation, and the class struggle between proletariat and bourgeoisie is intensifying . . . International capital and Japanese monopoly capital are proceeding along a path of deepening contradictions. This fated community,

> seeking a spiritual grounding in the Emperor system, is trying to move back to the Emperor system of Imperial Japan and the bureaucratic rule that prevailed before the defeat of 15 August, and down the path of fascism.[6]

Most of the leaders of the Utari Kyōkai, on the other hand, were wealthy farmers or businessmen with strong local links to the ruling LDP. The Chairman, Nomura Giichi, had served in the Imperial Army in Sakhalin, and after three years in Soviet POW camps had returned to his native Shiraoi to become a successful director of a local fishing cooperative, municipal councillor, and LDP member.[7] Nomura and the other conservative leaders of the Utari Kyōkai attempted to downplay political differences in favour of action on the 'three pillars' of Ainu welfare – education, housing and secure livelihood:

> Recently, discussion of the Ainu problem has been rife among the general public, and many Utari have become self-aware as a result. As it is, although I and the Utari Kyōkai have also been subject to criticism from various quarters, for me the Utari problem is not one of ideology or party politics. We must draw back from these and appeal to the Dōchō and the state on the three main issues.[8]

Between the views of Yūki and Nomura there existed a wide spectrum of opinion. One way to bridge the differences between the diverging wings of the movement was to appeal to the common bonds of Ainu identity. While some activists like Narita and Yūki were aware of the power of 'ethnic' symbols to promote unity, for others, especially the alienated young, a rapidly growing interest in Ainu history and culture was part of a general movement to rediscover Ainu heritage that accompanied politicisation. The staff of *Anutari Ainu*, for instance, compared 'racial prejudice' against the Ainu to the situation of Blacks in America, and began a similar search for their roots, seeking out elders and publishing lengthy interviews. The Utari Kyōkai leaders, too, most of them older men brought up in the pre-war native villages where certain traditional practices and beliefs had been maintained, remained proud of their heritage even as they promoted assimilation. So when the Nibutani Ainu Bunka Shiryōkan (Nibutani Ainu Culture Museum) opened in July 1972, containing the collection of local Ainu Kayano Shigeru, most Ainu activists could unite around what one newspaper called 'the symbol of the Ainu self-awareness movement'.[9] The cultural manifestations of Ainuness – embroidered traditional costume, prayers in the Ainu language, oral literature, dance – were increasingly in evidence at Ainu events, for the benefit of Ainu, not tourists. Festivals and ceremonies, such as those enacted each year before the new statue of Shakushain in Shizunai, became occasions to celebrate this heritage and link the present struggle to the feats of past heroes. Narita Tokuhei was impressed by the Ainu dancing at the Shakushain Festival, 'not that seen in tourist areas, but real dancing from the heart', that had enabled him to see 'a splendid Ainu people', and led him to feel that the gathering had 'lit the lamp of the solidarity that the Utari have long lost'.[10]

In 1974, Yūki, advised by Kushiro elder Yamamoto Tasuke, carried this movement further by setting up a committee to organise an *icharpa* (Ainu memorial service) at Nokkamappu for the thirty-seven Ainu executed there in 1789. The first *icharpa*, held in September 1974, was attended by fifty Ainu from around Hokkaidō and this 'invented tradition' thereafter became an annual event.[11] A similar service for the Ainu dead of the Battle of Okinawa was inaugurated at a memorial stone in Okinawa in 1981, and has been held periodically since then.[12] Yukara Za, a group of young Ainu artists based in Akan and led by Toko Nuburi and elder Yamamoto Tasuke, performed modern dramatised versions of Ainu epics as part of a UNESCO cultural festival in Paris in 1976.[13] The Yai Yukara group organised various field trips into the countryside, again drawing on the knowledge of Yamamoto, to 'learn the wisdom of life with nature'.[14] The Utari Kyōkai also began to organise local groups among members for the preservation and transmission of Ainu dance and handicrafts, holding annual competitions, although much effort was still directed towards producing craft items for sale. While much of the traditional cultural expertise involved in the ceremonies or field trips came from elders in rural or tourist communities, the initiative for these events came mainly from the politically active, younger, urban Ainu. The Sapporo branch of the Utari Kyōkai, for instance, politically oriented towards the left and having grown from a small group of dedicated activists into a major power base within the Association, began holding the Ashiri Chep Nomi (Ceremony to Welcome the New Salmon) on the banks of the Toyohira river in Sapporo annually from 1982. Not all traditional Ainu, however, agreed with the changes to the old ways initiated by the activists; some expressed grave reservations or anger against what they saw as 'fake' (*detarame*) ceremonies and insults to the gods.[15] But a considerable number of Ainu did support such cultural activities. The surveys carried out for the Utari Taisaku reported that the preservation of Ainu culture was supported by 83.7 per cent in 1972 and 79.6 per cent in 1979, while the rates of support for active cultural transmission were 74.2 per cent and 66.2 per cent respectively.[16]

Along with its 'culture', a nation needs a history, a collective memory of a coherent, idealised past that provides a sense of continuity while enabling a group to mediate its experiences of the present. Ainu activists, following the early lead of Wajin radicals, emphasised a historical narrative based on heroic Ainu resistance to rapacious Wajin aggression and the 'Emperor system' that directly challenged the master-narrative of peaceful and orderly Hokkaidō *kaitaku*.[17] The Ainu version of the past was then objectified by the festivals honouring Shakushain and the victims of Nokkamappu as national heroes. The importance of reviving an Ainu version of the past was keenly felt by Yūki Shōji who, in common with most Ainu, had never heard of the Nokkamappu incident until the early 1970s.[18] But this entailed glossing over certain gaps and tensions in the historical record. The elevation of Shakushain to the position of attempted liberator of the national homeland, for instance, largely ignored his long conflict with the neighbouring territorial group led by Onibishi, his ambush and killing of Onibishi and extermination of Onibishi's successors (men and women) in a surprise attack, his failure to convince Haukase to join the 'war of liberation', and his interest in restoring trade with mainland Japan, aided by Wajin allies. The Nokkamappu story, too, was complicated by the role of leaders like Tsukinoe who sided with the Matsumae. Blaming the bias of Wajin documentary evidence as misinterpreting Ainu motives was one strategy adopted by activists. While some called Tsukinoe a 'traitor' (*goyō Ainu*), for Yūki he was a national leader engaged in delicate diplomacy while sandwiched between the forces of two imperial regimes, Japan and Russia.[19]

As with culture, this renewed interest in Ainu history was not just the preserve of radical activists. Since the early 1970s there had also been a movement within the Utari Kyōkai, led by Kaizawa Tadashi, for the production of a 'correct' Ainu history that would challenge the official narratives on Hokkaidō *kaitaku* and the Northern Territories, the islands of Shikotan, Kunashiri, Etorofu and the Habomai group which had been under Soviet control since 1945. Official Japanese policy regarded the Northern Territories as inalienable Japanese territory 'built by our forefathers'. In 1976 Kaizawa wrote the first of a series of instalments of Ainu history in *Senkusha no Tsudoi*, opening with the proverb 'revisiting the old, we discover the new' (*furuki o tazunete atarashiki o shiru*).[20] This coincided with a new movement for 'people's history' among sympathetic young Japanese historians and in the ranks of the left-wing teachers' unions. Within the Utari Kyōkai, Ogawa Ryūkichi became increasingly concerned with educational issues, including the promotion of a 'correct' Ainu history.

Besides revisiting or reformulating the old, activists created new symbols to reinforce their concept of the *Ainu minzoku*, the Ainu people, as what Anderson calls a 'deep, horizontal comradeship' or an imagined political community – a nation.[21] An Ainu flag first appeared at the 1973 May Day parade in Sapporo. Sunazawa Biki had designed the flag to 'symbolise Utari pride, struggle, and passion'.[22] Light-blue and green represented the sea, sky and earth of the homeland, while a stylised arrowhead in white and red symbolised snow and the Ainu god of fire, Abe Kamui. One of the most potent symbols became that of *Ainu Moshiri*, the homeland. Although the term 'Ainu Moshiri' appeared only rarely in the writings of the Ainu activists of the 1930s – Chiri Yukie expressed a nostalgic vision of the homeland but called it Hokkaidō, for instance, while Iboshi Hokuto referred to it only once in all his poems – the liberation of Ainu Moshiri and the creation of an Ainu Republic was widely used as the battle cry of the Wajin terrorists who had adopted the Ainu cause.[23] By the late 1970s Ainu Moshiri had become a common term in the vocabulary of Ainu struggle. Ainu Moshiri (usually translated as 'the quiet earth where humans live' – *ningen ga sumu shizuka na daichi*) had connotations in both space and time; besides national territory in a physical sense, it stood also for a golden age in which Ainu lived independent and happy communal lives in harmony with nature until these were destroyed by subsequent invasion and colonisation. This vision, first expressed fifty years previously by Chiri Yukie, was articulated by Yūki Shōji, who added:

> Ainu Moshiri was the Mother Earth that formed Ainu culture, and this remains unchanged to this day. The Gods in whom the people believe have not left Ainu Moshiri for ever. The present situation where magnificent ethnic ceremonies are carried out every year in various regions, and prayers are offered respectfully to the Gods of Nature, is confirming Mother Earth, Ainu Moshiri, as the territory, albeit spiritually, of our people.[24]

As Yūki's adoption of the concept of Mother Earth (*haha naru daichi*) suggests, what most stimulated the growth of Ainu nationhood was contact with indigenous movements in other countries. Whereas some pre-war Ainu, in particular Iboshi Hokuto, had clearly conceptualised the Ainu as an 'indigenous people', most Ainu activists of the 1960s and 1970s had first looked to domestic movements for inspiration and tactics, in particular those of the Burakumin and left-wing activists. From the early 1970s, however, they began to forge concrete links with indigenous and other minority peoples abroad. Knowledge of civil rights movements, and, particularly, indigenous activism in North America, Australia and New Zealand, was obtained through the media and personal contacts. Narita Tokuhei, for instance, who had met and discussed discrimination with Burakumin while working as a craftsman in Okayama Prefecture, was further stimulated when he began to find out about the American Civil Rights Movement, and particularly the situation of the American Indian. Hiramura Yoshimi, the young founder of *Anutari Ainu*, consciously identified with Native Americans after a trip to the United States in 1972, and the first issue of the paper devoted a page to the confrontation at Wounded Knee between activists of the American Indian Movement and Federal authorities, while subsequent issues referred to the struggles of American Blacks in both prose and poetry.[25]

The first delegation of Ainu to travel overseas, however, went not to link up with indigenous activists in Western states, but to tour autonomous minority regions in China, the result of an invitation by the Chinese Ambassador to Japan on a tour of Hokkaidō in December 1973. This was not a passing whim of the Ambassador, but the outcome of negotiations initiated by Kaizawa Tadashi, assisted by JSP Diet member Okada Haruo, with Chinese representatives in Tokyo in February 1973.[26] Led by Kaizawa, the group of fifteen Ainu arrived in China for a three-week tour in February 1974. The Ainu were impressed by what they saw of Chinese policies towards minority peoples. One member of the group, Narita Tokuhei, wrote:

> Public documents are in the language of the minority people, and so is education. As long as the pastoral life continues they will be able to preserve their culture and traditions. While watching the wonderful Mongol dances, I was plunged into thought on the various problems that are involved in our inheriting and perpetuating Ainu traditional culture.[27]

Both the Chinese and the Ainu regarded the tour as a success, and further groups travelled to China in 1976, 1978 and 1983.

But ultimately of more importance in shaping Ainu nationhood were direct contacts with other indigenous peoples. In December 1977, two Eskimo from Barrow attending a meeting in Japan of the International Whaling Commission visited Kayano Shigeru in Nibutani. This led to an official invitation from the Mayor of Barrow and a visit by an Ainu group led by Nomura Giichi to the North Slope Autonomous Region in July 1978. They returned to Hokkaidō impressed by the degree of autonomy possessed by the indigenous peoples of the American Arctic under the Alaskan Native Claims Settlement Act of 1971, and the fact that it was funded out of tax revenue from the natural resources of the region, oil in particular.[28] Contacts increased thereafter. A group led by Narita Tokuhei visited Canadian and American Indian groups in 1978. In May 1981 Narita became the first Ainu to attend the World Conference of Indigenous Peoples, travelling to the third conference in Canberra to join a thousand delegates from twenty-one states in discussions on the restoration of indigenous rights, and celebrations of indigenous culture.[29] Not just political strategies were borrowed as a result of such interaction but the symbols of a common underlying 'Aboriginality' based on similar historic lifestyles and experiences of colonisation; Yūki Shōji's characterisation of Ainu Moshiri as Mother Earth, for instance, was an adaptation of Native American indigenous belief.[30] Speaking to an academic gathering after his return, Narita commented:

> What was interesting was that rather than just watch other groups perform, people got up on the stage together and joined in each other's songs and dances. They just gently joined in without distinction, and it was a really natural feeling to sing and dance together. It's because we all have things in common, on the level of feelings too.[31]

As Ainu activists became increasingly confident overseas, they also improved their domestic alliances, seeking common cause with a variety of social movements within the framework of the language of universal human rights. Narita Tokuhei laid out the range of Ainu alliances at a Burakumin meeting in 1984.

> [We] are now editing our history, claiming our rights, understanding our identity, beginning to walk for ourselves. As we advance our work, we can gain solidarity with the Buraku Liberation movement, the movement of Koreans in Japan, the physically handicapped, the women's movement, and various citizens' movements. Some people have indicated that the anti-nuclear movement seen from an international viewpoint has close relation to us as a minority's problem.[32]

By their very nature, the narratives of Ainu nationhood and human rights struck at the heart of government attitudes and policies towards the Ainu. From the government's perspective the assimilation policies pursued since the 1880s had succeeded to the extent that the 'Ainu people' no longer existed in a Japan conceived of as essentially homogeneous. By the 1970s, the discourse of Japanese uniqueness and homogeneity, exemplified by the *Nihonjinron* boom, had achieved near-hegemonic status among officials and mass society alike. Such attitudes, and their acceptance as common-sense by those at the pinnacles of power, are illustrated by the reply of Prime Minister Miki Takeo to a question by Kawamura Seiichi, JSP Diet member and Head of the JSP Special Committee on Ainu Issues, in the Upper House in November 1975. Miki defended an earlier statement to the effect that Japan was free of 'racial problems' (*jinshu mondai*) with the following comments:

> I did not speak on the basis of careful analysis of the Ainu or other issues, but said that the problems the world generally refers to as racial problems, well, happily Japan does not have the racial problems experienced by some other countries. I did not base this on a detailed – if I can call it that – analysis of such problems. What I said was that, on the whole, Japan is a country without the racial problems of the outside world, well, a homogenous nation (*dōshitsu no minzoku*).[33]

The official absence of minority populations in Japan was graphically illustrated by Japan's first report to the Human Rights Committee of the United Nations after ratification of the International Covenant on Civil and Political Rights in 1979. With regard to Article 27 of the Covenant, which concerns the rights of minorities, the Japanese government reported:

> The right of any person to enjoy his own culture, to profess and practise his religion or to use his own language is ensured under Japanese law. However, minorities of the kind mentioned in the Covenant do not exist in Japan.[34]

A Japanese government representative elaborated on this response in 1981, stating that since 'minority' meant 'a group of nationals who ethnically, religiously or culturally differed from other nationals and could be clearly differentiated from them from a historical, social or cultural point of view', minorities did not exist in Japan. This celebration of homogeneity was then justified by dismissal of Burakumin and Korean issues as a result of individual 'social prejudices' or other factors. The obliteration of Ainu culture and history was attributed to modernisation and acculturation:

> As for the Ainu, who were more properly called 'Utari people', [Mr Tomikawa] stated that since the Meiji restoration in the nineteenth century, establishment of a rapid communication system had made the difference in their way of life indiscernible. The Utari were Japanese nationals and treated equally with other Japanese.[35]

This was not how Ainu leaders saw it. On the contrary, a sense of Ainu nationhood was gaining strength among both radical and moderate Ainu leaders angered by such official denials of their existence. The identity of the *Ainu minzoku* was located in the historical experiences of dispossession and colonisation as an indigenous people, and a discourse of ethnicity reinforced by the increased prominence of cultural symbols. In the early 1980s this renewed sense of Ainu identity was to be translated into a renewed political agenda.

AINU SHINPŌ: A NEW LAW FOR A NEW NATION

The 1970s had been a turbulent decade for Ainu politics. Radical young activists had challenged both the state and the conservative Ainu leadership with new political doctrines and tactics. But by the end of the decade the creative energies of this movement were largely exhausted. They had, however, succeeded in bringing about considerable change in the nature of Ainu politics itself. While the political relationship between Ainu and the state remained within traditional institutional channels, typified by those existing between the Utari Kyōkai and various government departments, the Association had been forced to respond to the challenge of the younger activists within its ranks. Serious divisions remained, but the leadership talked increasingly of cultural identity and human rights alongside the need for improved welfare measures. Leaders like Kaizawa Tadashi and Nomura Giichi had travelled abroad and become aware of the situation and activities of indigenous peoples elsewhere. This in turn had generated a greater awareness of the Ainu as a separate and indigenous people. The Association had also sought to strengthen its position within the institutional arena and create new alliances and channels of influence by establishing links with the opposition Socialist and Communist parties. With the election in 1983 of Yokomichi Takahiro, a young and generally sympathetic Socialist Governor of Hokkaidō, the political climate became more favourable. From the early 1980s the Utari Kyōkai came increasingly to represent the public interests of the 'Ainu people' as a whole, and although some activists like Narita and Yūki maintained their own groups outside the Association, they also worked from positions of influence within it. Those activists who had remained opposed to any cooperation with the Utari Kyōkai – like Hashine Naohiko, who had launched a bitter personal attack on Nomura while serving a prison sentence for manslaughter – were almost completely sidelined.[36]

While the strength of the Utari Kyōkai lay in its direct links to government and its role as a channel for the government funds provided by the Utari Taisaku, therein also lay its weakness. Dependent on the state for what power it possessed, and with a vested interest in maintaining the *status quo*, it could only challenge the established order with great caution. Moreover, a large proportion of its non-activist members were more interested in the practical benefits of increased welfare provisions than the restoration of a putative Ainu nationhood. The movement for the establishment of the Ainu Minzoku ni kansuru Hōritsu (An), the Draft Legislation for the Ainu People (or Ainu Shinpō – New Ainu Law – as it is more commonly known), expressed the realisation by the Association that the two aims, if properly balanced, were not necessarily incompatible. In essence, the New Law campaign marks the clear emergence of ethnopolitics; the political aim was to increase Ainu access to the wealth of society, for the benefit of a constituency defined in terms of a distinct identity, and not merely by the extent of its relative deprivation. By emphasising Ainu identity as indigenous, this aim was to be achieved through the restoration of some measure of rights to the resources once controlled by the Ainu in their ancestral homeland. Thus identity itself became a tactic in the political struggle.

Although expressed in terms of 'ethnic pride' and 'human rights', the New Law had its origins in welfare policy. After the 1969 meeting between Nomura Giichi and the LDP Dōwa Committee's Akita Daisuke at which the Ainu had been offered, and had subsequently refused, incorporation into the Dōwa Special Measures Law, the Utari Kyōkai had asserted that their 'problem' was fundamentally different from that of the Burakumin. As a result, the Utari Taisaku had come into being as a unique set of welfare measures, but in fact closely resembled Dōwa policy. By 1981, when the disappointing results of the first seven-year phase of the Utari Taisaku were considered, discontent over the policy among Utari Kyōkai members was increasing. Whereas the proportion of Ainu working in primary industry had fallen between 1972 and 1979 from 63 per cent to 43 per cent, it was still much higher than the figure for the whole of Hokkaidō, which had halved to 9.4 per cent over the same period. The numbers of Ainu on general welfare had fallen to 69 per thousand, but this was still three and a half times higher than the Hokkaidō average. The proportion of Ainu children continuing on to High School had increased from 41.6 per cent to 69.3 per cent, but again, this figure was much lower than that of Hokkaidō as a whole.[37] Besides the lack of progress in the raising of Ainu economic and educational standards, another cause of discontent concerned the Utari Taisaku itself. This piecemeal collection of welfare measures lacked strong enabling legislation as well as failing to address issues of discrimination or human rights. Furthermore, the Dōwa Special Measures Law, which the Utari Taisaku closely resembled, was due to expire in 1982 and the debate over its extension had stimulated calls among Burakumin for the enactment of new legislation with a stronger human rights emphasis, the Buraku Kaihō Kihon Hō (Fundamental Law for Buraku Liberation). Paralleling these developments, Utari Kyōkai leaders felt that the abolition of the Protection Act and the enactment of a New Law would strengthen the welfare policy, but doubts were also expressed as to whether welfare policies would ever enable the Ainu to catch up with Wajin standards of living.[38]

In May 1981 the Special Committee of the Utari Kyōkai, formed in

1979, began to study proposals for new legislation. The ten members of the Special Committee included Nomura Giichi, Kaizawa Tadashi, Ogawa Ryūkichi and the sole Wajin member, a long-time ally of the Ainu since his involvement in the literary movement in Hidaka in the 1960s, Yamakawa Tsutomu of the *Hokkaidō Shinbun*. Nomura Giichi and Kaizawa Tadashi were no longer the conservatives who had argued so strongly for assimilation twenty years previously. Both had travelled and encountered indigenous peoples in other nation-states who enjoyed certain levels of autonomy under specific minority policies. Nomura had also been stung by the lack of economic improvement under the Utari Taisaku. Moreover, the Association was now devoting considerable effort to the preservation and transmission of Ainu culture and language as a result of the cultural revival of the 1970s. Self-perceptions had changed; most Ainu activists identified themselves on the basis of membership in the *Ainu minzoku*, the Ainu people or nation, for whose common good they were working. These changed perceptions were reflected in the work of the Special Committee on the New Law. 'This resulted', said Nomura,

> in a demand for the guarantee of our rights as indigenous people, based on the fact that our ancestors have always inhabited Ainu Moshiri. Unless we made this the first issue the proposal would have no power of persuasion. We had to make clear our historical circumstances up to the present and make them recognise this. Therefore [the New Law] is not merely a demand for a strengthened Utari Taisaku system, but a demand for the guarantee of our rights in Ainu Moshiri from hundreds of generations of our ancestors. It is a basic policy in a completely different dimension.[39]

As Nomura emphasised, one of the main elements in the new strategy of the Utari Kyōkai was the articulation of Ainu history, the reclamation of the Ainu version of the past in the face of sanitised official histories of Hokkaidō and the adjoining islands. This new direction of the Utari Kyōkai was made clear by the General Assembly of the Association in 1982, when a proposal was adopted declaring that the Ainu, as the indigenous people of the disputed Northern Territories, possessed indigenous rights in the region and should be included in any discussions on its future. This was partly in response to the publication the previous year of a 'PR booklet' by the Foreign Ministry, entitled *Warera no Hoppō Ryōdo* (Our Northern Territories), which made no mention whatsoever of the Ainu. On occasions when the Ainu were mentioned in the discourse on the Northern Territories, statements followed the official interpretation of history that had been initially set out in a 1950 resolution of the Hokkaidō Prefectural Assembly. This continued the practice, well known to late nineteenth century diplomats, of using the Ainu as convenient justification for Japanese claims while obscuring the violence of conquest:

> Looking back [over the history of the Northern Territories], the process whereby our country developed these islands, invested capital, and brought in people to bring them to their present state of prosperity is not just a recent phenomenon. These islands, along with Hokkaidō, were originally inhabited by the Ainu. From several hundred years ago, our country was continually engaged in peaceful trade with the Ainu at Akkeshi, Kiritappu and Nemuro. As a result of such friendly relations, even when mainlander migrant workers began to settle of their own accord, they provided the indigenous inhabitants with welfare and guidance, and assimilated them.[40]

In 1983 the Utari Kyōkai published its own booklet, *Chishima Rettō no Ainu Minzoku Senjū ni Kansuru Shiryō* (Materials Concerning the Prior Habitation of the Kurile Islands by the Ainu People), a collection of historical documents that contested the official version of events in the islands. Protests were also made to the Ministry of Education over the inaccurate and simplistic references to the Ainu in school textbooks.[41]

Against this background the Special Committee continued to meet on a regular basis. After twenty-six sessions the Committee came up with a draft proposal for new legislation, and this was aired for comments and discussion at six regional meetings of branches of the Association. On 27 May 1984 the proposal was adopted unanimously by the General Assembly of the Utari Kyōkai.

The introductory sections of the New Law challenged the official version of Hokkaidō history and the narrative of Ainu non-existence, and laid out the Ainu version in no uncertain terms.[42] This version not only legitimised the existence of the Ainu nation but served also to justify the Ainu demands contained in the proposed legislation. Those demands themselves combined welfare politics with a weak concept of indigenous rights in an occasionally uneasy embrace. The welfare measures bore more than a passing resemblance to the policies originally outlined in 1974 by the JSP's Special Committee on Ainu Issues, whose meetings were periodically attended by Utari Kyōkai representatives.[43]

'Indigenous rights' had not at this time been established, and indeed, are still not established, in international law, although such concepts had begun to be articulated by indigenous activists around the world. Indigenous rights were loosely conceived in terms of the restoration of control over ancestral resources of which the original inhabitants of a territory had been deprived, usually forcibly, through colonisation. This concept, generally expressed as native title to land or in popular discourse as Land Rights, was accompanied by demands for other rights set out in international instruments relating to culture, language, education, and protection against racism or genocide. The most crucial of these rights, that in a sense encompasses all the others, was the right to self-determination as peoples, as stated in the United Nations Charter and other instruments such as the International Covenant on Civil and Political Rights, ratified by Japan in 1979.[44]

The Ainu New Law, however, stopped short of calling for complete political secession. Instead, the draft concentrated on 'ethnic' and 'economic self-reliance' (*jiritsu*), basic human rights and the elimination of 'racial discrimination' (Section 1), guaranteed political participation (Section 2), and rights pertaining to education, language and culture (Section 3). Programmes and projects to attain these goals were to be funded through a combination of increased access to the resources of Hokkaidō – Ainu were to be exempted, for instance, from legal restrictions on fishing (Section 4: Fishing, Article 1) – and national funding for an Ainu Self-Reliance Fund under the control of the Ainu people. The welfare pedigree of the New Law was evident, however, in sections on agriculture, forestry, commercial activities and employment; instead of demanding native title to land, the New Law was framed in terms of increased grants and assistance (Section 4). The Self-Reliance Fund, moreover, has clear antecedents in Utari Kyōkai policy of the early 1970s. While clearly a law for a group conceived of ethnically in terms of 'distinct language and culture' and common history, no definition of who was, or was not, Ainu was offered.

Nevertheless, the adoption of the New Law by the General Assembly of the Utari Kyōkai marked the clear emergence of Ainu ethnopolitics. Despite differences of class, generation, gender, or political opinion, many Ainu had come to imagine themselves as linked by history and culture as an indigenous nation. And it was for the benefit of those who identified with this nation that Ainu leaders campaigned. The 'imagined community' of the *Ainu minzoku*, the Ainu nation, had become a social and political force, albeit still marginal, within Hokkaidō society. With the continued campaign for the New Law and a strengthening in the understanding of indigenous rights, the symbols and rhetoric of Ainuness have become evermore prominent in Ainu politics since 1984. In their own eyes, and those of an increasing number of Wajin, the 'dying race' has become an 'indigenous people'.

EPILOGUE: THE AINU IN THE 1990S

Since the adoption of the Ainu Shinpō by the Utari Kyōkai in 1984, it has become the main item on the Ainu political agenda, giving coherent shape to a formerly disparate and fragmented movement. While a handful of Ainu leaders are against the Shinpō on the grounds that it will breed more discrimination and that assimilation should still be the ultimate aim, most radicals and moderates alike can find something of value in its proposals. As the worldwide indigenous peoples' movement gains in strength, the text itself is being retrospectively reinterpreted in terms of indigenous rights. The response of the authorities has been mixed. The Hokkaidō government reacted quickly to set up a deliberative body, including Ainu representatives, in October 1984. Known as the Utari Mondai Konwakai (Utari Affairs Council), this body concluded that the Protection Act had lost all validity. Only 1,360 hectares of Protection Act lands were still utilised by Ainu as of March 1987, and the sum total of Ainu communal property held in a special bank account by the Governor of Hokkaidō amounted to 991,138 yen (January 1988).[45] Moreover, Ainu still require the Governor's permission to sell or transfer Protection Act lands; in 1988 twenty-eight applications were received, and fifteen in 1989.[46] In March 1987 the Utari Mondai Konwakai reported on welfare matters, and in March 1988 sent a qualified recommendation of acceptance of the New Law to the Dōchō, expressing reservations over the constitutional legality of guaranteed Ainu political representation. The Hokkaidō Prefectural Assembly unanimously accepted the proposal in July, passing it to central government the following month. After taking well over a year to respond, Tokyo also set up a committee but progress was excruciatingly slow.[47] Ainu activism, however, received a major boost in 1986 when the widely reported remarks of then Prime Minister Nakasone Yasuhiro on the absence of 'racial' minorities and his own possible Ainu ancestry aroused much resentment.

The Utari Kyōkai were also stimulated by the increasing involvement of Japanese civil rights groups in human rights activities of the United Nations to take their case to international bodies, attending the United Nations Working Group on Indigenous Populations for the first time in 1987 as the Ainu Association of Hokkaidō. Delegations have attended annually since then, and in May 1991 the Chair of the Working Group, Erica Daes, visited Hokkaidō at the request of the Association. Ainu representatives also participated in the revision of ILO Convention 107 on Indigenous and Tribal Populations during 1988 and 1989. Such activity has achieved mixed results. Having denied the existence of minorities to the UN in its 1980 report to the Human Rights Committee, in its next report in 1987 the Japanese government admitted the presence of Ainu persons (as individuals but not as members of an ethnic group) but denied that they were discriminated against. Finally, in December 1991 it was admitted that the Ainu exist as a minority as defined under Article 27.[48]

They are still not recognised as an indigenous people, however. The government's reasoning is that no official definition of indigenous peoples exists and therefore they cannot determine if the Ainu are indigenous.[49] This ignores the existence of definitions in such instruments as ILO Convention 169.[50] Within the UN Centre for Human Rights, however, the Ainu are regarded as the indigenous people of Japan. The Ainu leadership achieved a major victory in December 1992 when Nomura Giichi addressed the UN General Assembly as part of the inauguration ceremonies for the United Nations International Year of the World's Indigenous People. The following year, the Guatemalan Indian and Nobel Peace Prize winner Rigoberta Menchu visited the Ainu while on a trip to Japan.

Another consequence of international involvement in the worldwide indigenous peoples' movement is a heightened awareness of the concepts of indigenous rights and the celebration of indigenous culture. As a result, the cultural symbols of Ainu identity are increasingly visible whenever and wherever Ainu campaign to be recognised as a separate and indigenous people in their homeland, Ainu Moshiri. This also reflects an increased pride in being Ainu. Elders are once more teaching the dances and crafts to the younger generation, while younger people themselves have formed groups such as Yukara-za or the jazz band Moshiri to blend the old with the new in music, art and drama to create a contemporary Ainu culture. The traditional patterns of embroidery handed down from mother to daughter have been incorporated into striking contemporary designs by artists like Chikap Mieko or Kawamura Noriko. Festivals, whether of traditional origin or 'invented' like the memorial services at Nokamappu and Hokkaidō University, continue to be occasions to celebrate ethnic identity and heritage. These events are also important occasions for the transmission of political messages; both overt, in the form of speeches supporting the New Law, or indirectly, by showing that the Ainu maintain a cultural heritage, however modified, as a separate and indigenous people. Even the nature of tourism has begun to change. Until recently, most Ainu involved in tourism endured the humiliation of exhibiting themselves to an ignorant and derisive public out of economic necessity. Economic considerations, while still important, are now balanced in communities like Akan by a pride in introducing Ainu culture to a more appreciative audience. Nevertheless, many Ainu resent the disaffected Wajin, like the dreadlocked and ear-ringed youths who gather each summer in Nibutani, who seek refuge in an idealised version of Ainu culture.[51] As for language, twelve Ainu language schools have been set up to serve Ainu communities and courses are run in some universities, and although Ainu is no longer the language of daily life this renewed interest indicates that relegation to the status of a 'dead language' is somewhat premature.[52] The rich oral tradition of heroic epics and folktales is being transcribed and translated into Japanese for modern readers. Most Ainu use Ainu words sprinkled throughout daily conversation, and prayers are said in Ainu on ceremonial occasions. This also serves to reinforce a sense of common heritage.

The Utari Kyōkai and other activist groups continue to campaign throughout Hokkaidō and Honshū. Besides denouncing expressions of racism and discrimination in education and the media, groups organise meetings and events designed to increase understanding among the Wajin. Action has also been taken against Hokkaidō University over the issue of human remains. After a series of negotiations with the Utari Kyōkai, the University agreed in 1984 to house all Ainu remains in a specially constructed charnel on the campus and host an annual Ainu *icharpa* memorial service. Some bodies were also returned to Ainu communities. In 1985 a court action was initiated by Chikap Mieko against famous Ainu scholars over photographic copyright, and a successful out-of-court settlement in 1988 passed on the message to academics that the Ainu are no longer mere objects of research.[53]

For the foreseeable future at least, it would seem that Ainu ethnopolitics is here to stay. But, as critics of the Utari Kyōkai are quick to point out, a basic paradox remains. While the Ainu have come to exercise more control over their lives and identity than at any other time since the Meiji Restoration, the central role of the Utari Kyōkai in the Shinpō movement means that Ainu political action is largely conducted within channels sanctioned, indeed financed, by the state. Reliant on the Dōchō for 80 per cent of its funding and with a career Dōchō bureaucrat on secondment as the Head of Administration (*Jimukyokuchō*), the Association has increasingly taken on the characteristics of a quasi-governmental organisation that assists in the formulation and implementation of policy, despite the fact that the Association is based on private membership. Symbolic of this relationship was the attendance of Nomura Giichi at the Imperial Garden Party in October 1984, at which Emperor Shōwa encouraged him to work to preserve Ainu 'historical culture'.[54] Such contradictions continue to fuel internal divisions that are exacerbated by ambitious individuals building their own power bases within the Association. Located in spacious offices in a brand new public building in central Sapporo, the Utari Kyōkai is presently overseeing the fourth phase of the Utari Taisaku welfare policy. Chairman Nomura himself has no regrets about this relationship, pointing to the real gains that have been made in economic and educational terms.[55] Nevertheless, although considerable progress towards economic and educational parity has been achieved, as a minority population the Ainu remain disadvantaged. The latest survey for the Utari Taisaku in 1993 revealed that 34.6 per cent of Ainu still worked in the primary industrial sector in contrast to a mere 6.9 per cent of Wajin.[56] Educational achievment continues to lag behind that of Wajin, with 11.8 per cent advancing to higher education compared to 27.5 per cent of Wajin high-school leavers.[57] Numbers on welfare, however, are now down to just over twice that of Wajin.[58]

The influence of institutional Ainu politics was further boosted when Kayano Shigeru became the first Ainu elected to national office, entering the Upper House in August 1994 on the death of a Socialist member. Besides resurrecting the colours and symbolism of Biki's Ainu flag in his lapel pin, Kayano's campaign had a strong environmental stance, reflecting the somewhat uneasy alliance between the indigenous and 'green' movements. In November 1994 the Ainu language was heard in the Diet for the first time. With the realignment of political forces in Japan in the early 1990s, and the subsequent elevation of old allies like Socialist politician Igarashi Kōzō to the Cabinet, further steps have been taken to consider the New Law. In March 1994 Igarashi formed a private council to advise him on Ainu issues, but the Ainu remain low on the government's list of priorities. Of a pragmatic mind, the leaders of the Utari Kyōkai continue to call for autonomy and self-reliance (*jiritsu*) at home and cultivate links with academics, citizens' groups and politicians of all hues. In international forums, while asserting a common 'Aboriginality' with all other indigenous peoples and supporting indigenous rights to self-determination (*jiketsuken*), Ainu leaders stress that the Ainu respect the territorial integrity of the Japanese state and have no wish to secede.

One final note of caution is required. Despite the advances made by the organised Ainu movement, by no means all of the people socially and officially categorised as Ainu are themselves convinced by the politics of Ainuness. While the imagined community of the Ainu nation clearly exists for Ainu leaders and activists, the articulation of Ainu identity at the individual level of everyday experience varies widely. For some it may be largely instrumental and related to the pursuit of increased access to welfare or influence, while for others it is integral to their sense of Self. Many undergo deeply felt experiences in which they 'discover' an Ainu identity that introduces new pride and meaning into their lives. This study has, of necessity, concentrated on the leaders and activists who have most shaped Ainu politics, but there remains a largely silent majority in whose name they claim to act. While it would seem that many people of Ainu ancestry share the aims of the activists to a greater or lesser degree, particularly with regard to increased access to wealth, there are also many who do not belong to the Utari Kyōkai, continue to conceal their Ainu ancestry, and express no interest in Ainu culture as they aim to live out their lives as Japanese. Many Ainu who have achieved real gains in economic terms, due as much to the general prosperity of the 1980s as to Ainu activism or government policy, are wary of the continued efforts of Ainu activists to stress 'racial' discrimination, marginalisation and indigenous rights, or see welfare policies as perpetuating a 'beggar mentality' (*kojiki konjō*). Despite the continuation of prejudice, most of those who identify as Ainu are married to Wajin. As their children increasingly leave the rural enclaves, and Hokkaidō itself, to merge into a mainstream society which knows very little about the Ainu, how they will react to pressures to conform to social norms is at present an unanswered, and largely ignored, question. While Ainu leaders have achieved real material and political gains, and Ainu culture is more vibrant than at any time since the early decades of the century, the health of the Ainu nation remains fragile.

Afterword

This study has aimed to show two things. First, the nature of Ainu dispossession and marginalisation cannot be fully grasped without reference to how the discourse of 'race' structured, explained and justified relations of inequality between Wajin and Ainu. Second, the recent Ainu 'ethnic revival' is not the latest manifestation of a timeless and essential 'Ainuness' but a historical phenomenon located within a specific context of colonial relations. The Ainu political and cultural resurgence of the past twenty years is the latest phase in a pattern of colonisation and response that has shaped interactions between Ainu and Wajin for centuries.

The Ainu are the indigenous people of Japan. Their story is that of most Fourth World populations – Native Americans, Australian Aborigines, Inuit, Maori, Sami and others – who make up an estimated global population of over 200 million indigenous people. The original inhabitants of an area rich in natural resources, the Ainu have gradually been dispossessed of these resources since the days of the *basho*, when the local representatives of the Bakuhan regime joined forces with the capital and entrepreneurial skills of Kansai merchants to exploit the region. This process intensified from the early eighteenth century when the control of Ainu labour itself, and not the products of such labour exchanged through trade, became the main focus of Japanese economic activity. Under brutal conditions in the *basho*, images of non-human and demonic barbarians originating in Chinese thought gradually crystallised into the notion that the Ainu were merely dogs. With the Meiji Restoration and the establishment of the Kaitakushi, Ezochi became Hokkaidō and was transformed into an internal colony of the new Japanese state, a strategic empty land to be settled by immigration and developed along capitalist lines. Both of these policies required the dispossession of the Ainu as a prerequisite. The pace of dispossession accelerated once again with the appropriation of Ainu land as *terra nullius* by the Kaitakushi, and the inauguration of modern capitalist development. Immigration, a market economy, and a colonial administration served to create an unequal order within which the indigenous and powerless Ainu were enmeshed.

Modernisation was accompanied by new concepts of 'race' and 'nation' that served to interpret and sustain changing economic, social and political relations between Wajin and Ainu. The barbarian was transformed into a member of a 'primitive race', a wandering savage incapable of using the land or progressing to higher levels of civilisation, and thus doomed to die out in the 'struggle for survival'. A humanitarian movement to halt the physical extermination of the 'dying race' resulted in the institutionalisation of Ainu inferiority with the enactment of protective legislation in 1899. By the beginning of the twentieth century, the activities of scholars, educators, colonial officials and journalists ensured that the image of an inferior 'dying race' informed both government policy and public opinion. Against a background of sustained ideological efforts to forge a 'sense of nation' and the colonial expansion of an increasingly powerful and assertive state, 'race' and nation became increasingly synonymous as common-sense categories of understanding for most Japanese. National identity was located within a consanguineous family-state. Although legally Japanese citizens, the Ainu were thus excluded from the racialised national community as an internally colonised 'native' population. In the view of the state, the economic and social inequality of the Ainu was due to innate 'racial' inferiority and justified their continued subordination. By the early decades of the twentieth century, the overarching narratives of Japanese uniqueness and superiority ensured that other subject populations within the expanding empire were similarly constructed as inferior 'racial' Others.

Although Ainu response was limited by their extreme lack of power and resources, especially after the military defeats of 1669 and 1789, traditional ways of life survived into the Meiji period until the resources of land, fish and game upon which this lifestyle depended were appropriated or destroyed by the development of Hokkaidō. By the early twentieth century, most Ainu were sunk in chronic destitution and only barely managing to survive. Hampered by poverty and isolation, lacking in education, money or any other resources, the Ainu response was limited to isolated acts of individual violence or attempts to come to terms with rapid change in the new colonial situation. Against the odds, a few Ainu succeeded in overcoming many of the constraints imposed by the colonial order to obtain an education, or even achieve economic prosperity. In the 1920s and 1930s younger Ainu like Iboshi Hokuto, Chiri Yukie and Ega Torazō became the forerunners of a movement to better the condition of those they perceived as Utari, their people. Lacking resources and dependent largely on Wajin allies in positions of authority or the Christians associated with John Batchelor, they sought assimilation within dominant society by attempting to influence the institutional and ideological structures through which they were controlled. Their movement therefore concentrated on the revision of the Protection Act and the denial of the image of the 'dying race'. Only in Chikabumi did Ainu protest take on an overtly confrontational nature as the land dispute politicised and divided the community. Formation of the first organisation for all Hokkaidō Ainu, the Ainu Kyōkai, took place in 1930. Although headed by a Wajin bureaucrat and operated as an extension of the Dōchō Welfare Section, the Ainu Kyōkai provided an important forum for like-minded young Ainu from previously isolated communities to come together. Despite their ultimate objective of assimilation, these men and women remained proud of their heritage and helped create a new, but fragile, sense of Ainu unity.

The failure of their efforts to assimilate became clear in the decades after the collapse of the Empire in 1945. Narratives of Japanese 'racial' homogeneity and superiority continued to shape Ainu lives and deny those so identified the opportunity to participate in Japan's economic and political renewal. Although the Ainu Kyōkai was resurrected, the momentum and vitality of the pre-war movement was never regained. Torn by division and deprived of resources, the Ainu were unable to challenge relations of domination until the social and political climate of the 1970s contributed to the emergence of a new, and often radical, Ainu politics. Influenced by both domestic and international movements for civil and human rights, young radicals challenged the comfortable institutional position of the Utari Kyōkai, the successor of the Ainu Kyōkai, as a distributor of government largesse, and also launched an attack on the assimilation policies of the government itself. In common with other indigenous populations around the world, the cultural symbols of identity were activated in an attempt to provide a broad sense of Ainuness around which to mobilise politically. And so the Ainu nation was born. A flag, a history, and a homeland, Ainu Moshiri – the quiet earth where humans live – legitimised the existence of the Ainu people and underscored their claims for increased access to wealth and power.

This study has attempted to trace the material and ideological patterns of subjugation and response over the course of Ainu history. It is this unfolding historical pattern, rather than any persistent essential 'Ainuness', that best explains the present phenomenon of a resurgent and assertive Ainu ethnicity and the motivations of those who identify with it. Shaped and controlled for a century by colonialism and racialisation, some Ainu are nevertheless attempting to make themselves anew after their own fashion. The 'dying race' has become the 'Ainu nation' – Japan's indigenous people. But much remains to be achieved. Within broader

Japanese society the dominant narratives of national homogeneity and peaceful development in Hokkaidō remain secure enough to ensure that, despite growing Wajin support, the majority of the population still know little, and care even less, about Ainu demands. The dominant perception of Japan as a homogeneous nation (*tan'itsu minzoku*) indicates that 'racial' identities are still firmly embedded as common-sense perceptions in the minds of many Japanese. The conflation of *minzoku* with 'race' and the use of 'racial' discourse as ideology, 'meaning in the service of power', may be far from the minds of men and women who know little or nothing about the Ainu. For the Ainu themselves, however, it remains a fact of life.

Appendices

APPENDIX 1: THE HOKKAIDŌ FORMER NATIVES PROTECTION ACT (LAW NO.27, 1 MARCH 1899)

Article 1

Those Former Natives of Hokkaidō who are engaged, or wish to engage, in agriculture shall be granted free of charge no more than 15,000 *tsubo* (3,954 sq. yards) of land per household.

Article 2

The land granted under the preceding Article is subject to the following conditions on rights of ownership.

1 It may not be transferred except by inheritance.
2 No rights of pledge, mortgage, lease or perpetual lease can be established.
3 No easement (servitude) can be established without the permission of the Governor of Hokkaidō.
4 It cannot become the object of a lien or preferential right. The land granted in the preceding Article shall not be subject to land tax or local taxes until 30 years from the date of grant. Land already owned by Former Natives shall not be transferred except by inheritance, nor shall any of the real rights (*jus in rem*) referred to in paragraphs 1 to 3 be established upon it without the permission of the Governor of Hokkaidō.

Article 3

Any part of the land granted under Article 1 shall be confiscated if it has not been cultivated after 15 years from the date of grant.

Article 4

Hokkaidō Former Natives who are destitute will be provided with agricultural equipment and seeds.

Article 5

Hokkaidō Former Natives who are injured or ill but cannot afford medical treatment shall be provided with medical treatment or expenses for medicine.

Article 6

Hokkaidō Former Natives who are too injured, ill, disabled, senile or young to provide for themselves shall be granted welfare under existing legislation and if they should die at or during the period of assistance funeral expenses will be provided.

Article 7

Children of destitute Hokkaidō Former Natives who are attending school will be provided with tuition fees.

Article 8

Expenses incurred under Articles 4 to 7 shall be appropriated from the proceeds of the communal funds of Hokkaidō Former Natives, or if these are insufficient, from the National Treasury.

Article 9

An elementary school will be constructed with funds from the National Treasury in areas where there is a Former Native village.

Article 10

The Governor of Hokkaidō will manage the communal funds of the Hokkaidō Former Natives.

The Governor of Hokkaidō, subject to the approval of the Home Minister, may dispose of the communal funds for the interests of the owners of the communal funds or may refuse to expend it if he deems necessary.

The communal funds managed by the Governor of Hokkaidō shall be designated by the Governor of Hokkaidō.

Article 11

The Governor of Hokkaidō may issue police orders with regard to the protection of the Hokkaidō Former Natives and may impose a fine of over 2 yen but no more than 25 yen or a period of imprisonment of over 11 days but no more than 25 days.

By-laws

Article 12

This Act will become effective from 1 April 1899.

Article 13

Regulations relevant to the implementation of this Act shall be set by the Home Minister.

(*Source*: *ASH*, pp.117–119; Ainu Association of Hokkaidō, *Statement Submitted to the Fifth Session of the United Nations Working Group on Indigenous Populations*, Geneva, August 1987, Material 1.)

APPENDIX 2: NEW LAW CONCERNING THE AINU PEOPLE (DRAFT) ADOPTED AT THE GENERAL ASSEMBLY OF THE UTARI KYŌKAI, 27 MAY 1984

Preamble

The objectives of this legislation are to recognise the existence of the Ainu people with their own distinct culture in the state of Japan; for their ethnic pride to be respected under the Constitution of Japan; and for their ethnic rights to be guaranteed.

Reasons for this legislation

The Ainu people are a group with a unique history, possessing a distinct language and culture and maintaining a common economic lifestyle in Ainu Moshiri (the land where Ainu live) – Hokkaidō, Karafuto, and the Kurile Islands. The Ainu have held fast to their ethnic independence while struggling against the inhumane invasion and oppression of the Tokugawa Shōgunate and the Matsumae Domain.

The Japanese government, having taken the first step to becoming a modern state with the Meiji Restoration, unilaterally incorporated Ainu Moshiri into state territory as ownerless land without any negotiation with the indigenous Ainu. Furthermore, the government concluded the Sakhalin–Kurile Exchange Treaty with Imperial Russia and forced the Ainu in Karafuto and the Northern Kuriles to leave their homelands where they lived in peace.

The Ainu were robbed of their land, forests and seas. Taking deer or salmon became poaching and collecting firewood was deemed theft. On the other hand, Wajin immigrants flooded into the land, destructive development began, and the very survival of the Ainu people was threatened.

The dignity of the Ainu people was trampled underfoot by a policy of assimilation based on discrimination and prejudice. The Ainu were confined to granted lands, and their freedom to move or pursue an occupation other than agriculture was restricted, while their distinct language was stolen from them through education.

The postwar agrarian reform extended to the so-called Former Native allotments, and the trend in agricultural modernisation scattered the poor small-scale Ainu farmers, destroying the *Kotan* [villages] one by one.

Several tens of thousand Ainu are now said to live in Hokkaidō, with several thousand more outside Hokkaidō. Most of them are not guaranteed equal opportunities for employment due to unfair racial prejudice and discrimination. Excluded from the modern corporate sector, the Ainu form a group of the disguised unemployed and their lifestyle is usually insecure. Discrimination increases poverty, while poverty engenders further discrimination. The present sees widening gaps in such areas as living conditions and educational advancement for children.

The so-called Hokkaidō Utari Welfare Countermeasures that are presently being implemented are no more than a random collection of legislation and regulations. Not only do they lack coordination, but, above all, they obscure the responsibility of the state towards the Ainu people.

What is demanded here is the establishment of a thorough and comprehensive system predicated on the restoration of the ethnic rights of the Ainu, to eliminate racial discrimination, promote ethnic education and culture, and provide a policy for economic independence.

The issue of the Ainu people is a shameful historical legacy that arose during the process of establishing Japan as a modern state. It is also an important issue with implications for the guarantee of basic human rights under the Constitution. It is the responsibility of the government to resolve this situation. Recognising the problem as one concerning all citizens of Japan, the government must abolish the humiliating and discriminatory Hokkaidō Former Natives Protection Act and enact new legislation for the Ainu people. This legislation must apply to all Ainu living in Japan.

Section 1: Basic human rights

The basic human rights of the Ainu have been clearly violated over the years in the educational, social and economic spheres by both concrete and intangible racial prejudice.

With regard to this, the new legislation for the Ainu people is based on the fundamental concept of the elimination of discrimination against the Ainu people.

Section 2: The right to political participation

Since the Meiji Restoration, under official designations of 'Native' or 'Former Native', the Ainu people have received discriminatory treatment different from that accorded to other Japanese. There is no need to discuss the pre-Meiji period here. To overcome this humiliating situation and correctly reflect the demands of the Ainu people in national and local politics, the government should immediately put in place a policy to guarantee seats for Ainu representatives in the National Diet and local assemblies.

Section 3: Education and culture

Institutional discrimination against the Ainu under the Hokkaidō Former Natives Protection Act not only clearly violates the human rights of the Ainu but also encourages discrimination against the Ainu among the public. This has hindered the normal development of the Ainu people in education and culture and contributed to their inferior situation socially and economically.

The government must take the position that breaking through this current situation is one of the most important issues in a policy for the Ainu people and implement the following policies.

1 The implementation of a general education policy for Ainu children.
2 The planned introduction of Ainu language lessons for Ainu children.

3 The implementation of a policy to completely eliminate discrimination against the Ainu, both within the school system and in education in society.
4 The initiation of courses in Ainu language, culture and history in university education. Moreover, the employment of Ainu with ability to conduct such courses in various fields as professors, associate professors, or lecturers, regardless of existing legislation. The establishment of a special admissions system for Ainu children to enter university and take such courses.
5 The establishment of a national research facility specialising in the study and maintenance of Ainu language and culture. Ainu should actively participate as researchers. Previous research has been fundamentally flawed since it was unilaterally conducted without respect to the wishes of the Ainu people and turned the Ainu into so-called objects of research. This must be corrected.
6 The reinvestigation of the existence of the problems surrounding the contemporary transmission and preservation of Ainu culture, with a view to perfecting methods.

Section 4: Agriculture, fishing, forestry, commercial and manufacturing activity

The Hokkaidō Former Natives Protection Act stipulates a grant of up to 15,000 *tsubo* (about 5 hectares) per household for those engaged in agriculture. However, it must be recognised that Ainu difficulties in agriculture clearly result from the presence of discriminatory regulations not applied to other Japanese. The Hokkaidō Former Natives Protection Act must be abolished and a policy appropriate for the modern age established.

The present situation with regard to fishing, forestry, commercial and manufacturing activity is that because the same lack of understanding of the conditions of Ainu life exists, they have been ignored and no appropriate policy implemented.

To promote the economic independence of the Ainu, the following necessary conditions should therefore be put in place.

Agriculture

1 The guarantee of an appropriate acreage

Since Hokkaidō agriculture can be broadly classified into wet-rice cultivation, arable cropping, and dairy farming, a fair and appropriate acreage must be guaranteed according to the local agricultural situation.

2 Provision and modernisation of the productive base

Projects to improve the productive base for Ainu-managed agricultural enterprises should be implemented without regard to existing legislation.

3 Miscellaneous

Fishing

1 The granting of fishing rights

For those managing fishing enterprises or engaged in fishing, such rights should be granted to those who wish them regardless of the presence of existing fishing rights.

2 Provision and modernisation of the productive base

Projects to improve the productive base for Ainu-managed fishing enterprises should be implemented without regard to existing legislation.

3 Miscellaneous

Forestry

1 The promotion of forestry

Necessary measures should be implemented for the promotion of forestry for those who manage or are engaged in forestry enterprises.

Manufacturing and commercial

1 The promotion of manufacturing and commerce

Necessary measures should be implemented for the promotion of commercial or manufacturing enterprises managed by Ainu.

Labour policy

1 The enlargement of employment opportunities

Historical circumstances have clearly chronically lowered the economic position of the Ainu people. One manifestation of this is the large number of seasonal workers who can be regarded as disguised unemployed. The government should actively promote a labour policy to widen opportunities for employment for the Ainu people.

Section 5: Fund for Ainu self-reliance

The so-called Hokkaidō Utari Welfare Countermeasures are supported from the budgets of the Hokkaidō and national governments, but these protective measures should be abolished and a fundamental policy must be implemented to make the Ainu people self-reliant. The rights to guaranteed political participation, the promotion of education and culture, and the improvement in the productive base in agricultural, fishing and other enterprises should be considered part of this. Of these policies, some should be undertaken on the responsibility of national, prefectural, or municipal authorities, while others should be undertaken under the responsibility of the Ainu people. In the latter case in particular, a fund called the Self-Reliance Fund of the Ainu People should be established. This fund should be under independent Ainu management.

The government should be responsible for providing resources for the Fund.

The Fund should be established at the latest by 1987, when the second seven-year stage of the welfare policy is completed.

Section 6: Consultative bodies

To justly and continually reflect Ainu policies in national and local politics, the following consultative bodies should be established.

1 A Central Consultative Council for Ainu Policy (provisional title) should be established, directly attached to the Prime Minister's Office or associated with it. Members should consist of relevant State Ministers, representatives of the Ainu people, Diet members representing all parties from both Upper and Lower Houses, experienced scholars, business leaders and others.
2 Along with this consultative body at the national level, a Hokkaidō Consultative Council for Ainu Policy (provisional title) should be established. Composition should follow the same lines as the Central Consultative Council.

(*Source*: *Senkusha no Tsudoi*, No.37 (October 1984), pp.4–6; Ainu Association of Hokkaidō, *Statement Submitted to the Fifth Session of the United Nations Working Group on Indigenous Populations*, Geneva, August 1987, Material 10.)

Notes

INTRODUCTION

1 For the full English text of the speech, see G. Nomura, 'Inauguration Speech, UN General Assembly, 10 December 1992', Appendix B, in 'No Longer Forgotten: The Ainu', Special Issue of *AMPO Japan-Asia Quarterly Review*, Vol.24, No.3 (1993), pp.33–34.

2 '"No Minority Races in Japan", says Nakasone', *Japan Times*, 24 October 1986.

3 *The Economist*, 30 September 1978.

4 I. Hilger, 'Japan's "Sky People": The Vanishing Ainu', *National Geographic*, Vol.131, No.2 (February 1967), pp.268–296; I. Hilger, *Together With the Ainu: A Vanishing People* (Norman: University of Oklahoma Press, 1971). J.B. Cornell, 'Ainu Assimilation and Cultural Extinction: Acculturation Policy in Hokkaidō', *Ethnology*, Vol.3, No.3 (1964), pp.287–304.

5 B. Attwood, *The Making of the Aborigines* (Sydney: Allen and Unwin, 1989), p.149.

1 'RACE', ETHNICITY AND THE AINU

1 W. Wetherall and G. DeVos (eds), *Japan's Minorities: Burakumin, Koreans, Ainu, Okinawans*, Minority Rights Group Report No.3, New Edition (London: Minority Rights Group, 1983), p.3. According to the report, population figures are estimated at two to three million for Burakumin, 650,000 Koreans, nearly a million Okinawans, and around half a million members of other groups. The latest official population statistics for Ainu show 23,830 resident in Hokkaidō. (Hokkaidō Minseibu, *Heisei 5–nen Hokkaidō Utari Seikatsu Jittai Chōsa Hōkokusho* (1993 Report on Socio-economic Conditions of the Hokkaidō Ainu) (Sapporo: Hokkaidō Minseibu, 1993), p.2.

2 For recent contributions to the debate, see, for instance, M. Weiner, *Race and Migration in Imperial Japan* (London and New York: Routledge, 1994); or K. Yoshino, *Cultural Nationalism in Contemporary Japan: A Sociological Enquiry* (London and New York: Routledge, 1992).

3 F.C.C. Peng and P. Geiser, *The Ainu: The Past in the Present* (Hiroshima: Hiroshima Bunka Hyōron, 1977), p.281; I. Hilger, 'Japan's 'Sky People': The Vanishing Ainu', *National Geographic*, Vol.131, No.2 (February 1967),

pp.268–296; I. Hilger, *Together With the Ainu: A Vanishing People* (Norman: University of Oklahoma Press, 1971).

4 S. Emori, *Ainu no Rekishi: Hokkaidō no Hitobito (2)* (A History of the Ainu: the People of Hokkaidō [2]) (Tokyo: Sanseidō, 1987); Y. Baba, 'A Study of Minority–Majority Relations: The Ainu and Japanese in Hokkaidō', *Japan Interpreter*, Vol.13, No.1 (1980), pp.60–92. This paper originally appeared in Japanese as 'Nihon ni okeru Mainoritii Kenkyū e no Ichi Shiron: Ainu Kei Jūmin no Jirei Kenkyū', *Minzokugaku Kenkyū*, Vol.37, No.3 (December 1972), pp.214–238.

5 K. Sjöberg, *The Return of the Ainu: Cultural Mobilisation and the Practice of Ethnicity in Japan* (Chur: Harwood Academic Publishers, 1993). This work is unfortunately marred by numerous errors and misinterpretations.

6 M. Banton, *Racial Consciousness* (London and New York: Longman, 1988), pp.20–23.

7 P. van den Berghe, in E. Cashmore, *Dictionary of Race and Ethnic Relations*, Second Edition (London: Routledge, 1988), p.238; emphasis in the original.

8 R. Jenkins, 'Social Anthropological Models of Inter-ethnic Relations', in J. Rex and D. Mason (eds), *Theories of Race and Ethnic Relations* (Cambridge: Cambridge University Press, 1986), pp.177, 178.

9 R. Miles, *Racism after 'Race Relations'* (London and New York: Routledge, 1993), p.42.

10 Miles, *Racism after 'Race Relations'*, p.101.

11 Miles, *Racism after 'Race Relations'*, pp.13, 87. For a discussion of cultural and other 'masks of race' see D.T. Goldberg, *Racist Culture: Philosophy and the Politics of Meaning* (Oxford, UK and Cambridge, Mass.: Blackwell, 1993), pp.61–89.

12 Miles, *Racism after 'Race Relations'*, p.44.

13 J. Beckett, 'Aboriginality in a Nation-State: The Australian Case', in M.C. Howard (ed.), *Ethnicity and Nation-building in the Pacific* (Tokyo: United Nations University, 1989), p.120.

14 For an overview of the arguments used by ideologues of the European colonial powers, see P. Curtin, 'Introduction: Imperialism as Intellectual History', in P. Curtin (ed.), *Imperialism* (London: Macmillan, 1971), pp.ix–xxiii.

15 R. Miles, entry for 'Ideology' in Cashmore, *Dictionary of Race and Ethnic Relations*, pp.135–136.

16 K. Pyle, *The New Generation in Meiji Japan: Problems of Cultural Identity, 1885–1895* (Stanford: Stanford University Press, 1969), p.16.

17 J. Dower, *War without Mercy: Race and Power in the Pacific War* (New York: Pantheon, 1986), p.204. A brief overview of scientific racism and other intellectual trends in the period can be found in E. Hobsbawm, *The Age of Capital 1848–1875* (London: Abacus, 1977), pp.294–323; and E. Hobsbawm, *The Age of Empire 1875–1914* (London: Sphere Books, 1989), pp.252–256.

18 From 'The Land of the Gods', excerpted in R. Tsunoda *et al.* (ed.), *Sources of Japanese Tradition: Volume Two* (New York: Columbia University Press, 1964), p.39. For Hirata's comments on the animalistic characteristics of the Dutch, see D. Keene, *The Japanese Discovery of Europe, 1720–1830*, Revised Edition (Stanford: Stanford University Press, 1969), p.170.

19 G.P. Leupp, 'Images of Black People in Late Medieval and Early Modern Japan, 1543–1900', *Japan Forum*, Vol.7, No.1 (Spring 1995), pp.2–6.

20 F. Dikötter, *The Discourse of Race in Modern China* (Stanford: Stanford University Press, 1992), pp.35–36; emphasis in the original.

21 For a brief summary of folk attitudes towards the Other, see Dower, *War Without Mercy*, pp.234–240.
22 E. Shimao, 'Darwinism in Japan', *Annals of Science*, No.38 (1981), pp.93–102. The rest of this paragraph is also based on this article.
23 C. Darwin, *The Descent of Man*, Second Edition (New York, 1922), excerpted in Curtin, *Imperialism*, pp.22–33. Quotes are from p.24.
24 There never was a school of this name; it is a label applied retrospectively to a number of writers who actually displayed a variety of positions on evolution and society. See M. Banton, 'Social Darwinism', in Cashmore, *Dictionary of Race and Ethnic Relations*, pp.287–289.
25 G. Sansom, *The Western World and Japan: A Study in the Interaction of European and Asiatic Cultures* (Rutland, Vt. and Tokyo: Tuttle, 1977), p.433.
26 C. Gluck, *Japan's Modern Myths: Ideology in the Late Meiji Period* (Princeton: Princeton University Press, 1985), p.209; Sansom, *The Western World and Japan*, p.433. *Yūshō reppai* is usually translated as 'survival of the fittest' but literally means 'the superior win, the inferior lose'. For newspaper circulation see Gluck, *Japan's Modern Myths*, p.171. By 1911, 236 papers were being published in Tokyo and the provinces, and the seven largest daily's had circulations of over 100,000. Most issues were read by more than one person.
27 Shimao, 'Darwinism in Japan', p.96.
28 K. Takeuchi, 'How Japan Learned About the Outside World: The Views of other Countries Incorporated in Japanese School Textbooks, 1868–1986', *Hitotsubashi Journal of Social Studies*, No.19 (1987), p.9. The impact of Buckle's thought is discussed in S. Tanaka, *Japan's Orient: Rendering Pasts into History* (Berkeley and Los Angeles: California University Press, 1993), pp.39–40.
29 For nationalism as ideology in Japan see Gluck, *Japan's Modern Myths*, esp. pp.21–26, Chapters 4 and 5; for the overlap with 'race' see M. Weiner, *Race and Migration,* Ch.1; Dower, *War Without Mercy*, Chs 8 and 10.
30 Gluck, *Japan's Modern Myths*, pp.53–58, 118–19, 176, 273.
31 The definition of the nation as an 'imagined political community' was first proposed by Anderson, for whom a nation 'is imagined because the members of even the smallest nation will never know most of their fellow members, meet them, or even hear of them, yet in the mind of each lives the image of their communion . . . it is imagined as a *community*, because, regardless of the actual inequality and exploitation that may prevail in each, the nation is always conceived as a deep, horizontal comradeship.' B. Anderson, *Imagined Communities: Reflections on the Origin and Spread of Nationalism*, Revised Edition, (London: Verso, 1991), pp.6–7; emphasis in the original.
32 Miles, *Racism after 'Race Relations'*, p.59.
33 N. Shimazu, 'The Japanese Attempt to Secure Racial Equality in 1919', *Japan Forum*, Vol.1, No.1 (1989), p.93.
34 H. Yasuda, 'Kindai Nihon ni okeru 'Minzoku' Kannen no Keisei' (The Formation of the Concept of Minzoku in Modern Japan), *Shisō to Gendai*, No.31 (1992), pp.61–72. This and the following paragraph draw on this source and Pyle, *New Generation* (1969).
35 Cited in R. Mitchell, *Censorship in Imperial Japan* (Princeton: Princeton University Press, 1983), p.101.
36 Onishi is cited in Yasuda, 'Minzoku Kannen no Keisei', p.70; for the rise in nationalism see also Pyle, *New Generation*, pp.192–203.

37 For an erudite contemporary example of the overlap between 'race', nation and culture, see I. Nitobe, *The Japanese Nation: Its Land, Its People, Its Life; With Special Consideration to Its Relations with the United States* (New York and London: G. Putnam's Sons, 1912), especially Chapter 4, 'Race and National Characteristics'.

38 For the notion of 'invented tradition' see E. Hobsbawm, 'Introduction: Inventing Traditions', in E. Hobsbawm and T. Ranger (eds), *The Invention of Tradition* (Cambridge: Cambridge University Press, 1983), pp.1–14; and E. Hobsbawm, 'Mass-Producing Traditions: Europe 1870–1914', in the same volume, pp.263–283. For the 'invented traditions' surrounding the Japanese Imperial institution, see T. Fujitani, 'Inventing, Forgetting, Remembering: Toward a Historical Ethnography of the Nation-State', in H. Befu (ed.), *Cultural Nationalism in East Asia: Representation and Identity* (Berkeley: Institute of East Asian Studies, University of California, 1993), pp.77–106.

39 The phrase is that of J.B. Thompson. For Thompson, ideology refers to 'the ways in which meaning is mobilized in the service of dominant individuals and groups, that is, the ways in which meaning constructed and conveyed by symbolic forms serves, in particular circumstances, to establish and sustain structured social relations from which some individuals and groups benefit more than others, and which some individuals and groups have an interest in preserving while others may seek to contest'. J.B. Thompson, *Ideology and Modern Culture* (Cambridge: Polity Press, 1990), p.73.

40 I. Neary, *Political Protest and Social Control in Pre-war Japan: The Origins of Buraku Liberation* (Manchester: Manchester University Press, 1989), p.42; Gluck, *Japan's Modern Myths*, p.176.

41 Gluck, *Japan's Modern Myths*, p.16.

42 S. Hiraoka, 'Ainu Jinshu Shobun Ron' (On the Disposal of the Ainu Race), appendix in T. Aoyama, *Kyokuhoku no Bettenchi* (The Different World of the Extreme North) (Tokyo: Nippon Seinen Tsushinsha, 1918), p.6.

43 Cited in M. Hane, *Peasants, Rebels and Outcastes: The Underside of Modern Japan* (New York: Pantheon, 1982), p.35.

44 For Europe, see Miles, *Racism after 'Race Relations'*, pp.88–97. For the USA see R. Takaki, *Iron Cages: Race and Culture in 19th-Century America* (New York and Oxford: Oxford University Press, 1989), pp.115–116.

45 Cited in Pyle, *New Generation*, p.183.

46 D. Irokawa, *The Culture of the Meiji Period* (Princeton: Princeton University Press, 1985), p.298.

47 For a consideration of Britain in this period, see Miles, *Racism after 'Race Relations'*, pp.65–71.

48 Yamagata to Prime Minister Ōkuma, August 1914. Excerpted in Tsunoda, *Sources of Japanese Tradition*, p.207.

49 M. Kawamura, 'Taishū Orientarizumu to Ajia Ninshiki' (Mass Orientalism and Consciousness of Asia), in Iwanami Kōza, *Kindai Nihon to Shokuminchi 7: Bunka no Naka no Shokuminchi* (Modern Japan and the Colonies 7: The Colonies in Culture) (Tokyo: Iwanami Shoten, 1993), p.119.

50 Kawamura, 'Taishū Orientarizumu'; for *Nora-kura* see Hane, *Peasants, Rebels and Outcastes*, p.75.

51 A detailed discussion of this point can be found in Dower, *War Without Mercy*, especially pp.234–261.

52 Dower, *War Without Mercy*, pp.267–290.

53 *History of Japan*, Japanese Government Railways, 1939. Cited in Dower, *War Without Mercy*, p.222.
54 M. Harries and S. Harries, *Soldiers of the Sun: The Rise and Fall of the Imperial Japanese Army* (New York: Random House, 1992), p.480. Dower, *War Without Mercy*, pp.285–286.
55 Thompson, *Ideology*, pp.24–25.
56 Mitchell, *Censorship in Imperial Japan*, p.339.
57 For an overview of *Nihonjinron*, see Yoshino, *Cultural Nationalism*, pp.9–38; H. Befu, 'Nationalism and *Nihonjinron*', in Befu (ed.), *Cultural Nationalism in East Asia*, pp.107–135.
58 Yoshino, *Cultural Nationalism*, p.24.
59 The term has been popularised by A.D. Smith in his book *The Ethnic Revival* (Cambridge: Cambridge University Press, 1981). To use the term, however, is not to accept Smith's argument for the existence of 'ethnic' identities in the premodern period, a point discussed further below.
60 G. Macdonald, 'Ainu and Aboriginal Rights: The Struggle goes International', in N. Loos and T. Osanai (eds), *Indigenous Minorities and Education: Australian and Japanese Perspectives of their Indigenous Peoples, the Ainu, Aborigines and Torres Straits Islanders* (Tokyo: Sanyūsha, 1993), p.401.
61 A. Gray, 'The Indigenous Movement in Asia', in R.H. Barnes, A. Gray and B. Kingsbury (eds), *Indigenous Peoples of Asia* (Ann Arbor: Association for Asian Studies, 1995), p.45.
62 R.H. Barnes, 'Introduction', in Barnes, Gray and Kingsbury, *Indigenous Peoples of Asia*, p.1.
63 C. Geertz, *The Interpretation of Cultures* (New York: Basic Books, 1973), p.259.
64 S. Devalle, 'Discourses of Ethnicity: The Faces and the Masks', in Howard, *Ethnicity and Nation-building*, p.54. An influential critique of this approach was E. Said, *Orientalism* (Harmondsworth: Penguin, 1978).
65 As an example, Greenfeld cites a survey of children in early twentieth century Russia. This revealed that half of those in rural areas did not even know their family names, while half of those in Moscow did not know they were living in the city. Although these individuals shared the same cultural and linguistic traits as self-conscious Russian nationalists, 'Russian' identity had no meaning for them and did not influence their actions in any way. They did not possess an 'ethnic' or 'national' identity (the two are synonymous here). L. Greenfeld, *Nationalism: Five Roads to Modernity* (Cambridge, Mass. and London: Harvard University Press, 1992), pp.13, 494–495. This is in contrast to the arguments of A.D. Smith in favour of pre-existing or dormant ethnic ties in the activation of ethnicity, and the applicability of 'ethnicity' to the analysis of ancient societies like the Sumerians. Smith, *The Ethnic Revival*, pp.63–86.
66 Anderson, *Imagined Communities*, pp.164–170. For a discussion of the censuses of the Habsburg Empire and the linguistic nationalisms they helped generate, see E. Hobsbawm, *Nations and Nationalism Since 1780: Programme, Myth, Reality* (Cambridge: Cambridge University Press, 1990), pp.97–100. Not all nationalisms are ethnic, of course; for the distinction between civic nationalism and the more prevalent ethnic nationalism, see Greenfeld, *Nationalism*, pp.9–14.
67 R. Tonkinson, 'Aboriginal Ethnicity and Nation-building within Australia', in Howard, *Ethnicity and Nation-building*, pp.138–139.

68 This is not universal, or necessarily accepted by many Indian groups. At an Indigenous Peoples' Conference I attended in Nibutani, Hokkaidō in August 1993, an elder of the Kwakiutl Indian nation from the North West Pacific Coast, Gloria Webster, criticised the tendency of the young people of her nation to mix up aboriginal beliefs and adopt practices from plains cultures (Mother Earth, sweetgrass ceremonies, sweat lodges). She referred to them as 'New Age Indians'. As she pointed out, 'We are a sea people. Mother Earth is a concept unknown to us.'

69 Tonkinson, 'Aboriginal Ethnicity', p.144.

70 J. Clifton, 'The Indian Story: A Cultural Fiction', in J.A. Clifton (ed.), *The Invented Indian: Iconoclastic Essays* (New Brunswick: Transaction Publishers, 1990), pp.37, 38.

71 E. Said, *Culture and Imperialism* (London: Vintage, 1994), p.276.

72 S. Gill, 'Mother Earth: An American Myth', in Clifton, *Invented Indian*, pp.129–143.

73 S. Cornell, *The Return of the Native: American Indian Political Resurgence* (New York and Oxford: Oxford University Press, 1988), p.212.

74 Said, *Culture and Imperialism*, pp.348–349.

75 Beckett, 'Aboriginality in a Nation-State', p.129. Moreover, many non-indigenous New Age mystics in settler states are adopting elements of what they perceive to be an indigenous spirituality. For a case study in Australia, see J. Marcus, 'The Journey out to the Centre: The Cultural Appropriation of Ayers Rock', in A. Rutherford (ed.), *Aboriginal Culture Today*, Special Issue of *Kunapipi*, Vol.10, Nos. 1 and 2, (Sydney: Dangeroo Press, 1988), pp.254–274.

76 L. Yoneyama, 'Hiroshima Narratives and the Politics of Memory', Ph.D. dissertation, Stanford University, California, 1993, p.6.

77 Clifton, 'The Indian Story', pp.32–38.

78 Population estimates from R. Stavenhagen, *The Ethnic Question: Conflicts, Development, and Human Rights* (Tokyo: United Nations University Press, 1990), p.100.

79 The best analysis of the position of international law with regard to indigenous peoples is P. Thornberry, *International Law and the Rights of Minorities* (Oxford: Clarendon Press, 1991), pp.331–382. See also Stavenhagen, *The Ethnic Question*, pp.93–119.

80 Stavenhagen, paraphrasing J. Rothschild, *The Ethnic Question*, p.27.

81 Beckett, 'Aboriginality in a Nation-State', p.119.

82 P. Weinreich, 'The Operationalisation of Identity Theory in Racial and Ethnic Relations', in Rex and Mason, *Theories of Race and Ethnic Relations*, p.308.

83 Weinreich, 'Operationalisation of Identity Theory', pp.303–306.

84 For a good case-study of this aspect of ethnic identity with reference to indigenous and 'mixed-blood' communities in nineteenth century Canada, see H. Gorham, 'Families of Mixed Descent in the Western Great Lake Region', in B. Cox (ed.), *Native Peoples, Native Lands; Canadian Indians, Inuit and Metis* (Ottawa: Carleton University Press, 1987), pp.37–55. This aspect of ethnicity is often seen in the modern world in the phenomenon of 'passing'; although this is usually taken to mean identification with the majority group it is not always a one-way process.

2 BARBARIANS AND DEMONS

1 For an overview of the prehistoric period, see H. Utagawa, *Ainu Bunka Seiritsu Shi* (History of the Formation of Ainu Culture) (Sapporo: Hokkaidō Shuppan Kikaku Sentā, 1988).

2 This is only an estimate; it was not until the late eighteenth century that the Wajin became interested in Ainu numbers, by which time Ainu society was beginning to disintegrate. A survey of 1807 put the figure at 26,256, though it is unlikely that remoter inland settlements were included. It is also unclear if this includes Sakhalin Ainu. See S. Emori, *Ainu no Rekishi: Hokkaidō no Hitobito (2)* (A History of the Ainu: the People of Hokkaidō [2]), (Tokyo: Sanseidō, 1987) p.103; S. Takakura, *Ainu Seisaku Shi: Shinpan* (A History of Ainu Policy: New Edition) (Tokyo: Sanichi Shobō, 1972) p.289.

3 For Ainu society see S. Takakura, 'The Ainu of Northern Japan: A Study in Conquest and Acculturation' (Trans. J. Harrison), *Transactions of the American Philosophical Society*, Vol.50, No.4 (1960), pp.12–23; H. Watanabe, *The Ainu Ecosystem* (Seattle and London: University of Washington Press, 1973).

4 See, for instance, T. Amano, 'Kuma no Tankō' (A Few Thoughts on Bears), *Cultura Antiqua*, Vol.42, No.10 (1990), pp.26–35.

5 Ancient Chinese attitudes to peripheral peoples are summarised in F. Dikötter, *The Discourse of Race in Modern China* (Stanford: Stanford University Press, 1992), pp.2–10.

6 W.G. Aston, *Nihongi: Chronicles of Japan from the Earliest Times to* AD *697* (Rutland, Vt. and Tokyo: Tuttle, 1972), Vol.1, p.203.

7 Emori, *Ainu no Rekishi*, p.9.

8 K. Komai, 'The Ainu in the Age of T'ang Dynasty', *Acta Asiatica*, No.6 (March 1964). Komai has argued that the term *mōjin* was 'descriptive of the Ainu' and that the T'ang and Sung scholars also mentioned that these people were skilled archers, again linking them to the Ainu. In contrast, Y. Kitakamae, *Kodai Emishi no Kenkyū* (Studies of the Ancient Emishi) (Tokyo: Yūzankaku, 1991) concludes (p. 593) that this was simply a classical allusion and not a realistic physical description of the indigenous inhabitants of northeast Japan.

9 Utagawa, *Ainu Bunka Seiritsu Shi*, pp.269–271; Emori, *Ainu no Rekishi*, p.18; Kitakamae, *Kodai Emishi no Kenkyū*, pp.598–601.

10 Matsumae-chō Shi Henshū Shitsu (ed.), *Matsumae-chō Shi* (History of Matsumae Town), Vol.1, (Matsumae: Matsumae-chō, 1984), p.213. Another word often used was *Ebisu* (also read *fushū* and written with ideographs that literally mean 'prisoners') which is usually taken to stand for groups of barbarians who had submitted to the rule of the Ritsuryō regime and were in the process of being assimilated.

11 The debate over whether the Emishi and the Ezo were the same people has been around in one form or another since the 1870s but is characterised by sweeping generalisations based on fragmentary and often contradictory evidence. See, for instance, the enthusiastic presentation of the Ainu as 'proto-Japanese' by T. Umehara and K. Hanihara, *Ainu wa Gen-Nihonjin ka* (Are the Ainu Proto-Japanese?) (Tokyo: Shōgakkan, 1982). Some physical anthropologists (for instance K. Hanihara, 'Emishi, Ezo and Ainu: An Anthropological Perspective', *Japan Review*, No.1, 1990) claim that skeletal remains show clear links. For a historical overview see Kitakamae, *Kodai*

Emishi no Kenkyū; M. Kudō, 'Kodai Emishi no Shakai – Kōeki to Shakai Soshiki' (Society of the Ancient Emishi – Trade and Social Organization), *Rekishi Hyōron*, No.434 (June 1986); or T. Kikuchi, 'Emishi Kōkogaku no Genjō to Kadai' (Present Situation and Issues in Emishi Archaeology) in the same issue. For a recent consideration of Ainu in Tsugaru during the Tokugawa period, see K. Namikawa, *Kinsei Nihon to Hoppō Shakai* (Early Modern Japan and Northern Society) (Tokyo: Sanseidō, 1992).

12 K. Kindaichi, *Kindaichi Kyōsuke Senshū* (Selected Works of Kindaichi Kyōsuke), Vol.3, (Tokyo: Sanseidō, 1962), pp.69–71.

13 See Takakura, 'Ainu of Northern Japan', pp.24n, 76–77n; I. Bird, *Unbeaten Tracks in Japan* (New York: G.P. Putnam's Sons, New York, 1880; republished Rutland, Vt. and Tokyo: Tuttle, 1973), pp.273–274n. This and all subsequent citations are from the Tuttle edition.

14 Utagawa, *Ainu Bunka Seiritsu Shi*, pp.269–271; I. Endō, 'Ezo Andō-shi Koron' (Discussion on Andō as an Ezo), *Rekishi Hyōron*, No.434 (June 1986), pp.36–50.

15 The Manchurian goods included Ezo brocades (*Ezo nishiki*), richly embroidered silk gowns which had been presented to northern continental peoples by Chinese officials as part of the Chinese system of 'tributary' relationships on its borders. These then passed through a chain of other northern peoples, including the Ainu, to finally end up in the hands of daimyō and other members of the elites. See U. Hatakeyama, 'Ainu Clothing', in N. Loos and T. Osanai, *Indigenous Minorities and Education: Australian and Japanese Perspectives of their Indigenous Peoples, the Ainu, Aborigines and Torres Straits Islanders* (Tokyo: Sanyūsha, 1993), p.109. When Kakizaki Yoshihiro first visited Tokugawa Ieyasu in 1593 he presented him with one of these gowns, indicating their high status and value.

16 Takakura, 'Ainu of Northern Japan', p.49.

17 Kitakamae, *Kodai Emishi no Kenkyū*, p.414.

18 Cited in M. Kaiho, *Shiryō to Kataru Hokkaidō no Rekishi* (The History of Hokkaidō as Related by Historical Records) (Sapporo: Hokkaidō Shuppan Kikaku Sentā, 1985), p.24.

19 Kaiho, *Shiryō to Kataru*, p.30.

20 K. Sakurai, *Ainu Hishi* (Secret History of the Ainu) (Tokyo: Kadokawa Shoten, 1967), p.102.

21 T. Sasaki, 'Ainu-e ga Egaita Sekai' (The World Illustrated by Ainu Pictures), in Sapporo Gakuin Daigaku Jinbungakubu (ed.), *Ainu Bunka ni Manabu* (Learn From Ainu Culture) (Sapporo: Sapporo Gakuin Daigaku, 1990), pp.180–181.

22 Reproduced in Sasaki, 'Ainu-e', p.164.

23 The Ainu had long before given up making pottery and working iron. Although very few excavations have been carried out, one archaeological dig at an Ainu fort (*chashi*) has shown the extent to which Japanese goods had penetrated Ainu society by the seventeenth century, Sakurai, *Ainu Hishi*, p.122. Equally importantly, trade goods had become integrated into Ainu culture on other dimensions. Lacquer vessels and swords were important indicators of wealth and status and were used in religious ceremonies and as items of compensation in the settlement of disputes. See also D. Howell, 'Ainu Ethnicity and the Boundaries of the Early Modern Japanese State', *Past and Present*, No.142 (February 1994), pp.74–77.

24 H. Tabata, 'Some Historical Aspects of Ainu–Japanese Relations: Treachery, Assimilation and the Myth of Ainu Counting', in Loos and Osanai, *Indigenous*

Minorities and Education, pp.32–33. For *charanke* see also Takakura, 'Ainu of Northern Japan', p.20.

25 S. Kodama, *Ainu: Historical and Anthropological Studies* (Sapporo: Hokkaidō University School of Medicine, 1970), p.13.

26 Kodama, *Ainu*, p.15.

27 Cited in Takakura, 'Ainu of Northern Japan', pp.49–50.

28 N. Kamiya, 'Japanese Control of Ezochi and the Role of Northern Koryō', *Acta Asiatica*, Vol.67 (1994), pp.49–68.

29 *Matsumae-chō Shi*, p.580.

30 Cited in Takakura, 'Ainu of Northern Japan', p.28.

31 M. Kaiho, *Kinsei no Hokkaidō* (Early Modern Hokkaidō) (Tokyo: Kyōikusha, 1979), pp.93–95; and Kaiho, *Shiryō to Kataru*, pp.99–103. Kaiho's analysis has recently been criticised by H. Ohyi, 'Shakushain no Ran (Kanbun Kyū-nen Ezo no Ran) no Saikentō' (A Reinvestigation of the Rebellion of Shakushain), *Hoppō Bunka Kenkyū*, No.21 (1992). Ohyi claims Kaiho's interpretation of the historical sources is faulty and that there is no current archaeological evidence for the theory of strong regional groups.

32 Takakura, 'Ainu of Northern Japan', p.15. For a contemporary account of the troubles and the subsequent war see the unattributed 'Ezo Hōki' (The Ezo Uprising) [1671] in S. Takakura, (ed.), *Nihon Shomin Seikatsu Shiryō Shūsei, Vol.4 – Hoppō Hen* (Collection of Historical Materials on the Life of Common People in Japan, Vol.4 – The Northern Regions) (Tokyo: Sanichi Shobō, 1969), pp.639–650 (this collection is hereafter cited as *NS4*).

33 Takakura, 'Ainu of Northern Japan', p.51.

34 *Matsumae-chō Shi*, Vol.1, p.346.

35 Cited in Kaiho, *Kinsei no Hokkaidō*, p.78.

36 For the Christian interpretation see Sakurai, *Ainu Hishi*, p.123. The other view is represented by Kaiho, *Kinsei no Hokkaidō*, pp.101–102, who emphasises the importance of trading rights as a cause of the war. As for the incorporation of Wajin as kin, a similar phenomenon was observed among traders and Indians in the American northwest during the eighteenth century, and also between Aboriginals and early settlers in some parts of Australia in the mid-nineteenth century. See B. Attwood, *The Making of the Aborigines* (Sydney: Allen and Unwin, 1989), p.69. A differing perspective on Ainu and Wajin 'ethnicities' in this and subsequent periods is offered by Howell, 'Ainu Ethnicity', pp.69–93.

37 These are cited in Takakura, 'Ainu of Northern Japan', p.29.

38 Kamiya, 'Japanese Control of Ezochi', p.67–68.

39 Takakura, 'Ainu of Northern Japan', p.31.

40 Cited in Kaiho, *Kinsei no Hokkaidō*, pp.121–122.

41 These developments towards 'proto-industrialisation' are analysed in D. Howell, *Capitalism from Within: Economy, Society and the State in a Japanese Fishery* (Berkeley and Los Angeles: University of California Press, 1995), pp.24–49; Takakura, 'Ainu of Northern Japan', pp.30–47; Kaiho, *Kinsei no Hokkaidō*, pp.115–125; and for later development Takakura, *Ainu Seisaku Shi*, Ch.4.

42 The phrase is that of Toby. For a full discussion, see R. Toby, *State and Diplomacy in Early Modern Japan: Asia in the Development of the Tokugawa Bakufu* (Princeton: Princeton University Press, 1984), pp.211–230.

43 For *Kokugaku* and the Mito School, see B.T. Wakabayashi, *Anti-Foreignism and Western Learning in Early-Modern Japan* (Cambridge, Mass. and London: Harvard University Press, 1986).

44 Russian activity and Japanese response are described in J.J. Stephan, *The Kuril Islands: Russo–Japanese Frontier in the Pacific* (Oxford: Clarendon Press, 1974), pp.36–80.
45 Wakabayashi, *Anti-Foreignism*, p.27.
46 S. Hayashi, 'Sangoku Tsuran Zusetsu' (Illustrated Survey of Three Countries) [1785] cited in Takakura, 'Ainu of Northern Japan', p.55.
47 Honda Toshiaki, 'Keisai Hisaku Hōi' (Secret Plan for Managing the Country) [1798], in D. Keene, *The Japanese Discovery of Europe 1720–1830* (Revised Edition, Stanford: Stanford University Press, 1969), p.180.
48 For details of Bakufu policy, see Takakura, 'Ainu of Northern Japan', pp.58–80.
49 Cited in Takakura, *Ainu Seisaku Shi*, p.139.
50 'Kyūmei Kōki' (The True Record) [1807], cited in Takakura, 'Ainu of Northern Japan', p.55.
51 Murakami Shimanogyō, 'Ezo Seikei Zusetsu' (Illustrated Life of the Ezo) [1823], in *NS4*, p.603.
52 Keene, *Japanese Discovery of Europe*, pp.128,134.
53 T. Sasaki, 'Inu wa Sosen nari ya' (Perhaps Their Ancestors were Dogs) in Hokkaidō-Tōhoku Kenkyūkai (ed.), *Kita kara no Nihon Shi (2)* (Japanese History from the North, Vol.2) (Tokyo: Sanseidō, 1990), pp.216–222.
54 Y. Kaiho, *Kindai Hoppō Shi: Ainu Minzoku to Josei to* (Modern History of the Northern Regions: The Ainu People and Women) (Tokyo: Sanichi Shobō, 1992), p.193.
55 Matsumiya Kanzan, 'Ezo Dan Hikki' (Narratives of Ezo) [1710], *NS4*, p.394.
56 Mutō Kanzō, 'Ezo Nikki' (Ezo Diary) [1798], *NS4*, p.15.
57 See, for example, Kushiwara Masamine, 'Igen Zokuwa' (Tales of Ezo Customs) [1792], *NS4*, pp.488–489.
58 Mutō, 'Ezo Nikki', *NS4*, p.16.
59 Kushiwara, 'Igen Zokuwa', *NS4*, p.488.
60 See for example Koyama Norinari, 'Ezo Nikki' (Ezo Diary) [1808], *NS4*, p.57. Although Wajin commentators laid great stress on this lack of culture and civilisation among the Ainu, it is actually doubtful whether small and tenant farmers in rural Japan enjoyed a better standard of living under the Tokugawa. See I. Kikuchi, *Hoppō Shi no Naka no Kinsei Nihon* (Early Modern Japan in the History of the Northern Regions) (Tokyo: Azekura Shobō, 1991), p.40.
61 Toby, *State and Diplomacy*, pp.12–22.
62 Honda, 'Secret Plan', in Keene, *Japanese Discovery of Europe*, p.182.
63 For the argument that this was indeed the case, and that such manipulation of 'ethnic' boundaries was vital to Matsumae legitimacy, see Howell, 'Ainu Ethnicity', pp.85–90.
64 Mogami Tokunai, 'Ezo Kuni Fūzoku Ninjō no Sata' (Notes on the Customs and People of the Country of Ezo) [1790], in *NS4*; Keene, *Japanese Discovery of Europe*, p.132.
65 T. Yamamoto, 'Ezo Nōkō Kinshi Kō' (Thoughts on the Banning of Agriculture among the Ezo), *Monbetsu Shiritsu Kyōdo Hakubutsukan Hōkoku*, No.5 (1991).
66 Takakura, 'Ainu of Northern Japan', p.38.
67 Takakura, 'Ainu of Northern Japan', p.43.
68 Kikuchi, *Hoppō Shi no Naka*, pp.48–49; also I. Kikuchi, *Ainu Minzoku to Nihonjin: Higashi Ajia no Naka no Ezochi* (The Ainu and the Japanese: Ezochi in East Asia) (Tokyo: Asahi Shinbunsha, 1994), pp.230–232; Howell, 'Ainu Ethnicity', pp.88–89.

69 This also reflected ancient Chinese usage. For this human–barbarian dichotomy in Chinese images of barbarians see Dikötter, *Discourse of Race*, p.6.
70 See documents cited in Takakura, *Ainu Seisaku Shi*, pp.362, 370.
71 Matsuura Takeshirō, 'Kinsei Ezo Jinbutsu Shi' (Stories of Recent Ezo Personalities) [1860], *NS4*, pp.785, 790.
72 For a detailed overview of the variations of this myth, see Sasaki, 'Inu wa Sosen nari ya'.
73 *NS4*, p.541n; Dikötter, *Discourse of Race*, p.4.
74 Mogami Tokunai, 'Watarishima Hikki' (Notes on Watarishima) [1808], *NS4*, p.523.
75 E. Greey, *The Bear Worshippers of Yezo and the Island of Karafuto (Saghalin), or the Adventures of the Jewett Family and Their Friend Otto Nambo* (Boston: Lee and Shepard, 1884), p.62.
76 Bird, *Unbeaten Tracks*, p.315.
77 Takakura, *Ainu Seisaku Shi*, p.254.
78 Kikuchi, *Hoppō Shi no Naka*, pp.341–342.
79 Cited in Takakura, 'Ainu of Northern Japan', p.41.
80 Cited in Takakura, 'Ainu of Northern Japan', p.42.
81 Takakura, 'Ainu of Northern Japan', p.42.
82 'Ezo Kuni Fūzoku', *NS4*, p.473.
83 Cited in Takakura, *Ainu Seisaku Shi*, p.278.
84 For an insight into the folk beliefs of Tōhoku, see the collection of tales from the Iwate village of Tōno, not far from the Miyako home of the Etorofu *dekasegi* mentioned above, in K. Yanagita (trans. R. Morse), *The Legends of Tōno* (Tokyo: The Japan Foundation, 1975). Interestingly, one term used for mountain men or goblins is *ijin*, which can also be used to refer to outsiders or foreigners (p.30). The same word, usually written with another ideograph standing for 'barbarian', was used in Ezochi to mean Ainu. Whether the use of different ideographs actually denoted different semantic categories that were distinguished by the illiterate *dekasegi* is an interesting subject for further inquiry.
85 Takakura, *Ainu Seisaku Shi*, pp.278–280.
86 Matsuura, 'Kinsei Ezo Jinbutsu Shi', *NS4*, pp.786–787. Takakura has argued that although 'the great majority were counted as Ezo', there were 'many cases' in areas where Wajin were firmly consolidating control where 'mixed-bloods' (*konketsuji*) were able to escape from Ezo status and were employed as overseers. In contrast, in areas where Ainu were still powerful these individuals were despised. See *Ainu Seisaku Shi*, pp.299–300. Unfortunately Takakura, usually meticulous with his sources, cites no evidence whatsoever for either of these views. Historical and ethnological evidence tends to contradict this argument.
87 Kikuchi, *Hoppō Shi no Naka*, p.330.
88 This census (*Komin ninbetsu chō*) is reproduced in Shari-chō Shi Henshū Iinkai (ed.), *Shari-chō Shi* (History of Shari Town) (Shari, Shari-chō, 1955), pp.762–773. Out of 220 individuals, 43 are listed as having a Wajin father.
89 Kubota Shizō, 'Kyōwa Shieki' (Private and Official Diary) [1856], *NS4*, p.261.
90 Takakura, *Ainu Seisaku Shi*, pp.280–281.
91 Matsuura, 'Kinsei Ezo Jinbutsu Shi', *NS4*, p.786.
92 Matsuura, 'Kinsei Ezo Jinbutsu Shi', *NS4*, p.745.
93 Emori, *Ainu no Rekishi*, p.103. While these statistics are not entirely reliable the trend is clear, but probably also includes numbers of Ainu relocated to *basho* in East Ezochi.

94 Takakura, *Ainu Seisaku Shi*, pp.369–370.
95 Matsuura, 'Kinsei Ezo Jinbutsu Shi', *NS4*, p.733.
96 Namikawa, *Kinsei Nihon to Hoppō Shakai*, p.301.
97 Cited in Takakura, *Ainu Seisaku Shi*, p.365n.
98 Matsuura, 'Kinsei Ezo Jinbutsu Shi', *NS4*, p.787.
99 Matsuura Takeshirō (1818–1888) was an inveterate traveller and explorer who made six trips into the interior of Ezochi and Karafuto on official surveying missions for the Bakufu. He spoke Ainu and was usually accompanied by Ainu guides, whose company he preferred to that of the Wajin *dekasegi* of the *basho*. In his journals he is consistently critical of the exploitation and cruelty inflicted on the Ainu. Much of the information that exists on labour practices, the mistreatment of Ainu women, and the plight of those left behind in the villages in the early nineteenth century comes from his writings.
100 Tabata, 'Some Historical Aspects of Ainu–Japanese Relations', pp.33–35.
101 Sakakura Genjirō, 'Hokkai Zuihitsu' (Writings on the North Seas) [1739], *NS4*, p.410.
102 Tabata, 'Historical Aspects of Ainu–Japanese Relations', pp.34–35.
103 H. Kakizaki, *Ishū Retsuzō* (Pictures of Barbarian Chiefs) [1790] (Hakodate: Tosho Rikai [Hakodate Toshokan], 1988).
104 Murakami, 'Ezo Seikei Zusetsu', *NS4*, pp.545–638.
105 H. Wagatsuma and T. Yoneyama, *Henken no Kōzō: Nihonjin no Jinshu Kan* (The Structure of Prejudice: The Japanese Image of Race) (Tokyo: Nihon Hōsō Shuppan Kyōkai, 1967), pp.53–56; Keene, *Japanese Discovery of Europe*, p.170.
106 Bird, *Unbeaten Tracks*, p.233.

3 FORMER NATIVES

1 M. Peattie, 'Japanese Attitudes Towards Colonialism, 1895–1945', in R. Myers and M. Peattie (eds), *The Japanese Colonial Empire, 1895–1945* (Princeton: Princeton University Press, 1984), p.80.
2 B. Attwood, *The Making of the Aborigines* (Sydney: Allen and Unwin, 1989), p.1.
3 Y. Kaiho, *Kindai Hoppō Shi: Ainu Minzoku to Josei to* (Modern History of the Northern Regions: The Ainu People and Women) (Tokyo: Sanichi Shobō, 1992), p.15.
4 M. Gabe, 'Nihon no Kindaika to Okinawa' (Okinawa and the Modernisation of Japan), in Iwanami Kōza, *Kindai Nihon to Shokuminchi 1: Shokuminchi Teikoku Nihon* (Modern Japan and the Colonies 1: Colonial Empire Japan) (Tokyo: Iwanami Shoten, 1992), pp.101–104; S. Tamura, 'Naikoku Shokuminchi to shite no Hokkaidō' (Hokkaidō as an Internal Colony) in the same volume, pp.87–91.
5 Kaiho, *Kindai Hoppō Shi*, pp.42–77.
6 For the 1867 Convention, see J.A. Harrison, *Japan's Northern Frontier* (Gainesville: University of Florida Press, 1953), pp.51, 53 (note 42), 168–169. For Russian views on Japanese treatment of the Ainu, see p.53 (note 42). For Etorofu, see Y. Kosaka, *Ryubō: Nichirō ni Owareta Kita Chishima Ainu* (Exile: Driven out by Japan and Russia – The Northern Kurile Ainu) (Sapporo:

Hokkaidō Shinbunsha, 1992), p.139. Concerning Russian mistreatment of Sakhalin Ainu, see Y. Yamabe and K. Kindaichi, *Ainu Monogatari* (An Ainu Story) (Tokyo: Hakubunkan, 1913), pp.9–10; also J.J. Stephan, *Sakhalin: A History* (Oxford: Clarendon Press, 1971), p.55.

7 M. Kōno (ed.), 'Tai Ainu Seisaku Hōki Ruishū' (Collection of Legislation relating to Ainu Policy), in *Ainu Shi Shiryō Shū: Hōki, Kyōiku Hen* (Collected Materials on Ainu History: Laws and Education), Series 1, Vol. 2, (Sapporo: Hokkaidō Shuppan Kikaku Sentā, 1981), pp.31–32. Hereafter cited as *ASH*.

8 Harrison, *Japan's Northern Frontier*, pp.39–56; Stephan, *Sakhalin*, pp.59–64; M. Ogawa, 'Kotan e no Gyōkō/Gyōkei to Ainu Kyōiku' (Royal Visits to Ainu Communities and Ainu Education), *Kyōiku Shi Gakkai Kiyō*, No.34 (October 1991), p.53.

9 Harrison, *Japan's Northern Frontier*, p.116.

10 Tamura, 'Naikoku Shokuminchi', pp.92–94.

11 Kaitakushi proclamation of November 1869. Reproduced in M. Kōno (ed.), 'Ainu Sōshi: 5' (Collected Documents Relating to the Ainu: 5), *Ainu Shi Shiryō Shū: Abe Masami Bunkō Hen 3* (Collected Materials on Ainu History, Archives of Abe Masami 3) Series 2, Vol.6 (Sapporo: Hokkaidō Shuppan Kikaku Sentā, 1985), p.23.

12 *ASH*, p.37.

13 Hokkaidō-chō (Hokkaidō Shi Henshūsho ed.), *Shin Hokkaidō Shi* (New History of Hokkaidō) (Sapporo: Hokkaidō-chō, 9 Vols, 1969–1981), Vol.9 (Statistics), pp.880, 809.

14 Harrison, *Japan's Northern Frontier*, p.99.

15 The best survey of immigration and development is contained in *Shin Hokkaidō Shi*. For *kaitakuron* see Vol.4, pp.45–52; for later immigration and land policy see pp.229–285 in the same volume. See also S. Emori, *Ainu no Rekishi: Hokkaidō no Hitobito(2)* (A History of the Ainu: the People of Hokkaidō [2]) (Tokyo: Sanseidō, 1987), pp.108–128; and Y. Baba, 'A Study of Minority–Majority Relations: The Ainu and Japanese in Hokkaidō', *Japan Interpreter*, Vol.13, No.1 (1980), pp.65–66; F.C. Jones, *Hokkaido: Its Present State of Development and Future Prospects* (London: Oxford University Press, 1958), pp.10–23.

16 M. Ogawa, 'Ainu Gakkō no Settchi to Hokkaidō Kyūdojin Hogohō – Kyūdojin Jidō Kyōiku Kitei no Seiritsu' (The Establishment of Ainu Schools and the Hokkaidō Former Natives Protection Act – Regulations for the Education of Former Native Children), *Hokkaidō Daigaku Kyōikugakubu Kiyō*, No.55 (1991), p.294.

17 Emori, *Ainu no Rekishi*, p.117.

18 Emori, *Ainu no Rekishi*, p.118.

19 *Shin Hokkaidō Shi*, Vol.9, p.792.

20 *Shin Hokkaidō Shi*, Vol.9, p.809.

21 Hokkaidō (ed.), *Shin Hokkaidō Shi Nenpyō* (The New Chronology of Hokkaidō History) (Sapporo: Hokkaidō Shuppan Kikaku Sentā, 1989), p.434. The 1919 immigration figures are on p.430. For details of group immigration, areas of origin and new places of settlement, see the entries for respective years. Natural population increase is noted by Jones, *Hokkaido*, p.22.

22 Table adapted from Emori, *Ainu no Rekishi*, p.126. For more detailed statistics, see *Shin Hokkaidō Shi*, Vol.9, pp.764–766 for Wajin, 768–770 for Ainu.

23 For convicts in the mines, see M. Kuwabara, *Kaitaku no Kage ni: Hokkaidō no Hitobito (1)* (In the Shadow of Development: The People of Hokkaidō [1]) (Tokyo: Sanseidō, 1987), pp.184–191.

24 For Hokkaidō as a colonial economy, see Y. Komatsu, 'Gendankai no Henkyō/Naishoku Shokuminchi Ron ni tsuite no Kōsatsu (Ge): Hokkaidō Keizai Shi/Keizai Ron ni Kanren shite' (Considerations on the Present Stage of the Debate on Frontier Lands/Internal Colonies (3): Concerning the Economic History and Theory of Hokkaidō), *Ohotsuku Sangyō Keiei Ronshū*, Vol.3, No.1 (1992), especially pp.67–73.

25 Kaiho, *Kindai Hoppō Shi*, p.316.

26 Kaiho, *Kindai Hoppō Shi*, p.303.

27 K. Pyle, *The New Generation in Meiji Japan: Problems of Cultural Identity, 1885–1895* (Stanford: Stanford University Press, 1969), p.57. It should also be noted that the College produced other famous graduates, like Shiga Shigetaka, who were decidedly non-Christian.

28 I. Bird, *Unbeaten Tracks in Japan: An Account of Travels in the Interior Including Visits to the Aborigines of Yezo and the Shrine of Nikko* (Rutland, Vt. and Tokyo: Tuttle, 1973), p.217.

29 Bird, *Unbeaten Tracks*, p.232.

30 J. Bachira (J. Batchelor), 'Nihon Zaijū Rokujūninen no Kansō' (Findings After 62 Years in Japan), *Hokkaidō Shakai Jigyō*, No.80 (Jan. 1939), p.32. I have corrected the spelling and misprints in the original.

31 Harrison, *Japan's Northern Frontier*, p.67.

32 Kaitakushi proclamation, 8 October 1871. *ASH*, p.49.

33 Cited in Hokkaidō-chō, *Hokkaidō Kyūdojin Hogo Enkaku Shi* (History of the Protection of the Former Natives of Hokkaidō), (Sapporo, Hokkaidō-chō, 1934), p.243.

34 Kōno, 'Ainu Sōshi: 5', p.75.

35 *ASH*, p.33. See also the Shari *ninbetsuchō* of 1877 mentioned in the previous chapter (see p.45, n.88).

36 Kaitakushi Regulation No.22, 4 November 1878. *ASH*, pp.49–50.

37 S. Takakura, *Ainu Seisaku Shi: Shinpan* (A History of Ainu Policy: New Edition) (Tokyo: Sanichi Shobō, 1972), pp.408–409.

38 Cited in Takakura, *Ainu Seisaku Shi*, p.471.

39 *Hokkai Shinbun*, 25 March 1887; H. Murakami, *Ainu Jitsuwa Shū* (Collection of True Ainu Stories) (Asahikawa: Asahikawa Shiritsu Kyōdo Hakubutsukan, 1964), pp.45–46.

40 Takakura, *Ainu Seisaku Shi*, p.393.

41 Emori, *Ainu no Rekishi*, p.111.

42 Cited in Kaiho, *Kindai Hoppō Shi*, p.100.

43 For a full account of the Tsuishikari Ainu, see Karafuto Ainu Shi Kenkyūkai (ed.), *Tsuishikari no Ishibumi* (The Tsuishikari Monument) (Sapporo: Hokkaidō Shuppan Kikaku Sentā, 1992). For a briefer treatment, see Takakura, *Ainu Seisaku Shi*, pp.418–440 (the remark on women and children is cited on p.427); Kaiho, *Kindai Hoppō Shi*, pp.100–105.

44 Nemuro Prefecture to Naimushō and Nōshōshō, 21 November 1882. Cited in Takakura, *Ainu Seisaku Shi*, p.444.

45 Kaiho, *Kindai Hoppō Shi*, pp.105–110.

46 Bird, *Unbeaten Tracks*, p.223.

47 'Kushiro Dojin Iten no Riyū' (Reasons for Relocating the Kushiro Natives),

reproduced in Kushiro-shi, *Shin Kushiro-shi Shi* (New History of Kushiro City) (Kushiro: Kushiro-shi, 1974), pp.600–602.

48 J. Batchelor, *The Ainu and Their Folklore* (London: The Religious Tract Society, 1901), p.170. For agriculture, see p.177.

49 A.H.S. Landor, *Alone With the Hairy Ainu. Or, 3800 Miles on a Pack Saddle in Yezo and a Cruise to the Kurile Islands* (London: John Murray, 1893), p.101.

50 Karafuto Ainu Shi Kenkyūkai, *Tsuishikari no Ishibumi*, pp.276–277. For general overview see Emori, *Ainu no Rekishi*, pp.112–114; for Niikappu see Y. Yamamoto, *Hidaka-kuni Niikappu Goryō Bokujō Shi* (History of the Niikappu Imperial Ranch) (Tokyo: Miyama Shobō, 1985), pp.271, 273; for Shintotsugawa, Takikawa-shi Shi Hensan Iinkai (ed.) *Takikawa-shi Shi* (History of Takikawa City) Vol.1 (Takikawa: Takikawa-shi, 1981), p.106.

51 Teshikaga-chō Shi Hensan Iinkai (ed.), *Teshikaga-chō Shi* (History of Teshikaga Town) (Teshikaga: Teshikaga-chō, 1981), p.151.

52 Hokkaidō, *Shin Hokkaidō Shi Nenpyō*, p.191.

53 Bird, *Unbeaten Tracks*, p.219.

54 See, for instance, *Hokkai Taimuzu*, 15 October and 4 December 1909. In Biratori, a large Ainu village in the Hidaka region, there were three suicides between 1892 and 1905, but this rose to twelve between 1906 and 1916. M. Tomikawa, 'Ainu Minzoku no Jisatsu ni tsuite' (On Suicide Among the Ainu), *Hokudai Kaibō Kenkyū Hōkoku*, No.126 (1959), p.26–27.

55 Batchelor, *The Ainu and Their Folklore*, p.168.

56 B. Ohlson (ed.), *Ainu Material Culture from the Notes of N.G. Munro in the Archive of the Royal Anthropological Institute*, British Museum Occasional Paper No.96 (London: British Museum, 1994), p.43.

57 Hokkaidō Shinbunsha (ed.), *Hokkaidō Shinbun Yonjūnen Shi* (A Forty Year History of the Hokkaidō Shinbun Newspaper) (Sapporo: Hokkaidō Shinbunsha, 1983), pp.21–44.

58 Takakura, *Ainu Seisaku Shi*, pp.538–539.

59 J. Batchelor, 'Steps by the Way' (unpublished MS), p.120. I am indebted to Sir Hugh Cortazzi for a copy of this manuscript, dictated by Batchelor to his late wife's niece during his final years in Sapporo.

60 I. Nitami, *Ikyō no Shito: Eijin Jon Bachira Den* (The Foreign Apostle: A Biography of the Englishman John Batchelor) (Sapporo: Hokkaidō Shinbunsha, 1991), pp.50–51.

61 This discussion on the Protection Act draws on T. Tomita, 'Hokkaidō Kyūdojin Hogohō to Dōzu Hō: Jon Bachira, Shirani Takeshi, Parapita, Sanrottee' (The Hokkaidō Former Natives Protection Act and the Dawes Act: John Batchelor, Shirani Takeshi, Parapita and Sanrottee), *Jinbungakkai Kiyō*, No.48 (December 1990); and T. Tomita, 'Hokkaidō Kyūdojin Hogohō to Dōzu Hō: Hikakushiteki Kenkyū no Kokoromi' (The Hokkaido Former Natives Protection Act and the Dawes Act: An Attempt at a Comparative Historical Study), *Jinbungakkai Kiyō*, No.45 (August 1989).

62 *ASH*, pp.118–119. For full text, see Appendix 1.

63 For Meiji policies see T. Fujitani, 'Inventing, Forgetting, Remembering: Toward a Historical Ethnography of the Nation-State', in H. Befu (ed.), *Cultural Nationalism in East Asia: Representation and Identity* (Berkeley: Institute of East Asian Studies, University of California, 1993), p.99.

64 See Hokkaidō-chō, *Hokkaidō Kyūdojin Hogo Enkaku Shi*, pp.328–339. The statistics given here show that Ainu actually lived within the limits of 226

administrative hamlets (*buraku*) and one city (Muroran), although 118 of these had five or less Ainu households.

65 Emori, *Ainu no Rekishi*, p.142.

66 Hokkaidō Utari Kyōkai (ed.), *Ainu Minzoku no Jiritsu e no Michi* (The Road to Ainu Autonomy) (Sapporo: Hokkaidō Utari Kyōkai, 1991), p.28.

67 Hokkaidō (ed.), *Hokkaidō Nōchi Kaikaku Shi: Gekan* (History of Land Reform in Hokkaidō) Vol.2 (Sapporo: Hokkaidō-chō, 1957), p.235.

68 Hokkaido-chō, *Kyūdojin ni Kansuru Chōsa* (Survey of the Former Natives) (Sapporo, Hokkaidō-chō, 1922), pp.138–139.

69 M. Ogawa, 'The Hokkaidō Former Aborigines Protection Act and Assimilatory Education', in N. Loos and T. Osanai, *Indigenous Minorities and Education: Australian and Japanese Perspectives of their Indigenous Peoples, the Ainu, Aborigines and Torres Straits Islanders* (Tokyo: Sanyūsha, 1993), p.246.

70 Hokkaidō-chō, *Kyūdojin ni Kansuru Chōsa*, pp.105–106.

71 Ogawa, 'Protection Act and Assimilatory Education', pp.237–249. For the role of the teacher in the Ainu community, see M. Ogawa, 'Hokkaidō Kyūdojin Hogohō, Kyūdojin Jidō Kyōiku Kitei no shita no Ainu Gakkō' (Ainu Schools under the Hokkaidō Former Natives Protection Act and the Regulations for the Education of Former Native Children), *Hokkaidō Daigaku Kyōikugakubu Kiyō*, No.58 (1992), pp.242–252.

72 Hokkaidō-chō, *Kyūdojin ni Kansuru Chōsa*, p.119.

73 Hokkaidō-chō, *Kyūdojin ni Kansuru Chōsa*, pp.117–118.

74 Takakura, *Ainu Seisaku Shi*, p.520.

75 Hokkaidō-chō, *Hokkaidō Kyūdojin Gaikyō* (General Conditions of the Hokkaidō Former Natives) (Sapporo: Hokkaidō-chō, 1926), p.129.

76 Hokkaidō, *Nōchi Kaikaku Shi*, Vol.2, pp.235–236.

77 Emori, *Ainu no Rekishi*, pp.169–172; for an example of the personal enquiries made by Commissioners see *ASH*, p.267. For community organisations, see Kaiho, *Kindai Hoppō Shi*, pp.142–150; Ogawa, 'Protection Act and Assimilatory Education', pp.243–244; also Ogawa, 'Kyūdojin Hogohō no shita no Ainu Gakkō', pp.246–248.

78 Stephan, *Sakhalin*, pp.90, 111.

79 Stephan, *Sakhalin*, pp.86–90, 111–118, 131–141.

80 Ainu policy in Karafuto is briefly covered in Karafuto Ainu Shi Kenkyūkai, *Tsuishikari no Ishibumi*, pp.274–288. For Ainu and other indigenous population statistics, see *Karafuto Dojin Chōsa Sho* (Survey of Karafuto Natives) (Toyohara: Karafuto-chō 1931), and *Ainu Gai Dojin Chōsa* (Survey of non-Ainu Natives) (Toyohara: Karafuto-chō, 1933) which also mentions Otasu. For Otasu see also R. Tanaka and D. Gendānu, *Gendānu: Aru Hoppō Shōsu Minzoku no Dorama* (Gendānu: The Drama of a Northern Minority People) (Tokyo: Gendaishi Shuppankai, 1978), pp.30–44; Hokkaidō Rekishi Kyōikusha Kyōgikai (ed.), *Ainu, Orokko no Mondai to Kyōiku* (Ainu, Orok Issues and Education) (Sapporo: Hokkaidō Minkan Kyōiku Kenkyū Dantai Renraku Kyōgikai, 1976), pp.95–97.

4 THE DYING RACE

1 For the development of Ainu Studies, see S. Takakura, *Ainu Seisaku Shi: Shinpan* (A History of Ainu Policy: New Edition) (Tokyo: S. Sanichi Shobō,

1972), pp.534–540; Ainu Bunka Hozon Taisaku Kyōgikai (ed.), *Ainu Minzoku Shi* (Ainu Ethnology) (Tokyo: Daiichihōki Shuppan, 1970), pp.26–62; H. Fujimoto, *Ainugaku e no Ayumi* (Steps towards Ainu Studies) (Sapporo: Hokkaidō Shuppan Kikaku Sentā, 1983).

2 *Kaitaku Nisshi* (Daily Records of the Kaitakushi), No.24, 1874. Reproduced in Hokkaidō-chō, *Shin Hokkaidō Shi* (New History of Hokkaidō) (Sapporo: Hokkaidō-chō, 1969–1981), Vol.7. Lyman's arguments appear on pp.952–955.

3 Albert Bickmore, writing in 1868. Cited in J. Kreiner, 'European Images of the Ainu and Ainu Studies in Europe', in J. Kreiner (ed.), *European Studies on Ainu Language and Culture*, German Institute for Japanese Studies Monograph No.6 (Munchen: Iudicium Verlag, 1993), pp.33–34.

4 R. Hitchcock, 'The Ainos of Yezo, Japan', in *Annual Report of the Board of Regents of the Smithsonian Institution, Showing the Operations, Expenditures and Condition of the Institution for the Year Ending June 30 1890. Report of the U.S. National Museum* (Washington: Smithsonian, 1891), pp.433, 442, 443; I. Bird, *Unbeaten Tracks in Japan: An Account of Travels in the Interior Including Visits to the Aborigines of Yezo and the Shrine of Nikko* (Rutland, Vt. and Tokyo: Tuttle, 1973), pp.231, 274, 280, 307 (to be fair to Isabella, she later changed her mind about Ainu physical extinction when she observed the robust health still enjoyed in some inland communities at that time); A.H.S. Landor, *Alone with the Hairy Ainu. Or, 3800 Miles on a Pack Saddle in Yezo and a Cruise to the Kurile Islands* (London: John Murray, 1893), pp.268, 269, 271, 274, 295–296; B.H. Chamberlain, *The Language, Mythology, and Geographical Nomenclature of Japan, Viewed in the Light of Aino Studies* (Tokyo: Tokyo Imperial University, 1887), pp.43, 74–75; E. Morse, *Japan Day by Day* (Boston and New York: Houghton Mifflin Co., 1917), Vol.2, pp.1, 26.

5 Landor, *Alone with the Hairy Ainu*, p.280.

6 Bird, *Unbeaten Tracks*, p.255.

7 Bird, *Unbeaten Tracks*, p.254.

8 Hitchcock, 'Ainos of Yezo', pp.442–443.

9 For Morse and the Tokyo Anthropological Society, see Fujimoto, *Ainugaku e no Ayumi*, pp.31–40. Chamberlain's life and work in Japan is covered in R. Bowring, 'An Amused Guest In All: Basil Hall Chamberlain (1850–1935)', in Sir H. Cortazzi and G. Daniels (eds), *Britain and Japan 1859–1991: Themes and Personalities* (London and New York: Routledge, 1991), pp.128–136.

10 S. Tanaka, *Japan's Orient: Rendering Pasts into History* (Berkeley and Los Angeles: California University Press, 1993), pp.70–86.

11 *Hokkaidō Mainichi Shinbun*, 20 February, 1897. For theories of 'racial' origins in the Tokugawa and later periods, see C.T. Hayashida, 'Identity, Race and the Blood Ideology of Japan' (Ph.D. dissertation, University of Washington, Seattle, 1976), pp.19–29; also Kreiner, 'European Images of the Ainu'. The *koropokkuru* debate is discussed in Fujimoto, *Ainugaku e no Ayumi*.

12 Ainu Bunka Hozon Taisaku Kyōgikai, *Ainu Minzoku Shi*, p.31; Takakura, *Ainu Seisaku Shi*, p.538; Tanaka, *Japan's Orient*, pp.70–77.

13 K. Pyle, *The New Generation in Meiji Japan: Problems of Cultural Identity, 1885–1895* (Stanford University Press, 1969), p.152.

14 Tanaka, *Japan's Orient*, p.77.

15 I. Nitobe, *The Japanese Nation: Its Land, Its People, Its Life; With Special Consideration to Its Relations with the United States* (New York and London: G. Putnam's Sons, 1912), pp.86–87, 248–253.

16 J.E. Hoare, 'Mr. Enslie's Grievances: The Consul, the Ainu and the Bones', *Japan Society of London Bulletin*, No.78, pp.14–19.
17 Y. Koganei, 'Ainu no Jinshugakuteki Chōsa no Omoide' (Recollections of Ethnographical Investigations of the Ainu), *Dolmen*, Vol.4, No.7 (1935), pp.54–65.
18 Takakura, *Ainu Seisaku Shi*, p.538.
19 J. Batchelor, *The Ainu and Their Folklore* (London: The Religious Tract Society, 1901), p.7.
20 Other scholars also believed this to be the origins of *Aino*. However, the confusion probably stems from the fact that the vowel in question in the Ainu language was intermediate between Japanese *o* and *u* and was thus frequently mistaken by outsiders. S. Kodama, *Ainu: Historical and Anthropological Studies* (Sapporo: Hokkaidō University School of Medicine, 1970), pp.13–33. For Batchelor's opposition, see *Hokkai Taimuzu*, 25 October 1919; also J. Patric, *Why Japan was Strong: A Journey of Adventure* (London: Methuen, 1944), p.169. Ultimately Batchelor's efforts were in vain, since the similarity between the words *Ainu* and *inu* (dog) has caused torment for untold numbers of Ainu children to the present day.
21 Hokkaidō Kyōiku Kenkyūsho (ed.), *Hokkaidō Kyōiku Shi* (History of Education in Hokkaidō) (Sapporo: Hokkaidō Kyōiku Shi Hakkankai, 1963), p.234.
22 S. Tsuboi, 'Hokkaidō Kyūdojin Kyūiku Jigyō' (Welfare Projects for the Former Natives of Hokkaidō), *Tokyo Jinruigakkai Zasshi*, No.245 (August 1906), pp.431–434.
23 S. Kodama, 'Kinkyū o Yōshita Ainu Kenkyū' (Ainu Studies Required Urgency), *Hokkaidō no Bunka*, No.21 (March 1971), p.7.
24 Cited in M. Kaiho, *Shiryō to Kataru Hokkaidō no Rekishi* (The History of Hokkaidō as Related by Historical Records) (Sapporo: Hokkaidō Shuppan Kikaku Sentā, 1985), p.13.
25 Kodama, 'Kinkyū o Yōshita', p.9.
26 M.R. Peattie, *Nan'yō: The Rise and Fall of the Japanese in Micronesia, 1885–1945* (Honolulu: University of Hawaii Press, 1988), p.89.
27 T. Yamakawa, *Kono Ningen no Jidai* (These Human Times) (Tokyo: Renga Shobō Shinsha, 1991), pp.110–112; Tanaka, *Japan's Orient*, pp.239–262.
28 For a discussion of the work of these two scholars, see Hayashida, 'Blood Ideology of Japan', 144–159. Quote is cited on p.153. I have altered Hayashida's translation of *minzoku* to read 'race' rather than 'ethnic group' in line with the general argument.
29 T. Furukawa, 'Ketsuekigata yori Mita Taiwan Banjin to Hokkaidō Ainujin no Minzokusei' (The Racial Character of Taiwanese Aborigines and Hokkaidō Ainu Viewed through Blood Type), *Hanzaigaku Zasshi*, Vol.4, No.2 (March 1931), pp.130–136.
30 T. Ishibashi, F. Oka and T. Wada, 'Ainu no Seikaku: Seishōnen ni okeru Chōsa ni mototsuite' (Ainu Character Based on a Survey of Young People), *Minzoku Eisei*, Vol.12, No.6 (November 1944), p.352.
31 Kodama, *Ainu*, p.82.
32 J. Kanazeki, 'Ainu no Wakiga' (Ainu Body Odour), *Seirigaku Kenkyū*, Vol.11. No.8 (1934), pp.542–546.
33 Y. Kubo, 'Karafuto ni okeru Ainu Jidō to Nihon Jidō tono Hikkaku' (A Comparison Of Japanese and Ainu Children in Karafuto), *Jidō Kenkyūsho Kiyō*, Vol.9 (1926), pp.415–417.

34 T. Ishibashi *et al.*, 'Ainu Jidō no Chinō Chōsa: Chinō no Jinshuteki Sai oyobi Chinō ni oyobasu Konketsu no Eikyō ni kansuru – Chiken' (Survey of Intelligence among Ainu Children: Racial Difference in Intelligence and the Influence of Mixed Blood on Intelligence – an Opinion), *Minzoku Eisei*, Vol.10, No.4 (August 1942), pp.288–294.
35 Y. Yamabe and K. Kindaichi, *Ainu Monogatari* (An Ainu Story) (Tokyo: Hakubunkan, 1913), pp.26–28.
36 First Reading of Hokkaidō Natives Protection Act, House of Representatives, 29 November 1893. *Teikoku Gikai Gijiroku* (Transcripts of Imperial Diet Proceedings), in Hokkaidō Utari Kyōkai Ainu Shi Henshū Iinkai (ed.), *Ainushi Shiryō Hen 3: Kingendai Shiryō 1* (Collected Materials on Ainu History 3: Modern and Contemporary Materials 1) (Sapporo: Hokkaidō Utari Kyōkai, 1990), pp.32–33. Hereafter cited as *ASS3*.
37 *ASS3*, pp.32, 44, 47.
38 First reading of the Hokkaidō Former Natives Protection Act, House of Representatives, 6 December 1898, *ASS3*, p.76.
39 House of Representatives, 18 January 1899, *ASS3*, p.78. For the statements of Shirani Takeshi, see House of Representatives, 21 January 1899, *ASS3*, pp.91, 93, 99.
40 'Hokkaidō Kyūdojin Hogohō Shikō Saisoku' (By-laws for the Implementation of the Hokkaidō Former Natives Protection Act), Hokkaidō Government Ordinance 51, 13 June 1899, *ASH*, p.230.
41 Cited in M. Ogawa, 'The Hokkaidō Former Aborigines Protection Act and Assimilatory Education', in N. Loos and T. Osanai (eds), *Indigenous Minorities and Education: Australian and Japanese Perspectives of their Indigenous Peoples, the Ainu, Aborigines and Torres Straits Islanders* (Tokyo: Sanyūsha, 1993), p.239.
42 23rd Imperial Diet, Special Committee on the Laws for Karafuto, House of Peers, 23 March 1907, *ASS3*, pp.189–190.
43 Cited in Takakura, *Ainu Seisaku Shi*, pp.524–525.
44 E. Iwaya and N. Hōsei, 'Ainu Kyōiku no Hōhō' (Ways for Ainu Education), *Hokkaidō Kyōiku Zasshi*, No.9 (July 1893). Cited in M. Ogawa, 'Ainu Gakkō no Settchi to Hokkaidō Kyūdojin Hogohō – Kyūdojin Jidō Kyōiku Kitei no Seiritsu' (The Establishment of Ainu Schools and the Hokkaidō Former Natives Protection Act – Regulations for the Education of Former Native Children), *Hokkaidō Daigaku Kyōikugakubu Kiyō*, No.55 (1991), p.299.
45 E. Iwaya, 'Ainu no Genshō' (The Decrease in Ainu Numbers), *Hokkaidō Kyōiku Zasshi*, No.6 (1891), p.11. For a discussion of the career of Iwaya, see Y. Takegahara, 'Kindai Nihon no Ainu Kyōiku: Dōka Kyōiku no Shisō to Jissen' (Ainu Education in Early Modern Japan: The Theory and Practice of Assimilationist Education), in M. Kuwabara (ed.), *Hokkaidō no Kenkyū: Dai Rokkan* (Studies on Hokkaidō, Vol.6) (Osaka: Seibundō Shuppan, 1983), pp.463–470.
46 E. Iwaya, 'Hokubei Dojin Hogohō o Ronjite Ainu Jinshu Hogohō ni oyobu (2)' (On the Protection Act for the North American Natives With Reference to the Protection Act for the Ainu Race, Part 2), *Hokkaidō Kyōiku Zasshi*, No.88 (May 1901), pp.1–3.
47 E. Iwaya, 'Kyūdojin Kyōikudan' (On Ainu Education), *Hokkaidō Kyōiku Zasshi*, No.123 (April 1903), pp.34–37; and *Hokkaidō Kyōiku Zasshi*, No.125 (June 1903), pp.29–33.

48 S. Hiraoka, 'Ainu Jinshu Shobun Ron', (On the Disposal of the Ainu Race), appendix in T. Aoyama, *Kyokuhoku no Bettenchi* (The Different World of the Extreme North) (Tokyo: Nippon Seinen Tsushinsha, 1918), pp.1–17.

49 Hiraoka, 'Ainu Jinshu Shobun Ron', pp.4–6.

50 S. Emori, *Ainu no Rekishi: Hokkaidō no Hitobito (2)* (A History of the Ainu: the People of Hokkaidō [2]) (Tokyo: Sanseidō, 1987), pp.165–166.

51 Hokkaidō-chō, *Kyūdojin ni Kansuru Chōsa* (Survey of the Former Natives) (Sapporo: Hokkaidō-chō, 1922), p.115.

52 'Hokkaidō Kyūdojin Hogohō Kaisei ni Kansuru Hokkaidō-chō Shiryō' (Hokkaidō Government Materials Relating to the Revision of the Hokkaidō Former Natives Protection Act), 1937, *ASH*, p.297.

53 'Gojokumiai Setsuritsu ni Kansuru Ken' (Concerning the Establishment of Cooperatives), Hokkaidō Government Instruction No.65, 1924. In *ASH*, p.275.

54 M. Ogawa, 'Kotan e no Gyōkō/Gyōkei to Ainu Kyōiku' (Royal Visits to Ainu Communities and Ainu Education), *Kyōiku Shi Gakkai Kiyō*, No.34 (October 1991).

55 See for example, the poems and essays of the pupils of the Nisshin Elementary School composed in honour of the visit of Prince Chichibu in 1928. I. Yoshida, *Kokoro no Ishibumi* (Monument of the Spirit) (Tokyo: Hokkai Shuppan, 1935), in Kōno, Series 2, Vol.1, pp.239–245. For similar poems in honour of the future Emperor Taishō during his visit in 1911, see the magazine *Ryōyū*, No.17 (November 1911), reprinted in K. Tanikawa (ed.), *Kindai Minshū no Kiroku (5) – Ainu* (Records of the Masses in the Modern Period, Vol.5: The Ainu) (Tokyo: Shinjinbutsu Ōraisha, 1972), pp.129–142. This collection is cited hereafter as *KMK5*.

56 *Hokkaidō Kyōiku Shi*, p.290.

57 Cited in Ogawa, 'Protection Act and Assimilatory Education', p.242.

58 M. Ogawa, 'Hokkaidō Kyūdojin Hogohō, Kyūdojin Jidō Kyōiku Kitei no shita no Ainu Gakkō', (Ainu Schools under the Hokkaidō Former Natives Protection Act and the Regulations for the Education of Former Native Children), *Hokkaidō Daigaku Kyōikugakubu Kiyō*, No.58 (1992), pp.230–232.

59 T. Nishida, 'Kakusei o Nozomu' (Wishing for Awakening), *Ezo no Hikari*, No.2 (March 1931), p.21.

60 Nishida, 'Kakusei o Nozomu', p.19.

61 Kita Kōyō (M. Kita), 'Dojin Hogo no Enkaku to Hogohō no Seishin' (A History of Native Welfare and the Spirit of the Protection Act), *Hokkaidō Shakai Jigyō*, No.15 (July 1933), p.27.

62 Kita, 'Dojin Hogo no Enkaku', p.28.

63 M. Kita, 'Ainu yo Izuko e Iku (1)' (Ainu, Where are you Going? Part 1), *Hokkaidō Shakai Jigyō*, No.63 (August 1937), pp.43–44.

64 S. Okabe, 'Kyūdojin Zakki (2): Jinkō Ron to Iseki Hozon' (Notes on the Former Natives No.2: Population and Preservation of Relics), *Hokkaidō Shakai Jigyō*, No.60 (May 1937), p.50. Interestingly, there was at this time a mini-boom in writings on the Ainu in Nazi Germany, stimulated by a pro-Japanese attempt in 1934 to link the Japanese people to these 'northern Aryans' – see Kreiner, 'European Images of the Ainu', p.50.

65 K. Sonoda, 'Kyūdojin Seikatsu Zakken' (A Look at Ainu Life), *Hokkaidō Shakai Jigyō*, No.75 (August 1938), pp.24–27.

66 70th Imperial Diet, House of Representatives, 23 February 1937, *ASS3*, p.442.

67 70th Imperial Diet, Special Committee on Interim Revision of Military Relief Law, House of Representatives, 26 February 1937, *ASS3*, pp.456, 458, 473.

68 For example, see articles in *Hakodate Shinbun*, 3 September 1886; *Hokkaidō Mainichi*, 31 July 1891, 25 October 1892, 14 February 1895, 26 July 1899; *Kokumin Shinbun*, 27 January 1895; *Karafuto Nichi Nichi Shinbun*, 24 September 1910; *Otaru Shinbun*, 9 October 1905, also twelve-part series on 'Kyūdojin Mondai' (The Former Native Problem) in July 1905.

69 'Dojin no Ko' (Native Children), *Hokkaidō Mainichi*, 10 June 1897.

70 This ignored the fact that Hokkaidō Ainu men and women in traditional society had expended much effort at certain times of year gathering and processing certain plants, and catching and preserving salmon and deer meat to sustain the family unit through winter. The best source on Ainu subsistence activity in English remains H. Watanabe, *The Ainu Ecosystem* (Seattle and London: University of Washington Press, 1973). For a recent and accessible work in Japanese based on fieldwork among Ainu elders, see M. Haginaka *et al.*, *Kikigaki: Ainu no Shokuji* (Field Notes: Ainu Food), Nihon Shokuseikatsu Zenshū No.48 (Tokyo: Nōsangyōson Bunka Kyōkai, 1992).

71 'Tokachi no Dojin' (The Tokachi Natives), *Hokkai Taimuzu*, 12 March 1910.

72 For example, see 'Chishima Shikotan no Dojin' (The Natives of Shikotan) *Hokkai Taimuzu*, 19 June 1923; 'Horobitsutsu aru Shikotan Dojin no Konshaku' (The Past and Present of the Dying Shikotan Natives), *Hokkai Taimuzu*, 18 March 1930.

73 'Kyūdojin Jōtai' (The Situation of the Former Natives), *Hokkai Taimuzu*, 18 March 1918.

74 H. Iwano, 'Ryōchū Inshō Zakki' (Record of Impressions During my Journey), No. 14, *Hokkai Taimuzu*, 30 October 1909.

75 G. Fujinami, 'Ainu no Buraku o Otozureru' (Visits to an Ainu Village), March 1919. Articles reproduced in Kōno, 'Ainu Kankei Shinbun Kiji' (Newspaper Articles on the Ainu), in *Ainu Shi Shiryō Shū: Kōno Tsunekichi Shiryō Shū 1* (Collected Materials on Ainu History: Collected Materials of Kōno Tsunekichi 1), Series 2, Volume 7, (Sapporo: Hokkaidō Shuppan Kikaku Sentā, 1984), pp.166–172.

76 'Konketsu Ainu ga Shimesu Nihonjin Chi no Yūshūsei' (Mixed Blood Ainu Display the Superiority of Japanese Blood), *Hokkai Taimuzu*, 7 September 1939.

77 For Chiri, see 'Chōkan to Chiri-kun' (The Governor and Mr Chiri), *Hokkai Taimuzu*, 6 March 1937. Kindaichi's remarks on the 'dying race' are cited in H. Fujimoto, *Kindaichi Kyōsuke* (Tokyō: Shinchōsha, 1991), p.30.

78 K. Satō, *Hokkaidō Bungaku Shikō* (History of Hokkaidō Literature) (Sapporo: Nire Shobō, 1956), pp.148–163; K. Hayakawa, 'Bungaku ni Egakareta Ainu Minzoku' (The Ainu People in Literature), *Kyōdo Kenkyū*, No.8 (April 1969), pp.29–33. *Ainu no Gakkō, Kaze ni Notte kuru Koroppokuru* and *Koshamain Ki* can be found in S. Inoue *et al.* (eds), *Hokkaido Bungaku Zenshū Dai Jūikkan: Ainu Minzoku no Tamashii* (Collected Hokkaidō Literature, Vol.11: The Soul of the Ainu People) (Tokyo: Tachikaze Shobō, 1970).

79 Okabe, 'Kyūdojin Zakki', p.48.

80 S. Yoshimi, *Hakurankai no Seijigaku: Manazashi no Kindai* (The Politics of Expositions: Modernity on Show) (Tokyo: Chūkō Shinsho, 1992), pp.108–144. For Japanese participation in international, in particular American, expositions, see N. Harris, 'All the World a Melting Pot? Japan at American Fairs, 1876–1904', in A. Iriye (ed.), *Mutual Images: Essays in American–Japanese Relations* (Cambridge, Mass. and London: Harvard University Press, 1975), pp.24–54.

81 Y. Kaiho, *Kindai Hoppō Shi: Ainu Minzoku to Josei to* (Modern History of the Northern Regions: The Ainu People and Women) (Tokyo: Sanichi Shobō, (1992), pp.157–162; 'Jinruikan to Ainu' (The Hall of Mankind and the Ainu), *Hokkai Taimuzu*, 15 April 1903. It has to be admitted, however, that some Ainu benefited from participation in expositions; Batchelor recounts how one Ainu woman made 700 yen from the sale of handicrafts at St Louis, money that she used to build a Japanese-style house. J. Batchelor, 'Steps by the Way', p.148.

82 Meiji Kinenkai (ed.), *Takushoku Hakurankai Kinen Shashin Chō* (Commemorative Photographs of the Colonial Exposition) (Tokyo: Meiji Kinenkai, 1912). The quote is from one of the captions.

83 Yoshimi, *Hakurankai no Seijigaku*, p.127.

84 P. Bigelow, *Japan and Her Colonies* (London: Edward Arnold, 1923), p.185.

85 J. Hunter, *The Emergence of Modern Japan: An Introductory History Since 1853* (London and New York: Longman, 1989), pp.192–194.

86 K. Takeuchi, 'How Japan Learned About the Outside World: The Views of Other Countries Incorporated in Japanese School Textbooks, 1868–1986', *Hitotsubashi Journal of Social Studies*, No.19 (1987), pp.5–9.

87 S. Akiyama, *Nihon Chiri Shōshi* (Outline of Japanese Geography) (Tokyo: Chūōdō, 1887), Vol.2.

88 Gakkai Shihōsha, *Nihon Chiri Shōhō* (First Step in Japanese Geography) (Tokyo: Shūōdō, 1892).

89 Fukkyūsha Henshūjo, *Shōgaku Chiri* (Elementary Geography) (Tokyo: Fukkyūsha, 1901), Vols.2 and 4.

90 Cited in Y. Kaiho, 'Kindai ni okeru Ainu Kei Minshū Zō no Keisei: Nihonjin no Ainu-kan' (Formation of the Image of the Ainu Masses in the Early Modern Period: The Japanese Image of the Ainu), *Hokkaidō Chihō Shi Kenkyū*, No.90 (February 1973), p.40.

91 Monbushō, *Junjō Shōgaku Tokuhon* (Elementary School Reader) (Tokyo: Monbushō, 1910), Vol.10, Lesson 22.

92 *Kokutei Kyōkasho Iken Hōkoku Isan* (Report on Opinions on the State Textbooks), Monbushō, emphasis added. This extract from the report was included in the materials presented by Yukio Takegahara at a public lecture in Sapporo on 17 September 1992. I am deeply indebted to Mr Takegahara for this and other information by which this section benefits.

93 The expression is that of Yamanaka Hisashi. For his discussion of how stereotyped images of colonial peoples were diffused through elementary school history textbooks, see H. Yamanaka, 'Shōkokumintachi no Shokuminchi' (The Colonies of the Little Citizens), in Iwanami Kōza, *Kindai Nihon to Shokuminchi (7): Bunka no naka no Shokuminchi* (Modern Japan and the Colonies: The Colonies in Culture) (Tokyo: Iwanami Shoten, 1993), pp.57–79.

94 M. Komatsu, 'Ainu Shukōgeihin Tenrankai' (The Ainu Handicrafts Exhibition), *Hokkaidō Shakai Jigyō*, No.42 (October 1935), p.75.

95 The *Shūhokuroku* (Records of the Far North) of 1808 noted that the Ainu of Yubutsu were 'skilled in carving and their livelihood depended on the making of toys and other articles'. Cited in S. Takakura, 'The Ainu of Northern Japan: A Study in Conquest and Acculturation', (trans. J. Harrison), *Transactions of the American Philosophical Society*, Vol.50, No.4 (1960), p.61n. For Chikabumi and Matsui Umetarō see K. Sunazawa, *Ku Sukup Orushipe: Watashi no Ichidai no Hanashi* (The Story of My Life) (Tokyo: Fukutake Shoten, 1990), pp.48, 190. This remarkable autobiography of an Ainu woman from Chikabumi also

includes a section describing her work in tourism at Noboribetsu in the 1930s (pp.214–219). For Ainu handicraft exhibitions, see *Hokkaidō Shakai Jigyō*, No.62 (July 1937), pp.32–34; *Hokkaidō Shakai Jigyō*, No.42 (October 1935), pp.71–85.

96 T.P. Terry, *Terry's Japanese Empire: A Guidebook for Travelers* (Boston and New York: Houghton Mifflin Company, 1914), pp.353–354.

97 K. Kindaichi, *Ainu Life and Legends*, Tourist Library No.36 (Tokyo: Board of Tourist Industry, Japanese Government Railways, 1941), pp.76–81.

98 Ogawa, 'Hokkaidō Kyūdojin Hogohō', p.232.

99 'Otaru no Kuma Matsuri' (Bear Festival at Otaru), *Hokkaidō Mainichi*, 11 December 1889.

100 K. Sasaki, 'Hidaka Yuki' (Bound for Hidaka), *Hokkaidō Kyōiku Shinbun*, No.37 (November 1928), p.26.

101 Y. Baba, 'A Study of Minority–Majority Relations: The Ainu and Japanese in Hokkaidō', *Japan Interpreter*, Vol.13, No.1 (1980), pp.70–71.

102 Ogawa, 'Protection Act and Assimilatory Education', p.243.

103 Sunazawa, *Ku Sukup Orushpe*, p.311.

104 'Ainu ni taisuru Nihonjin no Jinshuteki Sabetsu Taigū' (Racially Discriminatory Treatment of the Ainu by Japanese), *Hokkai Taimuzu*, 25 October 1919.

105 Recorded in the diary of Ega Torazō, October 1928. In T. Umeki (ed.), *Ainu Dendōsha no Shōgai: Ega Torazō Ikō* (The Life of an Ainu Missionary: The Posthumous Writings of Ega Torazō) (Sapporo: Hokkaidō Shuppan Kikaku Sentā, 1986), p.169.

106 T. Chiri, 'Ainu no Ke ni tsuite' (On the Hair of the Ainu) *Kita no Hikari*, No.1 (December 1948), pp.28–29.

107 Ekashi to Fuchi Henshū Iinkai (ed.), *Ekashi to Fuchi: Kita no Shima ni Ikita Hitobito no Kiroku* (The Ainu Elders: A Record of the People who Lived on the Northern Island) (Sapporo: Sapporo Terebi Hōsō, 1983), pp.341–342.

108 H. Murakami, *Ainu Jitsuwa Shū* (Collection of True Ainu Stories) (Asahikawa: Asahikawa Shiritsu Kyōdo Hakubutsukan, 1964), p.112.

109 Cited in Ogawa, 'Ainu Gakkō no Settchi', p.298.

110 Cited in M. Ogawa, 'Ainu Kyōiku Seido no Haishi: Kyūdojin Jidō Kyōiku Kitei Haishi to 1937–nen Hokkaidō Kyūdojin Hogohō Kaisei' (The End of the Ainu Education System: The Abolition of the Regulations for the Education of Former Native Children and the 1937 Revision of the Hokkaidō Former Natives Protection Act), *Hokkaidō Daigaku Kyōikugakubu Kiyō*, No.61 (1993), p.59.

111 S. Kayano, 'Ainu Ethnic and Linguistic Revival', in N. Loos and T. Osanai (eds), *Indigenous Minorities and Education: Australian and Japanese Perspectives of their Indigenous Peoples, the Ainu, Aborigines and Torres Straits Islanders* (Tokyo: Sanyūsha, 1993), p.360.

112 Y. Hayasaka, *Shizen to Jinbun Shumi no Hokkaidō* (Nature, Culture, Tastes of Hokkaidō) (Sapporo: Hokkōsha, 1926), p.229.

113 K. Itagaki, 'Hokkaidō Kyūdojin no Koseki ni Kansuru Kōsatsu' (Considerations on the Family Registers of Hokkaidō Former Natives), *Hokkaidō Shakai Jigyō*, No.87 (August 1939), pp.24–27.

114 For ritual pollution and blood, see Hayashida, 'Blood Ideology of Japan', pp.120–123.

115 Osami, 'Ainu no Gakkō', in Inoue, *Hokkaidō Bungaku Zenshū*, p.223.

116 See the personal accounts of nineteen Ainu women contained in M. Takahashi, *Zoku Hokkaidō no Onnatachi: Utari Hen* (Women of Hokkaidō Continued: The Ainu) (Sapporo: Hokkaidō Josei Shi Kenkyūkai, 1981).

117 Another collection of oral histories that includes many pre-war memories is *Ekashi to Fuchi*. Useful autobiographies include those of Kayano Shigeru, *Our Land was a Forest: An Ainu Memoir* (Boulder: Westview Press, 1994), and the long-lived Sunazawa Kura, *Ku Sukup Orushipe*.

118 M. Kita, 'Ainu yo Izuko e Iku', p.44.

5 WITH SHINING EYES: AINU PROTEST AND RESISTANCE, 1869–1945

1 S. Takakura, 'The Ainu of Northern Japan: A Study in Conquest and Acculturation' (trans. J. Harrison), *Transactions of the American Philosophical Society*, Vol.50, No.4 (1960), p.79,79n.

2 T. Matsuura, 'Kinsei Ezo Jinbutsu Shi' (Stories of Recent Ezo Personalities), 1860, in *NS4*, pp.809–810.

3 See, for example, I. Bird, *Unbeaten Tracks in Japan: An Account of Travels in the Interior Including Visits to the Aborigines of Yezo and the Shrine of Nikko* (Rutland, Vt. and Tokyo: Tuttle, 1973), p.253.

4 For the life of Kannari, see K. Urata, 'Meiji no Ainu Seinen Kannari Tarō' (The Meiji Ainu Youth Kannari Tarō), in S. Matsumoto (ed.), *Kusuri*, Vol.2 (Kushiro: Kushiro Seikatsu Bunka Denshō Hozon Kenkyūkai, 1993), pp.63–75.

5 Hokkaidō-chō, *Shin Hokkaidō Shi Nenpyō* (The New Chronology of Hokkaidō History) (Sapporo: Hokkaidō Shuppan Kikaku Sentā, 1989), p.307.

6 Cited in S. Emori, *Ainu no Rekishi: Hokkaidō no Hitobito (2)* (A History of the Ainu: the People of Hokkaidō [2]) (Tokyo: Sanseidō, 1987), pp.152–153.

7 Emori, *Ainu no Rekishi*, pp.155–157; H. Murakami, *Ainu Jitsuwa Shū* (Collection of True Ainu Stories) (Asahikawa: Asahikawa Shiritsu Kyōdo Hakubutsukan, 1964), pp.107–111; G. Arai (Y. Katō, ed.), *Arai Genjirō Ikō: Ainu Jinbutsu Den* (The Posthumous Writings of Arai Genjirō: The Biographies of Famous Ainu) (Sapporo: Y. Katō, 1992), pp.38–40.

8 Y. Yamabe and K. Kindaichi, *Ainu Monogatari* (An Ainu Story) (Tokyo: Hakubunkan, 1913); Murakami, *Ainu Jitsuwa Shū*, pp.38–44.

9 Most of the information on the Chikabumi land disputes is taken from the following sources; Emori, *Ainu no Rekishi*, pp.190–217; T. Matsui, 'Chikabumi Ainu to Kyūdojin Hogohō' (The Chikabumi Ainu and the Former Natives Protection Act), *KMK5*, pp.566–575; Asahikawa-shi Shi Henshū Iinkai (ed.), *Asahikawa-shi Shi: Dai Ikkan* (History of Asahikawa City, Volume 1) (Asahikawa: Asahikawa Shiyakusho, 1959), pp.250–263.

10 Cited in *Asahikawa-shi Shi*, p.251.

11 *Asahikawa-shi Shi*, pp.250–255. For media response, see 'Chikabumi Genya o Toriage' (Chikabumi Wastelands to be Confiscated), *Jiji Shinpō*, 25 April 1900; 'Ōkura to Miura Anyaku' (Secret Manoeuvres of Ōkura and Miura), *Mainichi Shinbun*, 30 April 1900; 'Sonoda Chōkan Hokkaidō Dojin Mondai ni kanshite Kenseki seraru' (Governor Sonoda Reprimanded over Hokkaidō Native Issue), *Hōchi Shinbun*, 23 May 1900.

12 For politics and labour, see J. Hunter, *The Emergence of Modern Japan: An Inroductory History Since 1853* (London and New York: Longman, 1989), pp.220–224, 245–253. Tenant disputes are detailed in M. Hane, *Peasants, Rebels and Outcastes: The Underside of Modern Japan* (New York: Pantheon, 1982), pp.108–114.

13 Cited in Hane, *Peasants, Rebels and Outcastes*, p.146.

14 For a brief overview see Hane, *Peasants, Rebels and Outcastes*, pp.139–171. The most comprehensive treatment of the *Suiheisha* and *Yūwa* movements is I. Neary, *Political Protest and Social Control in Prewar Japan: The Origins of Buraku Liberation* (Manchester: Manchester University Press, 1989).

15 Neary, *Political Protest*, p.39.

16 Dokutōru Manrō (N.G. Munro), 'Kyūdojin ni kansuru Chōsa: Ge' (Survey of the Former Natives: 2), *Hokkai no Kyōiku*, No.303 (March 1918), p.13.

17 See M. Weiner, *The Origins of the Korean Community in Japan 1910–1923* (Manchester: Manchester University Press, 1989).

18 'Kiristo no Ai mo, Shaka no Jihi mo: Ainu ni wa Ichiwan no Doboroku' (Love for Christ, Mercy for the Buddha: For the Ainu a Cup of Alcohol), *Hokkai Taimuzu*, 5 May 1923.

19 'Dōhaku to Kyūdojinkan' (Former Natives' Feelings on the Prefectural Exhibition), *Hokkai Taimuzu*, 29 June 1918.

20 For the life of John Batchelor, see I. Nitami, *Ikyō no Shito: Eijin Jon Bachira Den* (The Foreign Apostle: A Biography of the Englishman John Batchelor) (Sapporo: Hokkaidō Shinbunsha, 1991); J. Batchelor, *Waga Kioku o Tadorite* (Tracing my Memory) (Sapporo: Bunrokusha, 1928); and J. Batchelor, 'Steps by the Way'. Where dates conflict (Batchelor is inconsistent; possibly his memory failed him in later years), I have followed Nitami.

21 See, for instance, H.D. Ölschleger, 'John Batchelor's Contributions to Ainu Ethnography', in J. Kreiner (ed.), *European Studies on Ainu Language and Culture*, German Institute for Japanese Studies Monograph No.6 (Munchen: Iudicium Verlag, 1993), pp.137–150.

22 Ölschleger, 'John Batchelor's Contributions to Ainu Ethnography', p.142.

23 J. Batchelor, *Ainu Life and Lore: Echoes of a Departing Race* (Tokyo: Kyōbunkan, 1927), p.5.

24 T. Takekuma, *Ainu Monogatari* (Ainu Tales) (Tokyo: Hakubunkan, 1918), English preface, p.1.

25 Takekuma, *Ainu Monogatari*, p.15.

26 Takekuma, *Ainu Monogatari*, p.57.

27 For the abolition of the Regulations, see M. Ogawa, 'Ainu Kyōiku Seido no Haishi: Kyūdojin Jidō Kyōiku Kitei Haishi to 1937-nen Hokkaidō Kyūdojin Hogohō Kaisei' (The End of the Ainu Education System: The Abolition of the Regulations for the Education of Former Native Children and the 1937 Revision of the Hokkaidō Former Natives Protection Act), *Hokkaidō Daigaku Kyōikugakubu Kiyō*, No.61 (1993), pp.56–61. Biographical sketches of Fushine, Ega and Takekuma are contained in Arai, *Ainu Jinbutsu Den*, pp.35–36, 68–69, 76–79.

28 B. Pilsudski, *Materials for the Study of Ainu Language and Folklore* (Cracow: Cracow University Press, 1912), p.ix.

29 I am indebted to Mr Satō Tomomi, a specialist in Ainu language and oral literature at the Hokkaidō University of Education at Iwamizawa, for drawing this to my attention and translating parts of the epic.

30 Pon Fuchi (Nogami Fusako), *Ainugo wa Ikite iru: Kotoba no Tamashii no Fukken* (The Ainu Language Lives: Restoration of the Soul of the Language) (Revised Edition, Tokyo: Shinsensha, 1987), pp.60–65; J. Batchelor, *The Ainu and Their Folklore* (London: The Religious Tract Society, 1901), p.167.
31 This can be seen in the case of Orita Suteno, an Ainu woman who worked closely with many academics to transmit her knowledge of premodern Ainu culture. When she was still a child in the Meiji Period, Orita was kept at home to learn traditional ceremonies and oral literature from her grandmother and uncle while her cousins were allowed to attend school. See M. Haginaka *et al.*, *Kikigaki: Ainu no Shokuji* (Field Notes: Ainu Food), Nihon Shokuseikatsu Zenshū No.48 (Tokyo: Nōsangyōson Bunka Kyōkai, 1992), pp. 207–215.
32 Hokkaidō-chō, *Hokkaidō Kyūdojin Hogohō Enkaku Shi* (History of the Protection of the Former Natives of Hokkaidō) (Sapporo: Hokkaidō-chō, 1934; Tokyo: Sanichi Shobō, 1981), p.343.
33 M. Ogawa, 'The Hokkaidō Former Aborigines Protection Act and Assimilatory Education', in N. Loos and T. Osanai (eds), *Indigenous Minorities and Education: Australian and Japanese Perspectives of their Indigenous Peoples, the Ainu, Aborigines and Torres Straits Islanders* (Tokyo: Sanyūsha, 1993), pp.244–245.
34 This information comes from conversations with an elderly Ainu resident of Kussharo.
35 Y. Chiri, *Gin no Shizuku: Chiri Yukie Ikō* (Silver Droplets: The Posthumous Writings of Chiri Yukie) (Tokyo: Sōfūkan, 1992), p.18.
36 See M. Chiri, 'A Song Sung by the Owl God Himself – from the Collected Songs of the Ainu Gods', in N. Loos and T. Osanai, *Indigenous Minorities and Education: Australian and Japanese Perspectives of their Indigenous Peoples, the Ainu, Aborigines and Torres Straits Islanders* (Tokyo: Sanyūsha, 1993), pp.119–128.
37 H. Fujimoto, *Chiri Mashiho no Shōgai* (The Life of Chiri Mashiho) (Tokyo: Shinchōsha, 1982), p.88.
38 F. Iha, 'Mezametsutsu aru Ainu Shuzoku' (The Awakening Ainu Race), in *Iha Fuyū Zenshū* (Collected Works of Iha Fuyū), Vol.11 (Tokyo: Heibonsha, 1976), p.307.
39 Iha, 'Mezametsutsu aru Ainu Shuzoku', p.307.
40 Iha, 'Mezametsutsu aru Ainu Shuzoku', p.307.
41 H. Fujimoto, 'Wajin Shinryaku to Ainu Kaihō Undō' (Wajin Invasion and the Ainu Liberation Movement), in *KMK5*, p.564.
42 H. Iboshi, *Kotan: Iboshi Hokuto Ikō* (Kotan: The Posthumous Writings of Iboshi Hokuto) (Tokyo: Sōfūkan, 1984), pp.52, 57, 62, 63, 139.
43 Iboshi, *Kotan*, pp.48, 53.
44 Iboshi, *Kotan*, pp.110–116.
45 Cited in Neary, *Political Protest*, p.80.
46 'Kenpaku kara Funki shite Ainu Zoku Kaihō no Undō' (Liberation Movement of the Ainu Race Arising from Oppression), *Tokyo Asahi Shinbun*, 22 October 1926.
47 I am indebted to Ishihara Makoto of the Sapporo-dō Shoten bookshop in Sapporo who kindly showed me one of these posters.
48 Y. Takegahara, 'Kaiheisha Sōritsu to Ainu Kaihō Undō' (The Establishment of the Kaiheisha and the Ainu Liberation Movement), *Kaihō Kyōiku*, No.284 (March 1992), p.41.

49 S. Wakaizumi, *Karafuto Kikō: Hokui Gojūdo no Tabi* (Karafuto Journal: A Journey at Fifty Degrees North) (Tokyo: Gokōsha, 1931), p.248.

50 M. Ogawa, 'Hokkaidō Kyūdojin Hogohō, Kyūdojin Jidō Kyōiku Kitei no shita no Ainu Gakkō' (Ainu Schools under the Hokkaidō Former Natives Protection Act and the Regulations for the Education of Former Native Children), *Hokkaidō Daigaku Kyōikugakubu Kiyō*, No.58 (1992), p.247.

51 Nitami, *Ikyō no Shito*, p.185.

52 Kita Masaaki states that the Kyokumeisha was originally founded by him in Obihiro in October 1922, with Fushine and other Ainu as Directors; if this is so, then the 1927 meeting could represent an attempt to relaunch or increase participation in the organisation. For Kita's account, including the original Charter, see M. Kita, *Ainu Enkaku Shi: Hokkaidō Kyūdojin Hogohō o megutte* (Ainu History: Concerning the Hokkaidō Former Natives Protection Act) (Sapporo: Hokkaidō Shuppan Kikaku Sentā, 1987), pp.110–117.

53 'Tokachi Ainu no Tsuretsu naru Sakebi' (The Fierce Cry of the Tokachi Ainu), *Hokkai Taimuzu*, 10 May 1927.

54 Ogawa, 'Ainu Kyōiku Seido no Haishi', pp.49–50.

55 A. Gordon, *The Evolution of Labor Relations in Japan: Heavy Industry, 1853–1955* (Council of East Asian Studies, Harvard University, Cambridge, Mass. and London: Harvard University Press, 1985), pp.220–230.

56 Kita, *Ainu Enkaku Shi*, pp.130–135.

57 Hokkaidō-chō, *Hokkaidō Kyūdojin Gaikyō* (General Conditions of the Hokkaidō Former Natives) (Sapporo: Hokkaidō-chō, 1936), pp.24, 26. Since the two households listed were located in Iburi and Nemuro Districts, it is tempting to speculate that they were the Kannari and Ōta families. For government expenditure on Ainu education and welfare, see Hokkaidō-chō, *Kyūdojin Hogo Enkaku Shi*, pp.352–357.

58 'Kagayaku Ainu' (Shining Ainu), *Hokkai Taimuzu*, 7 June 1933; Ogawa, 'Ainu Kyōiku Seido no Haishi', p.45.

59 This is essentially the argument of Y. Baba, 'A Study of Minority–Majority Relations: The Ainu and Japanese in Hokkaidō', *Japan Interpreter*, Vol.13, No.1 (1980).

60 S. Onobu, 'Dōzoku no Kanki o Unagasu' (Urging the Awakening of Our People), *Ezo no Hikari*, No.1 (November 1930), p.8.

61 S. Onobu, 'Itsumademo Gakusha no Kenkyū Zairyō taru nakare' (We Must Not Remain Research Materials for Scholars Forever), *Ezo no Hikari*, No.2 (January 1931), p.28.

62 H. Kaizawa, 'Wajin yo, Ōseki no Ezo o Wasureru nakare; Utari yo, Chishiki no Kōjō o Hakare' (Wajin, Do Not Forget the Ezo of the Past; Ainu, Plan to Increase Your Knowledge), *Ezo no Hikari*, No.2 (January 1931), p.25.

63 Y. Hiramura, 'Ainu to shite Ikiru ka? Hata Shamo ni Dōka suru ka?' (Do we Live as Ainu? Or Do we Assimilate to *Shamo*?), *Ezo no Hikari*, No.1 (November 1930), p.26.

64 S. Ogawa, 'Zento no Kōmei o Mokuhyō ni' (A Bright Future as Our Objective), *Ezo no Hikari*, No.3 (August 1931), p.20.

65 T. Kaizawa, *Ainu no Sakebi* (The Cry of the Ainu) (Sapporo: Ainu no Sakebi Kankōkai, 1931), *KMK5*, p.393. For a newspaper report of the Convention that concentrates on the Protection Act, see 'Ainu Seinen Taikai' (The Convention of Ainu Youth), *Hokkai Taimuzu*, evening edition, 5 August 1931.

66 Y. Nukishio, *Ainu Dōka to Senchō* (Ainu Assimilation and Its Examples)

(Obihiro: Hokkai Shōgun Kōseidan, 1934; reprinted Sapporo: Sapporo-dō Shoten, 1986), p.70–71.

67 See, for instance, F.C.C. Peng and P. Geiser, *The Ainu: The Past in the Present* (Hiroshima: Hiroshima Bunka Hyōron, 1977), pp.272–292.

68 'Horobiyuku to wa Nanigoto da' (What is Dying Out?), *Hokkai Taimuzu*, 20 September 1934; 'Ichi Ainu no Shūki' (Notes of an Ainu) 1–4, *Hokkai Taimuzu*, 14, 16, 18, 19 December 1934; 'Horobiyuku Minzoku no Hitsū Chi no Sakebi' (Cry of the Sad Blood of the Dying Race), *Karafuto Nichi Nichi Shinbun*, 16 October 1937.

69 Cited in Ogawa, 'Ainu Kyōiku Seido no Haishi', p.50.

70 T. Moritake, 'Zendō Utari ni Hakaru' (Calling Hokkaidō Utari), *Utari no Hikari*, No.15 (February 1934), *KMK5*, p.239.

71 This information was provided by the Ainu activist Ogawa Ryūkichi, himself the son of a Korean migrant labourer and an Ainu woman, at a lecture at Hokkaidō University of Education, Iwamizawa, 21 January 1993.

72 Emori, *Ainu no Rekishi*, pp.206–215.

73 G. Arai, *Ainu no Sakebi* (The Cry of the Ainu) (Sapporo: Hokkaidō Shuppan Kikaku Sentā, 1984), p.255.

74 Ainu Minzoku no Genzai to Mirai o Kangaeru Kai (ed.), *Ashita o Tsukuru Ainu Minzoku* (The Ainu Who Will Make Tomorrow) (Tokyo: Miraisha, 1988), p.205.

75 'Dojin Buraku no Bunri' (Division of the Native Village), *Karafuto Nichi Nichi Shinbun*, 24 September 1910.

76 'Waraware ni Gyoba o Kaese' (Give us back our Fishing Grounds), *Hokkai Taimuzu*, 17 May 1932.

77 'Waraware ni Gyoba o Kaese', *Hokkai Taimuzu*, 17 May 1932; *Utari no Tomo*, No.1 (January 1933), *KMK5*, p.249.

78 'Menoko no Koi wa Akumademo Shamo no Otoko ni' (The Love of Ainu Women is Always for Japanese Men), *Karafuto Nichi Nichi Shinbun*, 24 January 1930; 'Ainu Seinen no Kōgi' (An Ainu Youth's Protest), *Karafuto Nichi Nichi Shinbun*, 13 February 1930.

79 Nisen no Ainu mo Iyo-iyo Nihonjin ni naru' (Two Thousand Ainu Will at Last Become Japanese), *Karafuto Nichi Nichi Shinbun*, 26 July 1932; 'Ainu no Nyūseki' (Ainu to be Registered), *Karafuto Nichi Nichi Shinbun*, 4 December 1932; 'Dojin Zenpan Keihō Tekiyō' (All Natives to be Subject to Criminal Law), *Karafuto Nichi Nichi Shinbun*, 11 December 1932; 'Karafuto Ainu ni Kosekihō Tekiyō' (Karafuto Ainu to Come Under Family Registration Law), *Hokkai Taimuzu*, 14 December 1932; 'Karafuto Ainu mo Gunjin ni nareru' (Karafuto Ainu also Eligible for Military), *Karafuto Nichi Nichi Shinbun*, 14 December 1932; *Utari no Tomo*, *KMK5*, p.249.

80 'Shirahama no Ainutachi e Kokki o Kakuto ni Okuru' (National Flags Given to All Ainu Households in Shirahama), *Karafuto Nichi Nichi Shinbun*, 1 February 1933; 'Waraware no Ko mo Nihonjin' (Our Children Are Japanese Too), *Karafuto Nichi Nichi Shinbun*, 10 February 1933.

81 'Shamo to isshō nara Ora ya da' (I don't want Education with Wajin), *Karafuto Nichi Nichi Shinbun*, 1 April 1933.

82 Kita, *Ainu Enkaku Shi*, pp.137–139.

83 M. Komatsu, 'Kyūdojin Hogo Shisetsu Kaizen Zadankai Kiroku' (Record of the Symposium for the Improvement of Welfare Facilities for the Former Natives), *Hokkaidō Shakai Jigyō*, No.42 (October 1935), p.2.

84 Komatsu, 'Zadankai Kiroku', p.8.
85 Komatsu, 'Zadankai Kiroku', p.41.
86 Kita, *Ainu Enkaku Shi*, p.139.
87 M. Kita, 'Kyūdojin Dantai no Tabi' (The Trip of the Former Native Group), *Hokkaidō Shakai Jigyō*, No.59 (April 1937), p.54.
88 Emori, *Ainu no Rekishi*, p.216; Ogawa, 'Protection Act and Assimilatory Education', p.245.
89 'Kotan ni Haru no Taiyō' (Spring Sun in the Kotan), *Hokkai Taimuzu*, 13 March 1937.
90 'Kimun Utari no Tō Irei' (Memorial Service at the Kimun Utari Memorial), *Senkusha no Tsudoi* No.41 (January 1986), p.4.
91 S. Yanagi, 'Ainu e no Mikata' (A Viewpoint on the Ainu), *Kōgei*, No.106 (December 1941); 'Ainujin ni Okuru Sho' (A Letter to the Ainu), *Kōgei*, No.107 (March 1942). In S. Yanagi, *Yanagi Sōetsu Zenshū* (Collected Works of Yanagi Sōetsu), Vol.15, (Tokyo: Chikuma Shobō, 1981), pp.499–508, 528–537. For Yanagi and Korea, see Y. Kikuchi, 'Yanagi Sōetsu and Korean Crafts in the Context of the *Mingei* Movement', Paper presented at the Victoria and Albert/British Association of Korean Studies Korean Material Culture Study Day, 13 February 1993, esp. pp.13–15. I am indebted to Ms Kikuchi for this and other information on Yanagi.
92 Osaka Jinken Rekishi Shiryōkan (ed.), *Kindai Nihon to Ainu Minzoku* (Modern Japan and the Ainu) (Osaka: Osaka Jinken Rekishi Shiryōkan, 1993), p.70.
93 S. Takakura, 'Vanishing Ainu of Northern Japan', *Natural History*, Vol.75, No.8 (October 1966), p.24.
94 Chōsen Sōtokufu Hōmukyoku, 'Uji no Settei ni Kansuru Ken' (On the Establishment of Surnames), communication from Miyamoto Gen, Head of the Legal Bureau of the Government General of Korea, Tokyo Office, to Ishii Seiichi, Head of the Records Section of the Home Ministry, 30 January 1940; Chōsen Sōtokufu Hōmukyoku, 'Uji no Settei ni Kansuru Ken' (On the Establishment of Surnames), communication from Miyamoto Gen, Head of the Legal Bureau of the Government General of Korea, Tokyo Office, to Munei Toshikazu, Governor of Karafuto, 30 January 1940; Hokkaidō-chō Gakumubu, 'Ainujin no Uji ni Kansuru Ken' (On the Establishment of Ainu Surnames), communication from Hiramoto Yoshitaka, Head of the Education Section of the Hokkaidō Government, to Miyamoto Gen, Head of the Legal Bureau of the Government General of Korea, 21 February 1940; Karafuto-chō, 'Uji no Settei ni Kansuru Ken', communication from Governor of Karafuto to Head of Legal Bureau, Government General of Korea, 7 February 1940.

6 AINU LIBERATION AND WELFARE COLONIALISM: THE NEW AINU POLITICS AND THE STATE'S RESPONSE

1 For an account of the formation of the Ainu Kyōkai, see the recollections of Ogawa in Ekashi to Fuchi Henshū Iinkai (ed.), *Ekashi to Fuchi: Kita no Shima ni Ikita Hitobito no Kiroku* (The Ainu Elders: A Record of the People who Lived on the Northern Island) (Sapporo: Sapporo Terebi Hōsō, 1983), pp.75–80; for the Charter establishing the organisation, see *ASS3*, pp.961–966; for other information see 'Ainu Kyōkai no Yakunin to Yosan' (The Officials and Budget of the Ainu Association), *Ainu Shinbun*, No.2 (March 1946), *KMK5*, p.252.

2 One leader present at the meeting was Shiiku Kenichi, whose account is contained in *ASS3*, pp.925–931.
3 J. Hunter, *The Emergence of Modern Japan: An Introductory History Since 1853* (London and New York: Longman, 1989), pp.99–100. Statistics are from Hokkaidō (ed.), *Hokkaidō Nōchi Kaikaku Shi: Jōkan* (History of Land Reform in Hokkaidō, Vol.1) (Sapporo: Hokkaidō-chō, 1954), pp.5–6.
4 Petitions No.87 and 88, 18 February 1947. In *ASS3*, pp.860–864.
5 *Ekashi to Fuchi*, p.77.
6 'Hokkaidō Kyūdojin Hogohō Dai Ichijō ni yorite Kafu shitaru Tochi ni taishi Nōchi Kaikakuhō no Tekiyōgai Nōchi to shite Shitei Moshikomi' (On Designating the Land Granted Under Article 1 of the Hokkaidō Former Natives Act as Farmland Exempt from the Land Reform Laws), Communication No.951 from the Governor of Hokkaidō to the Minister of Agriculture and Forestry and the Minister of Welfare, 28 October 1947, *ASS3*, pp.880, 882.
7 Pete's report of this visit to the Ainu Kyōkai, on which this section is based, appears in *ASS3*, pp.900–911.
8 The Japanese versions of these petitions are given in *ASS3*, pp.891–900. Copies of the original English translations, which were the documents actually presented and from which I have quoted, are kept in the archives of the Hokkaidō Utari Kyōkai in Sapporo. This quote is from S. Ogawa, 'A Petition Regarding Farmland Owned by Ainu People in Hokkaido', p.3.
9 W. Pete, 'Petition: Concerning Ainu-owned farmland in Hokkaido', 10 December 1947.
10 Hokkaidō (ed.), *Hokkaidō Nōchi Kaikaku Shi* (History of Land Reform in Hokkaidō, Vol.2) (Sapporo: Hokkaidō-chō, 1957), p.241; 'Hokkaidō Kyūdojin Hogohō ni yori Kafu shitaru Tochi ni kansuru Nōchi Kaikaku Kankei Hōrei no Tekiyō ni tsuite' (Concerning the Application of the Land Reform Legislation to Land Granted under the Hokkaidō Former Natives Protection Act), Communication No.418 from Head of the Agricultural Administration Bureau of the Ministry of Agriculture and Forestry to the Governor of Hokkaidō, 10 February 1948, *ASS3*, p.922. It was not only Ainu who suffered from the land reform; many veterans whose families had been unable to till their lands while they were away on active service also lost their holdings.
11 Hokkaidō, *Nōchi Kaikaku Shi*, Vol.2, p.248.
12 'Hogohō wa Sonzoku Subeki da' (The Protection Act Should Continue), *Ainu Shinbun*, No.3 (April 1946), *KMK5*, p.258.
13 K. Yoshida, *Ainu Bunka Shi* (Ainu Cultural History) (Makubetsu: Hokkaidō Ainu Bunka Hozon Kyōkai, 1958), p.5 and frontispiece photographs.
14 H. Passin, *Encounter with Japan* (Tokyo, New York and San Francisco: Kodansha International, 1982), p.163.
15 Passin, *Encounter*, p.164.
16 'Ainu Minzoku mo Shutsuba' (Ainu also Run), *Mainichi Shinbun* (Hokkaidō edition) 6 April 1946, and G. Arai, *Arai Genjirō Ikō: Ainu Jinbutsu Den* (The Posthumous Works of Arai Genjirō: The Biographies of Famous Ainu) (Sapporo: Y. Katō, 1992), p.71.
17 'Ainu Kyōkai e no Kitai' (My Expectations of the Ainu Association), *Ainu Shinbun*, No.1 (11 June 1946), *KMK5*, pp.261–262. This issue was the first from the newly organised *Ainu Shinbunsha* (Ainu News Ltd) which took over publication from the *Ainu Mondai Kenkyūsho*.
18 For Communists and labour, see *Ainu Shinbun*, No.2 (March 1946), in *KMK5*,

p.255; for Koreans, 'Takahashi Honsha Shuhitsu Chōsen Minzoku o Gekirei' (Your Chief Editor Takahashi Fiercely Encourages the Korean People), *Ainu Shinbun*, No.1 (June 1946), *KMK5*, pp.265–266.

19 S. Tsuru, *Japan's Capitalism: Creative Defeat and Beyond* (Cambridge: Cambridge University Press, 1993), p.67.

20 F.C. Jones, *Hokkaido: Its Present State of Development and Future Prospects* (London: Oxford University Press, 1958), pp.41–52.

21 Hokkaidō Hidaka Shichō, *Hidaka Chihō ni okeru Ainu Kei Jūmin no Seikatsu Jittai to sono Mondaiten* (The Socio-economic Conditions of Residents of Ainu Descent in the Hidaka Region and Associated Problems) (Urakawa: Hidaka Shichō, 1965), pp.7, 16. This source is hereafter cited as *HAS*.

22 *HAS*, p.26.

23 *HAS*, p.7, p.20.

24 *HAS*, p.52, Chart 56.

25 *HAS*, p.43, Chart 41; p.44.

26 Y. Baba, 'A Study of Minority–Majority Relations: The Ainu and Japanese in Hokkaidō', *Japan Interpreter*, Vol.13, No.1 (1980) pp.80–82.

27 K. Yoshida, 'Hidaka Chihō ni okeru Ainu–Wajin no Tsūkon ni tsuite' (On Ainu–Wajin Intermarriage in the Hidaka region), *Jinruigaku Zasshi*, Vol.80, No.1 (1972), p.60.

28 F.C.C. Peng and P. Geiser, *The Ainu: The Past in the Present* (Hiroshima: Hiroshima Bunka Hyōron, 1977), pp.272–292; K. Seki, 'The Ainu of Nisshin: Family Life and Social Residues', in Peng and Geiser, *Past in the Present*, pp.62–84.

29 K. Sugawara, *Gendai no Ainu: Minzoku Idō no Roman* (The Modern Ainu: Drama of a People in Motion) (Tokyo: Genbunsha, 1966).

30 K. Yoshino, *Cultural Nationalism in Contemporary Japan: A Sociological Enquiry* (London and New York: Routledge, 1992), p.24.

31 Hidaka Chiku Shizunai Shibu Higashi Shizunai Chūgakkō Hidaka Chiku Tokubetsu Kenkyū Gurūpu, 'Hidaka, Iburi Chiku ni okeru Ainu-kei Jidō, Seitō o meguru Jittai to sono Taisaku' (Conditions and Countermeasures for Children and Students of Ainu Descent in the Hidaka and Iburi Regions), *Dai Go Bukai Hōkokusho* (Report of the Fifth Working Group), Hokkyōso Daiyonji Zendō Kyōiku Kenkyū Taikai (Fourth Hokkaidō Teachers' Union Convention on Educational Research), undated, early 1950s, pp.9–18.

32 T. Narita, 'Ainu Mondai ni Omou' (Thoughts on the Ainu Problem), *Hoppō Bungei*, Vol.5, No.2 (1972), p.38.

33 Reproduced in Ainu Association of Hokkaidō, Material 4, *Statement Submitted to the International Labour Conference 75th Session, 1988*, Geneva, June 1988.

34 M. Kaizawa, 'Ainu no Chi sae Usumereba' (If We Only Dilute Ainu Blood), in 'Nihonjin ni yoru Jinshu Sabetsu Higaisha Hyakunin no Shōgen' (The Statements of One Hundred Victims of Racial Discrimination by Japanese), Special Feature, *Ushio*, No.150 (February 1972), p.145.

35 See, for instance, a study on negative Ainu stereotypes held by Wajin children in Asahikawa, in I. Nishi, 'Jinshu Henken no Shakaiteki Bunseki – Hokkaidō Ainu o megutte' (A Social Analysis of Racial Prejudice: Concerning the Hokkaidō Ainu), in Asahikawa Jinken Yōgo Iin Rengōkai (ed.), *Kotan no Konseki* (Remains of the Kotan) (Asahikawa: Asahikawa Jinken Yōgo Iin Rengōkai, 1971), pp.57–61.

36 For instance, see the recollections of Kitahara Kyōko in R. Siddle and

K. Kitahara, 'Deprivation and Resistance: Ainu Movements in Modern Japan', and 'My Heritage of Pride and Struggle', in J. Maher and G. Macdonald (eds), *Diversity in Japanese Culture and Language* (London: Kegan Paul International, 1995), pp.147–159.

37 Sugawara, *Gendai no Ainu*, pp.31–48.

38 S. Kayano, *Our Land was a Forest: An Ainu Memoir* (Boulder: Westview Press, 1994), pp.98–100; Peng and Geiser, *Past in the Present*, p.292; Sugawara, *Gendai no Ainu*, p.220; I. Hilger, 'Japan's "Sky People": The Vanishing Ainu', *National Geographic*, Vol.131, No.2 (February 1967), p.285.

39 Y. Ozawa and Y. Takegahara, 'Seishōnen no Ainu Kan' (The Image of Ainu Among Young People), *Jinbun Gakuhō*, No.15 (March 1980), pp.11–19.

40 Sugawara, *Gendai no Ainu*, pp.78–88; Kayano, *Our Land was a Forest*, 115–123.

41 S. Hatozawa, *Wakaki Ainu no Tamashii* (The Soul of a Young Ainu) (Tokyo: Shinjinbutsu Ōraisha, 1972), p.64.

42 *Senkusha no Tsudoi*, No.1 (March 1963), p.25.

43 Sugawara, *Gendai no Ainu*, p.219.

44 Sugawara, *Gendai no Ainu*, pp.214-219; Peng and Geiser, *Past in the Present*, pp.276–278.

45 'Hidoi, Ainu no Seikatsu' (Ainu Life is Terrible), *Mainichi Shinbun*, 9 July 1959.

46 'Kokko Hojo wa Nozomi Usui' (Little Hope for National Aid), *Hokkaidō Shinbun*, 31 January 1960.

47 Sugawara, *Gendai no Ainu*, pp.209–210.

48 Corporatism in Japan, in the words of Aurelia George, entails a relationship of interdependence; the 'formal inclusion of interest groups in government administration for purposes of assistance in policy implementation, in exchange for guaranteed access to government officials, legitimation of interest groups in ministerial advisory and consultation processes and, in some cases, a direct role in the authoritative allocation of values'. A. George, 'Japanese Interest Group Behaviour: An Institutional Approach', in J.A.A. Stockwin *et al.*, *Dynamic and Immobilist Politics in Japan* (London: Macmillan, 1988), p.122.

49 'Ainu no Seikatsu ni Uruoi o' (Bringing Benefits to Ainu Life), *Hokkaidō Shinbun*, 30 September 1962.

50 Despite denials by local authorities to foreign researchers that separate lists of Ainu were kept (Peng and Geiser, *Past in the Present*, p.294, note 13), one Ainu from Asahikawa who went to get a copy of his family register (*koseki tōhon*) in 1971 found the word *Kyūdojin* written on it. K. Ozawa, 'Koseki Tōhon wa Ima mo "Kyūdojin"' (Former Native Still Appears on Family Registers), in 'Nihonjin ni yoru Jinshu Sabetsu', p.142. This has been of concern to Ainu up to the present. In 1975, a group of Ainu in Chitose campaigned to have public access to family registers restricted. See 'Koseki Kōkai Seigen' (Limits on Public Access to Family Registers), *Hokkaidō Shinbun*, 9 May 1975. This problem surfaced again in Asahikawa in 1987 when marks identifying Ainu were discovered on registers stored on microfilm. This information comes from an internal document of the Section for Protection of Human Rights of the Legal Bureau of Sapporo City that logs Ainu-related incidents.

51 'Kuma Matsuri o Haishi' (Bear Festival Abolished), *Hokkaidō Shinbun*, 16 March 1955.

52 Sugawara, *Gendai no Ainu*, pp.99–100; S. Kodama, *Ainu: Historical and Anthropological Studies* (Sapporo: Hokkaidō University School of Medicine, 1970), p.164; Ainu Association of Hokkaidō, *Statement Submitted to the Ninth Session of the United Nations Working Group on Indigenous Populations*, Geneva, July 1991, unpublished, p.5. Although Sugawara does not give the exact date or details of the team, there seems little doubt that it was the 1956 field trip to Shizunai referred to by Kodama and the Ainu Association of Hokkaidō. As a result of such activities, Kodama was almost universally hated by Ainu; few were saddened by news of his death. See S. Kayano, 'Kanashimarenai Ainu Gakusha no Shi' (Cannot be Sad on Death of Ainu Scholar), in 'Nihonjin ni yoru Jinshu Sabetsu Higaisha Hyakunin no Shōgen' (The Statements of One Hundred Victims of Racial Discrimination by Japanese), Special Feature, *Ushio*, No.150 (February 1972), p.151. Although not mentioned by name, the scholar in question would appear to be Kodama.

53 Hatozawa, *Wakaki Ainu no Tamashii*, p.37.

54 Sugawara, *Gendai no Ainu*, p.101.

55 K. Sakurai, *Ainu Hishi* (Secret History of the Ainu) (Tokyo: Kadokawa Shoten, 1967), p.15.

56 'Hachigatsu ni Zendō Ainu Matsuri' (Hokkaidō Ainu Festival to be held in August), *Hokkaidō Shinbun*, 8 January 1964.

57 Sugawara, *Gendai no Ainu*, pp.89–98.

58 Hilger, 'Japan's "Sky People"'; J.B. Cornell, 'Ainu Assimilation and Cultural Extinction: Acculturation Policy in Hokkaidō', *Ethnology*, Vol.3, No.3 (1964), pp.287–304. Japanese newspapers continued to use 'dying race' (*horobiyuku minzoku*) throughout the 1950s and 1960s. For an example of this kind of reporting, see the articles on Ainu ceremonies in *Mainichi Shinbun*, 21 October 1963.

59 Tokyo-to Kikaku Chōseikyoku Chōsabu, *Tokyō Zaijū Utari Jittai Chōsa Hōkokusho* (Report on the Socio-economic Survey of Ainu Residing in Tokyo) (Tokyo-to Kikaku Chōseikyoku Chōsabu, 1975), p.2.

60 Peure Utari no Kai published a handwritten and mimeographed newsletter, *Peure Utari*, featuring news, poems, and essays on Ainu issues. The information on the *Ainu Mondai Kenkyūkai* comes from T. Hagiwara, 'Ainu Mondai Kenkyūkai ni tsuite' (On the Ainu Mondai Kenkyūkai), *Peure Utari*, No.3 (April 1965), pp.91–92.

61 For Akan Ainu, see Sugawara, *Gendai no Ainu*, pp.182–189; for the Shakushain Festival, pp.126–136.

62 Hokkaidō, *Shin Hokkaidō Shi Nenpyō* (The New Chronology of Hokkaidō History) (Sapporo: Hokkaidō Shuppan Kikaku Sentā, 1989), pp.678–681.

63 Y. Takegahara, 'The Ainu in the New Textbooks for Social Studies', in N. Loos and T. Osanai (eds), *Indigenous Minorities and Education: Australian and Japanese Perspectives of their Indigenous Peoples, the Ainu, Aborigines and Torres Straits Islanders* (Tokyo: Sanyūsha, 1993), p.289.

64 'Ainu o Wasurenaide' (Don't Forget the Ainu), 'Dokusha no Koe' (Readers' Voices), *Hokkaidō Shinbun*, 13 May 1968, evening edition. The writer was Totsuka Miwako.

65 'Kieyuku Unmei no Kyūdojin Hogohō' (Protection Act Fated to Disappear), *Hokkai Taimuzu*, 8 April 1968.

66 *Senkusha no Tsudoi*, No.40 (August 1985), p.7.

67 'Dō Utari Kyōkai wa Hantai' (The Utari Association are Opposed), *Hokkaidō*

Shinbun, 18 June 1970; 'Keizaiteki Uratsuke ga Hitsuyō' (Economic Backup is Necessary), *Hokkaidō Shinbun*, 8 July 1970, evening edition; 'Kyūdojin Hogohō no Mayakashi' (The Swindle of the Protection Act), Readers' Voices, *Hokkaidō Shinbun*, 4 September 1970, evening edition.

68 G.C. Sala, 'Protest and the Ainu of Hokkaido', *Japan Interpreter*, Vol.10, No.1 (1975), pp.50–51; F. Miyoshi, 'Ainu ga Horobiru to Iu no ka' (Can you Say the Ainu are Dying?), in Asahikawa Jinken Yōgo Iin Rengōkai, *Kotan no Konseki*, pp.449–480.

69 G.C. Sala, 'Terrorism and Ainu People of Hokkaido', *Mainichi Daily News*, 8 May 1976. For Ainu organisation, see K. Suga, *Kono Tamashii Utari ni: Hatozawa Samio no Sekai* (Pass this Spirit to the Ainu: The World of Hatozawa Samio) (Tokyo: Eikō Shuppansha, 1976), pp.195–201.

70 A good account of the incidents and their impact on the Ainu is provided by Gary Sala, an American researcher who was present in Hokkaidō during the period. See Sala, 'Protest and the Ainu', and also 'Terrorism and Ainu People of Hokkaido', *Mainichi Daily News*, 8 May 1976. One of the Dōchō bombers recently had his death sentence upheld in the Supreme Court, eighteen years after the incident. 'Ōmori Hikoku ni Shikei Hanketsu' (Verdict of Death for Ōmori), *Asahi Shinbun*, 16 July 1994.

71 For a consideration of the terrorist campaign and the arrest of Yūki and his companions, see Sala, 'Protest and the Ainu'. For Yūki's account of the trial of the Ainu Kaihō Dōmei member, whom he alleges was framed and beaten by the police, see S. Yūki, *Ainu Sengen* (The Ainu Manifesto) (Tokyo: Sanichi Shobō, 1980), pp.89–114. For complaints of discriminatory attitudes among the police, see, for instance, 'Dōkei ga Futō na Kensa' (Unfair Investigation by Hokkaidō Police), *Hokkaidō Shinbun*, 27 December 1974.

72 *Senkusha no Tsudoi*, No.9 (July 1975), p.4 (back page).

73 For a detailed discussion of the theory and practice of denunciation see F.K. Upham, *Law and Social Change in Postwar Japan* (Cambridge, Mass. and London: Harvard University Press, 1987), pp.78–123.

74 R. Siddle, 'Academic Exploitation and Indigenous Resistance: The Case of the Ainu', in Loos and Osanai, *Indigenous Minorities and Education*, pp.43–45.

75 M. Fukuzawa, *Honoo ni Narite: Ainu Byōin Ki* (Turning into Flame: Record of an Ainu Hospital) (Sapporo: Hoppō Gun, 1990), p.353.

76 Suga, *Kono Tamashii*, pp. 201–202.

77 'Ainu de Shōbai Yurusenu' (We Will Not Permit Ainu to be Used For Commerce), *Asahi Shinbun*, 28 October 1974.

78 *Senkusha no Tsudoi*, No.6 (September 1974), p.4.

79 Information on the *Pureiboi* incident comes from the unpublished log of Ainu-related incidents kept by the Section for the Protection of Human Rights within the Legal Bureau of the Hokkaidō Government.

80 For Japan Travel Bureau, see T. Narita and K. Hanazaki (eds), *Kindaika no naka no Ainu Sabetsu no Kōzō* (The Structure of Ainu Discrimination within Modernisation) (Tokyo: Akaishi Shoten, 1985); adverts appear on p.312.

81 'Sabetsu no Jittai Shōgen e' (Evidence to be Given on State of Discrimination), *Hokkai Taimuzu*, 25 November 1973. Hashine, with the help of allies like the self-proclaimed revolutionary Ōta Ryū, turned his life story – a depressing tale of discrimination, criminality and underclass mentality – and new political affiliations into two books, published while he was in prison. N. Hashine, *Ezochi Horobite mo Ainu Moshiri wa Horobizu* (Ezochi may Disappear but

Ainu Moshiri will Never Die) (Tokyo: Shinsensha, 1973); N. Hashine, *Ware Ainu, Koko ni Tatsu* (We Ainu Stand Here) (Tokyo: Shinsensha, 1974).

82 'Ainujin Sabakenu' (You Can't Try an Ainu), *Hokkaidō Shinbun*, 16 July 1974; 'Bengojin ni Kōgibun' (Letter of Protest to the Lawyers), *Hokkaidō Shinbun*, 21 July 1974; 'Watashitachi wa Nihonjin da' (We are Japanese), Readers' Voices, *Hokkaidō Shinbun*, 21 July 1974.

83 'Ainu-kei Jūmin no Satsujin Kōhan' (Murder Trial of Resident of Ainu Descent), *Hokkaidō Shinbun*, 29 May 1975.

84 'Kainushi no Jōkoku Kikyaku' (Purchaser's Appeal Rejected), *Hokkaidō Shinbun*, 3 October 1979. For an outline of the case, see Pon Fuchi (Nogami Fusako), *Ureshipa Moshiri e no Michi* (The Road to Ureshipa Moshiri) (Revised edition, Tokyo: Shinsensha, 1992), pp.246–247.

85 'Ainu Sonchō no Tane o Maita' (I Sowed a Seed of Respect for the Ainu), *Hokkaidō Shinbun*, 12 July 1977.

86 The JCP stated its Ainu policy as follows: 'To secure their rights as an ethnic minority, to protect and preserve Ainu culture, to completely eliminate discrimination, and implement special measures for living conditions.' In Nihon Kyōsantō Chūō Iinkai, 'Ainu Kei Jūmin no Kenri no Hoshō to Sabetsu no Issō' (Securing the Rights of Residents of Ainu Descent and the Elimination of Discrimination), in 'Sangiin Senkyō de no Sōten to Nihon Kyōsanto no Yon Dai Kihon Seisaku' (Issues in the Upper House Election and the Four Main Basic Policies of the JCP), *Zenei*, Special Extra Edition, August 1974, pp.57–58. The JSP similarly stated that its broad aims were 'the extinction of the cruel exploitation and discrimination suffered by the Ainu people (*Ainu minzoku*), the elimination of ethnic oppression and the establishment of ethnic equality', then proceeded to lay out a more detailed set of policies. Nihon Shakaitō Seisaku Shingikai Ainu Minzoku Mondai Tokubetsu Iinkai, 'Ainu Minzoku Seisaku' (Policy on the Ainu People), *Gekkan Shakaitō*, No.207 (April 1974), pp.223–226.

87 T. Teshima, 'Utari Taisaku o meguru Jakkan no Yobiteki Kōsatsu' (Some Preliminary Considerations on the Utari Countermeasures), *Buraku Kaihō Kenkyū*, No.73 (April 1990), pp.88–92.

88 *Senkusha no Tsudoi*, No.13 (July 1976), appendix.

89 J. Beckett, 'Aboriginality in a Nation-State The Australian Case', in M.C. Howard (ed.), *Ethnicity and Nation-building in the Pacific* (Tokyo: United Nations University, 1989), p.122.

90 Yūki, *Ainu Sengen*, pp.39–40.

91 71st Diet, Third Subcommittee of the House of Representatives Budget Committee, 5 March 1973, in *ASS3*, p.594.

92 Head of Prime Minister's Office and Head Of Okinawa Development Agency Ueki Mitsunori, 77th Diet, House of Representatives Accounts Committee, 20 May 1976, in *ASS3*, pp.710–711. The term *minzoku* had by now acquired yet another sense as the sociological concepts of ethnicity began to enter popular use in the 1970s, although the English loan-word *esunishitii* is more often used in academic discourse.

7 BEGINNING TO WALK FOR OURSELVES: THE EMERGENCE OF THE AINU NATION

1 T. Narita, 'Ainu Mondai ni Omou' (Thoughts on the Ainu Problem) *Hoppō Bungei*, Vol.5, No.2 (1972), p.42.
2 'Ainu Mondai Mizukara Dakai e' (Ainu Will Find Solutions to Ainu Problem Themselves), *Hokkai Taimuzu*, 18 January 1973.
3 *Anutari Ainu*, No 1. (June 1973), p.8.
4 T. Narita, '"O Mikata Shamo" ni tsuite' (On 'Shamo Allies'), *Anutari Ainu*, No.2 (July 1973), p.5.
5 Osaka Jinken Rekishi Shiryōkan (ed.), *Kindai Nihon to Ainu Minzoku* (Modern Japan and the Ainu) (Osaka: Osaka Jinken Rekishi Shiryōkan, 1993), p.100.
6 Address by Yūki Shōji to provisional meeting of the *Tokyo Ainu Kaihō Kenkyūkai*, 1 July 1978. In Ifunke no Kai (ed.), *Ifunke: Aru Ainu no Shi* (Ifunke [Lullaby]: The Death of an Ainu) (Tokyo: Sairyūsha, 1991), pp.181–182.
7 K. Honda, *Hinkon naru Seishin: B Shū* (The Impoverished Spirit: Collection B) (Tokyo: Asahi Shinbunsha, 1989), pp.189–210.
8 *Senkusha no Tsudoi*, No.5 (January 1974), pp.2, 3.
9 'Ainu Jikaku Undō no Shinboru' (Symbol of the Ainu Self-awareness Movement), *Shakai Shinpō*, 23 July 1972.
10 Narita, 'Ainu Mondai ni Omou', pp.38–39.
11 'Eiyū no Rei Yasuraka ni' (Put the Souls of the Heroes at Rest), *Hokkaidō Shinbun*, 8 September 1974; 'Nokkamappu Misaki ni Keuntanke Hibiku' (Keuntanke echoes round Cape Nokkamappu), *Anutari Ainu*, No.12 (September 1974), p.1.
12 See *Senkusha no Tsudoi*, No.29 (January 1982), pp.1, 5–6.
13 'Parikko Kandō' (The Parisians are Moved), *Asahi Shinbun*, 1 May 1976.
14 *Anutari Ainu*, No.12, p.1; *Senkusha no Tsudoi*, No.13, p.3.
15 See, for instance, the comments of Elder Yamakawa Hiro in Ekashi to Fuchi Henshū Iinkai (ed.), *Ekashi to Fuchi: Kita no Shima ni Ikita Hitobito no Kiroku* (The Ainu Elders: A Record of the People who Lived on the Northern Island) (Sapporo: Sapporo Terebi Hōsō, 1983), p.383.
16 Hokkaidō Minseibu, *Shōwa 54–nen Hokkaidō Utari Seikatsu Jittai Chōsa Hōkokusho* (Report of the 1979 Survey of Socio-economic Conditions of the Hokkaidō Utari) (Sapporo: Hokkaidō Minseibu, 1979), p.30. Care needs to be taken with these figures, however, since they are based on a narrow sample and marred by a high proportion of respondents (around half) who ignored questions relating to culture in 1979.
17 A good example of this is provided by the work of Shinya Gyō, an early Wajin ally of Yūki Shōji. G. Shinya, *Ainu Minzoku Teikō Shi* (A History of Ainu Resistance) (Tokyo: Sanichi Shobō, 1977). Such activities were also aided by an academic movement among younger Japanese historians, including Emori Susumu and Kaiho Mineo, to write 'history from below' and recover the experiences of the 'masses' that led many to sympathise with the Ainu cause.
18 This is according to Yūki's Wajin friend and ally, Shinya Gyō, who relates how he first told Yūki about the incident. After describing the background and events of the executions in detail, Yūki vaguely recalled hearing something similar from his grandmother. The two then agreed that publicising such historical events was vital to the movement to eliminate discrimination and

restore Ainu rights. G. Shinya, *Kotan ni Ikiru Hitobito* (People who Live in the Kotan) (Tokyo: Saninchi Shobō, 1979), pp.36–38.

19 S. Yūki, *Ainu Sengen* (The Ainu Manifesto) (Tokyo: Sanichi Shobō, 1980), pp.125–128.

20 *Senkusha no Tsudoi*, No.11 (March 1976).

21 B. Anderson, *Imagined Communities: Reflections on the Origin and Spread of Nationalism* (Revised Edition, London: Verso, 1991), p.7.

22 *Anutari Ainu*, No.1, p.2. For a picture of the flag at the 1975 parade, see *Anutari Ainu*, No.16 (May 1975), p.4.

23 The revolutionary rhetoric (and cavalier disregard of the laws of libel) of these radicals is best illustrated by the work of Ōta Ryū, as in R. Ōta, *Ainu Kakumei Ron: Yukara no Sekai e no 'Taikyaku'* (On Ainu Revolution: 'Retreat' to the World of Yukara) (Tokyo: Ainu Moshiri Jōhōbu [Shinsensha], 1973).

24 Yūki, *Ainu Sengen*, p.43.

25 Narita, 'Ainu Mondai ni Omou', pp.36, 39–40; Y. Hiramura, 'Ainu to "Nihon" no Naka de Nanoru toki: Ashi no Kai kara Anutari Ainu e' (Identifying as Ainu in Japan: From Ashi no Kai to Anutari Ainu), *Hoppō Bungei*, Vol.6, No.6 (1973), p.28; *Anutari Ainu*, No.1 (June 1973), p.5. For a poem empathising with the experience of American Blacks, see 'Ima wa Naki Kokujin Seinen e Sasageru Shi' (Poem Offered to a Black Youth Now Dead) by Totsuka Miwako in *Anutari Ainu*, Nos. 6 and 7 (January 1974), p.4.

26 Hokkaidō Ainu Chūgoku Hōmondan (ed.), *Hokkaidō Ainu Chūgoku Hōmondan Ki* (Record of the Hokkaidō Ainu China Tour Group) (Sapporo: Hokkaidō Ainu Chūgoku Hōmondan, 1975), p.7.

27 *Chūgoku Hōmondan Ki*, p.85.

28 *Senkusha no Tsudoi*, No.19 (October 1978), supplement.

29 'Indean to Kōryū no Tabi' (Visit to the Indians), *Hokkaidō Shinbun*, 7 September 1978; 'Ainu Daihyō ga Hatsu Sanka' (First Attendance by Ainu Representative), *Hokkai Taimuzu*, 23 April 1981, evening edition; 'Fukken Neppoku' (Passion over Restoration of Rights), *Hokkaidō Shinbun*, 14 May 1981.

30 Yūki, *Ainu Sengen*, p.43.

31 Narita Tokuhei, in the collected reports edited by N. Egami, *Shimupojiumu: Ainu to Kodai Nihon* (Symposium: The Ainu and Ancient Japan) (Tokyo, Shōgakkan, 1982), p.304.

32 T. Narita, 'Discrimination Against Ainus and the International Covenant on the Elimination of All Forms of Racial Discrimination', in Buraku Kaihō Kenkyūsho (ed.), *The United Nations, Japan and Human Rights: To Commemorate the 35th Anniversary of the Universal Declaration of Human Rights* (Osaka: Kaihō Shuppansha, 1984), p.138.

33 76th Diet, House of Councillors Budget Committee, 6 November 1975, in *ASS3*, p.696.

34 Human Rights Committee, 12th Session, Document No. CCPR/C/10/Add.1, 14 November 1980. In Ainu Association of Hokkaidō, *Statement Submitted to the Fifth Session of the United Nations Working Group on Indigenous Populations*, Geneva, August 1987, Material 4.

35 Human Rights Committee, 14th Session, Document No. CCPR/C/SR.324, 10 November 1981, p.11. In Ainu Association of Hokkaidō, *Statement Submitted to the Fifth Session of the United Nations Working Group on Indigenous Populations*, Geneva, August 1987, Material 5.

36 Echoing Ōta Ryū, Hashine labelled Nomura the 'guard dog of the Japanese government'. N. Hashine, *Ware Ainu, Koko ni Tatsu* (We Ainu Stand Here) (Tokyo: Shinsensha, 1974), pp.82–84.

37 T. Teshima, 'Utari Taisaku o meguru Jakkan no Yobiteki Kōsatsu' (Some Preliminary Considerations on the Utari Countermeasures), *Buraku Kaihō Kenkyū*, No.73 (April 1990), pp.95, 96, 98.

38 For the background to the New Law, see *Senkusha no Tsudoi*, No.40, p.7; Honda, *Hinkon naru Seishin*, pp.211–222.

39 Nomura Giichi, cited in Honda, *Hinkon naru Seishin*, p.213.

40 'Habomai Shotō oyobi Chishima Rettō Henkan Konsei Ketsugi' (Resolution Earnestly Requesting the Return of the Kurile Islands and the Habomai Group), Hokkaidō Prefectural Assembly, 13 March 1950, reproduced in Hokkaidō Utari Kyōkai (ed.), *Chishima Rettō no Ainu Minzoku Senjū ni kansuru Shiryō* (Materials Concerning the Prior Inhabitation of the Kurile Islands by the Ainu People) (Sapporo: Hokkaidō Utari Kyōkai, 1983), pp.51–55. Quote is on p.53. The Japanese government, of course, has no option but to stress the peaceful development of the islands after the Cairo Declaration of 27 November 1943 called for Japan to be expelled from all territories taken by 'violence and greed'.

41 See, for instance, 'Monbushō ni Kōgi' (Protest to the Ministry of Education), *Hokkaidō Shinbun*, 25 August 1982.

42 Hokkaidō Utari Kyōkai, *Ainu Minzoku ni kansuru Hōritsu (An)* (Legislation Concerning the Ainu People – Proposal). See Appendix 2.

43 Nihon Shakaitō Seisaku Shingikai Ainu Minzoku Mondai Tokubetsu Iinkai, 'Ainu Minzoku Seisaku' (Policy on the Ainu People), *Gekkan Shakaitō*, No.207 (April 1974).

44 In 1984, the only international instrument specifically relating to indigenous peoples was ILO Convention 107 of 1957, on the Protection and Integration of Indigenous and other Tribal or Semi-Tribal Populations in Independent States. For the legal background to indigenous rights, see P. Thornberry, *International Law and the Rights of Minorities* (Oxford: Clarendon Press, 1991), pp.331–382.

45 Utari Mondai Konwakai, 'Ainu Minzoku ni Kansuru Shinpō Mondai ni tsuite' (On the Enactment of New Legislation Concerning the Ainu) March 1988, p.2.

46 Hokkaidō Shinbun Shakaibu, *Gin no Shizuku: Ainu Minzoku wa Ima* (Silver Droplets: The Ainu Today) (Sapporo: Hokkaidō Shinbunsha, 1991), p.147.

47 Utari Affairs Council, 'On the Enactment of New Legislation'; N. Owaki, 'On "A Proposal for New Legislation for the Ainu People": Its Meaning and Future Prospects', in N. Loos and T. Osanai (eds), *Indigenous Minorities and Education: Australian and Japanese Perspectives of their Indigenous Peoples, the Ainu, Aborigines and Torres Sraits Islanders* (Tokyo: Sanyūsha, 1993), pp.380–384; H. Uemura, 'Ainu Minzoku ni Kansuru Hōritsu ni tsuite' (On the New Law for the Ainu People), *Buraku Kaihō Kenkyū*, No.76 (1990), pp.14–22.

48 'Third Periodic report of Japan under Article 40 Paragraph 1(b) of the International Covenant on Civil and Political Rights', 16 December 1991, reproduced in Ainu Association of Hokkaidō, 'Statement Submitted to the Tenth Session of the United Nations Working Group on Indigenous Populations', Geneva, July 1992 (unpublished), p.19. The unofficial Japanese translation by the Foreign Ministry is *shōsu minzoku* – minority ethnic group, but its use is ambiguous. See T. Teshima, 'From the Assimilation Policy to the Guarantee of the Rights of the Ainu as an Indigenous People: A Critique Based

on the Reality of Discrimination Against the Ainu', in Buraku Kaihō Kenkyūsho (eds), *Human Rights in Japan from the Perspective of the International Covenant on Civil and Political Rights: Counter-Report to the Third Japanese Government Report* (Osaka: Buraku Kaihō Kenkyūsho, 1993), pp.30–33.

49 Statement of the Observer Delegation of Japan to the 11th session of the Working Group on Indigenous Populations, Geneva, July 1993.

50 International Labour Organisation, 'Convention Concerning Indigenous and Tribal Peoples in Independent Countries', Article One, Paragraph 1(b).

51 I am grateful to Katerina Sjöberg for bringing this to my attention.

52 See J. Maher, 'Ainugo no Fukkatsu' (Revival of the Ainu Language), in J. Maher and K. Yashiro (eds) *Nihon no Bairingarisumu* (Japan's Bilingualism) (Tokyo: Kenkyūsha Shuppan, 1991), pp.149–175.

53 For Hokkaidō University and the portrait rights case, see R. Siddle, 'Academic Exploitation and Indigenous Resistance: The Case of the Ainu', in N. Loos and T. Osanai (eds), *Indigenous Minorities and Education: Australian and Japanese Perspectives of their Indigenous Peoples, the Ainu, Aborigines and Torres Straits Islanders* (Tokyo: Sanyūsha, 1993), pp.45–48.

54 *Senkusha no Tsudoi* No.38 (January 1985), p.1.

55 Interview with Nomura Giichi, 28 August 1995.

56 Hokkaidō Minseibu, *Heisei 5-nen Hokkaidō Utari Seikatsu Jittai Chōsa Hōkokusho* (Report on the 1993 Survey of Socio-economic Conditions of the Hokkaidō Ainu) (Sapporo: Hokkaidō Minseibu, 1993), p.5, (hereafter *USJC*).

57 *USJC*, p.9.

58 Ainu: 39 per thousand; Wajin: 16. *USJC*, p.7.

Bibliography

1 Published collections of primary materials

Hokkaidō Utari Kyōkai (ed.) *Ainu Shi: Hokkaidō Ainu Kyōkai/Hokkaidō Utari Kyōkai Katsudō Shi Hen* (Ainu History: Activities of the Hokkaidō Ainu/Utari Association), Sapporo, Hokkaidō Utari Kyōkai, 1994. All original materials from this collection cited in the text are listed separately and followed by *AKS*.

Hokkaidō Utari Kyōkai Ainu Shi Henshū Iinkai (ed.) *Ainu Shi Shiryō Hen 4: Kingendai Shiryō 2* (Materials on Ainu History 4: Modern and Contemporary Materials 2), Sapporo, Hokkaidō Utari Kyōkai, 1989.

—— *Ainu Shi Shiryō Hen 3: Kingendai Shiryō 1* (Materials on Ainu History 3: Modern and Contemporary Materials 1), Sapporo, Hokkaidō Utari Kyōkai, 1990. Cited in notes as *ASS3*.

Kōno, M. (ed.) *Ainu Shi Shiryō Shū* (Collected Materials on Ainu History), 15 volumes in two series, Sapporo, Hokkaidō Shuppan Kikaku Sentā, 1980–1987. All original materials from this collection cited in the text are listed separately and followed by the relevant series and volume number (e.g. Kōno, Series 2, Vol.3).

—— 'Tai Ainu Seisaku Hōki Ruishū' (Collection of Legislation Relating to Ainu Policy), in *Ainu Shi Shiryō Shū: Hōki, Kyōiku Hen* (Collected Materials on Ainu History: Laws and Education), Series 1, Vol. 2, Sapporo, Hokkaidō Shuppan Kikaku Sentā, 1981. Cited in notes as *ASH*.

—— 'Ainu Kankei Shinbun Kiji' (Newspaper Articles on the Ainu), in *Ainu Shi Shiryō Shu: Kōno Tsunekichi Shiryō Shū 1* (Collected Materials on Ainu History: Collected Materials of Kōno Tsunekichi 1), Series 2, Vol.7, Sapporo, Hokkaidō Shuppan Kikaku Sentā, 1984.

—— 'Ainu Sōshi: 5' (Collected Documents Relating to the Ainu: 5), in *Ainu Shi Shiryō Shū: Abe Masami Bunkō Hen 3* (Collected Materials on Ainu History, Archives of Abe Masami 3), Series 2, Vol.6, Sapporo, Hokkaidō Shuppan Kikaku Sentā, 1985.

Takakura, S. (ed.) *Nihon Shomin Seikatsu Shiryō Shūsei Vol.4: Hoppō Hen* (Collection of Historical Materials on the Life of the Common People in Japan, Vol.4: The Northern Regions), Tokyo, Sanichi Shobō, 1969. Edo period materials cited in the text from this collection are listed separately and followed by *NS4*.

Tanikawa, K. (ed.) *Kindai Minshū no Kiroku 5: Ainu* (Records of the Masses in the Modern Period, Vol.5: The Ainu), Tokyo, Shinjinbutsu Ōraisha, 1972. Materials cited in the text from this collection are listed separately and followed by *KMK5*.

2 Newspapers

Asahi Shinbun
Hakodate Shinbun
Hōchi Shinbun
Hokkai Shinbun
Hokkai Taimuzu
Hokkaidō Mainichi Shinbun
Hokkaidō Shinbun
Jiji Shinpō
Karafuto Nichi Nichi Shinbun
Kokumin Shinbun
Mainichi Shinbun
Otaru Shinbun
Shakai Shinpō
Tokyo Asahi Shinbun

Japan Times
Mainichi Daily News

3 Ainu magazines and newsletters

Ainu Shinbun (Ainu News)
Anutari Ainu (We Ainu)
Ezo no Hikari (Light of Yezo)
Kita no Hikari (Light of the North)
Peure Utari
Ryōyū (Good Friends)
Senkusha no Tsudoi (Pioneer's Meeting)
Utari no Tomo (The Ainu's Friend)
Utari no Hikari (Light of the Ainu)

4 Unpublished materials

Batchelor, J., 'Steps by the Way', undated MS (late 1930s).

Hidaka Chiku Shizunai Shibu Higashi Shizunai Chūgakkō Hidaka Chiku Tokubetsu Kenkyū Gurūpu, 'Hidaka, Iburi Chiku ni okeru Ainu-kei Jidō, Seitō o meguru Jittai to sono Taisaku' (Conditions and Countermeasures for Children and Students of Ainu Descent in the Hidaka and Iburi Regions), *Dai Go Bukai Hōkokusho* (Report of the Fifth Working Group), Hokkyōso Daiyonji Zendō Kyōiku Kenkyū Taikai (Fourth Hokkaidō Teachers' Union Convention on Educational Research), undated (early 1950s). (Hokkaidō University Library).

Ogawa, S., 'A Petition Regarding Farmland Owned by Ainu People in Hokkaidō', December 1947.

Pete, W., 'Petition: Concerning Ainu-owned Farmland in Hokkaidō', 10 December 1947.

Sapporo Hōmukyoku [Log of Ainu-Related Incidents, 1975–1988].

5 Japanese language sources

Ainu Bunka Hozon Taisaku Kyōgikai (ed.) *Ainu Minzoku Shi* (Ainu Ethnology), Tokyo, Daiichihōki Shuppan, 1970.

Ainu Minzoku no Genzai to Mirai o Kangaeru Kai (ed.) *Ashita o Tsukuru Ainu Minzoku* (The Ainu Who Will Make Tomorrow), Tokyo, Miraisha, 1988.

Akiyama, S., *Nihon Chiri Shōshi* (Outline of Japanese Geography), Vol.2, Tokyo, Chūōdō, 1887.

Amano, T., 'Kuma no Tankō' (A Few Thoughts on Bears), *Cultura Antiqua*, Vol.42, No.10 (1990), pp.26–35.

Arai, G., *Ainu no Sakebi* (The Cry of the Ainu), Sapporo, Hokkaidō Shuppan Kikaku Sentā, 1984.

Arai, G., (Y. Katō, ed.) *Arai Genjirō Ikō: Ainu Jinbutsu Den* (The Posthumous Writings of Arai Genjirō: The Biographies of Famous Ainu), Sapporo, Y. Katō (private publication), 1992.

Asahikawa-shi Shi Henshū Iinkai (ed.) *Asahikawa-shi Shi: Dai Ikkan* (History of Asahikawa City, Volume 1), Asahikawa, Asahikawa Shiyakusho, 1959.

Baba, Y., 'Nihon ni okeru Mainoritii Kenkyū e no Ichi Shiron: Ainu Kei Jūmin no Jirei Kenkyū', *Minzokugaku Kenkyū*, Vol.37, No.3 (December 1972), pp.214–238.

Bachira, J. (Batchelor, J.) *Waga Kioku o Tadorite* (Tracing my Memory), Sapporo, Bunrokusha, 1928.

—— 'Nihon Zaijū Rokujūninen no Kansō – Findings After 62 Years in Japan', *Hokkaidō Shakai Jigyō*, No.80 (January 1939), pp.26–33.

Chiri, T., 'Ainu no Ke ni tsuite' (On the Hair of the Ainu) *Kita no Hikari*, No.1 (December 1948), pp.27–29. (*AKS*).

Chiri, Y., *Gin no Shizuku: Chiri Yukie Ikō* (Silver Droplets: The Posthumous Writings of Chiri Yukie), Tokyo, Sōfūkan, 1992.

Chōsen Sōtokufu Hōmukyoku, 'Uji no Settei ni kansuru Ken' (On the Establishment of Surnames), Communication from Miyamoto Gen, Head of the Legal Bureau of the Government General of Korea, Tokyo Office, to Ishii Seiichi, Head of the Records Section of the Home Ministry, 30 January 1940.

—— 'Uji no Settei ni kansuru Ken' (On the Establishment of Surnames), Communication from Miyamoto Gen, Head of the Legal Bureau of the Government General of Korea, Tokyo Office, to Munei Toshikazu, Governor of Karafuto, 30 January 1940.

Egami, N. (ed.) *Shimupojiumu: Ainu to Kodai Nihon* (Symposium: The Ainu and Ancient Japan), Tokyo, Shōgakkan, 1982.

Ekashi to Fuchi Henshū Iinkai (ed.) *Ekashi to Fuchi: Kita no Shima ni Ikita Hitobito no Kiroku* (The Ainu Elders: A Record of the People who Lived on the Northern Island), Sapporo, Sapporo Terebi Hōsō, 1983.

Emori, S., *Ainu no Rekishi: Hokkaidō no Hitobito (2)* (A History of the Ainu: the People of Hokkaidō [2]), Tokyo, Sanseidō, 1987.

Endō, I., 'Ezo Andō-shi Koron' (Discussion on Andō as an Ezo), *Rekishi Hyōron*, No.434 (June 1986), pp.36–50.

Fujimoto, H., 'Wajin Shinryaku to Ainu Kaihō Undō' (Wajin Invasion and the Ainu Liberation Movement), in K. Tanikawa (ed.), *Kindai Minshū no Kiroku 5: Ainu* (Records of the Masses in the Modern Period, Vol.5: The Ainu), Tokyō, Shinjinbutsu Ōraisha, 1972, pp.558–565.

—— *Chiri Mashiho no Shōgai* (The Life of Chiri Mashiho), Tokyo, Shinchōsha, 1982.

—— *Ainugaku e no Ayumi* (Steps towards Ainu Studies), Sapporo, Hokkaidō Shuppan Kikaku Sentā, 1983.

—— *Kindaichi Kyōsuke*, Tokyō, Shinchōsha, 1991.

Fukkyūsha Henshūjo (ed.) *Shōgaku Chiri* (Elementary Geography), Tokyo, Fukkyūsha, 1901.

Fukuzawa, M., *Honoo ni Narite: Ainu Byōin Ki* (Turning into Flame: Record of an Ainu Hospital), Sapporo, Hoppō Gun, 1990.

Furukawa, T., 'Ketsuekigata yori Mita Taiwan Banjin to Hokkaidō Ainujin no Minzokusei' (The Racial Character of Taiwanese Aborigines and Hokkaidō Ainu Viewed through Blood-type), *Hanzaigaku Zasshi*, Vol.4, No.2 (March 1931), pp.130–136.

Gabe, M., 'Nihon no Kindaika to Okinawa' (Okinawa and the Modernisation of Japan), in Iwanami Kōza, *Kindai Nihon to Shokuminchi 1: Shokuminchi Teikoku Nihon* (Modern Japan and the Colonies 1: Colonial Empire Japan), Tokyo, Iwanami Shoten, 1992, pp.101–138.

Gakkai Shihōsha, *Nihon Chiri Shōhō* (First Step in Japanese Geography), Tokyo, Shūōdō, 1892.

Haginaka, M., *et al.*, *Kikigaki: Ainu no Shokuji* (Field Notes: Ainu Food), Nihon Shokuseikatsu Zenshū No.48, Tokyo, Nōsangyōson Bunka Kyōkai, 1992.

Hagiwara, T., 'Ainu Mondai Kenkyūkai ni tsuite' (On the Ainu Mondai Kenkyūkai), *Peure Utari*, No.3 (April 1965), pp.91–92.

Hashine, N., *Ezochi Horobite mo Ainu Moshiri wa Horobizu* (Ezochi may Disappear but Ainu Moshiri will Never Die), Tokyo, Shinsensha, 1973.

—— *Ware Ainu, Koko ni Tatsu* (We Ainu Stand Here), Tokyo, Shinsensha, 1974.

Hatozawa, S., *Wakaki Ainu no Tamashii* (The Soul of a Young Ainu), Tokyo, Shinjinbutsu Ōraisha, 1972.

Hayakawa, K., 'Bungaku ni Egakareta Ainu Minzoku' (The Ainu People in Literature), *Kyōdo Kenkyū*, No.8 (April 1969), pp.29–41.

Hayasaka, Y., *Shizen to Jinbun Shumi no Hokkaidō* (Nature, Culture, Tastes of Hokkaidō), Sapporo, Hokkōsha, 1926.

Hiramura, Yoshimi, 'Ainu to 'Nihon' no naka de Nanoru toki: Ashi no Kai kara Anutari Ainu e' (Identifying as Ainu in Japan: From Ashi no Kai to Anutari Ainu), *Hoppō Bungei*, Vol.6, No.6 (1973), pp.27–29.

Hiramura, Yukio, 'Ainu to shite Ikiru ka? Hata Shamo ni Dōka suru ka?' (Do We Live as Ainu? Or Do We Assimilate to *Shamo*?), *Ezo no Hikari*, No.1 (November 1930), pp.24–26. (*AKS*).

Hiraoka, S., 'Ainu Jinshu Shobun Ron' (On the Disposal of the Ainu Race), appendix in T. Aoyama, *Kyokuhoku no Bettenchi* (The Different World of the Extreme North), Tokyo, Nippon Seinen Tsushinsha, 1918, pp.1–17.

Hokkaidō (Hokkaidō-chō) *Kyūdojin ni Kansuru Chōsa* (Survey of the Former Natives), Sapporo, Hokkaidō-chō, 1922. (Kōno, Series 1, Vol.1).

—— *Hokkaidō Kyūdojin Gaikyō* (General Conditions of the Hokkaidō Former Natives), Sapporo, Hokkaidō-chō, 1926. (Kōno, Series 1, Vol.1).

—— *Hokkaidō Kyūdojin Hogohō Enkaku Shi* (History of the Protection of the Former Natives of Hokkaidō), Sapporo, Hokkaidō-chō, 1934; Reprinted Tokyo, Sanichi Shobō, 1981.

—— *Hokkaidō Kyūdojin Gaikyō* (General Conditions of the Hokkaidō Former Natives), Sapporo, Hokkaidō-chō, 1936. (Kōno, Series 1, Vol.1).

—— *Hokkaidō Nōchi Kaikaku Shi: Jōkan* (History of Land Reform in Hokkaidō, Vol.1), Sapporo, Hokkaidō-chō, 1954.

—— *Hokkaidō Nōchi Kaikaku Shi: Gekan* (History of Land Reform in Hokkaidō, Vol.2), Sapporo, Hokkaidō-chō, 1957.

—— *Shin Hokkaidō Shi* (New History of Hokkaidō), 9 Volumes, Sapporo, Hokkaidō-chō, 1969–1981.

—— *Shin Hokkaidō Shi Nenpyō* (The New Chronology of Hokkaidō History), Sapporo, Hokkaidō Shuppan Kikaku Sentā, 1989.

Hokkaidō Ainu Chūgoku Hōmondan (ed.) *Hokkaidō Ainu Chūgoku Hōmondan Ki* (Record of the Hokkaidō Ainu China Tour Group), Sapporo, Hokkaidō Ainu Chūgoku Hōmondan, 1975.

Hokkaidō-chō Gakumubu, 'Ainujin no Uji ni kansuru Ken' (On the Establishment of Ainu Surnames), Communication from Hiramoto Yoshitaka, Head of the Education Section of the Hokkaidō Government, to Miyamoto Gen, Head of the Legal Bureau of the Government General of Korea, 21 February 1940.

Hokkaidō Hidaka Shichō, *Hidaka Chihō ni okeru Ainu Kei Jūmin no Seikatsu Jittai to sono Mondaiten* (The Socio-economic Conditions of Residents of Ainu Descent in the Hidaka Region and Associated Problems), Urakawa, Hidaka Shichō, 1965.

Hokkaidō Kyōiku Kenkyūsho (ed.) *Hokkaidō Kyōiku Shi* (History of Education in Hokkaidō), Sapporo, Hokkaidō Kyōiku Shi Hakkankai, 1963.

Hokkaidō Minseibu, *Shōwa 47-nen Hokkaidō Utari Jittai Chōsa Hōkoku* (Report of the 1972 Survey of Socio-economic Conditions of the Hokkaidō Ainu), Sapporo, Hokkaidō Minseibu, 1972.

—— *Shōwa 54-nen Hokkaidō Utari Seikatsu Jittai Chōsa Hōkokusho* (Report of the 1979 Survey of Socio-economic Conditions of the Hokkaidō Ainu), Sapporo, Hokkaidō Minseibu, 1979.

—— *Shōwa 61-nen Hokkaidō Utari Seikatsu Jittai Chōsa Hōkokusho* (Report of the 1986 Survey of Socio-economic Conditions of the Hokkaidō Ainu), Sapporo, Hokkaidō Minseibu, 1986.

—— *Heisei 5-nen Hokkaidō Utari Seikatsu Jittai Chōsa Hōkokusho* (Report on the 1993 Survey of Socio-economic Conditions of the Hokkaidō Ainu), Sapporo, Hokkaidō Minseibu, 1993.

Hokkaidō Rekishi Kyōikusha Kyōgikai (ed.) *Ainu, Orokko no Mondai to Kyōiku* (Ainu, Orok Issues and Education), Sapporo, Hokkaidō Minkan Kyōiku Kenkyū Dantai Renraku Kyōgikai, 1976.

Hokkaidō Shinbunsha (ed.) *Hokkaidō Shinbun Yonjūnen Shi* (A Forty Year History of the Hokkaidō Shinbun Newspaper), Sapporo, Hokkaidō Shinbunsha, 1983.

Hokkaidō Shinbun Shakaibu, *Gin no Shizuku: Ainu Minzoku wa Ima* (Silver Droplets: The Ainu Today), Sapporo, Hokkaidō Shinbunsha, 1991.

Hokkaidō Utari Kyōkai (ed.) *Chishima Rettō no Ainu Minzoku Senjū ni kansuru Shiryō* (Materials Concerning the Prior Inhabitation of the Kurile Islands by the Ainu People), Sapporo, Hokkaidō Utari Kyōkai, 1983.

—— *Ainu Minzoku no Jiritsu e no Michi* (The Road to Ainu Autonomy), Sapporo, Hokkaidō Utari Kyōkai, 1991.

Honda, K., *Hinkon naru Seishin: B Shū* (The Impoverished Spirit: Collection B), Tokyo, Asahi Shinbunsha, 1989.

Iboshi, H., *Kotan: Iboshi Hokuto Ikō* (Kotan: The Posthumous Writings of Iboshi Hokuto), Tokyo, Sōfūkan, 1984.

Ifunke no Kai (ed.) *Ifunke: Aru Ainu no Shi* (Ifunke [Lullaby]: The Death of an Ainu), Tokyo, Sairyūsha, 1991.

Iha, F., 'Mezametsutsu aru Ainu Shuzoku' (The Awakening Ainu Race), in *Iha Fuyū Zenshū* (Collected Works of Iha Fuyū), Vol.11, Tokyo, Heibonsha, 1976, pp.302–312.

Inoue, S., *et al.* (ed.) *Hokkaidō Bungaku Zenshū Dai Jūikkan: Ainu Minzoku no Tamashii* (Collected Hokkaidō Literature, Vol.11: The Soul of the Ainu People), Tokyo, Tachikaze Shobō, 1970.

Ishibashi, T., F. Oka and T. Wada, 'Ainu no Seikaku: Seishōnen ni okeru Chōsa ni mototsuite' (Ainu Character Based on a Survey of Young People), *Minzoku Eisei*, Vol.12, No.6 (November 1944), pp.339–352.

Ishibashi, T., *et al.*, 'Ainu Jidō no Chinō Chōsa: Chinō no Jinshuteki Sai oyobi ni Chinō ni oyobasu Konketsu no Eikyō ni kansuru – Chiken' (Survey of Intelligence among Ainu Children: Racial Difference in Intelligence and the Influence of Mixed Blood on Intelligence – an Opinion), *Minzoku Eisei*, Vol.10, No.4 (August 1942), pp.237–294.

Itagaki, K., 'Hokkaidō Kyūdojin no Koseki ni kansuru Kōsatsu' (Considerations on the Family Registers of Hokkaidō Former Natives), *Hokkaidō Shakai Jigyō*, No.87 (August 1939), pp.24–27.

Iwaya, E., 'Ainu no Genshō' (The Decrease in Ainu Numbers), *Hokkaidō Kyōiku Zasshi*, No.6 (1891), pp.11–19.

—— 'Hokubei Dojin Hogohō o Ronjite Ainu Jinshu Hogohō ni oyobu (2)' (On the Protection Act for the North American Natives With Reference to the Protection Act for the Ainu Race, Part 2), *Hokkaidō Kyōiku Zasshi*, No.88 (May 1901), pp.1–3.

—— 'Kyūdojin Kyōikudan' (On Ainu Education), *Hokkaidō Kyōiku Zasshi*, No.123 (April 1903), pp.34–37.

—— 'Kyūdojin Kyōikudan' (On Ainu Education), *Hokkaidō Kyōiku Zasshi*, No.125 (June 1903), pp.29–33.

Kaiho, M., *Kinsei no Hokkaidō* (Early Modern Hokkaidō), Tokyo, Kyōikusha, 1979.

—— *Shiryō to Kataru Hokkaidō no Rekishi* (The History of Hokkaidō as Related by Historical Records), Sapporo, Hokkaidō Shuppan Kikaku Sentā, 1985.

Kaiho, Y., 'Kindai ni okeru Ainu Kei Minshū Zō no Keisei: Nihonjin no Ainu Kan' (Formation of the Image of the Ainu Masses in the Early Modern Period: The Japanese Image of the Ainu), *Hokkaidō Chihō Shi Kenkyū*, No.90 (February 1973), pp.37–42.

—— *Kindai Hoppō Shi: Ainu Minzoku to Josei to* (Modern History of the Northern Regions: The Ainu People and Women), Tokyo, Sanichi Shobō, 1992.

Kaizawa, H., 'Wajin yo, Ōseki no Ezo o Wasureru nakare; Utari yo, Chishiki no Kōjō o Hakare' (Wajin, Do Not Forget the Ezo of the Past; Ainu, Plan to Increase Your Knowledge), *Ezo no Hikari*, No.2, (January 1931), pp.24–26. (*AKS*).

Kaizawa, M., 'Ainu no Chi sae Usumereba' (If We Only Dilute Ainu Blood) in 'Nihonjin ni yoru Jinshu Sabetsu Higaisha Hyakunin no Shōgen' (The Statements of One Hundred Victims of Racial Discrimination by Japanese), special feature, *Ushio*, No.150 (February 1972), pp.144–145.

Kaizawa, T., *Ainu no Sakebi* (The Cry of the Ainu), Sapporo, Ainu no Sakebi Kankōkai, 1931. (*KMK5*, pp.380–393).

Kakizaki, H., *Ishū Retsuzō* (Pictures of Barbarian Chiefs) [1790], Hakodate, Tosho Rikai [Hakodate Toshokan], 1988.

Kanazeki, J., 'Ainu no Wakiga' (Ainu Body Odour), *Seirigaku Kenkyū*, Vol.11, No.8 (1934), pp.542–546.

Karafuto (Karafuto-chō) *Karafuto Dojin Chōsa Sho* (Survey of Karafuto Natives), Toyohara, Karafuto-chō, 1931. (Kōno, Series 1, Vol.6).

—— *Ainu Gai Dojin Chōsa* (Survey of non-Ainu Natives), Toyohara, Karafuto-chō, 1933. (Kōno, Series 1, Vol.6).

—— 'Uji no Settei ni kansuru Ken' (On the Establishment of Surnames), Communication from Governor of Karafuto to Head of Legal Bureau, Government General of Korea, 7 February 1940. (National Diet Library, Kensei Shiryōshitsu, Ōno Rokuichirō Bunsho 1278).

Karafuto Ainu Shi Kenkyūkai (ed.) *Tsuishikari no Ishibumi* (The Tsuishikari Monument), Sapporo, Hokkaidō Shuppan Kikaku Sentā, 1992.

Kawamura, M., 'Taishu Orientarizumu to Ajia Ninshiki' (Mass Orientalism and Consciousness of Asia), in Iwanami Kōza, *Kindai Nihon to Shokuminchi 7: Bunka no naka no Shokuminchi* (Modern Japan and the Colonies 7: The Colonies in Culture), Tokyo, Iwanami Shoten, 1993.

Kayano, S., 'Kanashimarenai Ainu Gakusha no Shi' (Cannot be Sad on Death of Ainu Scholar), in 'Nihonjin ni yoru Jinshu Sabetsu Higaisha Hyakunin no Shōgen' (The Statements of One Hundred Victims of Racial Discrimination by Japanese), special feature, *Ushio*, No.150 (February 1972), pp.151–152.

Kikuchi, I., *Hoppō Shi no Naka no Kinsei Nihon* (Early Modern Japan in the History of the Northern Regions), Tokyo, Azekura Shobō, 1991.

—— *Ainu Minzoku to Nihonjin: Higashi Ajia no Naka no Ezochi* (The Ainu and the Japanese: Ezochi in East Asia), Tokyo, Asahi Shinbunsha, 1994.

Kikuchi, T., 'Emishi Kōkogaku no Genjō to Kadai' (Present Situation and Issues in Emishi Archaeology), *Rekishi Hyōron*, No.434 (June 1986), pp.2–12.

Kindaichi, K., *Kindaichi Kyōsuke Senshū* (Selected Works of Kindaichi Kyōsuke), Vol.3, Tokyo, Sanseidō, 1962.

Kita, M. (Kita Kōyō), 'Dojin Hogo no Enkaku to Hogohō no Seishin' (A History of Native Welfare and the Spirit of the Protection Act), *Hokkaidō Shakai Jigyō*, No.15 (July 1933), pp.21–29.

—— 'Kyūdojin Dantai no Tabi' (The Trip of the Former Native Group), *Hokkaidō Shakai Jigyō*, No.59 (April 1937), pp.50–55.

—— 'Ainu yo Izuko e Iku (1)' (Ainu, Where are you Going? Part 1), *Hokkaidō Shakai Jigyō*, No.63 (August 1937), pp.40–47.

—— *Ainu Enkaku Shi: Hokkaidō Kyūdojin Hogohō o megutte* (Ainu History: Concerning the Hokkaidō Former Natives Protection Act), Sapporo, Hokkaidō Shuppan Kikaku Sentā, 1987.

Kitakamae, Y., *Kodai Emishi no Kenkyū* (Studies of the Ancient Emishi), Tokyo, Yūzankaku, 1991.

Kodama, S., 'Kinkyū o Yōshita Ainu Kenkyū' (Ainu Studies Required Urgency), *Hokkaidō no Bunka*, No.21 (March 1971), pp.7–13.

Koganei, Y., 'Ainu no Jinshugakuteki Chōsa no Omoide' (Recollections of Ethnographical Investigations of the Ainu), *Dolmen*, Vol.4, No.7 (1935), pp.54–65.

Komatsu, M., 'Kyūdojin Hogo Shisetsu Kaizen Zadankai Kiroku' (Record of the Symposium for the Improvement of Welfare Facilities for the Former Natives), *Hokkaidō Shakai Jigyō*, No.42 (October 1935), pp.2–70.

—— 'Ainu Shukōgeihin Tenrankai' (The Ainu Handicrafts Exhibition), *Hokkaidō Shakai Jigyō*, No.42 (October 1935), pp.71–85.

Komatsu, Y., 'Gendankai no Henkyō/Naikoku Shokuminchi Ron ni tsuite no Kōsatsu (Ge): Hokkaidō Keizai Shi/Keizai Ron ni Kanren shite' (Considerations on the Present Stage of the Debate on Frontier Lands/Internal Colonies (3): Concerning the Economic History and Theory of Hokkaidō), *Ohotsuku Sangyō Keiei Ronshū*, Vol.3, No.1 (1992), pp.47–76.

Kosaka, Y., *Ryubō: Nichirō ni Owareta Kita Chishima Ainu* (Exile: Driven out by Japan and Russia – The Northern Kurile Ainu), Sapporo, Hokkaidō Shinbunsha, 1992.

Koyama, N., 'Ezo Nikki' (Ezo Diary), 1808 (*NS4*, pp.45–75).

Kubo, Y., 'Karafuto ni okeru Ainu Jidō to Nihon Jidō tono Hikkaku' (A Comparison Of Japanese and Ainu Children in Karafuto), *Jidō Kenkyūsho Kiyō*, Vol.9 (1926), pp.363–417.

Kubota, S., 'Kyōwa Shieki' (Private and Official Diary), 1856 (*NS4*, pp.223–270).

Kudō, M., 'Kodai Emishi no Shakai – Kōeki to Shakai Soshiki' (Society of the Ancient Emishi – Trade and Social Organization), *Rekishi Hyōron*, No.434 (June 1986), pp.13–35.

Kushiro-shi, *Shin Kushiro-shi Shi* (New History of Kushiro City), Kushiro, Kushiro-shi, 1974.

Kushiwara, M. 'Igen Zokuwa' (Tales of Ezo Customs), 1792 (*NS4*, pp.485–520).

Kuwabara, M., (ed.) *Kaitaku no Kage ni: Hokkaidō no Hitobito (1)* (In the Shadow of Development: The People of Hokkaidō [1]), Tokyo, Sanseidō, 1987.

Maher, J., 'Ainugo no Fukkatsu' (Revival of the Ainu Language), in J. Maher and K. Yashiro (eds), *Nihon no Bairingarisumu* (Japan's Bilingualism), Tokyo: Kenkyūsha Shuppan, 1991, pp.149–175.

Matsui, T., 'Chikabumi Ainu to Kyūdojin Hogohō' (The Chikabumi Ainu and the Former Natives Protection Act), in K. Tanikawa (ed.), *Kindai Minshū no Kiroku 5: Ainu* (Records of the Masses in the Modern Period, Vol.5: The Ainu), Tokyō, Shinjinbutsu Ōraisha, 1972, pp.566–575.

Matsumae-chō Shi Henshū Shitsu (ed.) *Matsumae-chō Shi* (History of Matsumae Town), Vol.1, Matsumae, Matsumae-chō, 1984.

Matsumiya, K., 'Ezo Dan Hikki' (Narratives of Ezo), 1710 (*NS4*, pp.387–400).

Matsuura, T., 'Kinsei Ezo Jinbutsu Shi' (Stories of Recent Ezo Personalities), 1860 (*NS4*, pp.731–813).

Meiji Kinenkai (ed.) *Takushoku Hakurankai Kinen Shashin Chō* (Commemorative Photographs of the Colonial Exposition), Tokyo, Meiji Kinenkai, 1912.

Miyoshi, F., 'Ainu ga Horobiru to Iu no ka' (Can you say the Ainu are dying?), in Asahikawa Jinken Yōgo Iin Rengōkai (ed.), *Kotan no Konseki* (Remains of the Kotan), Asahikawa, Asahikawa Jinken Yōgo Iin Rengōkai, 1971, pp.449–480.

Mogami, T., 'Ezo Kuni Fūzoku Ninjō no Sata' (Notes on the Customs and People of the Country of Ezo), 1790 (*NS4*, pp.439–484).

—— 'Watarishima Hikki' (Notes on Watarishima), 1808 (*NS4*, pp.521–543).

Monbushō (ed.) *Junjō Shōgaku Tokuhon* (Elementary School Reader), Tokyo, Monbushō, 1910.

Moritake, T., 'Zendō Utari ni Hakaru' (Calling the Hokkaidō Utari), *Utari no Hikari*, No.15 (February 1934). (*KMK5*, pp.239–240).

Munro, N.G. (Dokutōru Manrō) 'Kyūdojin ni kansuru Chōsa: Ge' (Survey of the Former Natives: 2), *Hokkai no Kyōiku*, No.303 (March 1918), pp.13–18.

Murakami, H., *Ainu Jitsuwa Shū* (Collection of True Ainu Stories), Asahikawa, Asahikawa Shiritsu Kyōdo Hakubutsukan, 1964.

Murakami, S., 'Ezo Seikei Zusetsu' (Illustrated Life of the Ezo), 1823 (*NS4*, pp.545–638).

Mutō, K., 'Ezo Nikki' (Ezo Diary), 1798 (*NS4*, pp.13–21).

Namikawa, K., *Kinsei Nihon to Hoppō Shakai* (Early Modern Japan and Northern Society), Tokyo, Sanseidō, 1992.
Narita, T., 'Ainu Mondai ni Omou' (Thoughts on the Ainu Problem), *Hoppō Bungei*, Vol.5, No.2 (1972), pp.34–42.
—— '"O Mikata Shamo" ni tsuite' (On 'Shamo Allies'), *Anutari Ainu*, No.2 (July 1973), p.5.
Narita, T. and K. Hanazaki (eds) *Kindaika no naka no Ainu Sabetsu no Kōzō* (The Structure of Ainu Discrimination within Modernisation), Tokyo, Akaishi Shoten, 1985.
Nihon Kyōsantō Chūō Iinkai, 'Ainu Kei Jūmin no Kenri no Hoshō to Sabetsu no Issō' (Securing the Rights of Residents of Ainu Descent and the Elimination of Discrimination), in 'Sangiin Senkyō de no Sōten to Nihon Kyōsanto no Yon Dai Kihon Seisaku' (Issues in the Upper House Election and the Four Main Basic Policies of the JCP), *Zenei*, special extra edition, August 1974, pp.57–58.
Nihon Shakaitō Seisaku Shingikai Ainu Minzoku Mondai Tokubetsu Iinkai, 'Ainu Minzoku Seisaku' (Policy on the Ainu People), *Gekkan Shakaitō*, No.207 (April 1974), pp.223–226.
Nishi, I., 'Jinshu Henken no Shakaiteki Bunseki – Hokkaidō Ainu o megutte' (A Social Analysis of Racial Prejudice: Concerning the Hokkaidō Ainu), in Asahikawa Jinken Yōgo Iin Rengōkai (ed.), *Kotan no Konseki* (Remains of the Kotan), Asahikawa, Asahikawa Jinken Yōgo Iin Rengōkai, 1971, pp.57–77.
Nishida, T., 'Kakusei o Nozomu' (Wishing for Awakening), *Ezo no Hikari*, No.2 (March 1931), pp.19–21. (*AKS*).
Nitami, I., *Ikyō no Shito: Eijin Jon Bachira Den* (The Foreign Apostle: A Biography of the Englishman John Batchelor), Sapporo, Hokkaidō Shinbunsha, 1991.
Nogami, F. (Pon Fuchi) *Ainugo wa Ikite iru: Kotoba no Tamashii no Fukken* (The Ainu Language Lives: Restoration of the Soul of the Language), Revised Edition, Tokyo, Shinsensha, 1987.
—— *Ureshipa Moshiri e no Michi* (The Road to Ureshipa Moshiri), Revised edition, Tokyo, Shinsensha, 1992.
Nukishio, Y. (H.) *Ainu Dōka to Senchō* (Ainu Assimilation and Its Examples), Obihiro, Hokkai Shōgun Kōseidan, 1934, reprinted Sapporo, Sapporo-dō Shoten, 1986.
Ogawa, M., 'Ainu Gakkō no Settchi to Hokkaidō Kyūdojin Hogohō – Kyūdojin Jidō Kyōiku Kitei no Seiritsu' (The Establishment of Ainu Schools and the Hokkaidō Former Natives Protection Act – Regulations for the Education of Former Native Children), *Hokkaidō Daigaku Kyōikugakubu Kiyō*, No.55 (1991), pp.257–325.
—— 'Kotan e no Gyōkō/Gyōkei to Ainu Kyōiku' (Royal Visits to Ainu Communities and Ainu Education), *Kyōiku Shi Gakkai Kiyō*, No.34 (October 1991), pp.50–65.
—— 'Hokkaidō Kyūdojin Hogohō, Kyūdojin Jidō Kyōiku Kitei no shita no Ainu Gakkō' (Ainu Schools under the Hokkaidō Former Natives Protection Act and the Regulations for the Education of Former Native Children), *Hokkaidō Daigaku Kyōikugakubu Kiyō*, No.58 (1992), pp.197–266.
—— 'Ainu Kyōiku Seido no Haishi: Kyūdojin Jidō Kyōiku Kitei Haishi to 1937-nen Hokkaidō Kyūdojin Hogohō Kaisei' (The End of the Ainu Education System: The Abolition of the Regulations for the Education of Former Native Children and the 1937 Revision of the Hokkaidō Former Natives Protection Act), *Hokkaidō Daigaku Kyōikugakubu Kiyō*, No.61 (1993), pp.37–79.

Ogawa, S., 'Zento no Kōmei o Mokuhyō ni' (A Bright Future as Our Objective), *Ezo no Hikari*, No.3 (August 1931), pp.20–21. (*AKS*).

Ohyi, H., 'Shakushain no Ran (Kanbun Kyū-nen Ezo no Ran) no Saikentō' (A Reinvestigation of the Rebellion of Shakushain), *Hoppō Bunka Kenkyū* No.21 (1992), pp.1–66.

Okabe, S., 'Kyūdojin Zakki (2): Jinkō Ron to Iseki Hozon' (Notes on the Former Natives No.2: Population and Preservation of Relics), *Hokkaidō Shakai Jigyō*, No.60 (May 1937), pp.46–50.

Onobu, S., 'Dōzoku no Kanki o Unagasu' (Urging the Awakening of Our People), *Ezo no Hikari*, No.1 (November 1930), pp.8–10. (*AKS*).

—— 'Itsumademo Gakusha no Kenkyū Zairyō taru nakare' (We Must Not Remain Research Materials for Scholars Forever), *Ezo no Hikari*, No.2 (January 1931), pp.27–28. (*AKS*).

Osaka Jinken Rekishi Shiryōkan (ed.) *Kindai Nihon to Ainu Minzoku* (Modern Japan and the Ainu), Osaka, Osaka Jinken Rekishi Shiryōkan, 1993.

Ōta, R., *Ainu Kakumei Ron: Yukara no Sekai e no 'Taikyaku' (On Ainu Revolution: 'Retreat' to the World of Yukara), Tokyo, Ainu Moshiri Jōhōbu [Shinsensha], 1973.*

Ozawa, K., 'Koseki Tōhon wa Ima mo "Kyūdojin"' (Former Native Still Appears on Family Registers), in 'Nihonjin ni yoru Jinshu Sabetsu Higaisha Hyakunin no Shōgen' (The Statements of One Hundred Victims of Racial Discrimination by Japanese), special feature, *Ushio*, No.150 (February 1972), p.142.

Ozawa, Y. and Y. Takegahara, 'Seishōnen no Ainu Kan' (The Image of Ainu Among Young People), *Jinbun Gakuhō*, No.15 (March 1980), pp.1–80.

Pon Fuchi (see Nogami, F.).

Sakakura, G., 'Hokkai Zuihitsu' (Writings on the North Seas), 1739 (*NS4*, pp.401–414).

Sakurai, K., *Ainu Hishi* (Secret History of the Ainu), Tokyo, Kadokawa Shoten, 1967.

Sasaki, K., 'Hidaka Yūki' (Bound for Hidaka), *Hokkaidō Kyōiku Shinbun*, No.37 (November 1928), pp.26–27.

Sasaki, T., 'Ainu-e ga Egaita Sekai' (The World Illustrated by Ainu Pictures), in Sapporo Gakuin Daigaku Jinbungakubu (ed.), *Ainu Bunka ni Manabu* (Learn From Ainu Culture), Sapporo, Sapporo Gakuin Daigaku, 1990, pp.147–213.

—— 'Inu wa Sosen nari ya' (Perhaps Their Ancestors were Dogs) in Hokkaidō-Tōhoku Kenkyūkai (ed.), *Kita kara no Nihon Shi (2)* (Japanese History from the North, Vol.2), Tokyo, Sanseidō, 1990, pp.189–225.

Satō, K., *Hokkaidō Bungaku Shikō* (History of Hokkaidō Literature), Sapporo, Nire Shobō, 1956.

Shari-chō Shi Henshū Iinkai (eds) *Shari-chō Shi* (History of Shari Town), Shari, Shari-chō, 1955.

Shinya, G., *Ainu Minzoku Teikō Shi* (A History of Ainu Resistance), Revised Edition, Tokyo, Sanichi Shobō, 1977.

—— *Kotan ni Ikiru Hitobito* (People Who Live in the Kotan), Tokyo, Sanichi Shobō, 1979.

Sonoda, K., 'Kyūdojin Seikatsu Zakken' (A Look at Ainu Life), *Hokkaidō Shakai Jigyō*, No.75 (August 1938), pp.24–27.

Suga, K., *Kono Tamashii Utari ni: Hatozawa Samio no Sekai* (Pass this Spirit to the Ainu: The World of Hatozawa Samio), Tokyo, Eikō Shuppansha, 1976.

Sugawara, K., *Gendai no Ainu: Minzoku Idō no Roman* (The Modern Ainu: Drama of a People in Motion), Tokyo, Genbunsha, 1966.

Sunazawa, K., *Ku Sukup Orushipe: Watashi no Ichidai no Hanashi* (The Story of My Life), Tokyo, Fukutake Shoten, 1990.

Takahashi, M., *Zoku Hokkaidō no Onnatachi: Utari Hen* (Women of Hokkaidō Continued: The Ainu), Sapporo, Hokkaidō Josei Shi Kenkyūkai, 1981.

Takakura, S., *Ainu Seisaku Shi: Shinpan* (A History of Ainu Policy: New Edition), Tokyo, Sanichi Shobō, 1972.

Takegahara, Y., 'Kindai Nihon no Ainu Kyōiku: Dōka Kyōiku no Shisō to Jissen' (Ainu Education in Early Modern Japan: The Theory and Practice of Assimilationist Education), in M. Kuwabara (ed.), *Hokkaidō no Kenkyū: Dai Rokkan* (Studies on Hokkaidō, Vol.6), Osaka, Seibundō Shuppan, 1983, pp.453–492.

—— 'Kaiheisha Sōritsu to Ainu Kaihō Undō' (The Establishment of the Kaiheisha and the Ainu Liberation Movement), *Kaihō Kyōiku*, No.284 (March 1992), pp.34–43.

Takekuma, T., *Ainu Monogatari* (Ainu Tales), Tokyo, Hakubunkan, 1918. (Kōno, Series 1, Vol.5).

Takikawa-shi Shi Hensan Iinkai (ed.) *Takikawa-shi Shi* (History of Takikawa City), Vol.1, Takikawa, Takikawa-shi, 1981.

Tamura, S., 'Naikoku Shokuminchi to shite no Hokkaidō' (Hokkaidō as an Internal Colony) in Iwanami Kōza, *Kindai Nihon to Shokuminchi 1: Shokuminchi Teikoku Nihon* (Modern Japan and the Colonies 1: Colonial Empire Japan), Tokyo, Iwanami Shoten, 1992, pp.87–99.

Tanaka, R., and D. Gendānu, *Gendānu: Aru Hoppō Shōsu Minzoku no Dorama* (Gendānu: The Drama of a Northern Minority People), Tokyo, Gendaishi Shuppankai, 1978.

Teshikaga-chō Shi Hensan Iinkai (ed.) *Teshikaga-chō Shi* (History of Teshikaga Town), Teshikaga, Teshikaga-chō, 1981.

Teshima, T., 'Utari Taisaku o meguru Jakkan no Yobiteki Kōsatsu' (Some Preliminary Considerations on the Utari Countermeasures), *Buraku Kaihō Kenkyū*, No.73 (April 1990), pp.87–109.

Tokyo-to Kikaku Chōseikyoku Chōsabu, *Tokyō Zaijū Utari Jittai Chōsa Hokokusho* (Report on the Socio-economic Survey of Ainu Residing in Tokyo), Tokyo, Tokyo-to Kikaku Chōseikyoku Chōsabu, 1975.

Tomikawa, M., 'Ainu Minzoku no Jisatsu ni tsuite' (On Suicide Among the Ainu), *Hokudai Kaibō Kenkyū Hōkoku*, No.126 (1959), pp.1–32.

Tomita, T., 'Hokkaidō Kyūdojin Hogohō to Dōzu Hō: Hikakushiteki Kenkyū no Kokoromi' (The Hokkaidō Former Natives Protection Act and the Dawes Act: An Attempt at a Comparative Historical Study), *Jinbungakkai Kiyō*, No.45 (August 1989), pp.5–21.

—— 'Hokkaidō Kyūdojin Hogohō to Dōzu Hō: Jon Bachera, Shirani Takeshi, Parapita, Sanrottee' (The Hokkaidō Former Natives Protection Act and the Dawes Act: John Batchelor, Shirani Takeshi, Parapita and Sanrottee), *Jinbungakkai Kiyō*, No.48 (December 1990), pp.1–22.

Tsuboi, S., 'Hokkaidō Kyūdojin Kyūiku Jigyō' (Welfare Projects for the Former Natives of Hokkaidō), *Tokyo Jinruigakkai Zasshi*, No.245 (August 1906), pp.431–434.

Uemura, H., 'Ainu Minzoku ni Kansuru Hōritsu ni tsuite' (On the New Law for the Ainu People), *Buraku Kaihō Kenkyū*, No.76 (1990), pp.14–22.

—— *Kita no Umi no Kōekishatachi: Ainu Shakai Keizai Shi* (The Traders of the Northern Seas: A History of Ainu Society and Economy), Tokyo, Dōbunkan, 1990.

Umehara T., and K. Hanihara, *Ainu wa Gen-Nihonjin ka* (Are the Ainu Proto-Japanese?), Tokyo, Shōgakkan, 1982.

Umeki, T. (ed.) *Ainu Dendōsha no Shōgai: Ega Torazō Ikō* (The Life of an Ainu Missionary: The Posthumous Writings of Ega Torazō), Sapporo, Hokkaidō Shuppan Kikaku Sentā, 1986.

Unattributed, 'Ezo Hōki' (The Ezo Uprising), 1671 (*NS4*, pp.639–650).

Urata, K., 'Meiji no Ainu Seinen Kannari Tarō' (The Meiji Ainu Youth Kannari Tarō), in S. Matsumoto (ed.), *Kusuri*, Vol.2, Kushiro, Kushiro Seikatsu Bunka Denshō Hozon Kenkyūkai, 1993, pp.63–75.

Utagawa, H., *Ainu Bunka Seiritsu Shi* (History of the Formation of Ainu Culture), Sapporo, Hokkaidō Shuppan Kikaku Sentā, 1988.

Utari Mondai Konwakai, 'Ainu Minzoku ni Kansuru Shinpō Mondai ni tsuite' (On the Enactment of New Legislation Concerning the Ainu) March 1988. *AKS*, pp.1387–1400.

Wagatsuma H., and T. Yoneyama, *Henken no Kōzō: Nihonjin no Jinshu Kan* (The Structure of Prejudice: The Japanese Image of Race), Tokyo, Nihon Hōsō Shuppan Kyōkai, 1967.

Wakaizumi, S., *Karafuto Kikō: Hokui Gojūdo no Tabi* (Karafuto Journal: A Journey at Fifty Degrees North), Tokyo, Gokōsha, 1931.

Yamabe, Y. and K. Kindaichi, *Ainu Monogatari* (An Ainu Story), Tokyo, Hakubunkan, 1913. (Kōno, Series 1, Vol.6).

Yamakawa, T., *Kono Ningen no Jidai* (These Human Times), Tokyo, Renga Shobō Shinsha, 1991.

Yamamoto, T., 'Ezo Nōkō Kinshi Kō' (Thoughts on the Banning of Agriculture among the Ezo), *Monbetsu Shiritsu Kyōdo Hakubutsukan Hōkoku*, No.5 (1991), pp.18–33.

Yamamoto, Y., *Hidaka-kuni Niikappu Goryō Bokujō Shi* (History of the Niikappu Imperial Ranch), Tokyo, Miyama Shobō, 1985.

Yamanaka, H., 'Shōkokumintachi no Shokuminchi' (The Colonies of the Little Citizens), in Iwanami Kōza, *Kindai Nihon to Shokuminchi (7): Bunka no naka no Shokuminchi* (Modern Japan and the Colonies: The Colonies in Culture), Tokyo, Iwanami Shoten, 1993, pp.57–79.

Yanagi, S., *Yanagi Sōetsu Zenshū* (Collected Works of Yanagi Sōetsu), Vol.15, Tokyo, Chikuma Shobō, 1981.

Yasuda, H., 'Kindai Nihon ni okeru "Minzoku" Kannen no Keisei' (The Formation of the Concept of Minzoku in Modern Japan), *Shisō to Gendai*, No.31 (1992), pp.61–72.

Yoshida, I., *Kokoro no Ishibumi* (Monument of the Spirit), Tokyo, Hokkai Shuppan, 1935. (Kōno, Series 2, Vol.1).

Yoshida, Kikutarō, *Ainu Bunka Shi* (Ainu Cultural History), Makubetsu: Hokkaidō Ainu Bunka Hozon Kyōkai, 1958.

Yoshida, Kōzō, 'Hidaka Chihō ni okeru Ainu–Wajin no Tsūkon ni tsuite' (On Ainu–Wajin Intermarriage in the Hidaka region), *Jinruigaku Zasshi*, Vol.80, No.1 (1972), pp.60–61.

Yoshimi, S., *Hakurankai no Seijigaku: Manazashi no Kindai* (The Politics of Expositions: Modernity On Show), Tokyo, Chūkō Shinsho, 1992.

Yuki, S., *Ainu Sengen* (The Ainu Manifesto), Tokyo, Sanichi Shobō, 1980.

6 English language sources

Ainu Association of Hokkaidō, *Statement Submitted to the Fifth Session of the United Nations Working Group on Indigenous Populations*, Geneva, August 1987. (*AKS*).

—— *Statement Submitted to the International Labour Conference 75th Session, 1988*, Geneva, June 1988. (*AKS*).

—— *Statement Submitted to the Ninth Session of the United Nations Working Group on Indigenous Populations*, Geneva, July 1991. (*AKS*).

Anderson, B., *Imagined Communities: Reflections on the Origin and Spread of Nationalism*, Revised edition, London, Verso, 1991.

Aston, W.G., *Nihongi: Chronicles of Japan from the Earliest Times to A.D. 697*, Rutland, Vt. and Tokyo, Tuttle, 1972.

Attwood, B., *The Making of the Aborigines*, Sydney, Allen and Unwin, 1989.

Baba, Y., 'A Study of Minority–Majority Relations: The Ainu and Japanese in Hokkaidō', *Japan Interpreter*, Vol.13, No.1 (1980), pp.60–92.

Banton, M., *Racial Consciousness*, London and New York, Longman, 1988.

Barnes, R.H., 'Introduction', in R.H. Barnes, A. Gray and B. Kingsbury (eds), *Indigenous Peoples of Asia*, Ann Arbor, Association for Asian Studies, 1995, pp.1–12.

Batchelor, J., *The Ainu and their Folklore*, London, The Religious Tract Society, 1901.

—— *Ainu Life and Lore: Echoes of a Departing Race*, Tokyo, Kyōbunkan, 1927.

Beckett, J., 'Aboriginality in a Nation-State: The Australian Case', in M.C. Howard (ed.), *Ethnicity and Nation-building in the Pacific*, Tokyo, United Nations University, 1989, pp.118–135.

Befu, H., 'Nationalism and *Nihonjinron*', in H. Befu (ed.), *Cultural Nationalism in East Asia: Representation and Identity*, Berkeley: Institute of East Asian Studies, University of California, 1993, pp.107–135.

Bigelow, P., *Japan and Her Colonies*, London, Edward Arnold, 1923.

Bird, I., *Unbeaten Tracks in Japan: An Account of Travels in the Interior Including Visits to the Aborigines of Yezo and the Shrine of Nikko*, Rutland, Vt. and Tokyo, Tuttle, 1973. (First published in 1880 by G.P. Putnam's Sons, New York.)

Bowring, R., 'An Amused Guest In All: Basil Hall Chamberlain (1850–1935)', in Sir H. Cortazzi and G. Daniels (eds), *Britain and Japan 1859–1991: Themes and Personalities*, London and New York, Routledge, 1991, pp.128–136.

Cashmore, E. (ed.) *Dictionary of Race and Ethnic Relations*, London, Routledge, 1988.

Chamberlain, B.H., *The Language, Mythology, and Geographical Nomenclature of Japan, Viewed in the Light of Aino Studies*, Tokyo, Tokyo Imperial University, 1887.

Chiri, Mutsumi, 'A Song Sung by the Owl God Himself – from the Collected Songs of the Ainu Gods', in N. Loos and T. Osanai (eds), *Indigenous Minorities and Education: Australian and Japanese Perspectives of their Indigenous Peoples, the Ainu, Aborigines and Torres Strait Islanders*, Tokyo, Sanyūsha, 1993, pp.119–128.

Clifton, J.A., 'The Indian Story: A Cultural Fiction', in J.A. Clifton (ed.), *The Invented Indian: Iconoclastic Essays*, New Brunswick, Transaction Publishers, 1990, pp.29–47.

Cornell, J.B., 'Ainu Assimilation and Cultural Extinction: Acculturation Policy in Hokkaidō', *Ethnology*, Vol.3, No.3 (1964), pp.287–304.

Cornell, S., *The Return of the Native: American Indian Political Resurgence*, New York and Oxford, Oxford University Press, 1988.

Curtin, P. (ed.) *Imperialism*, London, Macmillan, 1971.

Devalle, S., 'Discourses of Ethnicity: The Faces and the Masks', in M.C. Howard (ed.), *Ethnicity and Nation-building in the Pacific*, Tokyo, United Nations University, 1989, pp.50–73.

Dikötter, F., *The Discourse of Race in Modern China*, Stanford, Stanford University Press, 1992.

Dower, J., *War Without Mercy: Race and Power in the Pacific War*, New York, Pantheon, 1986.

Fujitani, T., 'Inventing, Forgetting, Remembering: Toward a Historical Ethnography of the Nation-State', in H. Befu (ed.), *Cultural Nationalism in East Asia: Representation and Identity*, Berkeley, Institute of East Asian Studies, University of California, 1993, pp.77–106.

Geertz, C., *The Interpretation of Cultures*, New York, Basic Books, 1973.

George, A., 'Japanese Interest Group Behaviour: An Institutional Approach', in J.A.A. Stockwin *et al.*, *Dynamic and Immobilist Politics in Japan*, London, Macmillan, 1988.

Gill, S., 'Mother Earth: An American Myth', in J.A. Clifton (ed.), *The Invented Indian: Iconoclastic Essays*, New Brunswick, Transaction Publishers, 1990, pp.129–143.

Gluck, C., *Japan's Modern Myths: Ideology in the Late Meiji Period*, Princeton, Princeton University Press, 1985.

Goldberg, D.T., *Racist Culture: Philosophy and the Politics of Meaning*, Oxford, UK and Cambridge, Mass., Blackwell, 1993.

Gordon, A., *The Evolution of Labor Relations in Japan: Heavy Industry, 1853–1955*, Council of East Asian Studies, Harvard University, Cambridge, Mass. and London, Harvard University Press, 1985.

Gorham, H., 'Families of Mixed Descent in the Western Great Lake Region', in B. Cox (ed.), *Native Peoples, Native Lands; Canadian Indians, Inuit and Metis*, Ottawa, Carleton University Press, 1987, pp.37–55.

Gray, A., 'The Indigenous Movement in Asia', in R.H. Barnes, A. Gray and B. Kingsbury (eds), *Indigenous Peoples of Asia*, Ann Arbor, Association for Asian Studies, 1995, pp.35–58.

Greenfeld, L., *Nationalism: Five Roads to Modernity*, Cambridge, Mass. and London, Harvard University Press, 1992.

Greey, E., *The Bear Worshippers of Yezo and the Island of Karafuto (Saghalin), or the Adventures of the Jewett Family and Their Friend Otto Nambo*, Boston, Lee and Shepard, 1884.

Hane, M., *Peasants, Rebels and Outcastes: The Underside of Modern Japan*, New York, Pantheon, 1982.

Hanihara, K., 'Emishi, Ezo and Ainu: An Anthropological Perspective', *Japan Review*, No.1 (1990), pp.35–48.

Harries, M. and S. Harries, *Soldiers of the Sun: The Rise and Fall of the Imperial Japanese Army*, New York, Random House, 1992.

Harris, N., 'All the World a Melting Pot? Japan at American Fairs, 1876–1904', in A. Iriye (ed.), *Mutual Images: Essays in American–Japanese Relations*, Cambridge, Mass. and London, Harvard University Press, 1975, pp.24–54.

Harrison, J.A., *Japan's Northern Frontier*, Gainesville, University of Florida Press, 1953.

Hatakeyama, U., 'Ainu Clothing', in N. Loos and T. Osanai (eds), *Indigenous Minorities and Education: Australian and Japanese Perspectives of their Indigenous Peoples, the Ainu, Aborigines and Torres Straits Islanders*, Tokyo, Sanyūsha, 1993, pp.104–118.

Hayashida, C.T., 'Identity, Race and the Blood Ideology of Japan', Ph.D. dissertation, University of Washington, Seattle, 1976.

Hilger, I., 'Japan's "Sky People": The Vanishing Ainu', *National Geographic*, Vol.131, No.2 (February 1967), pp.268–296.

—— *Together With the Ainu: A Vanishing People*, Norman, University of Oklahoma Press, 1971.

Hitchcock, R., 'The Ainos of Yezo, Japan', in *Annual Report of the Board of Regents of the Smithsonian Institution, Showing the Operations, Expenditures and Condition of the Institution for the Year Ending June 30 1890. Report of the U.S. National Museum*, Washington, Smithsonian, 1891.

Hoare, J.E., 'Mr. Enslie's Grievances: The Consul, the Ainu and the Bones', *Japan Society of London Bulletin*, No.78, pp.14–19.

Hobsbawm, E., *The Age of Capital 1848–1875*, London, Abacus, 1977.

—— 'Introduction: Inventing Traditions', in E. Hobsbawm and T. Ranger (eds), *The Invention of Tradition*, Cambridge, Cambridge University Press, 1983, pp.1–14.

—— 'Mass-Producing Traditions: Europe, 1870–1914', in E. Hobsbawm and T. Ranger (eds), *The Invention of Tradition*, Cambridge, Cambridge University Press, 1983, pp.263–307.

—— *The Age of Empire 1875–1914*, London, Sphere Books, 1989.

—— *Nations and Nationalism since 1780: Programme, Myth, Reality*, Cambridge, Cambridge University Press, 1990.

Howell, D., 'Ainu Ethnicity and the Boundaries of the Early Modern Japanese State', *Past and Present*, No.142 (February 1994), pp.69–93.

—— *Capitalism from Within: Economy, Society and the State in a Japanese Fishery*, Berkeley and Los Angeles, University of California Press, 1995.

Hunter, J., *The Emergence of Modern Japan: An Introductory History Since 1853*, London and New York, Longman, 1989.

Irokawa, D. (trans. and ed. M. Jansen) *The Culture of the Meiji Period*, Princeton, Princeton University Press, 1985.

Jenkins, R., 'Social Anthropological Models of Inter-ethnic Relations', in J. Rex and D. Mason (eds), *Theories of Race and Ethnic Relations*, Cambridge: Cambridge University Press, 1986, pp.170–186.

Jones, F.C., *Hokkaido: Its Present State of Development and Future Prospects*, London, Oxford University Press, 1958.

Kamiya, N., 'Japanese Control of Ezochi and the Role of Northern Koryō', *Acta Asiatica*, Vol.67 (1994), pp.49–68.

Kayano, S., 'Ainu Ethnic and Linguistic Revival', in N. Loos and T. Osanai (eds), *Indigenous Minorities and Education: Australian and Japanese Perspectives of their Indigenous Peoples, the Ainu, Aborigines and Torres Straits Islanders*, Tokyo, Sanyūsha, 1993, pp.360–367.

—— *Our Land was a Forest: An Ainu Memoir*, Boulder, Westview Press, 1994.

Keene, D., *The Japanese Discovery of Europe, 1720–1830*, Revised Edition, Stanford, Stanford University Press, 1969.

Kikuchi, Y., 'Yanagi Sōetsu and Korean Crafts in the Context of the *Mingei* Movement', Paper presented at the Victoria and Albert/British Association of Korean Studies Korean Material Culture Study Day, 13 February 1993.

Kindaichi, K., *Ainu Life and Legends*, Tourist Library No.36, Tokyo, Board of Tourist Industry, Japanese Government Railways, 1941. (Kōno, Series 1, Vol.7).

Kodama, S., *Ainu: Historical and Anthropological Studies*, Sapporo, Hokkaidō University School of Medicine, 1970.

Komai, K., 'The Ainu in the Age of T'ang Dynasty', *Acta Asiatica*, Vol.6 (March 1964), pp.1–10.

Kreiner, J., 'European Images of the Ainu and Ainu Studies in Europe', in J. Kreiner (ed.), *European Studies on Ainu Language and Culture*, German Institute for Japanese Studies Monograph No.6, Munchen, Iudicium Verlag, 1993, pp.13–60.

Landor, A.H.S., *Alone With the Hairy Ainu. Or, 3800 Miles on a Pack Saddle in Yezo and a Cruise to the Kurile Islands*, London, John Murray, 1893.

Leupp, G.P., 'Images of Black People in Late Mediaeval and Early Modern Japan, 1543–1900', *Japan Forum*, Vol.7, No.1 (Spring 1995), pp.1–13.

Macdonald, G., 'Ainu and Aboriginal Rights: The Struggle goes International', in N. Loos and T. Osanai (eds), *Indigenous Minorities and Education: Australian and Japanese Perspectives of their Indigenous Peoples, the Ainu, Aborigines and Torres Straits Islanders*, Tokyo, Sanyūsha, 1993, pp.399–417.

Marcus, J., 'The Journey out to the Centre: The Cultural Appropriation of Ayers Rock', in A. Rutherford (ed.), *Aboriginal Culture Today*, special issue of *Kunapipi*, Vol.10, Nos. 1 and 2, Sydney, Dangeroo Press, 1988, pp.254–274.

Miles, R., *Racism after 'Race Relations'*, London and New York, Routledge, 1993.

Mitchell, R., *Censorship in Imperial Japan*, Princeton: Princeton University Press, 1983.

Morse, E., *Japan Day by Day*, Two Volumes, Boston and New York, Houghton Mifflin Co., 1917.

Narita, T., 'Discrimination Against Ainus and the International Covenant on the Elimination of All Forms of Racial Discrimination', in Buraku Kaihō Kenkyūsho (ed.), *The United Nations, Japan and Human Rights: To Commemorate the 35th Anniversary of the Universal Declaration of Human Rights*, Osaka, Kaihō Shuppansha, 1984, pp.135–139.

Neary, I., *Political Protest and Social Control in Prewar Japan: The Origins of Buraku Liberation*, Manchester, Manchester University Press, 1989.

Nitobe, I., *The Japanese Nation: Its Land, Its People, Its Life; With Special Consideration to Its Relations with the United States*, New York and London, G. Putnam's Sons, 1912.

Nomura, G., 'Inauguration Speech, UN General Assembly, 10 December 1992', *AMPO Japan–Asia Quarterly Review*, Vol.24, No.3 (1993), pp.33–34.

Ogawa, M., 'The Hokkaidō Former Aborigines Protection Act and Assimilatory Education', in N. Loos and T. Osanai (eds), *Indigenous Minorities and Education: Australian and Japanese Perspectives of their Indigenous Peoples, the Ainu, Aborigines and Torres Straits Islanders*, Tokyo, Sanyūsha, 1993, pp.237–249.

Ohlson, B. (ed.), with Introduction by B. Durrans, *Ainu Material Culture from the Notes of N.G. Munro in the Archive of the Royal Anthropological Institute*, British Museum Occasional Paper No.96, London, British Museum, 1994.

Ölschleger, H.D., 'John Batchelor's Contributions to Ainu Ethnography', in J. Kreiner (ed.), *European Studies on Ainu Language and Culture*, German Institute for Japanese Studies Monograph No.6, Munchen, Iudicium Verlag, 1993, pp.137–150.
Owaki, N., 'On "A Proposal for New Legislation for the Ainu People": Its Meaning and Future Prospects', in N. Loos and T. Osanai (eds), *Indigenous Minorities and Education: Australian and Japanese Perspectives of their Indigenous Peoples, the Ainu, Aborigines and Torres Straits Islanders*, Tokyo, Sanyūsha, 1993, pp.375–384.
Passin, H., *Encounter with Japan*, Tokyo, New York and San Francisco, Kodansha International, 1982.
Patric, J., *Why Japan was Strong: A Journey of Adventure*, London, Methuen, 1944.
Peattie, M.R., 'Japanese Attitudes Towards Colonialism, 1895–1945', in R. Myers and M. Peattie (eds), *The Japanese Colonial Empire, 1895–1945*, Princeton, Princeton University Press, 1984.
—— *Nan'yō: The Rise and Fall of the Japanese in Micronesia, 1885–1945*, Honolulu, University of Hawaii Press, 1988.
Peng, F.C.C., and P. Geiser, *The Ainu: The Past in the Present*, Hiroshima, Hiroshima Bunka Hyōron, 1977.
Pilsudski, B., *Materials for the Study of Ainu Language and Folklore*, Cracow, Cracow University Press, 1912.
Pyle, K., *The New Generation in Meiji Japan: Problems of Cultural Identity, 1885–1895*, Stanford, Stanford University Press, 1969.
Said, E., *Orientalism*, Harmondsworth, Penguin, 1978.
—— *Culture and Imperialism*, London, Vintage, 1994.
Sala, G.C., 'Protest and the Ainu of Hokkaido', *Japan Interpreter*, Vol.10, No.1 (1975), pp.44–65.
—— 'Terrorism and Ainu People of Hokkaido', *Mainichi Daily News*, 8 May 1976.
Sansom, G., *The Western World and Japan: A Study in the Interaction of European and Asiatic Cultures*, Rutland, Vt. and Tokyo, Tuttle, 1977.
Seki, K. 'The Ainu of Nisshin: Family Life and Social Residues', in F.C.C. Peng and P. Geiser, *The Ainu: The Past in the Present*, Hiroshima, Hiroshima Bunka Hyōron, 1977, pp.62–84.
Shimao, E., 'Darwinism in Japan', *Annals of Science*, No.38 (1981), pp.93–102.
Shimazu, N., 'The Japanese Attempt to Secure Racial Equality in 1919', *Japan Forum*, Vol.1, No.1 (1989), pp.93–100.
Siddle, R., 'Academic Exploitation and Indigenous Resistance: The Case of the Ainu', in N. Loos and T. Osanai (eds), *Indigenous Minorities and Education: Australian and Japanese Perspectives of their Indigenous Peoples, the Ainu, Aborigines and Torres Straits Islanders*, Tokyo, Sanyūsha, 1993, pp.40–51.
Siddle, R. and K. Kitahara, 'Deprivation and Resistance: Ainu Movements in Modern Japan: and My Heritage of Pride and Struggle', in J. Maher and G. Macdonald (eds), *Diversity in Japanese Culture and Language*, London, Kegan Paul International, 1995, pp.147–159.
Sjöberg, K., *The Return of the Ainu: Cultural Mobilization and the Practice of Ethnicity in Japan*, Chur, Harwood Academic Publishers, 1993.
Smith, A.D., *The Ethnic Revival*, Cambridge, Cambridge University Press, 1981.
Stavenhagen, R., *The Ethnic Question: Conflicts, Development, and Human Rights*, Tokyo, United Nations University Press, 1990.

Stephan, J.J., *Sakhalin: A History*, Oxford, Clarendon Press, 1971.

—— *The Kuril Islands: Russo–Japanese Frontier in the Pacific*, Oxford, Clarendon Press, 1974.

Tabata, H., 'Some Historical Aspects of Ainu–Japanese Relations: Treachery, Assimilation and the Myth of Ainu Counting', in N. Loos and T. Osanai (eds), *Indigenous Minorities and Education: Australian and Japanese Perspectives of their Indigenous Peoples, the Ainu, Aborigines and Torres Straits Islanders*, Tokyo, Sanyūsha, 1993, pp.32–39.

Takaki, R., *Iron Cages: Race and Culture in 19th-Century America*, New York and Oxford, Oxford University Press, 1989.

Takakura, S., 'The Ainu of Northern Japan: A Study in Conquest and Acculturation' (trans. J. Harrison), *Transactions of the American Philosophical Society*, Vol.50, No.4 (1960).

—— 'Vanishing Ainu of Northern Japan', *Natural History*, Vol.75, No.8 (October 1966), pp.16–25.

Takegahara, Y., 'The Ainu in the New Textbooks for Social Studies', in N. Loos and T. Osanai (eds), *Indigenous Minorities and Education: Australian and Japanese Perspectives of their Indigenous Peoples, the Ainu, Aborigines and Torres Strait Islanders*, Tokyo, Sanyūsha, 1993, pp.288–297.

Takeuchi, K., 'How Japan Learned About the Outside World: The Views of other Countries Incorporated in Japanese School Textbooks, 1868–1986', *Hitotsubashi Journal of Social Studies*, No.19 (1987), pp.1–13.

Tanaka, S., *Japan's Orient: Rendering Pasts into History*, Berkeley and Los Angeles, California University Press, 1993.

Terry, T.P., *Terry's Japanese Empire: A Guidebook for Travelers*, Boston and New York, Houghton Mifflin Company, 1914.

Teshima, T., 'From the Assimilation Policy to the Guarantee of the Rights of the Ainu as an Indigenous People: A Critique Based on the Reality of Discrimination Against the Ainu', in Buraku Kaihō Kenkyūsho (eds), *Human Rights in Japan from the Perspective of the International Covenant on Civil and Political Rights: Counter-Report to the Third Japanese Government Report*, Osaka: Buraku Kaihō Kenkyūsho, 1993, pp.29–36.

Thompson, J.B., *Ideology and Modern Culture*, Oxford, Polity Press, 1990.

Thornberry, P., *International Law and the Rights of Minorities*, Oxford, Clarendon Press, 1991.

Toby, R., *State and Diplomacy in Early Modern Japan: Asia in the Development of the Tokugawa Bakufu*, Princeton, Princeton University Press, 1984.

Tonkinson, R., 'Aboriginal Ethnicity and Nation-building within Australia', in M.C. Howard (ed.), *Ethnicity and Nation-building in the Pacific*, Tokyo, United Nations University, 1989, pp.136–151.

Tsunoda, R., *et al.* (ed.) *Sources of Japanese Tradition: Volume Two*, New York, Columbia University Press, 1964.

Tsuru, S., *Japan's Capitalism: Creative Defeat and Beyond*, Cambridge: Cambridge University Press, 1993.

Upham, F.K., *Law and Social Change in Postwar Japan*, Cambridge, Mass. and London, Harvard University Press, 1987.

Wakabayashi, Bob T., *Anti-Foreignism and Western Learning in Early-Modern Japan*, Cambridge, Mass. and London, Harvard University Press, 1986.

Watanabe, H., *The Ainu Ecosystem*, Seattle and London, University of Washington Press, 1973.

Weiner, M., *The Origins of the Korean Community in Japan 1910–1923*, Manchester, Manchester University Press, 1989.

—— *Race and Migration in Imperial Japan*, London and New York, Routledge, 1994.

Weinreich, P., 'The Operationalisation of Identity Theory in Racial and Ethnic Relations', in J. Rex and D. Mason (eds), *Theories of Race and Ethnic Relations*, Cambridge, Cambridge University Press, 1986, pp.299–320.

Wetherall, W. and G. DeVos (eds) *Japan's Minorities: Burakumin, Koreans, Ainu, Okinawans*, Minority Rights Group Report No.3, New Edition, London, Minority Rights Group, 1983.

Yanagita K., *The Legends of Tōno* (trans. R. Morse), Tokyo, The Japan Foundation, 1975.

Yoneyama, L., 'Hiroshima Narratives and the Politics of Memory', Ph.D. dissertation, Stanford University, California, 1993.

Yoshino, K., *Cultural Nationalism in Contemporary Japan: A Sociological Enquiry*, London and New York, Routledge, 1992.

Index